Black Los Angeles

Black Los Angeles

American Dreams and
Racial Realities

EDITED BY

Darnell Hunt and
Ana-Christina Ramón

New York University Press

NEW YORK AND LONDON

NEW YORK UNIVERSITY PRESS
New York and London
www.nyupress.org

Library of Congress Cataloging-in-Publication Data
Black Los Angeles : American dreams and racial realities /
edited by Darnell Hunt and Ana-Christina Ramón.
p. cm.
Includes bibliographical references and index.
ISBN-13: 978-0-8147-3734-7 (cl : alk. paper)
ISBN-10: 0-8147-3734-X (cl : alk. paper)
ISBN-13: 978-0-8147-3735-4 (pb : alk. paper)
ISBN-10: 0-8147-3735-8 (pb : alk. paper)
1. African Americans—California—Los Angeles. 2. Los Angeles (Calif.)—
Race relations.   I. Hunt, Darnell M. II. Ramón, Ana-Christina.
F869.L89N3194 2010
305.896'073079494—dc22   2009048945

New York University Press books are printed on acid-free paper,
and their binding materials are chosen for strength and durability.
We strive to use environmentally responsible suppliers and materials
to the greatest extent possible in publishing our books.

Manufactured in the United States of America

c 10 9 8 7 6 5 4 3 2 1
p 10 9 8 7 6 5 4 3 2 1

Contents

vi

Acknowledgments

An original volume of this scope would have been impossible to produce without the input of dozens of scholars and community stakeholders. Throughout this eight-year project, we indeed have been fortunate to benefit from such input, particularly from our contributors, to whom we are deeply indebted. We are especially grateful to Dawn Jefferson, who logged countless hours helping us edit the following chapters into what we hope is a coherent whole. Of course, we also would be remiss if we did not thank our editor at NYU Press, Ilene Kalish, and her assistant, Aiden Amos, for believing in the project and for keeping it on track.

The following alphabetical list recognizes the other people and organizations that have contributed to this project, from concept to page: Muhtarat Agoro, Meron Ahadu, H. Samy Alim, Mark Alleyne, Teresa Barnett, Wren Brown, Bunche Center Staff, Bunche Center Community Advisory Board, Kenny Burrell, Shani Byard, California African American Museum, Marne Campbell, Brandy Chappell, Robyn Charles, Nicole Chase, Avery Clayton, Edward Comeaux, Jacqueline DjeDje, Winston Doby, Faustina DuCros, Shirley Jo Finney, Ford Foundation, J. Paul Getty Trust, Kevin Fosnacht, Lorn Foster, Franklin Gilliam, David Grant, Jamel Greer, Jasmine Greene, Lucy Florence Cultural Center, Nandini Gunewardena, C. R. D. Halisi, Tina Henderson, William and Flora Hewlett Foundation, Jennifer Hinton, Cynthia Hudley, Pamela Huntoon, Angela James, Uma Jayakumar, Amber Johnson, Birgitta Johnson, J. Daniel Johnson, Robin Nicole Johnson, Tiffany Jones, Mandla Kayise, Jonathan "J" Kidd, Mei-Ling Malone, Beza Merid, Derrick Mims, Eric Moore, Nicole Moore, Ernest Morrell, Cynthia Mosqueda, Worku Nida, Chinyere Osuji, Bernard Parks, Jennifer Payne, Karisa Peer, Theri Pickens, Virgil Roberts, Mark Sawyer, Woody Schofield, Robert Singleton, Anton Smith, Alva Stevenson, Peter Taylor, Jervey Tervalon, Roena Rabelo Vega, Christine Vu, Tara Watford, Steve Wesson, Christopher d Jimenez y West, Kelvin L. White, Theresa White, UCLA Center for Oral History Research, UCLA Center for Community Partnerships, UCLA Chicano Studies Research Center, and Christina Zanfagna.

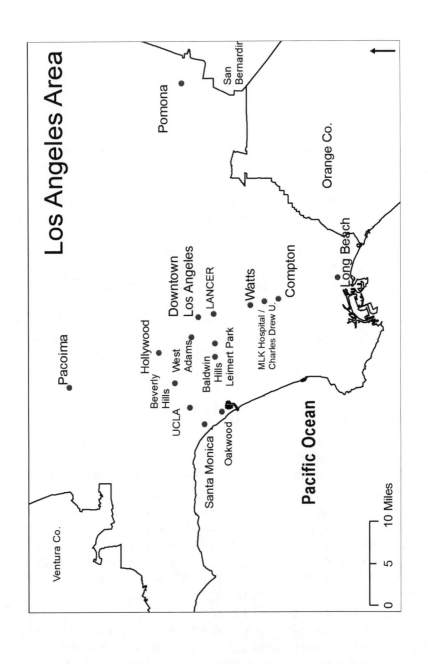

Los Angeles Area

Ventura Co.

Pacoima

Beverly
Hills

UCLA

Santa Monica

Oakwood

Hollywood

West
Adams

Baldwin
Hills

Leimert Park

Downtown
Los Angeles

LANCER

MLK Hospital /
Charles Drew U.

Watts

Compton

Pacific Ocean

Pomona

San
Bernardin

Orange Co.

Long Beach

0   5   10 Miles

Introduction

Dreaming of Black Los Angeles

Darnell Hunt

Over a fast-paced montage of images—Los Angeles's downtown skyline, home-lined hillsides, street signs—and accompanied by a hip-hop–inspired musical theme, we hear the voices of several black teenagers:

Male #1: Welcome to Los Angeles . . .
Female #1: . . . our Los Angeles
Male #1: Baldwin Hills.
Female #1: City in the Clouds.
Jonathan: Not all black people live in the 'hood.
Moriah: Some of us live in big houses with amazing vistas.
Ashley: We are the sons and daughters of doctors, actors, and athletes . . .
Seiko: . . . as well as policemen, nurses, and teachers.
Lor'Rena: This is where the Black Beverly Hills meets.
Staci: The mean streets of Crenshaw and Inglewood below.
Aungel: Some of us are blessed with opportunities . . .
Justin: . . . and some of us will always struggle for a better tomorrow.
Gerren: But what unites us is greater than what separates us . . .
Sal: . . . because we share more than just a neighborhood.
Female #2: This is Baldwin Hills . . . and this is our reality.

So begins a typical episode of Black Entertainment Television's *Baldwin Hills*,[1] a scripted "reality" program that debuted on the black-oriented cable network in 2007. Developed by a white production company,[2] *Baldwin Hills* was among BET's most popular shows in 2007. It was seen in nearly 1 million black homes coast to coast when it debuted and was reviewed

1

in the nation's most influential media. The *New York Times*, for example, headlined its review "The Posh Princes and Princesses of the Hills," and described the title-sequence voice-overs presented above as "unabashed sociological pleading."[3] At issue, of course, was the teen-targeted show's apparent status as a counternarrative to a more dominant narrative that placed black people in the ghetto, their children at constant risk of being swept up by drug and gang culture, and their dreams for a "better tomorrow" permanently on hold. Wrote the *New York Times*:

> [T]he show's 11 cast members, ages 16 to 19, whose upper-middle-class parents include two former NBA stars, are the smartest, funniest, most charming and generally most well-behaved group of teenagers imaginable. Instead of the drama of racial inequality, we get the more ordinary drama of spoiled kids trying, very politely, to take advantage of their parents.[4]

This example of "highly satisfying, if not exactly exciting, television," as the newspaper put it, provides us with an apt point of entry for introducing the issues that concern us in this volume. It is telling that white sensibilities played such a defining role in a show airing on a black-oriented cable network and targeted at black teens. The history of American television, after all, is one of white domination.[5] The "Hood and the Hills" concept that drives the show, as one of the white creators labeled it,[6] highlights the drama of black diversity in Los Angeles at the expense of the "drama of racial inequality." As a consequence, the history of a place like Baldwin Hills is erased. The static snapshots circulated by the show offer little context for making sense of the black lives depicted on the screen. Baldwin Hills just is. The black people who live there just are.

The Black Los Angeles Project

This book, by contrast, has everything to do with context. *Black Los Angeles: American Dreams and Racial Realities* is a historically grounded, multidisciplinary exploration into the ups and downs of black life in a huge American metropolis. It is an attempt to connect the dots between the past, present, and future of a space that was seeded centuries ago with a profound black presence, that has attracted hundreds of thousands of black migrants in the intervening years, but that, oddly enough, is only marginally understood as a black place. *Black Los Angeles: American Dreams and Racial Realities* aims to situate black-identified places like Baldwin Hills, as well as the people who live, work, and play there, within the context of a much broader space my colleagues and I think of as "Black Los Angeles."

Over the past eight years, the Ralph J. Bunche Center for African American Studies at the University of California, Los Angeles (UCLA) has hosted a series of workshops involving scholars and community members, all under the rubric of the "Black Los Angeles Project," in order to identify relevant questions and effective methods for interrogating this book's rather complex object of inquiry. A term like "Black Los Angeles," we found, raises interesting questions about what is meant by "black" and by "Los Angeles." With "black," we ultimately agreed that we were invoking all of the racial meanings that have been applied to people of African descent throughout American history. These "racial projects"[7] have distinguished "black people" from "white people" (e.g., skin color, facial features, cultural differences), primarily as a means of subordinating the former to the latter (e.g., slavery, Jim Crow, institutional racism). In this sense, our decision to center the concept of "black" in this book had much more to do with power and politics than with any objectively verifiable differences between the "races" that may exist in nature. And even though chapters in this book consider the rather remarkable multicultural history of Los Angeles, it was the fundamental binary relationship between "blackness" and "whiteness" that framed our inquiry.[8]

"Los Angeles," of course, is a city that has objectively defined, geographic boundaries. Its 498.3 square miles—among the largest of American cities—was home to 3.8 million residents in 2006.[9] But when we speak of "Los Angeles" in this book we invoke the much broader understanding of a place that incorporates areas of the Southern California region lying beyond the formal city limits.[10] The notion of the Los Angeles metropolitan area gets us a bit closer to the space we have in mind. Nearly 13 million people resided in this area in 2005,[11] people who hailed from all over the globe and who spoke more than 200 different languages. The idea of "Black Los Angeles" brings it all together to define a unique urban space in which people of African descent—who both struggle with and celebrate the meanings associated with "blackness" in America—have developed and continue to develop a sense of community. Five core themes have anchored our efforts to understand "Black Los Angeles:" communities and neighborhoods; religious life; political participation; cultural production; and social justice. Each of the sixteen chapters that comprise this book presents a case study or historical vignette that traverses the entire range of these themes. The book is organized into four sections: "Space," three chapters that trace the evolution of black communities in Los Angeles; "People," four chapters that tell the stories of people who've faced particular challenges in the city; "Image," five chapters that attempt to make sense of media representations and self-representations about Black Los Angeles; and "Action," four chapters that document community interventions successful in bringing about progressive change.

No single volume can tell the whole story that is Black Los Angeles. Collectively, the chapters comprising this book merely aim to make clearer what the complexities of day-to-day life in a big city often obfuscate. They attempt to stitch together a big picture from meaningful details, specific cases carefully selected by scholars and community members from the myriad possibilities, because of their potential for revealing what lies at the heart of black life in Los Angeles.

Throughout its history, Los Angeles has been imagined as the city of dreams.[12] Whether it was the region's reputation as a temperate paradise with expansive, palm tree–lined beaches and mountain vistas, the real estate boosterism that attracted white midwesterners to the area throughout the late nineteenth and early twentieth centuries, or the association of the city with the Hollywood image factories that later took root there, Los Angeles has figured prominently in the popular American imagination. Often this imagery portrayed the West Coast, which Los Angeles has come to anchor, as a final frontier. This wide-open destination, teeming with possibilities, has at times symbolized the pursuit of the American Dream.

The idea of the "American Dream" is the subject of countless artistic and academic works. This is so because the idea has been such a cornerstone of American culture, one that has inspired people to strive for a better tomorrow, while also functioning as an ideology masking the fundamentally unequal distribution of power and privilege in American society. The idea is firmly rooted in the early days of what would become America, when Puritans came to North America to establish a society based on the Puritan ideal of the "good life." It has evolved throughout the centuries with focuses on upward mobility, home ownership, and equality.

But whereas for most Americans, the idea of the American Dream has resonated comfortably with the core of their being *as Americans*, for African Americans the dream has evoked significantly more ambivalence.

This is because "racial realities," which we invoke in the second half of this book's subtitle, are also a core component of the American landscape. As such, they create tensions and contradictions acutely felt by a people who have never enjoyed full citizenship in this country because of their race. Indeed, these realities have inspired poets like Langston Hughes to write of a "dream deferred," visionaries like Martin Luther King Jr. to talk about his "dream that one day this nation will rise up and live out the true meaning of its creed," and activists like Eldridge Cleaver to employ the idea of the American Dream in order to "struggle against the American nightmare." It is this basic tension between dreams and realities that each of the chapters in this book explores in its own way. It is this tension that the case of Baldwin Hills so effectively introduces.

The "Real" Baldwin Hills

It should surprise no one that a show like BET's *Baldwin Hills* would have captured the imagination of so many African American youth in the first decade of the 2000s. These viewers, as evidenced by the hundreds of posts to the show's BET message board, obviously derived pleasure from their struggles to reconcile what they were seeing with their own day-to-day experiences.[13] Despite the show's calculated focus on the "ordinary drama of spoiled kids trying, very politely, to take advantage of their parents," the imagery mass-communicated by the show necessarily invoked an enduring tension between American Dreams and racial realities, between the material trappings of success and the stubborn reality of race. This is a tension that less-affluent black viewers could not help but find provocative as they compared the privileged black lives depicted in the show to their own. Meanwhile, more affluent black youth (like my goddaughter who lived in an upscale, white neighborhood in Tennessee) likely found the show compelling because of its simultaneous depiction of upper-middle-class status infused with the flavor of black community—a happy marriage missing from their own, otherwise happy lives.

My wife and I moved to Baldwin Hills in 1994. Fresh out of graduate school, we stumbled upon a secluded community realtors referred to as "Baldwin Vista" and fell in love with a modestly sized, yet stylish two-bedroom-and-den home on a quiet street terminated by a cul-de-sac. When we saw the house we knew immediately that it was our dream first home. Boasting a tree-filtered, 180-degree view of the city—which included the famous Hollywood sign, Los Angeles's ever-evolving down-town skyline, and the high-rise buildings that line Wilshire Boulevard from downtown to the sea—the house was nestled in the Baldwin Hills among several other more impressive structures on the street, many of which, we would learn, were distinctive homes that had been featured in *Architectural Digest* in the 1950s and 1960s. I had come of age in Washington, DC, one of America's more conventional "chocolate cities." I hadn't seen another black community quite like the one we'd just moved into.

"Baldwin Hills" refers to prime real estate in Southwest Los Angeles, a community fifteen minutes from everywhere,[14] which received its name from E. J. "Lucky" Baldwin, a cattle rancher and horse racer who acquired the land in the nineteenth century from the original, Spanish land grant holders.[15] In chapter 1, Paul Robinson systematically chronicles the processes by which the Spanish era of the eighteenth century gave rise to the more familiar racial topography of twenty-first-century Los Angeles. For now, it's important to note that "Lucky" Baldwin's Rancho Cienega o Paso de la Tijera would eventually be parceled out, developed by the Baldwin Hills Company and other developers in the 1940s and 1950s, before becoming more recognizable today as the tony, majority-black communities of Baldwin Hills Estates, Baldwin Vista, Ladera Heights, and View Park —which collectively provide the backdrop for BET's *Baldwin Hills*.[16]

Baldwin Hills, in interesting ways, encapsulates many of the contradictions that comprise Black Los Angeles. On the one hand, it is recognized as one of the most affluent black communities in America. On the other, it is located in "South Los Angeles"—a relatively undesirable area of Los Angeles once referred to as "South Central," acquiring its name from one of the city's earliest black neighborhoods on South Central Avenue. As Dionne Bennett shows in chapter 8, this geographically ill-defined area has been associated with gangs, drugs, and violence in American popular culture, particularly since at least the mid 1980s. Alex Alonso pays particular attention to the presence of street gangs in the area in chapter 5, when he presents a history of black gangs in Los Angeles. Indeed, my wife and I were able to afford our first home in Baldwin Vista primarily because of what sits at the foot of the hill: less than half a mile away, rests Baldwin Village, or "The Jungle" as locals call it, a sprawling black and Latino low-income apartment complex infamous for gang violence and serving as the location for the apartment of actor Denzel Washington's rogue cop in *Training Day* (see fig. I.1). The moniker "The Jungle," of course, was a classic double entendre. So-named for the lush tropical

Figure I.1. Baldwin Village, with Baldwin Hills homes in background. Photo courtesy of Darnell Hunt.

foliage that engulfs the area's several surrounding blocks, it came to signify negative stereotypes associated with the mostly poor and working-class people who lived there. Our first home, perched in the hills directly above this community, would have been priced significantly out of our reach had it been located on Los Angeles's Anglo-identified Westside. But this property-value maxim didn't always apply to Baldwin Hills.

The case of Baldwin Hills exposes tensions between the promise of Los Angeles and racial realities related to the passage of time and the transition of space. When the sprawling area known as Baldwin Hills was first developed in the 1940s and 1950s, it was one of the most exclusive communities in all of Southern California. Indeed, the area was nicknamed "Pill Hill" because of the preponderance of doctors who called the hills home. Whereas Los Angeles's Westside would increasingly come to signify "white space" in the "colorblind" times of the late twentieth century, Baldwin Hills was explicitly *defined* as such during its conception. Despite a Supreme Court decision that challenged the legality of racially restrictive covenants in 1948, the declaration of restrictions attached to the deed for each home in the area sought to ensure that Baldwin Hills would remain a white space in perpetuity.[17] Accordingly, the original deed for our first home (which was built in 1953) included the following notable restrictions:

1. No part of any said realty shall ever be sold, conveyed, leased, or rented to any person not of the white or Caucasian race.
2. No part of any said realty shall ever at any time be used or occupied or be permitted to be used or occupied by any person not of the white or Caucasian race, except such as are in the employ of the resident owner or resident tenants of said property.[18]

In other words—housekeepers, maids, butlers, and gardeners aside —these declarations worked to assure affluent, white homebuyers that Baldwin Hills would be devoid of color. And so it was in the early days. This centrally located community of amazing vistas, cool ocean breezes, architecturally significant housing, and nearby, whites-only golf course, constituted, shortly after its development, an exclusive white wonderland. And far from being the property-values liability that it was in the early 2000s, "The Jungle" of the 1950s and early 1960s comprised trendy, luxury apartments that appealed to well-heeled whites who were all too happy to reside at the foot of the hills.

So what happened?

Scholars of residential segregation in America have written extensively about the role white fears of an impending minority threat play in motivating "white flight" from urban areas,[19] a phenomenon aided by realtors who exploit real or perceived declines in property values to encourage white homeowners to sell their homes to nonwhite families.[20] As more homes are sold, more trickle onto the market. Eventually a "tipping point" is reached, after which the process accelerates and rather dramatically transforms the neighborhood from white to minority space.[21] Paul Robinson's decade-by-decade mapping of racial demographics in chapter 1 shows how this process has helped shape the geographic contours of "Black Los Angeles" over the years. What happened in Baldwin Hills, to be sure, constitutes but a specific Los Angeles incarnation of a more general American racial process.

Nevertheless, there are several notable peculiarities about the case of Baldwin Hills that bear consideration here, with many of these peculiarities rooted in the particulars of Los Angeles. For example, white flight from Baldwin Hills clearly accelerated in the years following the 1965 Watts riots—not only the nation's costliest urban uprisings up to that point, but also a signature black rebellion that arguably signaled the end of the civil rights era and the rise of Black Power.[22] Although most of the activities associated with the Watts uprisings occurred several miles away from the tranquil environs of Baldwin Hills, many of the original white homeowners in the area undoubtedly found the explosion of black outrage too close for comfort.

One of these pioneers, a neighbor who lived across the street from our first home, provided us with stories about why he and his wife, unlike many of the original homeowners, decided to stay. In his eighties when we first moved into the neighborhood, he regularly talked to us about his attachment to his one-of-a-kind house with a view, about the natural beauty of the surrounding area that could not be easily duplicated elsewhere. A retired professor, he noted that the street and the one immediately below had been developed by a consortium of fifty-three professors from the University of Southern California in the early 1950s, after they acquired seventeen acres from the Baldwin Hills Company and divided it into individual lots.[23] "Troydale," as the close-knit community was known in honor of USC's "Trojans" nickname, would become virtually all black by the mid-1970s, after nearly all of my neighbor's white peers abandoned him and the area.

By late 1999, we had expanded our family and were looking to move to a larger home. We found one in the same neighborhood, a little farther up the hill, which doubled our living space and also provided a nice view of the city's skyline through a canyon. Then, a few years later, we moved again in the same neighborhood, this time to a comparable-sized home that was notable for its stunning, unobstructed, 180-degree view of the city from downtown to the hills of the Westside. Built in 1960 and featured in a 1962 edition of *Architectural Digest*, the home was designed by a white architect who had once served as chief designer for Los Angeles's famed black architect to the stars, Paul Williams.[24] The home underscored another peculiarity about Baldwin Hills that is quintessential Los Angeles: the area's association with black celebrity.

In the early years of racial transition, Baldwin Hills became home to dozens of black celebrities and athletes who happily snatched up the one-of-a-kind properties vacated by whites who had fled farther west. The last home we purchased in the neighborhood, in 2003, had been purchased by actress Roxie Roker in 1975 from the widow of the white dentist who built the house in 1960. Roker, her husband Sy Kravitz, and young son Lenny (who would attend Beverly Hills High School and later become a rock star) had moved from New York to Los Angeles so that Roker could co-star in the 1970s and 1980s hit sitcom, *The Jeffersons*.[25] Redd Foxx (*Sanford and Son*), Esther Rolle (*Good Times*), film director John Singleton (*Boyz N the Hood*), rapper Ice Cube, and basketball stars A. C. Green and Byron Scott of the Los Angeles Lakers are also among the "names" who called Baldwin Hills home at one point in their careers.

One of the themes emerging from this book is that Black Los Angeles has had a profound effect on how we think about Black America, particularly since the second half of the twentieth century, when the Hollywood television and film industries, in conjunction with professional sports, assumed center stage in the stories the nation told about itself. Nancy Yuen's work in chapter 9 shows how black actors invariably found themselves in the position of interpreting the roles they played in television and film— even when the story was set in other places—through the prism of their experiences of being black and living in Los Angeles. It is no accident that Motown Records moved to Los Angeles in 1972 or that the SOLAR label, as Scot Brown explores in chapter 11, became such a force in the black music world of the 1970s and 1980s. Late twentieth-century Los Angeles had become the nation's media capital.

Of course, not all of Los Angeles's black celebrities chose to live in Baldwin Hills nor were most of Baldwin Hills's black residents, after the transition, rich and famous. Some—like California's first black congresswoman, Yvonne Brathwaite Burke, or the state's first black female Speaker of the Assembly, Karen Bass—were public servants who, while well known, would not be considered celebrities by most. The reputations of these Baldwin Hills residents were grounded in their ability to engage the difficult, day-to-day work of politics, to connect with the common woman and common man and, in the end, to impact the material conditions faced by blacks in the city, region, and state. Burke's lengthy tenure as a Los Angeles County supervisor figures prominently in chapter 12, when Ana-Christina Ramón and I examine the politics behind the rise and fall of Martin Luther King Jr. Hospital, a facility erected in the aftermath of the Watts uprisings to serve the largely black community in the area. Melina Abdullah and Regina Freer examine Bass's contributions in chapter 13, which considers the rich legacy of black female leaders in the city who labored to bridge electoral politics with community organizing.

Despite the glamour often associated with Baldwin Hills, the majority of its residents since the transition have been more ordinary black Angelenos. They were upwardly mobile, middle-class professionals like the next-door neighbors we had when we lived in our first, modest-sized "Troydale" home. A postal worker and a schoolteacher, the couple had purchased their hillside home from the original white owners at the height of the neighborhood's racial transition in 1971. For this couple, for the hundreds of black police officers, nurses, doctors, lawyers, professors, and small business owners who also moved into the community during the early period, and for those, like us, who followed a generation later, Baldwin Hills represented the attainment of a distinctively black version of the American Dream. Ironically, it was a dream made possible for most by white flight, depressed property values, and declining amenities.

Driving south on La Brea Avenue, the house-lined Baldwin Hills looming ahead to either side of the road, one couldn't help but notice the aging strip malls and shopping centers that stood in the early 2000s and wonder what the area must have been like in its white heyday, when local businesses catered to a more upscale crowd, before residents who could do better abandoned neighborhood schools for other options, and before a shopping center at the foot of the hills burned down in the Los Angeles "riots" of 1992, forever singeing the boundaries of the community. Despite the distinctive hillside homes, despite the unparalleled views of the city, and despite the almost mythic allure Baldwin Hills had achieved over the years in the black imagination, the fact remains that residents of Baldwin Hills routinely found it necessary to leave this hallowed black space and head farther west in order to obtain the type of services—quality schooling for their children, well-stocked and adequately staffed stores, trendy restaurants—commensurate with the dream. Arguably, the dream represented by Baldwin Hills was a mixed blessing that had much to say about the experience of being black in Los Angeles and in America.

The Dream of Black Los Angeles

In "Colored California," an article published in a 1913 issue of *The Crisis*,[26] W. E. B. Du Bois writes about his first visit to Los Angeles. What immediately strikes the reader about the piece is the exuberance with which Du Bois, the era's eminent scholar of race, describes the promise that Los Angeles holds for black people. Sixty years before Baldwin Hills would become a signature black residential space, Du Bois had already proclaimed Los Angeles as something of a housing mecca for blacks. Speaking of the black residents who greeted him in Los Angeles, he writes, "They are without doubt the most beautifully housed group of colored people in the United States."[27] Du Bois goes on to devote considerable space in the article to several images that showcase the smart homes of enterprising black residents. Indeed, one such image, of the "beautiful home of Mr. and Mrs. William Foster," adorns the issue's cover.

But Du Bois concedes that the city was no racial paradise—"The color line is there and sharply drawn," he notes. He then describes the segregationist practices that organized public life in the city, much as they did in other cities throughout America during the period. "Women have had difficulty in having gloves and shoes fitted at the stores, the hotels do not welcome colored people, the restaurants are not for all that hunger."[28]

Du Bois's observations about the early color line in Los Angeles are echoed in the 1936 doctoral dissertation of a young black man who studied at the University of Southern California—the predominantly white, private university about two miles from the center of Los Angeles's black community of the day. Max Bond, uncle of future NAACP chairman Julian Bond, explains that Los Angeles's color line began to harden around the time of Du Bois's visit, as more and more enterprising blacks migrated to the city:

> Many old settlers report that twenty years ago Negroes were welcomed patrons of many of the downtown establishments; they could receive service at any of the downtown restaurants and hotels. . . . The change in attitudes occurred, as has been mentioned, after large increases in the population took place.[29]

It goes without saying that Los Angeles's color line, in all of its peculiarity and typicality, is a hulking presence in each of the chapters presented in this book. For example, Andrew Deener's ethnography of Oakwood (chap. 3) chronicles how Los Angeles's color line of the early 1900s resulted in the establishment of one of the earliest communities of black homeowners in the city—a seaside enclave that was in decline by the early 2000s due to the dynamics of a real estate market specific to another era. In chapter 2, Reginald Chapple examines how Los Angeles's color line also led to the establishment of the city's signature black community of the early twentieth century, Central Avenue, as well as to the rise of

Leimert Park, which eventually replaced Central Avenue as the cultural hub of Black Los Angeles in the late 1960s. Paul Von Blum's chapter on the history of black visual art in Los Angeles (chap. 10) underscores the centrality that Leimert Park assumed in a racialized art world, while Jooyoung Lee's chapter explores the experiences of aspiring young black male rappers who gravitated to the Leimert Park cultural scene in lieu of other opportunities for success (chap. 4).

Despite the reality of the color line throughout the city's history, an air of excitement permeates Du Bois's writing about the Los Angeles he encountered in 1913. One gets the sense that in an era constrained by the dictates of Jim Crow, he saw possibilities for black people in the city. Not only did there appear to be a reasonably high level of racial comity between the city's black and white residents, but the black residents did not strike him as accommodationists inclined to settle for their racial subordination: "[T]he better class of people, colored and white, can and do meet each other. There is a great deal of co-operation and good will and the black folk are fighters and not followers of the doctrine of surrender."[30]

Apparently, Du Bois wasn't alone in his optimism. Los Angeles became an increasingly popular destination for black Americans throughout the first half of the twentieth century. As Edna Bonacich, Lola Smallwood-Cuevas, Lanita Morris, Steven Pitts, and Joshua Bloom note in chapter 15, many of these migrants were pushed out of the South and pulled into Los Angeles because of the growing city's reputation of affording more opportunities for black employment.

Still, there seemed to be something more fundamental to the allure of Los Angeles in the black imagination, something more formative about black expectations regarding the group's place in the city. Park and Burgess's classic volume, *The City*, provides us with insight here when it looks beyond the material factors of the metropolis, typically captured in maps and statistics, and considers the city as a "state of mind." This approach pays particular attention to the "body of customs and traditions, and of the organized attitudes and sentiments" unique to Los Angeles. *Black* Los Angeles, as Park and Burgess might put it, is not "merely a physical mechanism and an artificial construction. It is involved in the vital processes of the people who compose it; it is a product of nature, and particularly of human nature."[31]

A unique "state of mind," as well as a distinctive ethos and history, indeed seems to have permeated what we think of as "Black Los Angeles." Not only was California named for a mythical black Amazonian queen,

"Califia," but more than half of the Spanish founders of the city in 1781, as Paul Robinson shows in chapter 1, were of African descent. Moreover, because California was admitted to the Union as a free state in 1850—a fact that Du Bois underscores in his article from *The Crisis*—the foundation was laid for a rather peculiar and flexible racial order in the region.[32] At the same time, the pioneering spirit associated with the opening of the West likely tickled the black migrant's imagination as well. Blacks who came west from more settled and rigidly racist regions of the country clearly saw promise in the growing city, a place where it might actually be possible for blacks to realize the American Dream.

But as the black population of Los Angeles swelled with the influx of migrants from Texas, Louisiana, and elsewhere during the first half of the twentieth century, racial realities more reflective of the Jim Crow South soon followed, eventually challenging the dream that so many had hoped to find in the growing metropolis. By the latter part of the twentieth century, prospects seemed more mixed than in Du Bois's day. The urban uprisings of 1965 and 1992, as well as the diminished opportunities associated with those living in communities like "The Jungle," stood side-by-side with black overrepresentation among local elected officials and the enviable lifestyles of black Angelenos living in places like Baldwin Hills. At the same time, a steady stream of immigrants from Central and South America, Asia, and elsewhere had transformed Los Angeles into one of the world's most diverse cities by the last decades of the twentieth century, a multicultural maze, some blacks feared, which threatened the political clout enjoyed by the region's large black population. Although the County of Los Angeles boasted the second largest black population in the nation in 2007—nearly a million people—this population represented a relatively small, 9.5 percent of the county's overall population.[33]

Not long after the University of California established a southern branch in Los Angeles in 1919, it enrolled perhaps its most celebrated alumnus. A young Ralph Bunche, who would go on to become the first African American awarded the Nobel Peace Prize in 1950, became the valedictorian of the school's 1927 class. UCLA would have important connections to Black Los Angeles from its beginnings, educating many of the city's black luminaries, including Bunche, the color-barrier-transcending Jackie Robinson, and Los Angeles's "second" black mayor, Tom Bradley,[34] among many others. But by the early years of the twenty-first century, as Ana-Christina Ramón and I examine in chapter 16, the local chapters of the National Urban League, NAACP, and other community-based advocacy groups would be forced to form an alliance to challenge campus admissions policies that threatened to erase the black student presence from the publicly funded campus.

Nonetheless, the dream of a better life lived on for many black Angelenos, despite the often harsh social and economic realities some confronted in the city. For all of the black families in Los Angeles able, for example, to celebrate the academic advancement of their young ones, there were others forced to endure the hardships associated with maintaining ties to loved ones behind bars—like the families interviewed by Belinda Tucker, Neva Pemberton, Mary Weaver, Gwendelyn Rivera, and Carrie Petrucci in chapter 6. While members of the black gay community studied by Mignon Moore in chapter 7 negotiated their place(s) in Black Los Angeles, others wrestled with environmental justice issues that, as Sonya Winton reveals in chapter 14, were largely ignored by mainstream environmental groups. To be sure, the struggle between American dreams and racial realities in Los Angeles continued in the early twenty-first century.

In the final analysis, this book aims to address several critical questions associated with this struggle: What is the nature of the "black" in the space we refer to as "Black Los Angeles?" How can the history of a place be employed to make sense of the racial present? What lessons can be learned that might help make black dreams of a brighter future a reality in the region and beyond? And what can the case of "Black Los Angeles" teach us about race in America? Black Los Angeles is and has always been a space of profound contradictions. Just as Los Angeles has come to symbolize the complexities of the early twenty-first-century city,[35] so too has Black Los Angeles come to embody the complex realities of race in so-called "colorblind" times.

NOTES

1. Transcript based on the opening sequence for season two of *Baldwin Hills*.

2. *Baldwin Hills* was produced by Michael McNamara (Director), Sheri Maroufkhani (Executive Producer) and Bill Rademaekers (Executive Producer) of MCFilmworks, according to a July 10, 2008, report from *PR Newswire US*. The first-season DVD and BET website (from July 10, 2008) also identified Mark Brown, an African American actor, as an Executive Producer for the show.

3. Mike Hale, "Posh Princes and Princesses of the Hills," *New York Times*, August 7, 2007, http://www.nytimes.com/2007/08/07/arts/television/07hale.html?_r= 1&scp=1&sq=baldwin%20hills%20show&st=cse (accessed August 20, 2008).

4. Ibid.

5. Elsewhere, I chronicle the history of business-as-usual practices in American popular television that, as of the early twenty-first century, still "virtually guaranteed the conservation of a radically insular industry under white control" (Hunt, *Channeling Blackness*, 269).

6. Director Michael McNamara, from interviews featured in "The Creators" on the first-season DVD for the series.

7. Omi and Winant, *Racial Formation in the United States*.

8. See Hunt, *Channeling Blackness*.

9. U.S. Census Bureau.

10. For a more detailed discussion of ways of thinking about "Los Angeles," see Hunt, "Representing 'Los Angeles.'"

11. U.S. Census Bureau.

12. For example, see M. Davis, *City of Quartz*.

13. For example, one viewer, "kris120379," had this to say about the show: "I am from L.A. We know how are [*sic*] people are. This show is so fake and gay. They are actors not reality. They are from Beverly Hills or Hollywood. Why can't people just be real? Why didn't BET get real people from L.A.???" (http://betboards.bet.com/forums/404219/ShowPost.aspx)

14. Baldwin Hills is centrally located in the Los Angeles Basin, with easy access to the 10 Interstate, the 405 Freeway, and the 110 Freeway. These major Los Angeles freeways surround the area in a triangle with sides about five miles long. Baldwin Hills is less than three miles from the studios of Culver City, less than five miles from the museums of Los Angeles's Wilshire Corridor, about six miles from Beverly Hills, eight miles from the beaches of Venice and Marina Del Rey, and eight miles from the heart of downtown Los Angeles.

15. Baldwin claims to have imported several hundred black laborers to Los Angeles in the nineteenth century, when the black population was still quite small (Bond, "The Negro in Los Angeles").

16. In 2000, blacks comprised 78.5 percent of the residents living in Los Angeles's 90008 zip code and 72.4 percent of the residents living in the city's 90043 zip code—areas that included most of the Baldwin Hills communities discussed here. Blacks comprised 70.8 percent of Ladera Heights, an unincorporated area of Baldwin Hills. The median income for this community was $103,174, which was more than twice the national median.

17. See chaps. 1 and 2 for more on this development.

18. Declaration of Restrictions made on April 27, 1951, between the Baldwin Hills Company and the original owner of my home.

19. See Massey and Denton, *American Apartheid*.

20. For example, see "Group to Explore Reason for Sale of Ladera Homes" *Los Angeles Times*, June 25, 1972, CS1.

21. Gladwell, *Tipping Point*.

22. Horne, *Fire This Time*.

23. "University Faculty Group Owns Tract," *Los Angeles Times*, May 20, 1951, E1.

24. Paul Williams became the first black certified architect west of the Mississippi in 1921 and later the first black member of the American Institute of Architects. He was known for designing dozens of celebrity homes throughout the Southern California region, as well as prominent public buildings like the Theme Building at Los Angeles International Airport. See Hudson and P. Williams, *Paul R. Williams, Architect*.

25. *The Jeffersons* aired on CBS from 1975 to 1985. Roxie Roker played "Helen Willis," one half of the interracial couple that befriended the Jeffersons as neighbors in their posh New York high-rise.

26. *The Crisis* has been the official journal of the National Association for the Advancement of Colored People (NAACP) since the journal was founded by Du Bois in 1910.

27. Du Bois, "Colored California," 193.

28. Ibid., 194.

29. Bond, "The Negro in Los Angeles," 288–89. Between 1910 and 1920, according to Bond, Los Angeles's black population grew from 7,599 to 15,579.

30. Du Bois, "Colored California," 194.

31. Cited in Hunt, "Representing 'Los Angeles,'" 322–23.

32. For a more detailed discussion of the peculiarities of California's racial order during the period compared to the rest of the nation, see Almaguer, *Racial Fault Lines*.

33. U.S. Census Bureau. Only Cook County in Illinois had a larger black population.

34. In chap. 1, Paul Robinson discusses the importance of Tom Bradley, Los Angeles's first black mayor in the American period.

35. See Dear, *From Chicago to L.A.* for a discussion of Los Angeles as a model for understanding urban processes in the twenty-first century.

||||||||||||||||||||||||||||||||||||||||||||||||||||||

Part 1

Space

People cut themselves off from their ties of the old life when they come to Los Angeles. They are looking for a place where they can be free, where they can do things they couldn't do anywhere else.

—Tom Bradley

Reality is wrong. Dreams are for real.

—Tupac Shakur

Chapter 1

|||||||||||||||||||||||||||||||||||||||||||||||||

Race, Space, and the Evolution of Black Los Angeles

Paul Robinson

First elected in 1973, Tom Bradley is usually credited as the first black mayor of Los Angeles. But a more comprehensive history of the city must recognize that Francisco Reyes was actually the first. His term began in 1793, when the city was still under the Spanish flag. To be sure, the African presence in Los Angeles dates back to the city's origins, and the story of the "Black City of Angels" has yet to be fully told. In this opening chapter, we journey through time to "map out" the spaces associated with the evolution of Black Los Angeles.

African Roots

Although there has long been recognition of the mixed Spanish, African and Native American origins of the first settlers in Los Angeles, there also has been a tendency for scholars to downplay the influence of their African and Native American roots, instead dwelling on their assimilation into the region's Spanish heritage. The multiracial pueblo that was formed on the banks of the Los Angeles River in the late eighteenth century played an important role in the Spanish Empire's northward expansion into "Alta California," yet that role was obscured by early Anglo-American historians who made unsubstantiated charges of the laziness, ignorance and uselessness of the original inhabitants.[1] These oversights and misrepresentations tended to overshadow the remarkable accomplishments of the society that developed on the western frontiers of the Spanish Empire. This multiracial society proved crucial to Spain's colonial expansion into

North America and set the stage for the modern development of the Los Angeles area.[2]

When El Pueblo de Nuestra Señora la Reina de Los Angeles Del Río de Porciúncula (The Town of Our Lady the Queen of the Angels on the River Porciúncula) was established in 1781, the majority of the pobladores (settlers) had African ancestry. The presence of these earliest blacks was the result of Spain's eighteenth-century expansion of its empire northward into what was then known as Alta California. The original settlers of Los Angeles came from areas that are now states in western Mexico, a region where the Spanish empire relied heavily on African and mulatto[3] populations as soldiers (black militiamen), and laborers in agriculture and mining. As a result, racial restrictions on upward social mobility of those with African heritage were more relaxed than in other parts of the empire. The shortage of Spaniards willing to serve on the Western frontera (frontier), led to the development of a substantial free black population living in the Pacific coastal areas of Sinaloa, Sonora, and Baja California. Estimates have placed Africans and mulattoes at greater than 25 percent of the overall population living in these regions during the eighteenth century.[4]

Despite Spain's rigid racial classification system that placed Africans (negros) and Indians (indios) at the bottom, Africans and mixed-race individuals enjoyed greater social mobility on the Western frontier.[5] Racial mixing was more common in California than in Anglo-dominated portions of North America, with men of all races tending to marry indigenous women (indias) or African/European/indigenous women of various mixtures (mulatas and mestizas). Spanish men also held African and Native American concubines. As a result, mulattoes and mestizos quickly outnumbered other groups, and many of the original African Californios exhibited gradual "browning" over time as people married into other ethnic groups.[6] By 1760 one Spanish observer noted that most of the soldiers on Spain's Western frontier were mulatto.[7] Africans and Indians who became Christians were considered part of the "gente de razon" or "people of reason," thus elevating their social standing.

When Spanish imperial authorities decided to head off the encroachment of Russians and English on the northern Pacific Coast by establishing a network of missions (clergy settlements), presidios (army forts), and pueblos (villages) in Alta California, many of the people recruited as settlers were free Africans or mulattoes from Baja, Sinaloa, and Sonora.[8] Of the original forty-six pobladores, at least twenty-six of them were at least part African (see table 1.1).

TABLE 1.1
Original Pobladores at Los Angeles, 1781[a]

Name	Race	Age	Spouse Name	Spouse Race	Spouse Age	Children: Name and Age
José Lara	Español	50	María Antonia Campos	India Ladina	23	José Julián, 4; Juana Jesús, 6; María Faustina, 2
José Antonio Navarro	Mestizo	42	María Rufina Dorotea	Mulata	None listed	José María, 10; José Clemente, 9; María Josefa, 4
Basilio Rosas	Indio	67	María Manuela Calixtra Hernández	Mulata	None listed	José Máximo, 15; Carlos, 12; Antonio Rosalino, 7; José Marcelino, 4; Juan Esteban, 2; María Josefa, 8
Antonio Mesa	Negro	38	Ana Gertrudis López	Mulata	27	Antonio María, 8; María Paula, 10
Antonio Villavicencio	Español	30	María de los Santos Seferina	India	26	María Antonia Josefa, 8, entenada
José Vanegas	Indio	28	María Máxima Aguilar	India	20	Cosmé Damién, 1
Alejandro Rosas	Indio	19	Juana Rodríguez	Coyota	20	
Pablo Rodríguez	Indio	25	María Rosalía Noriega	India	26	María Antonia, 1
Manuel Camero	Mulato	30	María Tomasa	Mulata	24	
Luís Quintero	Negro	55	María Petra Rubio	Mulata	40	José Clemente, 3; María Gertrudis, 16; María Concepción, 9; Tomasa, 7; Rafaela, 6
José Moreno	Mulato	22	María Guadalupe Gertrudis	Mulata	19	

[a] Spanish Soldiers (escorts) and their families not listed.
Source: First Padron (Census) of Los Angeles, 1781.

The early pueblo at Los Angeles was not isolated from nearby missions and presidios. Several of the Spanish soldiers who escorted the eleven pobladores families also lived in the settlement with their own families, and there was considerable exchange and movement back and forth between the pueblo at Los Angeles, the mission at San Gabriel (roughly ten miles away) and the presidios at Santa Barbara and San Diego (each about one hundred miles away). The pueblo also received regular supplies from other parts of New Spain that arrived by ship near San Pedro and were brought overland to Los Angeles. The lifestyles of pueblo residents were strictly controlled by the military, local government authorities, and the Catholic Church. Each poblador had to be registered to live in a settlement, and could not travel away from the pueblo without the permission of local authorities. The job of the pobladores was to grow crops and raise livestock to help provision the soldiers at Santa Barbara. In exchange, they were provided with the supplies and materials necessary for survival until they could become self-sufficient. There were strict guidelines governing conduct in each pueblo and restricting relations with local Indian tribes.[9]

Unlike in many other parts of the Spanish Empire, there was little social distance between poblador families. Mulattoes, Spaniards, mestizos, and indios (except the local Indians) tended to intermingle and marry with little restriction in colonial Los Angeles. Spanish military officers and their families were the closest to an isolated aristocratic class because the Spanish system imposed ceilings on how high persons of non-Spanish ancestry could rise in the military. However, all evidence supports the likelihood that, socially, even officers tended to intermingle freely with the enlisted and with the pobladores.[10] More evidence of the upward mobility of blacks in the early Los Angeles pueblo is found in the election of a mulatto, Francisco Reyes, as the alcalde (mayor) in 1793. The population of the pueblo by then had grown to 148 persons, including 59 Spaniards, 57 mulattoes, 17 mestizos, and 15 indios. However, even within the different ethnic groups then established at the pueblo, there was continued distinction made between the more Hispanicized indios and the local Native Americans, who continued to be forbidden from establishing residence in the pueblo.

By 1800 the success of the pueblo—then boasting 315 persons—had become fully apparent. The original settlement of mostly African ancestry from New Spain's Pacific Frontier had morphed into a successful and productive pueblo and become a great asset to Spain.[11] The pueblo at Los Angeles was the largest Spanish settlement in Alta California in 1807. The settlement experienced a continual influx of retired soldiers and their families from the nearby presidios of San Diego and Santa Barbara, and the descendants of the original pobladores continued to proliferate. As the population grew so did commerce, and soon foreign ships regularly visited the nearby ports.[12] Although forbidden to trade with these ships under Spanish law, the trading opportunities offered by these "Yankee Clippers" were too great for Californios (including some Angelenos) to pass up, and a brisk local trade in sea otter furs developed. Because of its lucrative nature, local authorities in California routinely overlooked this trade.[13] The early 1800s thus began an irreversible trend of contact with the young American nation that would eventually transform Los Angeles from its Spanish roots. During the struggle for Mexican independence from Spain that embroiled central Mexico between 1811 and 1821, foreign trade grew rapidly. Supply ships from New Spain dwindled during this time, increasing Angelenos' reliance on trade with foreign nations.

In 1822 Californios were informed that the Treaty of Cordoba had been signed and that they now lived in a province of the new nation of Mexico. Many Californios, especially the Catholic padres who closely identified with Spain, were displeased, but there was little they could do about it.[14] The political transition from Spanish colony to independent nation of Mexico did not drastically change the daily lives of the Spanish-speaking Afro-Californians, but if anything, the egalitarian ideals and prohibition against slavery introduced by Mexico's new government likely bolstered many of the colonists' feelings of self-esteem and their social standing. In fact, the Mexican period was a time when Africans and their descendents held some of the most important positions in California society.

Although the period of Mexican control in Alta California lasted only about twenty-five years, at least two of the Mexican governors, Manuel Victoria (1831–32), and Pio Pico (1832, 1845–46), had African ancestry. Manuel Victoria was reported by Mexican writers of the period to be a full blooded Negro,[15] and Pio Pico was the grandson of one of the early mulatta residents of the Los Angeles pueblo, and indeed Pio Pico's appearance reflected his African ancestry.

Pico—after whom today's Pico Boulevard is named (see fig 1.1)—is the most famous of the early Afro-Mexican residents of Los Angeles, and his success in civic and commercial life is remarkable. In 1821 Pico opened a dram shop (a bar serving alcohol) in Los Angeles. He earned substantial income from his bar, along with profits from his other enterprise, a nearby hide-tanning shop. In the years that followed, Pico and his brother, Andres Pico, grew to be important figures in Mexican California and played significant roles in the transition from Mexico to the United States in 1846. During the Mexican American War, Governor Pico fled to Baja California, where he unsuccessfully lobbied the Mexican congress to send troops on behalf of the Californios. After the war, Pio Pico returned

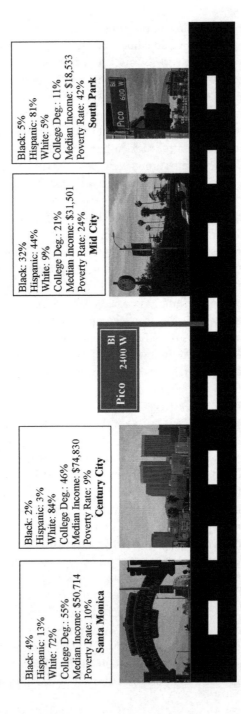

Black: 4%
Hispanic: 13%
White: 72%
College Deg.: 55%
Median Income: $50,714
Poverty Rate: 10%
Santa Monica

Black: 2%
Hispanic: 3%
White: 84%
College Deg.: 46%
Median Income: $74,830
Poverty Rate: 9%
Century City

Black: 32%
Hispanic: 44%
White: 9%
College Deg.: 21%
Median Income: $31,501
Poverty Rate: 24%
Mid City

Black: 5%
Hispanic: 81%
White: 5%
College Deg.: 11%
Median Income: $18,533
Poverty Rate: 42%
South Park

Figure 1.1. A Trip Down Pico Boulevard: From the Pacific to Downtown. From *left* to *right*, the data refer to the following geographical areas: Santa Monica City and zip codes 90067, 90019, 90015. Source: U.S. Census Bureau. Note: Statistics from the 2000 Census.

to Los Angeles and built the famous Pico House Hotel, a structure that still stood in the early 2000s near the site of the original pueblo in downtown Los Angeles.

The example of Pico illustrates how blacks were hardly limited by race in Alta California, where a multiracial society developed that was open to upward mobility and assimilation of people of African descent. Particularly in civic and commercial life, Africans and their descendents experienced few limitations on their prosperity. Certainly social prejudice existed, with dark-skinned settlers more likely than their lighter-skinned counterparts to experience personal discrimination because of their appearance, but that discrimination did not significantly retard their social and economic mobility.

With the coming of American settlers, the situation changed drastically. Because of their experiences under Spanish and Mexican rule, and the ease of their previous assimilation into mainstream life, black Angelenos of the period did not have a strong racial consciousness, most considering themselves as simply "Mexicans." For those Mexicans who retained their African features, the American period would change the way they were treated, and they would begin to suffer increasing institutional injustice alongside English-speaking blacks.

An early example of this change in racial climate is found in the reminiscences of Major Horace Bell, an early American resident of Los Angeles and an important figure in California Democratic politics of the period. Bell told the story of how during the 1853 elections, one of his aides, a Southerner, reported trouble at a polling place in the County of Los Angeles. The aide stated that a black man was attempting to vote, and that he wanted to use violence against the man. When Bell investigated, it turned out that the black man in question spoke only Spanish and considered himself to be a Mexican. The man told an interpreter that he had always voted and wanted to continue to vote under American rule. Upon finding out the man intended to vote for the Democratic candidate, Major Bell decided in favor of political expediency and sent his irate Southern aide to another polling place, thus permitting the black man to vote.[16]

Rise of a New Racial Order

The first English-speaking blacks arrived in the Los Angeles area some time during the early 1800s. Those who arrived by ship had made an arduous and dangerous passage around the tip of South America, or else had endured an overland journey through the Isthmus of Panama. Many others arrived on foot, by horse, or in wagons and coaches from the East.[17] The earliest English-speaking black Californians were an eclectic group engaging in everything from hunting and trapping on the frontier to domestic work in cities.[18] The famous mulatto mountain man and trapper James Beckwourth is known to have spent several years in California in the 1840s; another free black man, Jacob Dodson, took part as a volunteer in the Fremont exploration expeditions into California in the early 1840s. Both of these men worked with the U.S. troops in the battles against the Californios a few years later.[19]

Although the published reports of English-speaking blacks in Mexican California are numerous, there is no documentation of them in Los Angeles before the American period. The total population of the city at the time of the first U.S. Census in 1850 was 3,530.[20] Table 1.2 provides the earliest information available on blacks in the American period, listing fifteen black residents in the County of Los Angeles, twelve of whom lived in the city proper.

The individuals in the census shown were born in many different regions, and a closer look at their households reveals that they also had a variety of living situations that were clearly divided by the language spoken (English versus Spanish).[21] Peter Biggs, known around Los Angeles

TABLE 1.2
African Americans in Los Angeles County in the 1850 Census[a]

Name	Age	Birthplace	Residence
Manuel Agugue	48	Mexico	LA county
Tomasa Agugue	35	Mexico	LA county
Margarita Balenzuela	2	California	LA county
Peter Biggs	35	Virginia	LA city
Josefa U. Chosofo	18	California	LA city
Malvina Conway	20	Kentucky	LA city
William Davis	27	Mississippi	LA city
Julia Douglass	45	Georgia	LA city
Lucy Evertsen (Mulatto)	6	Florida	LA city
Ignacio Fernandez	30	Guatemala	LA city
Becky Hardige	16	Arkansas	LA city
Susan Hardige	14	Alabama	LA city
Clarissa Holman	27	Tennessee	LA city
William Roldan	24	New York	LA city
Maria Ruddle	17	Missouri	LA city

[a] Census likely an undercount.
Source: 1850 Census of Los Angeles County.

by the name of "Nigger Pete," was the only English-speaking black not listed as living in a white household at the time. Biggs became an important person in 1850 because he was the town's only English-speaking barber. He came to California originally as the slave of a U.S. military officer and had been freed at the close of the Mexican American War. He settled in Los Angeles and for a while his "New Orleans Shaving Saloon" enjoyed a monopoly on providing haircuts for Anglo-Angelenos. He married a Mexican woman and is known to have had a daughter named Juana.[22]

Other blacks are listed in the census as free persons living in the home of whites, and although their recorded status as free in 1850 remains dubious, eventually most of these people became part of the growing population of English-speaking free blacks living in the city after the Civil War. For example, Malvina Conway was living in the home of John Conway, a surveyor from Tennessee. Meanwhile, William Davis lived in a house with eight other men, including an American Indian (most likely Creek or Cherokee) from Georgia, and seven other white men from various states in the American South, most of whom listed their occupation as miners.[23]

Over the next decade these fifteen individuals would be joined by at least seventy-three others with African ancestry, including some of the most influential figures in Black Los Angeles history—such as members of the Robert Owens and Biddy Mason families. Through the acquisition of property, Owens and Mason, two former slaves, would eventually help to launch the beginnings of a spatially concentrated Los Angeles black community. How Mason and the others won their freedom and went on to participate in the development of what would become vibrant black neighborhoods by the turn of the century in many ways mirrors the path of the city's own growth.

Black Space, Black Community

After the United States seized control of California in 1846, English-speaking blacks continued to trickle into the Los Angeles area by land or by sea. Irrespective of their mode of entry into California's territory, some African Americans arrived as free persons, while others arrived held in a state of bondage.[24]

Although California was a "free state," many white Southerners who had moved west were determined to keep their African slaves. Despite being technically against California law, owning slaves was still practical for whites in California because the size and rural nature of the state made law enforcement unlikely. Also, a large proportion of the Anglo population in the 1850s consisted of Southerners who held pro-slavery attitudes, making the times difficult for blacks in the Los Angeles area and California in general.

Two early legislative acts initiated by state legislators in Sacramento symbolized these difficulties. The Fugitive Slave Law of California was passed in 1852 and stayed in effect until 1855. This law protected Southerners who brought slaves into California, making it illegal for them to run away from their "owners" while living in California. The act endangered free blacks as well, especially those who did not possess freedom papers. Another harmful statute was the ban on court testimony by non-white witnesses. Passed in 1850, this law freed whites to commit crimes against blacks and other non-whites with impunity, as long as there were no white witnesses present to testify against the perpetrators.

Thus, blacks living in 1850s Los Angeles needed to exercise caution regarding their surroundings or face certain trouble. Rape and other forms of violence were ever-present threats, and there are many accounts of random, unprovoked violence against blacks, usually at the hands of white Southerners.[25] During the pre–Civil War era, blacks in California struggled against the hostility of their environment and improved their legal standing by coming together to fight unjust laws and practices directed against them.

No story typifies the complexity of life for black Angelenos in the 1850s more than that of Robert "Uncle Bob" Owens and Bridget "Biddy" Mason. Although they came to Los Angeles under completely different circumstances, their lives became intertwined. Robert Owens came to California in 1853 after buying his entire family's freedom in Texas. Owens established a relationship with the U.S. Army and was awarded a contract to supply wood to the U.S. quartermaster in Los Angeles.[26] Like Peter Biggs, the 1850s black Los Angeles barber mentioned earlier, Owens and his wife Winnie were examples of newly freed slaves who had become economically prosperous by dealing with those U.S. Army personnel and other white Angelenos who were Northerners and Unionists, and in some cases with European immigrants. Owens rapidly acquired wealth, especially after he purchased land on San Pedro Road, began stocking domestic animals, and became a successful cattle and horse dealer who employed many Mexican vaqueros (cowboys).[27]

Biddy Mason, her daughters, and several other slaves (mostly females) were brought into California by a Georgian who had joined the Mormon Church. After a falling-out with the local Mormon leadership, which was based near San Bernardino, the slave owner sought to travel to Texas, bringing his slaves (including Biddy Mason and her daughters) along with him. For a short time he camped near Los Angeles, while preparing to travel to Texas. Free blacks in the Los Angeles area were aware of the situation faced by other blacks in the region, especially those being held illegally. Owens and other members of his family had befriended the group, and one of Owens's sons was attracted to one of Biddy Mason's daughters. When Robert Owens was told that the Masons' "owner" planned to take them to Texas, a state whose notorious slavery laws he was familiar with, he reported the encampment to the local sheriff and then participated in a rescue operation to remove the enslaved blacks from the Georgian's custody. When the matter was brought before Benjamin Hays, a judge in Los Angeles who was a Northerner and a Unionist, Mason and the others were granted their freedom, much to the dismay of many white Los Angeles residents. Owens sheltered the Mason family at his properties in Los Angeles and advised her on how to do business in the city.[28]

Free blacks in Los Angeles aggressively championed the rights of those who were being enslaved in the state. The actions of the Robert Owens family were instrumental in Biddy Mason's family and the other slaves winning their freedom and avoiding continued slavery in Texas. After Owens died in 1863 his widow, Winnie Owens, Biddy Mason, and their shared children and grandchildren became very successful business entrepreneurs, particularly in real estate. One of Owens's sons (Charles Owens) married one of Mason's daughters (Ellen Mason), and a family dynasty was born. By the turn of the century, the sons of Charles and Ellen had become some of the wealthiest blacks in the West.[29] The real estate activities of these two prominent families and other early financially successful blacks eventually created the nucleus for the formation of a burgeoning black community to the east and south of the old pueblo.

By the 1860s Los Angeles already had become an ethnically diverse city. Mexican Americans were still the dominant population, but the increasing number of whites from Northern states, European immigrants, Southern whites, Asians, and blacks were changing the city's makeup rapidly. English-speaking blacks in Los Angeles began to establish a base in the city, and started to participate in statewide politics. They joined other influential blacks in the state and formed the Colored Convention,

vigorously protesting in front of the California Legislature.[30] For example, as early as 1856 Biddy Mason, with her freedom papers fresh in hand,
participated in the Second Annual Convention of the Colored Citizens of
California in Sacramento, the state capital. She testified against the White
Witness Only Law stating, "This deprivation subjects us to many outrages
and aggressions by wicked and unprincipled white men."[31] The Colored
Convention movement (1855–57) was a key force in eventually overturn-
ing the restrictive and unjust laws that were being passed in the California legislature regarding African Americans—including the California
Fugitive Slave Law, the White Witness Law (which wasn't overturned for
Asians and Mexicans for another ten years[32]), the Separate Schools acts,
and other laws that were detrimental to black Californians.[33]

After the Civil War, blacks in Los Angeles began to achieve a more favorable social position than they had in the previous first two decades
of American rule. As the city became more connected to the rest of the
United States via the establishment of new railroad linkages in the 1870s,
its population grew more and more cosmopolitan. The numbers of blacks
in the County of Los Angeles remained small in the Reconstruction period, however, growing only from 134 in 1870 to 188 in 1880. The population of Los Angeles as a whole was growing more rapidly, and thus the
black share of the population dwindled from .008 percent to .006 percent
during this period. Though still small in number, Los Angeles's black population in this era found themselves in a position to form a unique and
vibrant black community in a space that was relatively free from the historical social relationships that existed between blacks and whites in other
parts of the country. Blacks living in the Los Angeles area at the time were
not isolated from other groups and were likely to have white neighbors.
The 1870 and 1880 censuses show virtually none of the black families living in Los Angeles County had black neighbors; instead they were likely
to live next to whites from the Northeast or North Central states, or European and/or Asian immigrants along with Mexican Americans. They were
not yet living in same-race neighborhoods and instead were loosely clustered into specific sectors of the city in the 1870s and '80s, based on their
occupations.[34]

There appears to have been some degree of social continuity between
the "Calle De Los Negros" of the Mexican period (later dubbed "Nigger Alley" by Anglos) and the later development of an English-speaking
black American settlement to the south and east of this street. Probably
attracted by the presence of Afro-Mexicans who are known to have lived

in and around Calle de Los Negros, English-speaking blacks had also settled in that core area by 1850, along with Mexican and Chinese families,
spreading out down Los Angeles Street toward the quartermaster's depot.
Biddy Mason also lived close to this area. She can be found in the 1860
census living in a home with a middle-aged laborer named James Davis,
along with her daughter and son-in-law, Ellen and Charles Owens, their
son Robert C. Owens, and Henderson Houston, a young laborer.[35]

During this period, Los Angeles was transitioning from an agrarian into
an industrial city, and this rise of local industry created new employment
opportunities for its residents. In 1870 the most common occupation for
black men was "barber," while for women it was "housekeeping." By 1880
"railroad porter" replaced "barber" as the most common occupation for
black men, with more than 20 percent of the black male workforce listing "railroad porter" as their occupation, while "housekeeping" remained
the primary occupation for women. The railroad, in particular, was becoming an important new force in the early economy of the Los Angeles
black community. Railroad companies tended to hire light-skinned men
to work as porters. In fact, 70 percent of the men who identified "railroad
porter" as their occupations in the 1880 census were listed as mulatto.[36]

Beginning in 1880, the U.S. Census included street names for all of the
households visited in the City of Los Angeles.[37] Already by 1880 there
were spatially isolated concentrations of blacks living to the south and
to the north of downtown. It bears repeating that although blacks in Los
Angeles at that time were almost certain to have white neighbors, they
also tended to cluster in only a few parts of the city. The clusters were
(1) a group of mulatto- and black-headed households composed of railroad porters and their families who were living near the Southern Pacific
Railroad's River Station that opened in 1875; this area is now part of Los
Angeles State Historic Park; (2) a large group of households immediately
to the south of the old Mexican pueblo; this area was the extension of
the original black encampments that had settled along Los Angeles Street,
between the old pueblo and the U.S. quartermaster's depot; and (3) young
black and mulatto house servants who lived in the homes of wealthier
whites; these individuals tended to be in their late teens and early twenties and were found scattered throughout the better homes on the southwestern periphery of the city.

Joshua W. Smart, patriarch of the Smart family, arrived in Los Angeles from Providence, Rhode Island, in the 1850s. He had set sail aboard
a "California Clipper" or a "China Clipper" heading for San Francisco to

trade for gold or perhaps across the Pacific to trade in China by way of Hawaii. At some point, young Smart left his ship and came to Los Angeles, where he quickly became established. By 1860 he had met and married Sarah J., who was quite likely the daughter of Robert Owens. The Smart Family continued to establish itself during the 1860s, and by 1870 Joshua Smart had become one of the wealthiest black men in the County of Los Angeles. The value of his estate was $1,450, making him not quite as wealthy as the Owens and Mason families but far wealthier than most of the other residents of Los Angeles. And like the Owens and Mason families, Smart had invested in real estate—a swampy area of land south of downtown on the old Dominguez Rancho, which was called "Nigger Slough" by local whites.[38] Although the Smarts lived in Los Angeles, it is very likely that he allowed other, more newly arrived African American migrants to live in the Slough in exchange for agricultural labor, and thus the offensive nickname developed. This term was used to refer to the area until the 1940s, when the area was drained and more aptly named the Dominguez Channel.

Sarah J. Smart and Joshua Smart are another example of the success of many of the early black pioneer families who lived in Los Angeles during the early years of the transition period from a Mexican to American city. They were able to take advantage of an existing climate of greater openness to African American mobility. Their English language skills and knowledge of American business practices certainly helped them to acquire land and homes. They were able to leverage this real estate to improve their material conditions in ways that would not have been possible in many other areas of the country. They were personally successful and attempted to transfer this wealth to their descendants. But changes in racial attitudes and the development of a massive local social engineering project would hinder the upward mobility of the Smart family as well as most other African Americans in the Los Angeles area in the decades ahead.

Black Mecca?

By 1900 the black population of Los Angeles county had increased to 1,817, a tenfold increase since 1880. This number would increase by more than five times by 1910, rising to 9,424. Although the black population grew slightly faster than the general population over this period, the black share of the city's population increased only from about 1 percent to 2 percent.[39]

The growth in both the black and overall population in Los Angeles took place during a time of rapid transition into an industrial city. Many areas of the city were remade in the 1880–1910 period, and previously un-developed areas were being developed. At the same time, migrants from other parts of the United States, Europe, Mexico, and East Asia continued to arrive. As the city became more diverse, blacks struggled to define their place in the urban hierarchy.

The catalyst for the initial rapid increase in the black population and the formation of a larger black community was the land boom of the 1880s, resulting in the expansion of the black population to 1,258 by 1890.[40] During the 1880s, many new subdivisions were built in the Los Angeles area; housing was abundant and cheap. Although blacks were still relegated to service jobs, they could own property in many areas of Los Angeles. Land ownership was an important factor in the success of the early black pioneer families and continued to be a means to prosperity for those who arrived between 1880 and 1920. The early migrants who clustered around Central Avenue (discussed by Reginald Chapple in chap. 2), as well as those who seeded the black seaside community of Oakwood (discussed by Andrew Deener in chap. 3), benefited from this expansion.

Early twentieth-century Los Angeles did not offer the abundance of industrial jobs that characterized other major U.S. cities, and as a result blacks were disproportionately represented in the menial services. Nearly a third of employed black males in Los Angeles in this period worked as janitors, porters, waiters, or house servants. Others worked as horsemen and later as chauffeurs, but only a few were conductors or motormen, the higher-level transportation jobs. Even greater discrimination occurred in the booming retail trade industry. By 1910 retail trade had become the largest source of employment in Los Angeles. At that time there were 6,177 store salesmen working in the city, of whom only eight were black. By 1920 there were 11,341 salesmen, of whom only twenty-eight were black.[41] Blacks seeking retail employment faced overwhelming competition from European and Mexican immigrants in the early twentieth century, which was accompanied by discriminatory hiring by management.[42]

Despite the discrimination and competition they faced, early twentieth-century black Angelenos formed a diverse community with many social organizations, such as the numerous churches, secret societies, and other community organizations that had sprung up in the years following the Civil War. As in earlier periods, blacks continued to live in all areas of the city, and many were able to improve their material conditions despite increasing hostility by the white population. Many whites resisted the attempts of blacks to redefine their social position in the growing city. Shut out of many sectors of the economy by discriminatory practices, blacks excelled in the professions and business opportunities that were open to them.

This was a time of great promise for blacks in Los Angeles. Given the success of many California blacks in the decades following slavery, there was much hope for the future. One of the key characteristics that promoted the success of the early black Angelenos was the high degree of social organization. For example, a group of black leaders in the city sought to establish a "Negro Cooperative" in 1901. This establishment was to be a "Stock Company organized to Publish Papers and Colonize the Negro Race." The *Los Angeles Times* noted at the time that "the colored people of Los Angeles appear to be thoroughly interested in the development of their race, on both social and industrial lines." Among the community leaders spearheading this effort was J. J. Neimore, publisher of the *California Eagle*. The leaders sought to establish "an industrial training school, an employment agency and an 'Old Virginia Kitchen' for the preparation and sale of old-time Southern cookery."[43]

In addition to business and industry, attaining high levels of education was another method that newly arriving blacks settling in Los Angeles used to combat effects of the mounting racial discrimination they were facing. Writers of mainstream newspapers such as the *Los Angeles Times* were not sure how to address the impressive strides being made by area blacks in the decades after the Mexican era ended. The following excerpt from a 1903 story about the first black lawyer to practice in the city reflects the racist, patronizing, and yet ambivalent attitudes toward black achievement that many white Angelenos held:

FIRST NEGRO TO PRACTICE
*He Bursts Upon Court and Makes Sensation. Gets Poor
Coon Off Scot Free in Crap-shooting Case. District Attorney
Didn't Know the Game, but Squire Blair Had It Pat.*

Coon crap shooters of this town have found a triumphant Moses. He is a little one Baltimore negro as black as a crow. He has come here to practice law. The name of this latest addition to the bar is Isador D. Blair, Esq.

There were three forlorn coons huddled together in the dock listening to the testimony of some police men that had arrested them for shooting craps in a basement on New High Street. Just as Deputy District Attorney Beebe was asking a question there came a complaining voice from the rear. "Mistah Prosecutor, Ah wish yo wouldn't leadt thet witness; yo are suggestin' th' ansehs." Beebe turned and his jaw dropped in blank amazement. As the case went on, the courtroom full of darkies sat listening with stunned admiration. The end of it was that Beebe got up and dismissed the charge against Blair's two clients (a "big yellow Buck" and a "little black fellow").[44]

The question of how blacks would be integrated into the newly burgeoning Los Angeles metropolis was a popular topic in the late nineteenth and early twentieth centuries. While the use of terms like "coon" and "darky" were commonly used by *Los Angeles Times* writers when referring to blacks, these derogatory terms did not go unchallenged. Part of the core mission of black newspapers like the *California Eagle* was to combat the negative stereotypes perpetuated by mainstream, white society. Churches and fraternal organizations such as the Los Angeles Forum (an open forum for black Angelenos) also shared their grievances with black leadership, including successful black clergy, businesspersons, and with each other. This and numerous other community meetings and events provided opportunities to organize for the uplift of the black community in Los Angeles. These black organizations attempted to fight the negative stereotypes they faced at the hands of the mainstream, white-dominated society. A 1906 article in the *Los Angeles Times* captures some of this resistance:

ONLY "AFRICAN" WILL DO.
Negroes Object to Being Called "Darky," "Coon," or Even "Negro."
The wrongs of the negro race were forcibly presented last night at . . . the African Methodist Episcopal Church at Pico and Paloma streets. . . . Two hundred or more gathered at the church to attend . . . an oration delivered by Dr. M. E. Sykes of Los Angeles. . . . Sykes referred to degradations he declared are daily heaped upon his people. A second speech was made by Paul Nash, a colored lawyer. Nash took exception to the treatment that the race question has received at the hands of the press, especially to the use of the terms "darky," "nigger," "negro" and "coon" which he says the paper commonly and indiscriminately use to refer to "Africans."[45]

A general feeling among the black elite in Los Angeles at the time was that if they could only dispel the myths about Africans living in America, they could overcome the social isolation and exclusion they confronted in the city.

The black population in the City of Los Angeles exceeded 7,500 by 1910 and by 1920 had doubled to more than 15,000. As the black population swelled, smaller and smaller proportions of the available residential land were open for black residence. Deed restrictions were increasingly used to prevent blacks from living in most areas of the city's expanding geography.

Expanding Black Space

The relatively small and diverse black communities of 1920s and 1930s Los Angeles were drowned under the enormous wave of in-migration from the South in the 1940s.[46] As this in-migration continued, the social character of the black communities in Los Angeles changed (see table 1.3).

We have good information on what Los Angeles area black communities were like prior to the influx of black migrants from the South during the war years. Max Bond's "The Negro in Los Angeles" documents the spatial layout for Black Los Angeles in the late 1920s and early 1930s and sets the context for the social transformations of the 1940s.[47] Bond's comparisons of the black communities that he researched are reproduced

TABLE 1.3
Birthplace of Los Angeles Blacks, 1920, 1940, 1950[a]

1920			1940			1950		
State	N	%	State	N	%	State	N	%
Texas	2,626	18	California	14,456	19	Texas	50,696	24
California	2,323	16	Texas	13,578	18	California	40,517	19
Tennessee	1,414	10	Louisiana	10,091	14	Louisiana	38,301	18
Arkansas	1,212	8	Oklahoma	4,936	7	Arkansas	14,133	7
Louisiana	1,111	8	Mississippi	3,963	5	Mississippi	12,199	6
Missouri	807	6	Georgia	3,574	5	Oklahoma	10,580	5
South Carolina	707	5	Alabama	3,448	5	Georgia	6,642	3
Illinois	606	4	Arkansas	2,400	3	Alabama	5,732	3
Kansas	505	3	Missouri	2,400	3	Missouri	4,478	2
Kentucky	504	3	Tennessee	2,191	3	Kansas	4,214	2
Other	2,622	18	Other	13,104	18	Other	26,918	13

[a] Author's calculations. Includes non-Hispanic blacks residing in the Los Angeles–Long Beach, CA, metropolitan area.
Source: S. Ruggles, M. Sobek, T. Alexander, C. A. Fitch, R. Goeken, P. K. Hall, M. King, and C. Ronnander, Integrated Public Use Microdata Series: Version 4.0 (Machine-readable database), Minneapolis, MN: Minnesota Population Center (producer and distributor), 2008.

TABLE 1.4

Comparative Analysis of Black Families in Los Angeles, 1934

	Nativity	Family Background	Family Tradition
Central Avenue	Most of the residents appear to be from Texas, Louisiana, and Oklahoma. In addition, Alabama, Georgia, and Arkansas are well represented.	Diversified culture patterns.	Very definite traditions of morality, education, thrift, and home ownership.
West-Side	Nativity so diversified that no state predominates.	In many cases training for successful urban life has been gained from residence in other urban communities both North and South; some lived on East side for a short time.	Very definite traditions of morality, education, thrift, and home ownership.
Temple Street	Appear to be predominately from Tennessee, Alabama, and Georgia. Many other states are represented.	Family pattern typical of rural sections of the South, primary contacts exist. Reorganization around values, which have raised level of culture.	Reasons given for home ownership and family unity center around traditions or morality, thrift, and desire to own property.
Holmes Avenue	Majority of families appear to be from Alabama. Large numbers from other Southern states.	Family pattern typical of rural sections of the South. Urban values leading to higher culture levels not included in pattern.	Only old home-owning families seem to have any definite family tradition.

Source: Bond, "The Negro in Los Angeles."

in tables 1.4, 1.5, and 1.6. According to Bond, black communities on the Westside were much more socially and economically stable than the more socially heterogeneous South Central Avenue community (see chap. 2) or the largely poor Holmes Avenue community. In 1930s Los Angeles, those blacks who had been able to secure professional, well-paid employment often successfully moved to the Westside community, one that was spatially isolated from the poorer ghettos that had developed along South Central Avenue or in Watts.

Throughout the 1940s and into the 1950s, most black Angelenos were forced to crowd into the established black zones of the city and denied opportunities in wartime employment and housing. In response to this discrimination, leaders within the black community rallied around the

TABLE 1.5
Comparative Analysis of Black Families in Los Angeles, 1934 (Continued)

	Mobility	Family Control	Employment
Central Avenue	Families in constant state of flux. Old settlers and more recent homeowners are exceptions.	Extreme disorganization of family and community resulting in lack of control. Some families, however, represent well-organized units.	Breadwinners, for the most part, unskilled. An area of contrasts. Many prosperous families. A large percentage dependent upon the county. Great unemployment.
West-Side	Residents are, in numerous instances, homeowners. Mobility occurs only among those who occupy courts and apartment houses.	Control grows out of internal family organization.	Occupations diversified. Apparent freedom from widespread poverty.
Temple Street	Majority of these families settled in this area when they first came to Los Angeles. Most of them are old settlers. Apartment houses and cheap rent houses beginning to appear.	Family, organized around the church, acts as a means of control. Family itself a well-organized unit in community.	Many city employees. Unskilled workers. Many unemployed.
Holmes Avenue	Recently populated by rural people seeking cheap living quarters. Due to isolation not much mobility out of community.	Lack of family control due to absence of restraints, which operated in rural districts.	Unskilled laborers. Excessive unemployment among breadwinners and homemakers. School provides free meals for many of the children.

Source: Bond, "The Negro in Los Angeles."

employment issue and battled against injustice. One such crusader was Charlotta Bass, co-founder of the *California Eagle* (see chap. 13). Increasingly, Los Angeles–area labor leaders joined with national labor leaders to fight for the opening up of nonmenial employment to blacks. A. Philip Randolph's March on Washington resulted in Executive Order 8802 in 1941, which made it illegal for government contractors to discriminate in hiring during World War II. In the wake of Executive Order 8802, hundreds of thousands of blacks migrated to Los Angeles to work in the newly opened defense industries. Subsequent overcrowding in Los Angeles's "Black Belts" caused the housing crisis to become the number-one issue facing Los Angeles's black community during this time.

An early turning point came in November 1939, when California Superior Court Judge Georgia Bullock ruled that Mr. and Mrs. Sam Deedman could legally live in their house at 690 East Fiftieth Street in Los Angeles. This decision was made despite the fact that the area had been covered by racial restrictions for thirteen years. This one favorable decision caused a renewed interest in legal efforts to open housing in Los Angeles. But another challenge came in 1941, when white members of a West Jefferson Homeowners Association attempted to have five black families that had "crossed over the line into White Los Angeles" evicted from their properties. A few years later, black celebrities who had broken into the Hollywood film industry fought to keep their homes in the nearby Sugar Hill area of the West Adams district.[48]

When the 1948 *Shelley v. Kraemer* Supreme Court decision rendered racially restrictive covenants illegal, there was an immediate impact on the black residents of Los Angeles County. Because *Shelley v. Kraemer* had been designated as a judicial test case, the decision settled all similar cases on file with the Los Angeles Superior court. This meant that white homeowners associations could no longer seek judicial support based upon violation of racially restrictive covenants. All black homeowners living in restricted areas were now legally able to remain in their houses.[49]

No longer able to count on the Los Angeles Police Department (LAPD) or the County Sheriff's Department to enforce restrictive covenants, White Neighborhood Protectives of 1950s Los Angeles adopted other

TABLE 1.6

Comparative Analysis of Black Families in Los Angeles, 1934 (Continued)

	Type of Home	Problems Facing Family
Central Avenue	Area of single dwellings, courts, and apartment house. "Doubling" and overcrowding occur.	Unemployment. Poverty. Prostitution. Family disorganization. Juvenile delinquency. Desertion.
West-Side	The Wilshire of the Negro communities. Homes well furnished; usually owned by occupants. For the most part, single dwellings. High rent area.	Some unemployment. Internal family problems common to middle-class homes.
Temple Street	Medium homes, usually owned by occupants. Nicely furnished and neatly kept.	Unemployment. Poverty. Lawless element recently moved into community.
Holmes Avenue	Cheap rent area. Small single residences, poorly furnished.	Unemployment. Poverty. Juvenile Delinquency.

Source: Bond, "The Negro in Los Angeles."

tactics to keep blacks out of their communities, including violence. This violence was aimed at exerting spatial control over blacks. In the aftermath of *Shelley v. Kraemer*, a wave of cross burnings, shootings, and bombings were directed at the property of those pioneer black families who attempted to make their homes in the restricted white communities. Racial conflict took place at geographic locations that seem to correspond to areas of black penetration into formerly all-white residential space. The geographic pattern of the early racial "flash points" seems to indicate that these were acts aimed at stopping the advance of a growing, increasingly prosperous black community into "white space."

Despite federal rulings on the unconstitutionality of racially restrictive housing areas, local authorities in Los Angeles continued to ignore area blacks' simple desire for equal protection under the law. In the 1950s, the situation escalated enough to alarm citizens of a possible race riot. For urban blacks, fear intensified following the March 1952 bombing of William Bailey's house on Dunsmuir, a residence that at the time was just outside of the westernmost part the ghetto.[50] The force of the explosion was felt throughout a twelve-square-block area. Bailey had been warned of the bombing by cryptic messages and fortunately was not at home during the explosion. However, he did sustain heavy property losses.[51] Bailey charged that the LAPD had known about the threat to his life and property but had done nothing to prevent it from happening. The grand jury assigned to investigate the bombing turned up no leads, and the bombing was never solved.[52]

The failure of police and judicial action in the Bailey case, along with the many other acts of racial intimidation taking place in the early 1950s, prompted the Los Angeles chapter of the NAACP to charge:

> The indifference of official Los Angeles to the serious lack of police protection for Negroes moving into the "new" areas in the city is a problem that may well explode into a race riot the next time an act of violence is visited upon a Negro family. I have noted this lack of concern from the mayor down to the Chief of Police. Even the Grand Jury has seemingly been convinced by police reports that "all is well" on Dunsmuir. Since the first of the year there has been two bombings, two cross burnings and numerous threatening letters reported in Los Angeles. The failure to apprehend one single suspect in any instance gives the go-signal to the bigots and lets minority group persons know beyond a shadow of a doubt just what to expect in the way of protection and effective investigation

on the part of the various law enforcement agencies of the city, state and federal government.[53]

The lack of equal protection under the law that black Angelenos experienced as they moved into white communities was simply an extension of the type of treatment they were subjected to in the ghetto. The LAPD was notorious for stopping and beating blacks for no cause in the Eastside black communities. So it was not surprising that they would ignore the sight of blacks being terrorized by white civilians outside of the ghetto. Not only did the LAPD not prosecute perpetrators of crimes against blacks, they often further victimized the victims.

As the 1950s progressed, the turbulent aftereffects of *Shelley v. Kraemer* subsided somewhat, and black Angelenos settled into a pattern of westward expansion. Whites rapidly fled from the southwest side of Los Angeles in the 1950s and 1960s. Between 1950 and 1956, more than 125,000 whites left the central city area of Los Angeles.[54] As whites fled central Los Angeles in the 1950s, what had been three separate black communities—each with a distinct regional identity—merged into one contiguous black residential space. Although the residents at the western edge of this new consolidated black ghetto continued to enjoy higher standards of living, geographic isolation and thus their ability to maintain class distinctions was gone—especially with respect to rental housing.

Subsequently, "black spaces" in Los Angeles became more and more class heterogeneous after the late 1950s. Part of the reason for the increases in social class heterogeneity can be found in the very processes by which the Los Angeles black ghetto expanded. Although initial penetration into white communities was usually accomplished by middle- or upper-class blacks, the white out-migration that resulted opened the way for increasing class heterogeneity. Shortly after penetration, the process of racial turnover would begin. Blacks of all strata, including intracity migrants from the Eastside and incoming migrants from the South, filled Westside vacancies, especially rented housing.[55]

Turbulent '60s

Upwardly mobile black Angelenos were on the move in the 1950s and 1960s. Typically they spearheaded the penetration of white residential areas. But these pioneers often found that while intracity moves brought

better housing stock, they didn't lead to long-term social or spatial transformation of the communities into middle-class, integrated space.

As one observer noted, "the continued expansion of the Negro ghetto
into the sixties closed the gaps that had provided temporary physical
separation of the Negro middle class from the poverty pockets of Watts,
Central Avenue and Avalon."[56] Throughout the 1960s, some blacks again
removed themselves (temporarily at least) from the expanding ghetto by
moving farther west into West Adams and the Baldwin Hills communities
(see Introduction). Nonetheless, less-desirable ghetto communities still
surrounded them. This constant westward expansion of the black ghetto
in Los Angeles represented the efforts of middle-class blacks to escape
from the clutches of the ghetto and all that it represented. The continued
movement by blacks into these previously white areas led to a decline in
the desirability of what was becoming "black space."

The changes in the geographic character of class within the black communities of Los Angeles during these years left many black Angelenos attempting to cling to regional identities that were increasingly less valid.
As one observer of black attitudes preceding the Watts uprisings noted:

The poor people of Watts divided Black Los Angeles in half, symbolically,
at Central Avenue. An "east-sider" was a "low-rider," a poor [b]lack, "a
brother." A "west-sider" was a middle class Negro, one who had little sym-
pathy for poor [b]lacks, a "White man's nigger, "a "house nigger," an Uncle Tom. It was not considered relevant that nearly as many poor [b]lacks
lived on the west side of town, or that one could find Uncle Toms a mile
east of Central Avenue, because class was not a fixed notion to the people
of Watts—it was a transitory state of mind. Although class standing usually correlated with income, education, and so on, this was not necessarily so. A poor [b]lack man who "put on airs" or "acted White" could
have been called a west-sider, an Uncle Tom or middle class. Similarly, a
wealthy Negro who "acted [b]lack" could have been considered a brother,
an east-sider, perhaps even a low-rider.[57]

Naturally, financially stable individuals desired to raise their children
in nice, safe areas, but the color of their skin limited their ability to find
housing in areas of the city defined as "white space." The difficulty that
prosperous blacks had in finding housing that was truly removed from
the ghetto is illustrated by these excerpts from an article in a 1962 issue of
the *California Eagle*:

It took a month of sitting in and picketing, a change of ownership of the tract, and wide local community support for one Negro family to get one home in the Monterey Highlands tract in Monterey Park. Bobby Liley, a physicist, was sold a house last Thursday by Earl P. Snyder of the Kembo Corporation, who acquired the tract by foreclosing on the developer, Montgomery Ross Fisher. Fisher had steadfastly refused to sell Liley a house, despite the fact that the tract was financed with FHA funds. "I commend Snyder for selling the home, he thought it was the right thing to do," Bobby Liley stated. Liley said the significance of this sale was "the fact that a person sold the house to a Negro." In some similar cases there have been back-door sales, homes sold to Whites who were buying for Negroes. This time the sale was really to a Negro."[58]

For middle- and upper-class blacks living in Los Angeles during the early 1960s, the fact that they were not wanted in White Los Angeles was hammered home by the passing of Proposition 14 by California voters in 1964. This measure was designed to repeal the Rumford Fair Housing Act and would allow racial discrimination in housing to continue legally in California. Proposition 14 was so popular among white Californians that it passed by a two-to-one margin.[59] Although Proposition 14 was eventually struck down by federal judicial action and never implemented, the wounds it caused could not be undone.[60] In August 1965, when the California Highway Patrol stopped Marquette Frye, Black Los Angeles entered a new era in its development. What started as a routine traffic stop conflagrated into an urban revolt where thirty-four people died, and a thousand more were injured. Four thousand people were arrested and property damage was estimated at $200 million.[61] A new militancy had swept through the black community.[62]

Black Crisis

As the 1970s began, it seemed as if things were looking up for black Angelenos. The turbulence of the 1960s had led to important gains for black Americans. The 1968 Fair Housing Act promised to open up new areas of the Los Angeles region for black residence. There appeared to be a new climate of openness and acceptance of blacks in the Los Angeles area, and fair housing legislation was a big part of this. As the center of the black community shifted from Central Avenue over to the Crenshaw Corridor, black regional identities shifted as well (see chap. 2). Nonetheless, articles in the city's black press warned of two distinct but related problems that emerged in the Los Angeles black community during the twenty-year period between 1970 and 1990—increasing social disorder in black communities, and a crisis in black leadership. These two problems were by no means new to the black community. However, they surfaced in Los Angeles at a time when many assumed that blacks living in the nation's urban areas had "turned the corner" on their way to equality with mainstream America.

The impact of the social breakdown in the 1970s and 1980s upon the Los Angeles black community was somewhat devastating, reaching black families wherever they lived in the metropolitan area. Although Max Bond had documented social disorder as a feature of Black Los Angeles as early as 1936, he also pointed out that the Westside black community was for the most part free of "ghetto behavior." By the 1970s, however, it was only in the Baldwin Hills/Windors Hills/View Park/Ladera Heights area that residential class isolation existed in an area predominately occupied by blacks. In the rest of Westside Black Los Angeles, racial turnover led to class heterogeneity—in the classic manner observed by the sociologists who had studied cities such as Chicago and Philadelphia in prior eras.[63] White out-migration, especially from rental housing, led to increasing class heterogeneity as the community transitioned from majority white to majority black. The mixing of social economic status that geographic proximity brought about was especially difficult for youth. As the 1970s and 1980s progressed, interneighborhood conflict between youth became more and more of a problem in the predominantly black portions of Los Angeles, regardless of the social-class standing of the participants (see chap. 5).

A tragic example of this can be found in the story of Robert Ballou, a Westside black youth and the son of a lawyer, who was killed by leather-jacket-seeking Eastside youths (from Washington High) in 1972 outside of a *Soul Train* concert at the Hollywood Palladium. The story surrounding this sensational event is an important example of a transformation in black intracommunity relations that took place after the 1968 Fair Housing Act. Ballou and his Westside friends were the victims of violence visited upon them by youth from the "other side" of the black community.

Ballou was living in a neighborhood that was on the fringe of the black community and that was undergoing racial transition (see table 1.7). The Ballou family was a classic example of middle- and upper-class black families that had moved far away from the core black community in an effort

TABLE 1.7
Community Educational Differences,
Adams/La Brea vs. Westmont/West Athens

	1970 (%)	1980 (%)	1990 (%)
Tract of Ballou's residence			
College Grads	15.8	27.2	34.6
Black	30.9	65.4	67.2
Tract of Washington High			
College Grads	1.7	4.3	3.3
Black	83.4	92.7	86.0

Source: U.S. Census, 1970, 1980, 1990.

to obtain better housing and class separation. The census tract that contained their home on Brushton was less than 1 percent (0.4 percent) black in 1960; by 1970 it had risen to 31 percent black. By 1980 this area at the border of Los Angeles and Culver City—known as the Adams/La Brea area—was more than 65 percent black. Like most early black penetration zones, however, the transition started out as a class-based movement: as the community became increasingly black in the 1960s and 1970s, the percentage of its residents who were college educated also rose.

A crisis in black leadership, by contrast, seemed all but avoided when Los Angeles elected it first black mayor since the Mexican period. In 1973 the Westside city councilman Thomas Bradley was elected mayor of Los Angeles, benefiting from overwhelming black support throughout the city. Blacks voted for Bradley not only out of a sense of racial affinity but also because they believed he would make positive changes in the conditions confronting Black Los Angeles. Black Angelenos, however, were doomed to be disappointed. Bradley was known as a nonconfrontational leader, a man who went out of his way not to choose sides on any issue and act instead as a mediator of conflict. Bradley's own election to city council and then later to mayor were the result of multiracial coalition building. Although the multiracial coalition Bradley assembled had its positives, it also hampered the will and ability of the Bradley administration to work for progressive change in the black community. This fact was observed early on by Booker Griffin, a journalist for the *Los Angeles Sentinel*. In June 1974, Griffin wrote:

I have lived in three cities—Gary, Cleveland, and Los Angeles, all of which have had [b]lack mayors. [. . .] I am used to [b]lack mayors and therefore have not experienced the same sensational fantasia as have some others in this town. I grew up in a town where there where always [b]lack elected officials and judges so I took [b]lack politicians off of their pedestals while I was still a child. This appears to make me unique in Los Angeles.[64]

Griffin went on to describe a disturbing direction in Bradley's first year of leadership, which he likened to a policy of "benign neglect" when it came to the problems confronting Black Los Angeles.

Bradley, of course, had run and was elected on the premise that he was going to "be a mayor for all Los Angeles." He pledged to serve the needs of the Valley, as well as the Harbor area, to be a leader concerned with each and every community. He attempted to show that favoritism and neglect would not be tolerated while he was mayor. Bradley was characterized by caution, contemplation, and the absence of controversy throughout his political career. He sought not to "rock the boat" and was considered to be more the arbitrator of conflict than the initiator of it.[65]

This mayoral style hampered Bradley's ability to get things done in neglected areas of the city (such as in South Central) and facilitated his ability to accomplish things in other, favored areas (such as in the Downtown district). Bradley's linkages to Los Angeles's business interests necessarily involved him in the allocation and location of development projects. As long as he made governmental decisions in accordance with the wishes of the local business elite, Bradley's regime was likely to be seen favorably by city powerbrokers. Conversely, any move to influence decision making to benefit the predominantly black or Latino sections of Los Angeles probably would have been viewed as controversial, due to widespread belief in the zero-sum principle that when one area gains, another loses.

Bradley had humble origins, yet while in office he became a symbol of the more bourgeois elements of Los Angeles's black society. He became synonymous with the "elite" Westside district of West Adams and the Crenshaw-Baldwin Hills, and not as much with the Central Avenue community of his early years. This disconnect was a product of the massive intracity migration that Black Los Angeles had experienced in the 1950s and 1960s.

As the population shifted in geographic location, the regional identity of black Angelenos shifted as well. By the late 1970s, the Crenshaw/Baldwin Hills area had become the new center of black space in the city. What had started out as a place of refuge, where middle-class blacks could enjoy a higher standard of living, became the new social and cultural center for blacks of all social classes—just like Central Avenue had been in earlier periods. The tendency for the Bradley regime to neglect Los Angeles's black community was facilitated by the solid support that Bradley continued to receive from much of the black electorate, regardless of where black voters resided.

Clearly black Angelenos saw Bradley as significantly more supportive of their interests than the white mayors that preceded him. But another very basic reason that Bradley continued to receive so much support from the black community was the mysterious nature of the decision-making process in urban politics. Important city issues were often resolved at the elite level, behind closed doors, and the average black voter didn't have a clue as to what was going on between Bradley and those who were part of the city-wide coalition. His symbolic value as "one of our own," allowed Bradley to remain extremely popular among black Angelenos—even though he often failed to speak out on issues of importance to the black community. One such issue was school busing.

In the early 1970s, federal attention was drawn to the extreme levels of segregation in Los Angeles public schools. As was the case in other cities, mandatory busing was considered to remedy the situation, and the court battles over this issue continued into the late 1970s. Of course, busing was seen as undesirable to many of Los Angeles's white residents, including Bradley's white coalition partners. Although the judge hearing the case requested that Bradley act as a community leader in the resolution of this issue, he remained silent throughout most of the period. Then, in a move suggesting that the Bradley regime had already shifted toward conservatism, Bradley came out strongly against massive cross-town busing[66] prior to his 1977 reelection, arguing that it would strain the city's budget and be an emotionally draining experience.[67]

During the 1980s, Los Angeles's black community continued to flirt with social disorder. Black Los Angeles became an increasingly dangerous space to live in, particularly for black youth. Although direct discrimination and racism against blacks had been declining since the 1960s, by the 1980s the expectations held by black youth in the city seemed to be largely out of sync with the actual structures of opportunity. On the one hand, blacks continued to experience symbolic social gains such as Bradley's continued visibility as mayor and the presidential candidacies of Jesse Jackson. On the other hand, black youth—both in the inner city and suburban black settlement areas—seemed to be growing more and more disaffected and farther and farther out of control as the decade progressed. Gang violence in Los Angeles reached record levels in the 1980s, and many of the victims were black youths. The social fabric of the heart of Black Los Angeles seemed torn by youth violence (see chap. 5).

Although the petty conflicts between teen street gangs caught the media's attention, there was a lot more happening under the surface. The police and other law enforcement authorities were active in the black community in many ways that had nothing to do with combating gangs. To be sure, many of the actions and tactics of the LAPD and other authorities served only to further inflame the feelings of injustice within the black community. The actual percentage of Los Angeles's young black community who were actively involved in street gangs was very small in most parts of the county. Yet, the gang and drug problems associated with inner-city Los Angeles (see chap. 8) became a favorite topic of news stories, television programming, and Hollywood movies, both entertaining and frightening people all over the nation and around the world. Many black Angelenos viewed police actions to stop the gang turf wars as anything but heroic. For many in Black Los Angeles, gangs were seen as an excuse for police to brutalize blacks who weren't actually affiliated with gangs, and there was evidence to support this view:

APARTMENT OWNERS SUE OVER LAPD GANG SWEEPS
The owners of a Los Angeles apartment damaged nearly a year ago in a police gang sweep filed a $10 million dollar suit last week, claiming police destroyed property out of a bias against [b]lacks. [. . .] The suit, brought by Cheri and Henry Lang, is one of several brought by neighbors claiming their homes were trashed while they were beaten and humiliated during the raids on Aug 1.[68]

Unlike other urban settings, the dichotomy within Los Angeles was not that of an inner-city underclass "left behind" as the talented middle class moved away to the suburbs.[69] Instead, if there was any dichotomy to be drawn, it was between the apparent increasing social freedom for blacks in the metropolis and the increasing failure of many to realize this opportunity—a failure rooted in the violence and social disorder that plagued Black Los Angeles throughout the 1980s.

Black Community Redefined?

Although the core African American areas of South Los Angeles had already begun losing large numbers of its population to the suburbs throughout the 1980s, the process accelerated in the 1990s. The first three years of the 1990s in particular were critical in changing the geographic and social realities of Black Los Angeles. The events that took place in the years before the 1992 urban rebellion were so damaging to the collective psyche of Black Los Angeles that many felt violence was the only way out. In the decades leading up to the 1990s, African American areas had been failed by their local institutions, ironically by those citywide institutions that were supposed to protect and serve the community. They were particularly affected by continually underperforming neighborhood schools, ineffective community policing, and the withdrawal of local blue-collar employers during the 1970s and 1980s, combined with the rising cocaine trade and the proliferation of local street gangs that eroded neighborhood safety.

The streets of Black Los Angeles had become more and more dangerous, and by 1992 they exploded with violence. The black community had been shocked by the 1991 videotaped beating of an unarmed black motorist by the LAPD and the acquittal of a Korean shopkeeper for the videotaped shooting of a black teenage girl in the back of the head over a bottle of orange juice.[70] An op-ed published in the *Los Angeles Times* represented the sentiments of many black Angelenos:

> It was the utterly senseless nature of Soon Ja Du's crime that made it so notorious: She shot Latasha Harlins at point-blank range in the back of the head as the girl walked away from an argument over a $1.79 bottle of orange juice. Judge Karlin knew the entire city was watching this case, and she knew her sentence would send a message. The message is clear: black life is worthless. Unlike 1950s' Mississippi, however, in 1991 Los Angeles such a message does not come without a price. Another frightening assumption underlies these calls for quiescence: that even in circumstances as outrageous as the King beating and the Du sentencing, other ethnic groups are so incapable of placing themselves in either the individual or collective shoes of the African-American community that they cannot understand why outrages and strong action are required. If this is truly the extent of the isolation in which the African-American community finds itself, then ultimately a path of political accommodation makes no sense.[71]

In the early 1990s, a sense of hopelessness and fear gripped much of the Black Los Angeles populace, particularly those residents of the former

African American ghettos, leading to increasing black out-movement to suburban areas.

Black out-migration opened the way for Latino in-migration into formerly black-dominated areas in South Los Angeles. Population pressures emanating out of Mexico and Central America led to rapid in-movement of Latinos into the Los Angeles area, with many Latino families choosing to live in areas that were dominated by African Americans. These areas tended to have lower home values than comparable non-black ghetto areas, so they were attractive to the incoming Latino migrant. As the population mix of formerly black areas changed, some tensions naturally arose. However, divisiveness between blacks and Latinos in South Los Angeles was often exaggerated by the media, particularly the *Los Angeles Times* and local television news outlets. These media rarely missed an opportunity to sensationalize the black-brown demographic shifts that had been occurring in South Los Angeles for decades. While the media sensationalized conflicts between blacks and Latinos and saturated their news coverage with stories about recent population shifts, the reality remained that the groups shared geographic space with very little social contact, especially by adults. Despite the tight spaces they shared in South Los Angeles, interethnic conflict remained minimal.

Nonetheless, many black old-timers were nostalgic about life in earlier decades, when the ghetto was more solidly black. A *Los Angeles Times* article about the period's demographic changes captures this nostalgia:

> "There used to be theaters everywhere, up and down Broadway," the 60-year-old North Carolina native said. "They're gone. Just like somebody came in and got them at night." South Los Angeles was once the core of the city's black community. Today, the area is home to tens of thousands of Latino immigrants. They have found hope in a neighborhood that blacks, young and old, have been leaving during the past decade to pursue their dreams of a better life in the suburbs.[72]

These feelings of a neighborhood turned bad were exacerbated by the events of April 29–May 3, 1992, events that served as a catalyst to further accelerate black out-movement from South Los Angeles. After the acquittal of officers involved in the highly publicized Rodney King beating, the city erupted in five days of rioting and looting, leading to the deaths of fifty-three persons, many of them black. The Los Angeles rebellion of 1992 has been well documented,[73] but I mention it here only to draw attention to its role as a catalyst for continued and increased out-migration of African Americans from what was formerly core, inner-city black space.

As the 1990s progressed, the increasing availability of cheaper housing at the Los Angeles periphery had quickened the redistribution of the region's African American population away from the traditional black residential areas in South Los Angeles County. Throughout the 1990s and into the early twenty-first century, blacks continually moved out to newly developing areas of Los Angeles County (e.g., Lancaster/Palmdale in the Antelope Valley), as well as to the suburban counties of Riverside, San Bernardino, and to a lesser extent Orange and Ventura.

This migration was fueled by an expansion in area housing values that lasted throughout most of the 1990s up until the financial collapse of 2008. The value of houses in Los Angeles proper rose steadily, and new houses in the far-flung suburbs were cheaper than those in older parts of the county, including the areas where most African Americans had traditionally resided. With the widespread availability of credit sparked by the rising home values, existing homeownership for Los Angeles area residents provided the ability to leverage housing equity to improve one's standard of living, including eventually trading up to better homes in the suburbs (see figs. 1.2 and 1.3).

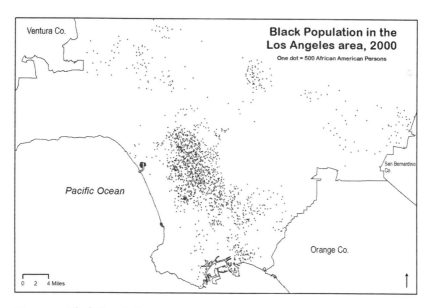

Figure 1.2. Black Population, 2000.

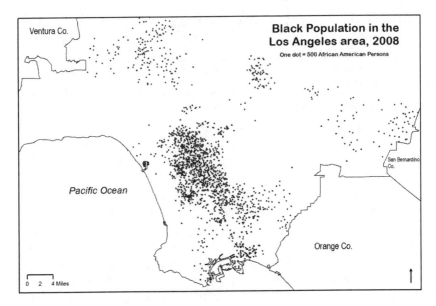

Figure 1.3. Black Population, 2008.

The impact that the Los Angeles Rebellion of 1992 had on African American population trends in the Los Angeles region is evident in tables 1.8 and 1.9. Table 1.8 reveals that the 1990s was the only decade in which the African American population of Los Angeles County actually declined (by 6 percent). This historic loss of black residents was triggered by the concerns that followed the civil unrest in the early period of the decade —the sense that blacks living in South Los Angeles were under siege by multiple forces, that they couldn't get equal treatment under the law, and that their communities had been taken over by gangs, drugs, and crime. This was a decade when many African Americans who could afford to do so moved to suburban areas, leading to a net loss in the county's black population for the first time since the city's colonial origins. As shown in table 1.9, Riverside and San Bernardino counties received the majority of the black population fleeing South Los Angeles. Black population growth in those counties tended to outpace overall growth, while Orange County and Ventura County remained largely resistant to black in-migration.

The African-origin population of Los Angeles has always been diverse, but never as diverse as it had become by the first decade of the 2000s. Black immigrants from the Caribbean, Africa, and the Americas

TABLE 1.8
Growth of Black Population after 1940

Year	Total Population	Black Population	% Black	% Growth
1940	2,790,359	70,781	3	
1950	4,281,997	222,534	5	214
1960	6,038,771	458,947	8	106
1970	7,044,641	759,091	11	65
1980	7,506,690	927,823	12	22
1990	8,863,164	992,674	11	7
2000	9,519,338	930,957	10	−6
2008	10,024,081	944,798	9	1

Source: U.S. Census 1940–2000.

TABLE 1.9
*Regional Share of the Black Population Living in Los Angeles Area
Counties 1960, 1990 and 2008*

County	Black Population	Share (%)	Total Population	Share (%)
Ventura				
1960	3,584	0.7	199,138	3.0
1990	15,629	1.3	669,016	5.0
2008	16,671	1.2	806,938	4.4
Orange				
1960	3,519	0.7	703,925	9.0
1990	42,681	3.0	2,410,556	16.0
2008	58,036	4.3	3,031,930	16.7
Riverside				
1960	12,554	2.6	306,191	4.0
1990	63,591	5.0	1,170,413	8.0
2008	149,471	10.9	2,233,496	12.3
San Bernardino				
1960	17,122	3.5	503,591	6.0
1990	114,934	9.0	1,418,380	10.0
2008	196,392	14.4	2,108,797	11.6
Los Angeles				
1960	458,947	92.5	6,038,771	78.0
1990	992,974	81.0	8,863,167	61.0
2008	944,798	69.0	10,024,081	55.1
Region Total				
1960	495,726	100	7,751,616	100
1990	1,229,809	100	14,531,529	100
2008	1,365,368	100	18,205,242	100

Source: U.S. Census, 1960 and 1990, and 2008 Population Estimates.

contributed larger and larger streams of new persons of African descent to the Los Angeles area during this period. By 2008 there were an estimated 90,391 persons of sub-Saharan African and/or Caribbean ancestry living in Los Angeles County, constituting nearly 10 percent of the county's total

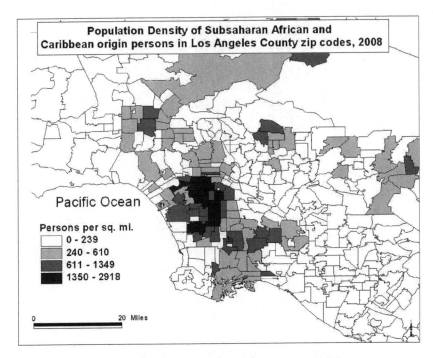

Figure 1.4. Population Density of sub-Saharan African and Caribbean Origin Persons in Los Angeles County zip codes, 2008.

black population. Over 61,000 sub-Saharan Africans resided in Los Angeles County, including more than 7,000 Nigerians, nearly 5,000 Ethiopians, and more than 1,000 Ghanaians. These continental Africans were joined by more than 28,000 Caribbean/West Indian blacks, including more than 11,500 Belizians, more than 9,900 Jamaicans, more than 1,900 Haitians, and more than 1,700 Trinidadians. These newer black immigrants tended to cluster in and around existing African American settlement areas, particularly around the Baldwin Hills/Crenshaw neighborhoods and other parts of South Los Angeles (see fig. 1.4).

As the first decade of the 2000s wound to a close, the question remained what these new sources of black immigration would mean for the cultural fabric of Black Los Angeles. Black immigrants from the Caribbean and Africa tended to share residential space with American-born blacks but their cultural backgrounds and social identities were often vastly divergent. As the county's non-native black population grew throughout the decade, the diverse groups comprising it increasingly challenged common assumptions about the people and spaces comprising "Black Los Angeles."

NOTES

1. Mason, *Los Angeles under the Spanish Flag.*
2. Bandini, *History of California.*
3. Defined as mixed African race, particularly of black and white ancestry.
4. Forbes, "The Early African Heritage of California."
5. Ibid.
6. Campbell, "Heaven's Ghetto?"
7. Forbes, "The Early African Heritage of California."
8. Mason, *Los Angeles under the Spanish Flag.*
9. Ibid.
10. Ibid.
11. Ibid.
12. Forbes, "The Early African Heritage of California."
13. Ibid.
14. Bandini, *History of California.*
15. Bancroft, *History of California*, vol. 2.
16. Lapp, *Blacks in Gold Rush California.*
17. Bancroft, *History of California*, vol. 1.
18. Ibid.
19. Forbes, "The Early African Heritage of California."
20. U.S. Census Bureau, "Seventh Census of the United States, 1850."
21. The racially mixed nature of the Californio population most likely made it very difficult for American census takers to consistently record the racial classification of these families. The job of the census taker was to record the race of the individuals in a household, but it must have been surprising to an American to encounter Spanish-speaking households with people of mixed skin tones and hair textures living together, with no clear lines of distinctions. This likely caused mistakes in calculating the Afro-Latino population at the time. The racial mixture and often crowded living conditions that necessitated families, extended families, friends, and servants all housed under one roof, probably further complicated the matter.
22. Bond, "The Negro In Los Angeles."
23. Ibid.
24. Lapp, *Blacks in Gold Rush California.*
25. Ibid.
26. Bond, "The Negro In Los Angeles."
27. De Graaf, Mulroy, and Taylor, *Seeking El Dorado.*

28. Campbell, "Heaven's Ghetto?"

29. Ibid.

30. Flamming, *Bound for Freedom.*

31. Wheeler, *Black California.*

32. Ibid..

33. Lapp, *Blacks in Gold Rush California.*

34. U.S. Census Bureau, "Tenth Census of the United States, 1880."

35. Ibid.

36. Ibid.

37. Using the street names and scanning to preceding and succeeding pages to get nearest cross-street information, it is possible to roughly determine the locations of black households living in the City of Los Angeles in 1880. Because of the street grid structure of Los Angeles, we can deduce that the margin of error for the location of these households is probably under 1/10 of a mile on average. This information was used to develop a small GIS database for historical spatial analysis of black household locations in the late nineteenth century.

38. Miramontes, "Research Resource Materials."

39. U.S. Census Bureau, "Tenth Census of the United States, 1880"; U.S. Census Bureau, "Twelfth Census of the United States, 1900"; U.S. Census Bureau, "Thirteenth Census of the United States, 1910."

40. De Graaf, *City of Black Angels.*

41. Ibid.

42. See Bonacich and colleagues' account of the black labor movement in Los Angeles in chap. 15.

43. "Colored Cooperative," *Los Angeles Times,* November 20, 1901, 9.

44. "First Negro to Practice," *Los Angeles Times,* September 3, 1903, A1.

45. "Only 'African' Will Do," *Los Angeles Times,* October 4, 1906, II1.

46. Sandoval, "Ghetto Growing Pains."

47. Bond, "The Negro in Los Angeles."

48. "Sugar Hill Residents Battle to Keep Homes," *California Eagle,* March 24, 1943, 1. For more on restrictive covenants, see chap. 2 and chap. 11.

49. Although no longer legally enforceable, restrictive covenants remained lawful as a private agreement until the 1968 Fair Housing Act outlawed them.

50. Bailey was a science teacher at George Washington Carver Middle School in southeast Los Angeles (two blocks from S. Central Ave. and off of E. Vernon Ave.).

51. See Stanley G. Robertson, "Police Reveal 'Leads' in Bombings: Local, State, National Agencies Delve into West Adams Blasts," *Los Angeles Sentinel,* March 20, 1952, A1.

52. O'Conner, "The Negro and the Police in Los Angeles."

53. Ibid., 139.

54. Sandoval, "Ghetto Growing Pains."

55. Recognizing the importance of this process to the development of the institutions and ideologies of Los Angeles's black community is crucial. This is especially important in light of the urban underclass debate and its fallout. See Wilson, *Declining Significance of Race,* and *Truly Disadvantaged*; Massey and Denton, *American Apartheid.*

56. Sandoval, "Ghetto Growing Pains."

57. O'Toole, *Watts and Woodstock,* 50.

58. Robert Farrell, "Sit-in Ends as New Homeowner Sells Tract Home to Negro: 34-Day Fight Brings Victory to Physicist," *California Eagle,* April 12, 1962, 1.

59. Tyler, *Black Radicalism in Southern California.*

60. Hunt and Ramón also discuss the negative impact of Proposition 14 in chap. 12.

61. Horne, *Fire this Time.*

62. See also Tyler, *Black Radicalism in Southern California.*

63. See Frazier, *Negro Family in Chicago;* and W. E. B. Du Bois, *Philadelphia Negro.*

64. Booker Griffin, "A Personal Evaluation: Tom Bradley's First Year," *Los Angeles Sentinel,* June 27, 1974, A7.

65. Barker, *Black Electoral Politics.*

66. Los Angeles required mandatory busing from 1978 to 1982. For more on the Los Angeles busing issue, see Ettinger, "The Quest to Desegregate Los Angeles Schools."

67. Payne and Ratzan, *Tom Bradley, the Impossible Dream.*

68. "Apartment Owners Sue Over LAPD Gang Sweeps," *Los Angeles Sentinel,* July 20, 1989, A1.

69. Wilson, *Truly Disadvantaged.*

70. See chap. 8 for a discussion on how both of these incidents were represented in mainstream media.

71. Geoffrey Taylor Gibbs, "Can African-Americans Now Truly Believe in Judicial Fairness?" *Los Angeles Times,* November 24, 1991, M6.

72. Charisse Jones, "Old Memories Confront New Realities in South L.A. Neighborhood: Some Blacks Adjust, Others Leave What Was Once the Core of the African-American Community," *Los Angeles Times,* February 17, 1992, 1.

73. For example, see Hunt, *Screening the Los Angeles "Riots"* and chaps. 5 and 8.

Chapter 2

From Central Avenue to Leimert Park
The Shifting Center of Black Los Angeles

Reginald Chapple

Since the turn of the twentieth century, there have been two prominent black centers in Los Angeles: the Central Avenue community from approximately 1900 to 1950, and the Crenshaw/Leimert Park Village community from approximately 1960 to the present. Central Avenue and Crenshaw Boulevard, respectively, form the main commercial spines of each center and are spatially connected by a seven-mile stretch of Martin Luther King Jr. Boulevard, which moves from the west at Rodeo Road to the east and terminates at Central Avenue.

One of the main elements that defined these two geographic areas as black centers in their respective time periods was their thriving commercial districts. Both areas were populated by black entrepreneurs who employed people of African descent and provided goods and services that catered to the black population. Central Avenue's heyday was during the Jim Crow era, which produced de jure racialized ghettos marked by the black entrepreneurship and homeownership clustered around the major thoroughfare. The Crenshaw/Leimert Park District emerged later, after the outlawing of restrictive housing covenants by the U.S. Supreme Court spurred an out-migration of blacks from the Central Avenue community. Although blacks had fanned out to other parts of Los Angeles County —including the West Adams District, Inglewood, Pico/LaBrea, Pacoima, and Watts—by the end of the first decade of the 2000s, the Crenshaw/ Leimert Park Village community was the largest resettlement community of African Americans in Los Angeles.

The process of placemaking by black Angelenos provides a window on understanding the spatial impact of black entrepreneurship, politics, homeownership, and cultural ways. "Placemaking" refers to the history of landscape, how places are planned, designed, built, inhabited, appropriated, celebrated, and discarded.[1] This conception intertwines cultural identity, social history, and urban design with the production of space; it describes a process that begins the moment residents relocate to a new landscape.[2] Such has been the case with black Angelenos. This chapter focuses on the movement of Black Los Angeles's center of gravity from 1880 to the present. It examines the push and pull factors that have shaped the production and decline of black space in the city.

Historic Central Avenue and the Creation of the Business District

Central Avenue was the first large settlement community for blacks migrating to Los Angeles in search of better housing, employment, and an improved quality of life during the post-Reconstruction Era. The lure of available real estate pulled black migrants into Los Angeles, eventually making Los Angeles the city with the highest black homeownership population in the nation. But Jim Crow laws kept early migrants squeezed within a relatively tight area (see chap. 1), which was bounded by First Street to the north and Main Street to the west. Early on, the area beyond Main Street was known as the "Westside," while the area east of Main Street was known as the "Eastside."

The formation of a distinct black district along Central Avenue may be traced to the years just prior to the turn of the twentieth century, when blacks expanded from their settlements of the 1890s, and whites sold their homes and abandoned the area. During the early 1900s, white residents on Central Avenue endeavored to restrict blacks at Seventh Street. One of the black families to settle south of that street was threatened by a mob. A decade later, one of the first blacks to settle on Eighteenth Street and Central had her house sacked by a white mob. Despite such occasional efforts at intimidation, blacks continued to obtain houses along Central Avenue.[3] Some blacks were able to move to the Westside, west of San Pedro, if they had the resources, but they were often met with white resentment and hostility.

The Central Avenue commercial district had three distinct hub locations, each associated with a different period: the 1890s Brick Block on San Pedro between First Street and Second Street; the 1900–1920s Negro

District on Central Avenue between Sixth Street and Washington Boulevard; and the late 1920s–1950 Historic Core between Forty-second Street
and Central Avenue. The black businesses that comprised these locations
were known and advertised as "Race Enterprises," with the idea driving
these businesses being a simple one: take care of your own.[4] The unfortu-
nate reality was that black businesses of the day were usually unsuccessful in their attempts to compete with white businesses—businesses that
typically were better capitalized and could cut prices in order to eliminate
black businesses as competitors. Race Enterprises ushered in a new type
of black entrepreneur that catered to black people exclusively. These enterprises were made possible by the increased quality of life, economic
mobility, and disposable income blacks in Los Angeles enjoyed compared
to their counterparts in other parts of the country. The other dynamic
that made the Race Enterprises of Black Los Angeles thrive was a result of
increased racism and Jim Crow laws, a spatial dynamic that contained the
growth of Black Los Angeles and resulted in what may be described as a
black ghetto.

Although Central Avenue between Sixth Street and Washington became the new hub of Race Enterprise, black businesses were not alone
on Central Avenue. They had competition from white businesses. George
Beavers Jr., one of the founders of Golden State Mutual Life Insurance
Company, recalled that this competition was typical for the period:

> The Jewish people and the Caucasians going into the Negro community
> to benefit from their trade. . . . They wanted Negro trade. They were not
> interested in developing any Negroes to be their competitors, naturally.[5]

J. J. Neimore's *California Eagle* was located next to Fred Roberts's *New
Age* race paper on Central Avenue. Roberts would later become the first
black State Assemblymember from the Central Avenue district. Both the
Eagle and the *New Age* were promoters of Race Enterprises and encouraged black Angelenos to support black businesses during this shift of center in Black Los Angeles. In 1915 Fred Roberts reported that the Chinese
people of California were boycotting Japanese produce because Japanese
merchants were discriminating against Chinese buyers. Roberts approved
of this tactic and added that any white retailers who discriminated against
blacks should be boycotted as well.

In an effort to promote the cause of supporting Race Enterprises, Roberts, Joe Bass, and other middle-class leaders formed a local branch of the

National Negro Business League. The national organization had been established in 1900 by Booker T. Washington in Boston, Massachusetts, and later incorporated in New York. With 320 chapters nationwide, its mission was "to promote the commercial and financial development of the Negro." The Los Angeles chapter was, in part, organized to fight against a prevailing belief amongst black buyers that white services were in some way superior to those of Race Enterprises.

As Darnell Hunt notes in the Introduction (p. 11), W. E. B. Du Bois visited Los Angeles for the first time in 1913. While there, he was struck by the Race Enterprises and the entrepreneurial mind-set of the black business owners and heralded the "snap and ambition" of Los Angeles's "new blood." In a photo taken during his visit, Du Bois can be seen standing next to a tall John A. Somerville, who would co-found the Hotel Somerville (Dunbar Hotel) with his wife, Vada, in 1928 and birth the local NAACP in their living room. It should be noted that the photo was taken in front of the Colored YMCA and Fred Roberts's *New Age* office on San Pedro Street.

In 1916 Sidney P. Dones, one of the most celebrated Black Los Angeles business owners and a promoter of Race Enterprises, opened the Booker T. Washington Building at Tenth and Central Avenue. The opening of this building announced the official birth of the Central Avenue Business District. Located two blocks south of the *Eagle*'s office, the building was a handsome three-story affair, with shops on the sidewalk level and offices and apartments above.[6] This "mixed-use" style would come to characterize the Black Los Angeles business district. Joe Bass touted the building in the *Eagle* with a booming headline that read: CENTRAL AVENUE ASSUMES GIGANTIC PROPORTION OF BUSINESS SECTION FOR COLORED MEN. He called it the "Largest and Best Appointed Edifice on Central Avenue."[7] His exclamations set the building and Race Enterprise apart from the other white, Jewish, Japanese, Chinese, and Mexican businesses that competed with black business along Central Avenue. The diversity of races within Black Los Angeles's core district was amplified by the crowd present at Du Bois's speech during his 1913 visit. Du Bois reported that the hall was "filled with 2,300 people from the white, yellow, and black races."[8]

Central Avenue, affectionately known as "the Avenue" by black Angelenos, soon acquired other entrepreneurial landmarks. These included Ida Wells's Southern Hotel on Central Avenue, between Twelfth and Pico, which opened in February 1916. A month later, F. A. Williams and a San

Diego–based business partner purchased the Angelus Theater at 932 Central Avenue, a "moving picture and vaudeville" house.[9] Although the Race papers simply advertised the location of the theater as "Central Avenue, Between 9th and 12th," Black Los Angeles knew the exact location.[10]

The *Eagle*'s Joe Bass called Central Avenue between Eighth and Twentieth Streets "one of the most remarkable Negro business sections anywhere in the country." Sidney Dones was given much of the credit for developments along the Avenue because of his real estate, insurance, and financing acumen. Dones, wrote Bass, "has said by his action no obstacle is too great for me to surmount on my way to success."[11] Bass also gave his *Eagle* credit for promoting Race Enterprises in the Central Avenue District.

By 1916 seventeen black churches were located in Los Angeles, and all of them congregated in or around the Central Avenue business district. The earliest black church in Los Angeles, First African Methodist Episcopal Church (First AME), was located at Eighth and Towne in the Negro business district.[12] Second Baptist Church—its name distinguishing it from the all-white First Baptist Church—was located nearby. The remaining fifteen churches were also in the district and clustered within one square mile, creating a hub of sacred urban space between Main Street and Alameda Street.

Amid the rapid growth of the district, the Progressive Business League of Los Angeles (PBL) replaced the Negro Business League. What remained unchanged was the boosting of Race Enterprises. In 1919 the PBL published its 185-member list and insisted that readers "get in the habit of spending money with your own people."[13] This echoed what the *Weekly Observer* and other booster Race papers had said thirty years earlier.[14] The key change in the Central Avenue district was the heightened level of Black Los Angeles's economic power and the plethora of black-owned enterprises on the Avenue within the Seventy-fourth Assembly District—representing the political power that would elect Fred Roberts to the State Assembly and pave the way for Augustus Hawkins to be elected to Congress. Indeed, a quarter of the black businesses were located on Central Avenue with other black-owned businesses within a few blocks of the Avenue.

During the 1920s, black-owned insurance companies emerged as the most successful black economic development venture because they provided blacks with a vital service.[15] Black Los Angeles gave birth to the largest black-owned insurance company west of the Mississippi, the Golden State Mutual Life Insurance Company, which was founded by William Nickerson Jr., Norman Oliver Houston, and George Allen

Beavers Jr. These three men would become dominant voices in the social and political scene of Central Avenue.

The PBL business roster showed a small clustering of businesses south of Washington Boulevard on Central Avenue, outside of the Seventy-fourth District. For example, at Thirty-seventh and Central, a Race man had opened a real estate office. This location would foreshadow the future movement of Black Los Angeles farther down the Avenue to the south.[16] This area would become the new hub of black entrepreneurship and the center of the historic Jazz Era in Los Angeles from the 1930s to the 1950s. The jewel of Central Avenue was the Hotel Somerville, later renamed the Dunbar Hotel. One of the most important landmarks in Los Angeles, it was more than just a resort for weary travelers of color. The lobby, restaurant, and conference room became a central meeting place for black Angelenos, hosting a wide range of social and community events. It was truly the symbol of black achievement in the city.[17] In 1933 the first office of the *Los Angeles Sentinel*—still the largest black newspaper in the West in the early 2000s—would open nearby.

Race Enterprises surged in Los Angeles at the same time Jim Crow sentiments were on the rise, and the two trends were related. As white prejudice increased, the idea of a group economy sounded better to blacks. And the same black population that sparked white discrimination also provided black entrepreneurs with a large pool of customers. Because the rising number of black businesses on Central Avenue made whites in the district uncomfortable, white flight ensued. Black Los Angeles took advantage of this abandonment and staked its homeownership claim on Central Avenue. The complex dance of race, space, and place was ever present and would continue as the black center shifted along Central Avenue.[18]

West Adams District

In the 1950s Black Los Angeles experienced another major geographical shift, when black Angelenos who could, moved to the West Adams District. It was mostly middle-class black Angelenos who moved out of the Central Avenue District to the previously forbidden Westside (see chap. 1). The Supreme Court's outlawing of restrictive housing covenants that had previously kept Black Los Angeles hemmed into the Eastside made this possible, but blacks had been integrating unrestricted blocks in the

Figure 2.1. Golden State Mutual Life Building in West Adams. Photo courtesy of Darnell Hunt.

area since 1900. This expanded area of black settlement became a broader northern and western extension of the West Jefferson neighborhood, radiating out from Jefferson and Adams Boulevards from Central Avenue.

West Adams did not have an easily identifiable "center."[19] There was no Dunbar Hotel, no concentration of jazz clubs and theaters or society meeting places like those on Central Avenue. The new community landmark was the Golden State Mutual Life Insurance Company building, designed by Paul R. Williams in 1948. Located at 1999 West Adams Boulevard (northeast corner of Western Avenue and Adams Boulevard) (see fig. 2.1), it was built furthest west of any other major Black Los Angeles institution and encouraged a relocation of Race Enterprises along Western Avenue. Williams also designed the new home of First AME Church (see fig. 2.2) located in the residential core near Golden State Mutual.[20] The two institutions were so close to one another that overflow congregants from First AME routinely parked their cars in the Golden State parking lot on Sundays.

West Adams qualifies as one of the oldest neighborhoods in Los Angeles. Oil barons, vintners, railroad magnates, and real estate developers hired top architects of the day to create West Adams mansions in a variety of styles. The district's wealthy residents of the 1920s included lawyers, doctors, oil baron Edward L. Doheny, Port of Los Angeles developer Randolph Huntington Minor, and a host of other prominent Los Angeles citizens. Included in this list is Thomas J. Furlong, whose father and siblings founded the industrial city of Vernon on the eastern border of the Central Avenue District. Thomas's son James Furlong is remembered in Los Angeles history as one of the first landowners in the city to sell land and homes to black families. The land was in the Central Avenue District closer to Slauson Avenue and worked to pull the black Central Avenue district to its southern edge around the Dunbar Hotel.[21] Many of the black families that James Furlong helped get started in Los Angeles would eventually become wealthy enough to join him on the Westside in the West Adams District.

Located to the south of downtown Los Angeles, West Adams's boundaries were Figueroa Street to the east, West Boulevard to the west, Pico

Figure 2.2. First AME Church in West Adams. Photo courtesy of Darnell Hunt.

Boulevard to the north, and Jefferson Boulevard to the south. Adams Boulevard is the main street of the District. The area along Adams Boulevard between Figueroa and Crenshaw became known as the Boulevard of Churches because of the numerous denominations that lined the thoroughfare. The area is filled with classic examples of the elaborate architectural styles of the times, including Victorian, Queen Anne, Stick/Eastlake, Shingle, Mission, Transitional Arts and Crafts, Beaux Arts and the Revival Styles, and Craftsman. These styles were in stark contrast to the small, wood, California bungalow-type homes that had come to characterize the Eastside. It was not long before well-off black Angelenos who could afford to move out of the Central Avenue District began looking west to the West Adams District for other housing opportunities.

Affluent blacks especially were drawn to the northeast corner of West Adams known as the Heights, because the area was slightly elevated above the rest of West Adams. Blacks would eventually dub the area "Sugar Hill" because it contained numerous stately, turn-of-the-century Victorian homes originally targeted for well-to-do whites. As early as 1935, black Angelenos were finding ways to purchase homes on nonrestricted blocks in West Adams. But they had only penetrated within a mile of Sugar Hill. Norman Houston, co-founder of Golden State Mutual Life Insurance Company, would break this trend in 1938 and purchase a home in the heart of Sugar Hill, even though he didn't move into it right away. He didn't want to subject himself to the racial hostility and slurs that were inflicted on blacks who integrated the city's neighborhoods, which could include cross burnings, bombings, and letters from neighbors warning blacks to vacate "or else." So Houston rented his home to a white tenant instead. Houston eventually moved his family into the home in 1941, despite opposition from the West Adams Heights Improvement Association, a local white homeowner's organization that would be at the center of the Supreme Court's restrictive housing covenant case.

By 1944 more wealthy black Angelenos were moving to Sugar Hill. It is perhaps best remembered as the place where Hattie McDaniel, the first African American to win an Academy Award, purchased her mansion.[22] Other prominent black Angelenos who purchased homes in the area included actress Louise Beavers, entertainer Pearl Bailey, John and Vada Somerville, who built the Hotel Somerville (Dunbar Hotel) and founded the Los Angeles Chapter of the NAACP, Horace Clark, owner of the Clark Hotel, one of the most famous hotels and cultural centers on Central Avenue, and Courtland G. Mitchell, the first black to run for city council.[23]

These and other wealthy blacks began a process of pulling other black Angelenos toward West Adams, thus pushing whites to other parts of the city, including Beverly Hills, Hollywood, and the new Westside communities closer to the ocean. Despite black gains in the early years, Sugar Hill would remain majority white.

The process of integrating Sugar Hill took a sharp legal turn in 1945, when the West Adams Heights Improvement Association filed a lawsuit in the California Superior Court. Its main argument was that by selling homes to blacks, white Sugar Hill homeowners had violated racially restrictive housing covenants that supposedly covered those properties until the year 2035.[24] Judge Thurman Clark ruled the covenants as unenforceable and threw out the case saying:

> It is time that members of the Negro race are accorded, without reservations or evasions, the full rights guaranteed them under the 14th Amendment to the Federal Constitution. Judges have been avoiding the real issue too long.[25]

West Adams Heights Improvement Association appealed the decision to the California Supreme Court. Loren Miller, the fiery, former journalist with the *Los Angeles Sentinel* who had become an NAACP attorney, represented the defendants. Reminiscing on why he had led the crusade to desegregate Black Los Angeles and ultimately urban America, he noted:

> Negro newcomers and old residents alike were hemmed in, penned up in racial ghettos—those sprawling black belts lying in the residentially least desirable heartlands of America's great cities.[26]

The best and brightest of Black Los Angeles attended the California Supreme Court hearing, dressed in their finest in order to create an atmosphere of black sophistication that would support Miller's dynamic presentation. Miller argued that the homeowners' requirement that residents be of the "pure white race" was absurd. Miller won the case and carried this message to the U.S. Supreme Court with Thurgood Marshall and a team of NAACP lawyers.[27] Above a large picture of Hattie McDaniel's Sugar Hill home, the *Los Angeles Sentinel*'s front page splashed the declaration, "California Negroes Can Now Live Anywhere! . . . Homes Like These No Longer Out of Bounds."[28] However, one loophole remained: rather than abolish racially restrictive housing covenants, the U.S. Supreme Court had just rendered them unenforceable. There would be one more court battle surrounding the matter, and Thurgood Marshall and Loren Miller would be the legal team to argue on behalf of blacks before the Court. The case was based on a white woman, Leola Jackson, who had decided to sell her property to blacks in Los Angeles. Olive Barrows, another covenanter, sued her for violation of the racially restrictive covenant associated with the property. In *Barrows v. Jackson*, the Court ruled that allowing covenanters to sue for damages would be a direct violation of the 1948 *Shelley v. Kraemer* ruling. The Sugar Hill defendants had finally won, but racial desegregation would prove to be a slow process throughout Los Angeles.

Racially restrictive housing covenants were not the only political battle that black West Adams residents had to fight. Early in 1954, West Adams residents began fighting their most determined battle against the proposed route for the Santa Monica (I-10) Freeway. The California State Highway Commission had selected a freeway route that cut a swath through what the *California Eagle* proudly described as the "most prosperous, best kept secret and most beautiful Negro owned property in the country, including Sugar Hill."[29] In response to this threat, a group of West Adams residents formed the Adams-Washington Freeway Committee and chose a delegation to present their grievances to the California State Highway Commission in Sacramento. Their main argument was that the selection of the route was at best insensitive and at worst racially motivated.

Composed of Floyd Covington, the former Urban League director and a Sugar Hill homeowner, and two other West Adams residents, including a Japanese American man, the delegation presented its case on February 18, 1954. Covington and the other delegates pleaded with the commission to reroute the freeway to the Washington Boulevard side, which was north of the proposed route and a mostly white neighborhood. One of their main arguments was that West Adams's non-white residents would not readily pick up and relocate to another neighborhood like their white counterparts. Black Angelenos from the City of Santa Monica also protested because the proposed freeway route bisected the city's small, 200-member black community at the Ink Well Beach.[30] The delegation got a temporary reprieve from the commission while it deliberated on their protest. But ultimately the commission insisted that the proposed route was the best, citing transit convenience and cost effectiveness as its rationale.

The Santa Monica (I-10) Freeway development was one of the key elements that prompted the decline of the black middle-class center of West Adams. In addition to West Adams, the freeway development snaked its way through the old San Pedro and Negro Districts on the old Eastside, taking out much of the physical fabric that might remind Black Los Angeles of its historical geography, as well as the social, political, economic, and cultural ways that it developed in these early black centers. Even the home of John and Vada Somerville, where W. E. B. Du Bois had stayed during his historic visit to Los Angeles in 1913, was in the path of the freeway.

The Leimert Park/Crenshaw District

Throughout the 1950s, well-employed black Angelenos continued moving west, pushed in part by the development of the I-10/Santa Monica Freeway out of West Adams and pulled by the lure of better housing, schools, and quality of life. By the late 1950s and early 1960s, Black Los Angeles moved west and south of West Adams into Leimert Park and the exclusive area of Baldwin Hills. These areas are part of the Crenshaw District, which became the new Black Los Angeles center in the wake of the 1965

Figure 2.3. Leimert Park Village. Photo courtesy of Darnell Hunt.

Watts riots. Leimert Park Village (see fig. 2.3) became the social, cultural and political heart of this new Black Los Angeles center.

Walter H. "Tim" Leimert developed Leimert Park, beginning in 1928. It was designed by the Olmsted Brothers firm, with principals Frederick L. Olmsted Jr. and John C. Olmsted at the helm. The firm was started by their father, Frederick L. Olmstead Sr., who is most noted for designing Central Park in New York City and other great urban parks. Leimert Park was one of the first comprehensively planned communities in Southern California designed for moderate-income families. As early as 1930, the area was advertised as being highly controlled:

> Leimert Park is admirably equipped with school facilities, but even more important is the system of safety streets and walks so planned that children going to and from school cross streets with very little traffic.[31]

In 1938, *Life* magazine sponsored the building of eight houses in various communities throughout the United States and selected Leimert Park Village, which was considered a model of urban planning, as the site for *Life*'s colonial-style home. Leimert Park's circulation patterns limited traffic near churches and schools. Utility wires were buried or hidden from view in alleys, which allowed for the dense planting of trees down the community's main streets. The trees gave the area a setting reminiscent of the Olmsted Brothers firm's other parklike residential developments.

The Olmstead Brothers designed the centerpiece park at Forty-third Place and Degnan Boulevard as the anchor for the area. The park was bounded by a commercial district on Forty-third Street, Degnan, and Leimert Boulevards. Small-scale apartment developments immediately radiated out from the main street commercial core known as Leimert Park Village, with its southern edge at Vernon Avenue. Beyond the apartments were low-scale, single-family homes that crossed Santa Barbara Boulevard (now King Boulevard) and terminated at Jefferson Boulevard. These boulevard boundaries to the north and south are the same ones that hemmed the historic Central Avenue District around the Dunbar Hotel. Ironically, Leimert Park was being developed around the same time that the Dunbar Hotel, Hudson-Liddell, and Golden State Mutual Life Insurance Company buildings were opening on Central Avenue and pulling the Black Los Angeles population farther south on Central Avenue below Washington Boulevard. Although Leimert Park was developed as a white family enclave, it would later become a pull community that the black middle class was drawn to after the relaxation of restrictive housing covenants in 1950. Leimert Park also pulled the last wave of the Second Great Migration of blacks to Los Angeles in the late 1950s.

Genethia Hudley Hayes, former school board president and executive director of the Southern Christian Leadership Conference, migrated to Los Angeles with her family in 1958 from the west side of Chicago. Her family was one of the first families to integrate their block. "We believed that this was the most progressive venue for us," she said. "L.A. was akin to Hollywood or Disneyland—no racism, no playing field that couldn't be leveled."[32]

The Hayes family purchased a single-family home in Leimert Park, sight unseen, from Chicago. "I believe that my dad's real estate agent really stuck his neck out when he decided to sell the home to our family," Hayes recalled. "Our last name, Hayes, didn't sound black or white and didn't send up any red flags in the process." But when the Hayeses arrived to see their house for the first time and move in, there was no welcoming wagon. "I remember I used to come outside with my mother to get in the car in the morning and our white neighbor would be outside going to work. I would say good morning to her and she would just look at me. I'd say to my mom, 'Gosh she's not very friendly.' Finally, I learned that the neighbors weren't pleased that we had moved in, which was something I could not comprehend at that age."

The Hayes family was accustomed to living in mixed communities in Chicago, but Leimert Park was a different experience. The large lawns, vibrant colors, and diverse array of stucco Spanish-style architecture of the neighborhood houses contributed to the general aura of middle-class well-being that pervaded the community. While Hayes believed that class lines in Chicago's black communities were not as deeply defined, the burgeoning middle-class black presence in Leimert Park was beginning to exhibit elitism that characterized the city's Eastside-Westside schism.[33]

According to the U.S. Census, Leimert Park had a population of 4,262 residents in 2000, of which 80.7 percent was African American. It was part of the larger Crenshaw District (fig. 2.4), which had a population that was 74 percent African American. These population numbers have enabled the communities to elect political leaders of African descent to the Los Angeles City Council, as well as provide heavy voting support for

Figure 2.4. Baldwin Hills Crenshaw Plaza. Photo courtesy of Darnell Hunt.

Mayoral, State Assembly, State Senate, and Los Angeles Unified School District races.

Black Politics of Space in Leimert Park Village

Leimert Park Village emerged as the new center of Black Los Angeles following the 1992 civil unrest in Los Angeles. Like the 1965 Watts riots, the 1992 Los Angeles rebellion involved ill-feelings between police and the black community—this time following a not-guilty verdict for police officers who were caught on videotape brutally beating Rodney King, a black suspect they had pulled over for a moving violation. For Black Los Angeles, the verdicts reinforced the political and economic divide that had grown between white and Black Los Angeles since 1965, reminding many of the injustices endured by blacks from the Eastside to West Adams. Unlike Watts, the 1992 uprisings were not contained to a central, largely black community. The entire city seemed to erupt in displeasure, with violence happening in Watts, the old Central Avenue district—by then 72 percent

Latino—West Adams, the Crenshaw District, Inglewood, East Los Angeles, and beyond.[34]

In 1992, Black Los Angeles was without an identified center for the first time since the earliest black settlements took shape around Central Avenue in the 1880s and 1890s. The 1965 Watts riots had divorced many black Angelenos from affiliation with the Eastside. Black Angelenos were in need of a public meeting place and a way to demonstrate support for each other economically and politically. They also needed to celebrate and reassert their social, cultural, and political identities. Leimert Park Village created a space for all of these things to occur. But while the Village took on the role of black center post-1992, it had been a center of black cultural and artistic activity since the late 1960s (see chap. 10). Made possible by an artist collective, the Village art center ran counter to the city's other black centers in terms of organization. The Brick Block, Central Avenue, and West Adams centers had been organized by the interplay of entrepreneurial activity and high homeownership rates in contained districts. The Leimert Park/Crenshaw area, by contrast, had a renter-occupied rate of 64 percent and a homeownership rate of just 29 percent, compared to a homeownership rate of 36 percent in the Central Avenue corridor.

Nevertheless, we should not underestimate the influence of the artists who led the charge in Leimert Park, as many were entrepreneurs and activists in their own right. Moreover, many of them played a significant role in different social justice movements throughout Los Angeles. To be sure, some of these black Leimert Park merchants came from families that have been entrenched in the creation of the early Black Los Angeles centers on the Eastside. This last point was illuminated for me in 2005, when I attended the ninety-second birthday of William Nickerson Jr., the son of William Nickerson, co-founder of Golden State Mutual. I learned that the Nickerson family counted sisters Mary and Jackie—who owned the Zambezi Bazaar gift shop in Leimert Park Village—as part of a long line of family members who were merchants and advocates in the community. Both had been active participants in the Village Merchants Association and vocal about a city councilmember's alleged abuse of political power. Their advocacy for due process in Leimert Park Village made perfect sense, as they had come from a lineage of Black Los Angeles entrepreneurs and advocates. Their pioneering position in Leimert Park Village had maintained continuity with their family's long-standing role in creating black spaces in Los Angeles.

Leimert Park as Contested Black Space

Despite the rise of Leimert Park as a post-1992 black center, a 1996 public debate over the installation of meters into the main parking area of the Village illustrates that it was also contested black space. The main actors in this conflict were the Leimert Park Merchants Association and Councilman Mark Ridley-Thomas. Each group had its own "imagined" ideal of what Leimert Park should and could be. The issue: parking meters.

The Merchants Association believed that Councilman Ridley-Thomas made a unilateral decision to turn two unmetered parking lots into metered lots without the input of local black merchants. Ridley-Thomas claimed that the lots were underutilized, arriving at this conclusion after commissioning a parking meter study for the area. The report concluded that meters could generate over $500,000 in revenue that could be returned to the community for improvements. But the councilman didn't pitch the meter idea to the merchant stakeholders as a revenue generator that could improve Leimert Park's infrastructure. His failure to do so created significant friction, as the merchants group felt they were being left out of the political process.

The Merchants Association viewed the Village parking lots as a free amenity (rare in Los Angeles) that would pull patrons into the district for long periods of shopping. They also contended that the free parking was what enticed residents from other parts of the city to come and participate in the numerous black cultural festivals hosted in the Village throughout the year—including the LA/LA,[35] Kwanzaa, and Juneteenth celebrations, blues festivals, and Martin Luther King Day Parade.

In a meeting with Ridley-Thomas, the Merchants Association threatened to oust him if he didn't comply with their wishes and drop his plan to install meters. The councilman rebutted the threat by saying, "I understand politics and I understand black people." The merchants never asked what he meant by the statement. But when later asked what they thought he meant, they interpreted his statement to mean, "I control these resources for this area and I know that you will never organize yourself enough to do anything."[36]

This conflict suggested that there had been a shift of sorts in the political position occupied by black merchants, particularly compared to what was common in earlier black centers. In the Eastside Central Avenue District of the early twentieth century, it was the merchants who drove the progress and development of the community with input and support from figures like Assemblymember Fred Roberts of the Seventy-fourth District. The community seemed to move as a whole on these types of issues. But in post-1992 Leimert Park Village, the input of the entrepreneurial community was subordinated to the development agenda of a single councilman. Ultimately, the meters were installed in Leimert Park.

While the new center community of Leimert Park Village served as an outward signifier of African American pride and culture, an inward struggle over identity, power, and resistance was being waged in the late 1990s to the present. The struggle could be seen in how merchants protested against the broad array of festivals that came into the village throughout the year. While it might seem at first glance that the festivals would be a benefit to local foot traffic, some merchants complained that festival booths blocked access to their stores. They also charged that many of the festival merchants sold the same items as local merchants, thus creating direct and unwanted competition. Eventually, merchants found ways to compromise with festival producers in the operation of the festivals, to limit competition and business disruptions, and to focus on promotion of Leimert Park Village as an important center for Black Los Angeles.

During this same period, other struggles over land ownership and increasing rent prompted several of the founding merchants and artists to move out of the village. The artist Ramesses left Leimert Park Village in 2002 after Jack Sidney, who owned the land on which nine Village businesses sat, fell into ill-health and had to sell his storefronts on the eastside of Degnan Boulevard, between an alley and Forty-third Street.[37] For years, Sidney had purposely kept the rents below market rates in order to nurture the arts and cultural activities that were taking root in Leimert Park. He sold the property to Russell Associates, a Sherman Oaks–based company that immediately began notifying the merchants of rent increases in August 2002, shortly after it completed the purchase. The Leimert Park Merchants Association president maintained that, "the new owners are not interested in anything other than receiving rent. We wrote a letter to them to let them know they didn't just invest in a building, they invested in a community that is proud and moving forward."[38]

Collectively, these developments demonstrate the tenuous nature of arts, culture, and entrepreneurship in Leimert Park Village—just as it was establishing itself as the black center in early twenty-first-century Los Angeles. The Jim Crow–era entrepreneurship stories of Golden State Mutual, the Dunbar Hotel, and Booker T. Washington Building along Central

Avenue should have taught Black Los Angeles that in order to firmly anchor a black center, the black community must control the land.

In the early 2000s, the Crenshaw District had all of the necessary elements to establish its position as the center of Black Los Angeles: high homeownership rates; majority black population; black entrepreneurship; black political representation at the city, county, state, and federal levels; and black Angelenos yearning for a place to call their own—whether they lived there or not. Black Los Angeles was at a key point in its development, when it could have learned much from its bittersweet Eastside legacy of struggle, power, and progress. To be sure, the gain of placemaking that was largely erased by the I-10 Freeway development in West Adams was a poignant lesson about the need to be united as a community and in control of political processes. This lesson—along with lessons from the expansion and later decline of the Central Avenue District—needs to be fixed in the collective memory of Black Los Angeles, carried forward, understood, and applied by future generations seeking to solidify the position of Crenshaw/Leimert Park Village as the center of Black Los Angeles.

NOTES

1. Hayden, *The Power of Place*, 15–17.
2. Lefebvre, *The Production of Space*. 46–48, 110.
3. De Graaf, "The City of Black Angels."
4. Ibid, 117.
5. George Beavers Jr., *Interview Conducted in 1982 by Ranford B. Hopkins*: Department of Special Collections, Young Research Library, University of California, Los Angeles. Audio recording, tape no. 2, side 1, May 4, 1982, transcript, 33.
6. Flamming, *Bound for Freedom*, 122.
7. "The Get Together Movement Spreads," *California Eagle*, February 12, 1916, vol. 29, no. 1, 1; "Central Avenue and the Eagle," *California Eagle*, April 8, 1916, vol. 29, no. 9, 4.
8. Du Bois, "Colored California."
9. "The Get Together Movement Spreads," *California Eagle*, February 12, 1916, vol. 29, no. 1, 1.
10. "Angelus Theater Advertisement," *California Eagle*, March 10, 1916, vol. 29, no. 5, 3.
11. "Central Avenue and the Eagle," *California Eagle*, April 8, 1916, vol. 29, no. 9, 4.

12. First AME was established in 1872.

13. "The Progressive Business League," *California Eagle*, October 4, 1919, vol. 33, no. 34, 8, back page.

14. This same cry to "Recycle Black Dollars" would play itself out in the 1990s and early twenty-first-century business center of Crenshaw/Leimert Park Village.

15. Butler, *Entrepreneurship and Self-Help*, 122.

16. "The Progressive Business League," *California Eagle*, October 4, 1919, vol. 33, no. 34, 8, back page.

17. Bunch, "Introduction."

18. Flamming, *Bound for Freedom*, 124.

19. Ibid., 377.

20. The original Eighth and Towne Building burned down in 1972, long after the First AME congregation had relocated to West Adams.

21. Cecilia Rasmussen, "Honoring L.A.'s Black Founders [includes description of the Furlong Tract]," *Los Angeles Times,* February 13, 1995, Metro Section, B3.

22. "Victory on 'Sugar Hill,'" *Time Magazine*, December 17, 1945, http://www.time.com/time/magazine/article/0,9171,776487,00.html (accessed April 1, 2009).

23. "West Adams History." West Adams Heights/Sugar Hill Neighborhood Association/West Adams Heritage Association, http://www.westadamsheightssugarhill.com/HistoricWestAdams.html, http://www.westadamsheritage.org/index.php?option=com_content&task=blogcategory&id=20&Itemid=53 (accessed April 5, June 15, 2009).

24. Sides, *L.A. City Limits*, 99.

25. "Victory on 'Sugar Hill,'" *Time* magazine, December 17, 1945.

26. Miller, *The Petitioners*, 321.

27. In 1947 the U.S. Supreme Court heard challenges to the 1926 *Corrigan v. Buckley* decision, allowing judicial enforcement of restrictive housing covenants based on race. Three cases were combined to form *Shelley v. Kraemer*. Thurgood Marshall and the NAACP team made persuasive arguments related to the constitutionality of state-sanctioned discrimination and the sociological impact of restrictive covenants. In May 1948, the U.S. Supreme Court handed down its historic decision, making racially restrictive covenants unenforceable.

28. Grace E. Simmons, "'Sugar Hill,' Other L.A. Areas Freed; Race Ban Outlawed," *Los Angeles Sentinel*, May 6, 1948, vol. 14, no. 7, 1.

29. Sides, *L.A. City Limits,* 124.

30. The Ink Well Beach was a 200-foot section of the Santa Monica State Beach that was once reserved for only African Americans. The Ink Well was roped off to separate black and white beachgoers. In the 1940s roughly 2,000 African Americans lived in Santa Monica and created a thriving community of well-attended churches and successful businesses at the neighborhood end of Ink Well Beach.

31. "Life Presents Eight Houses Especially Designed by Famous American Architects," *Life*, September 26, 1938, 45.

32. Genethia Hudley Hayes, interview by author, June 1–3, 2007.

33. Hutchinson, "The Northern Drive."

34. See Hunt, *Screening the Los Angeles "Riots."*

35. The Los Angeles to Louisiana Festival ("LA/LA") is held annually around Fat Tuesday (Mardi Gras) in February. It commemorates the migration of Louisianans from Louisiana to Los Angeles, the largest home space of Louisianans outside of Louisiana.

36. Mark Ridley-Thomas, quoted at a Leimert Park Merchants Association community meeting, May 16, 2001.

37. Ramesses was a long-term, live-work artist in Leimert Park Village. Working out of the old Brockman Gallery space (see chap. 10 in this volume for a further discussion of the Brockman Gallery), his specialty was glass work and graphic drawings. He became infamous during the "Leimert Park Village Parking Meter Debate" when he featured Councilman Ridley-Thomas in cartoon art as a sellout to the community. Ridley-Thomas summoned the FBI because he felt the protest art was a threat to his life. Ramesses continued to hold arts classes for children and adults while demonstrating his craft on the street until the sale of his space by his landlord in 2002.

38. John L. Mitchell, "Surrounding Leimert Park Village: Sudden Rise in Rents Threatens Area's Identity," *Los Angeles Times*, December 26, 2002, B2.

Chapter 3

The Decline of a Black Community by the Sea
Demographic and Political Changes in Oakwood

Andrew Deener

I attended a party at the small cottage of my wife's friend John, a white man in his late twenties, who recently moved to Oakwood and works in the film production industry. Oakwood, a one-square-mile area in Venice, California, was often recognized as a distinct neighborhood altogether. Many referred to it as the "black section" of Venice, and activists commonly described it as the last remaining "pocket of poverty" in this coastal neighborhood, due to the fourteen low-income, housing projects constructed during the 1970s. Sometimes Oakwood residents identified this location through more pejorative terms as "the ghetto," "the 'hood," "the projects," or as "Ghost Town." Despite these labels, Oakwood was a very diverse location that was no longer a predominantly black community.

John's cottage, which he rented for more than $2,000 a month, was a small two-bedroom structure and rests behind a larger, aging house. The only entranceway was through the gate out front, which was locked. Without a phone, we waited on the street trying to figure out how to get inside this blocked-out world, a world that escaped any public contact or visibility. As I looked around, the only public activity came from African American children running in the street, and African American teenagers leaning up against a concrete wall in front of a house. We watched them as they checked us out, standing there trying to enter our friend's home. John finally let us in, and we walked to the back of the property where about twenty people were standing around barbequing, drinking, listening to music, and talking. Attendees at the party were almost entirely from outside of the neighborhood, showing a disconnection from the local surroundings. Only one other person at the party lived in Venice. Everyone there was white and young, between twenty-five and thirty-five years old, and besides Alana and me, they knew John from either work or college.

During the evening, I asked John about the neighborhood. He explained that since moving in several months ago, he had pretty much kept to himself. He had yet to meet any of his neighbors. He knew a little bit about the culture and history of the street from his landlord, who explained to him that if something goes down—suspicious or bothersome—he should talk to an African American woman who lives across the way, who apparently knew everything about the street and everyone on it. But other than that, he had little knowledge about the rich and diverse social history of the neighborhood to which he moved, and little motivation to learn more. Instead, the proximity to the beach and the secluded lifestyle in his back cottage were enough to keep him content for the time being or until he eventually moved.

This party was one of many moments I noted as part of my research and writing about Venice. In 2002 I started an ethnographic study about the social and economic life of the Venice Boardwalk. I attended a number of neighborhood meetings during that time and came to understand that many of the problems on the boardwalk were part of a larger pattern of neighborhood change. For the next six years, I explored the impact of these changes from the perspectives of different groups, including those living in Oakwood, the most racially, ethnically and socioeconomically diverse section of Venice. As I came to know a number of long-term residents, I was compelled to explore the impact of demographic and political-economic changes on race, ethnicity, generation, and public and private life in Oakwood. What I discovered was an intricate process of intra- and intergroup conversion, and a multifaceted, longitudinal transformation of a neighborhood and community.

Demographic Change: From Black to Brown to White

The 1970 census showed that African Americans made up the largest racial category in Oakwood, at 45 percent of the population, with Latinos following at 32 percent (see table 3.1). The 1980 census illustrated an inversion of that, with Latinos making up 45 percent and African Americans

TABLE 3.1
Oakwood Population by Black and Hispanic, 1960–2000

	1960	1970	1980	1990	2000
Total Population	8,228	8,152	8,962	9,216	8,536
Black Population	3,191	3,660	2,729	2,022	1,244
Percent Black	39%	45%	30%	22%	15%
Hispanic Population	1,481	2,635	4,039	4,572	4,049
Percent Hispanic	18%	32%	45%	49.6%	47%

Source: U.S. Censuses, 1960–2000.

30 percent of the population. Twenty years later, the 2000 census revealed that Latinos still made up the largest percentage at 47 percent, but whites now followed at 33 percent, and blacks trailed at 15 percent of the Oakwood area.

This transition of Oakwood's demographic composition reveals three significant trends typical of the pattern of change throughout the City of Los Angeles during that period. First, a pattern of residential segregation by race and class[1] historically shaped Oakwood. Second, the number of Latinos increasingly overshadowed the number of African Americans, converting Oakwood into a mixed racial/ethnic locale by the first decade of the 2000s.[2] Third, long-term residents of Oakwood, like those living in Los Angeles neighborhoods where the majority of the population is composed of people of color and/or low-income residents are now experiencing the influx of wealthier white residents as well. While the census statistics are informative in understanding the dramatic changes in residential composition, they do not help us understand differences in community formation and transformation, or the effects of demographic and political-economic changes on intergroup relations between blacks, Latinos, and whites.

In Oakwood, African Americans, rooted in a multigenerational, home-owning community, largely had been compelled to disperse over time. However, remaining residents and community institutions continued to serve as a magnet for family members and friends who had moved away. This created the appearance of a concentrated African American community more significant than the actual numbers of residents.

Unlike African Americans, the number of Latinos has generally increased since 1960. Their trajectory is made up of successive waves of immigration to Venice from several places in Latin America, creating distinct problems of integration into the broader Oakwood community and between the different phases of Latino residents. Between 1990 and 2000, the (non-Hispanic) white population also began to change. Long-standing white Oakwood residents, similar to many of their black and Latino counterparts, were either low-income, working-, or middle-class. Yet, as coastal property values escalated, increasingly wealthier white people moved into the district. During the period of my research, they purchased aging homes, remodeled or even tore them down in order to build sleek, multilevel buildings. Sometimes, they acquired adjoining lots in order to construct standout homes that loomed large over smaller, aging, worn-out building structures. They often erected tall fences around their homes that exceeded the city-defined legal limit in order to manufacture an amplified feeling of security and privacy. Over time, Oakwood became a complex social environment created by a combination of long-term homeowner-ship, immigration, low-income housing projects, and gentrification. Complications arose when this area was coveted by individuals with highly variable levels of economic resources who all wanted to live, work, and/or play close to the beach.

Early African American Population Growth and Its Repercussions

For more than a century, Oakwood was considered a black neighborhood due to its multigenerational network of African American residents. This community created a vibrant society where barriers between public and private life were minimized. Regular interactions between black residents were facilitated by historically strong social links between black residents, many related through kinship, marriage, and childbirth, as well as the racial climate that restricted mobility beyond the boundaries of Oakwood. Combined, these factors reinforced the fluidity between new and old African American residents in public and private life.

There were three phases of African American population expansion in Venice. The first two were the direct result of migration from the South, as people sought better living conditions, greater financial opportunities, and increased freedoms by escaping racially hostile conditions. The first phase occurred in the early 1900s, when the population expanded from 33 African Americans in 1910 to 102 in 1920. Men and women worked as manual laborers, service workers, and servants to Abbot Kinney, the developer of Venice, as well as for many of the wealthier white residents who lived on the extensive canal system that structured the identity of the Venice neighborhood.[3] At this time, housing was sporadically scattered in the Oakwood area for all residents, much of the land was undeveloped, and it became an early site of black homeownership on the Westside of Los Angeles.

The second phase of migration from the southern states of Arkansas, Louisiana, Texas, and Mississippi, among others, accelerated due to job prospects before and during World War II; in particular, the need for defense workers at Hughes Aircraft in Culver City and McDonnell Douglass in Santa Monica. From 1940 to 1950, the black population in Oakwood tripled, from 346 to 1,157,[4] a much greater growth rate in comparison to the neighborhood's overall white population.[5]

The third phase of expansion came during a postwar population boom,[6] and the construction of the Santa Monica Freeway (an extension of Interstate 10).[7] Eminent domain laws targeting black and Latino residents living in nearby Santa Monica were used to force many out of the neighborhood. In search of homes, some moved to Venice, sparking a peak in the number of black residents during this decade. According to census figures, after 1970 the black population in Oakwood began to decline.

These three different tracts of migration culminated in a very stable Oakwood community that extended between cohorts. Friends and relatives commonly moved to Los Angeles, following the advice of those who had already arrived. This provided newcomers with the opportunity to improve their financial standing by staying for extended periods of time without rent. As Regina Stanton,[8] a ninety-year-old woman raised in Venice whose family was the first black family to arrive in 1905, recalls:

> They'd live with relatives or whatever. Because one family would come into the neighborhood and they'd ask their family to come on in, you know how people do. And they'd double up in the house and everything until they could get a place on their own.

Lila Riley, an African American woman and life-long resident in her sixties, adds:

> There were the black families that were down here for a while, some who were even here from the very beginning of Venice. And they would tell the other family members, wherever they were living, "Come on out to

Venice, California . . ." And it was still in development back then, so they would come and stay and find a place to live right around here. . . . [T]hey would move right next door, build a house, and before you knew it, you look around and the whole street was owned by black families.

Oakwood was the only location in Venice that would allow black residency. Housing covenants and racist encounters with residents from surrounding white neighborhoods and Los Angeles Police Department (LAPD) officers also limited African American mobility and strengthened community ties. During the early years, African American residents recalled a chapter of the Ku Klux Klan in Venice, and how they often withstood threats from Klan members. Both Regina Stanton and Myra Washington told me multiple stories from their childhoods about their fathers and uncles marching up and down the streets with shotguns to protect newly arriving black families from white residents who threatened and harassed them:

> AD: When you came here, how'd you know that you had to live behind West Washington Boulevard and Lincoln? Like how'd you know that this was the area?
> Regina: This was the only place that they would sell to you. We knew.

Others recounted clear racial boundaries that restricted their mobility. In particular, east of Lincoln Boulevard and south of West Washington Boulevard (later Abbot Kinney Boulevard) were off limits (see fig. 3.1). This restricted mobility, built upon a persistent fear of outside interrogation, was passed down between generations of residents.

Lila Riley, now in her sixties, remembers when she was a child:

> Then the blacks couldn't go east of Lincoln. . . . Brooks Avenue, they changed the name on the east side of Lincoln. West we called it "Brooks" and then on the east, when you cross Lincoln, they called it "Lake Street." They didn't want to be associated with poor black people. And you didn't really test the waters out in those days.

The restrictions on mobility were even passed down to younger—third- and fourth-generation residents—due to the fear of what lay beyond Oakwood's borders. Edward Morris, a third-generation resident in his early forties, expressed his perception about the geographic limitations facing Oakwood inhabitants:

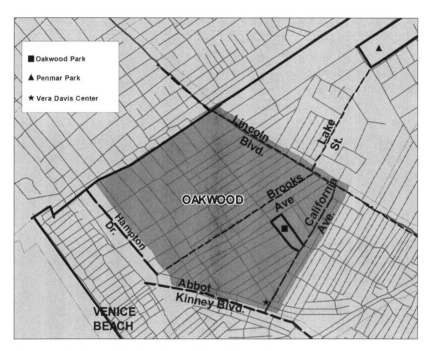

Figure 3.1. Oakwood Landmarks and Spatial Boundaries

> You walked outside of Oakwood, and they called the police. [Imitating a white man] "We need help. There's a black man in my neighborhood." And then the police come right away and they force you back into your community. [Imitating a police officer] "Boy, what are you doing here? Get your ass back over there!"

This fear of outside harassment continued for decades, demonstrating the historic impact of these geographic borders as a symbolic form of imprisonment for African American residents.

How Restrictions Helped Redefine Community

The coupling of the complex system of social networks and the external constraints on mobility produced a culture in Oakwood that blurred the boundary between public and private space, shaping self-presentation, family/community structure, and use of private property/shared space.

Longtime black residents recall how little mom-and-pop stores emerged in the area, catering to them, and when people went out to a local store it was acceptable to enter in your robe and slippers, as if you were still inside your home, not taking care to prepare a public presentation. Delia Montgomery, who was in her mid-sixties, recalled Oakwood when she was a child and young adult:

> Venice at that time was a very close-knit community. It was sort of like being in a big living room. . . . So, since the forties, fifties and at some level in my generation, everybody knows everybody. And if you don't know who they are, then you know somebody in their family. And so when I was growing up and everyone knew everyone, and it was a more neighborly community where they knew your grandparents, or they went to school with your kids, or something. And so you had a stronger community connection there.

People commonly blurred the distinction between family and community. In addition to their parents, children faced the authority of their neighbors, most commonly the older women of the neighborhood, who watched and monitored the streets as if they served as an extension of their parents outside of the home.[9] Lakesha Holt, in her late forties and from a family that boasted fourth- and fifth-generation residents in Oakwood, remembered the cultural dynamics of this public life:

> I knew all of San Juan, I knew all of Broadway, I knew all of Indiana.[10] That would be a real community, because they would watch us. And if anything would happen, Miss Reese would call my parents before I even got home. "I saw your little girl and she was doing this, or this, or that. She's on her way." . . . Older people watched you. They sat out on their front porches and they watched you. The way it is now, you can't see. I mean you can't visually see anybody.[11] We knew everybody. And they all knew you, because we were a family, we were a community.

Moreover, in tough times when financial resources were restricted, African American families repeatedly depicted their ability to band together, serving communal meals and helping one another out of a jam.[12] "You never went hungry," said Melinda Campbell. "We were always having picnics and barbeques and everyone came. If someone didn't have enough to put food on the table that week, everyone else helped out. Ya know, it was like, 'We're gonna barbeque tonight anyway, so come on over.' And everyone would come over. And people would bring different things and we'd all share." This culture of shared resources still functioned into the early 2000s, in a muted form.

Homes were another area where public and private boundaries blurred. Black residents were less likely to consecrate their neighbors' houses as private residences because of the close proximity between family members and friends who lived on the same blocks or streets. Instead, with many children living throughout the neighborhood, they ran into and out of their neighbors' homes with the rest of the children as if there was no ceremonial distinction between home ownership. Neighbors often used corridors to connect their backyards, readily allowing access to what people today commonly perceive as "private space." African American residents expressed how evenings were not scheduled as the time to retire into the house for "family time" or "private time," but instead it was an occasion to rekindle social bonds and catch up with others, including their children, through "community time." This promoted a village lifestyle rather than that of a more insular suburban one.

The Results of Generational Change within the African American Community

Although Oakwood never completely became a black community in terms of total demographic composition, according to longtime residents, certain streets became almost entirely filled with black residents.[13] This development is noteworthy when considered within the early 2000s context of the demand for beachfront property. Many of the elder black residents were very cognizant of the significance of their community placement and worked hard to pass this understanding down to their children, along with, to the extent possible, the homes where they were raised.

Some were able to acquire additional residences that provided their siblings, children, and grandchildren with places to live nearby. Regina Stanton, still living in the house her father built, remembered her father not only assembling houses on empty neighborhood lots but also bringing in houses on trucks into which family members would then move. Later in life, when her son became an adult, having a house on a double lot allowed her the opportunity to provide her son and grandson with land to construct another house behind hers and become third-generation Venice homeowners, despite the fact that the property values were increasing and the opportunity to purchase additional homes was becoming more difficult.

In other cases, the children or grandchildren of original black homeowners eventually purchased the homes in which they grew up from their parents, grandparents, uncles, and aunts. Over the years, a small number of black families were able to acquire multiple lots, creating a miniature (and in two cases I encountered, not so miniature) real estate empire, owning several properties on their own streets and throughout the Oakwood area (see table 3.2).

The combined outcome of black homeownership, constraints of limited mobility, and a culture of familial proximity, was that many of the third- and fourth- (and in some cases, even fifth- and sixth-) generation African Americans were raised in an environment that they viewed as "their neighborhood," the place into which they were born and the one that they symbolically controlled. They were members of the longest-standing community in the overall neighborhood, making this part of Venice the "black section."

TABLE 3.2
Oakwood in Black and White, 2000[a]

	Blacks	Whites
Population	1,284	2,809
Per Capita Income	$13,662	$40,870
Poverty Rate	22%	12%
Unemployment Rate	11%	5%
Labor Force Participation Rate	53%	77%
Education ≥ Baccalaureate	11%	59%
Occupation: Management/Professional	38%	58%
Occupation: Service	16%	12%
Occupation: Sales/Office	34%	18%
Home-ownership Rate	26%	21%
Age of Homeowners		
34 or less	5%	17%
35–64	40%	75%
65 or greater	55%	8%
Average Household Size	2.4	1.6
Nonfamily households	39%	76%
Rides Public Transit to Work	17%	5%

[a] 2000 data from Los Angeles County Census tracts 2732 and 2733; Income data from 1999; Whites refers to White, non-Hispanics.
Source: U.S. Census Bureau.

However, in the 1960s and 1970s, the economic context began to shift, including opportunities for jobs, which subsequently hindered possibilities for financial security among this generation and their children.[14] It was a highly politicized time, with the civil rights movement and the explosion of the Watts riots in 1965. These events precipitated extended federal, state, and local efforts to provide funding for communities in economic need in order to limit the likelihood of future uprisings.

During this time, African American activists from Oakwood began to search for ways to improve the livelihoods of their relatives, friends, and neighbors. Delia Montgomery, a longtime resident in her late sixties, wrote a grant for federal funding that was used to start Project Action, an organization providing job training, educational tutoring, and community-watch training. As the organization grew, members realized that there was a need for low-income housing, and they collaborated with the U.S. Department of Housing and Urban Development (HUD) and local housing activists to receive additional monies to construct fourteen low-income housing projects in Oakwood during the early 1970s; these projects would be managed at the community level.

The outcome of the new affordable housing was, by and large, extra living spaces for many who already lived in Oakwood as the children and grandchildren of long-term African American homeowners and renters in the area. Initially the housing was community-run by Project Action, but eventually due to financial difficulties, private owners purchased it and arranged new contracts with HUD to maintain the affordability of the housing units. Despite their official status as Project-Based Section 8 housing (a program run by the federal Department of Housing and Urban Development (HUD) that gives the developer stable subsidies from the government, while tenants are chosen on the basis of their exceptionally low incomes and special needs), units are often allocated in ways that circumvent the bureaucratic rules when tenants negotiate with a local building manager.

By the early 1970s, the first eight buildings were constructed, and 98 percent of the residents living in the 176 units were black, 92 percent of whom were receiving some form of federal aid.[15] When the fourteen buildings were completed, they were not concentrated on one street or in one section of Oakwood, but instead, separate structures were scattered throughout the entire one-mile radius area (see fig. 3.2), which in turn, created a feeling of amplified stability and territorial control for black residents, who found their way into these apartments.

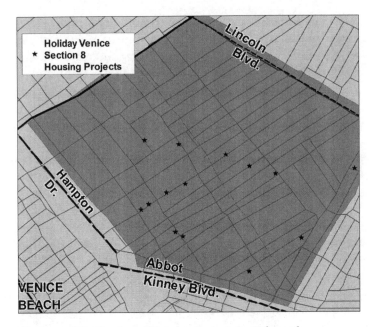

Figure 3.2. Distribution of Housing Projects in Oakwood.

Even with changes mounting in the demographic makeup of the neighborhood, blacks continued to control the growth of low-income housing
and the uses and symbolism of neighborhood public spaces. For example,
the directors of the Oakwood Park were generally black men, who continued to hire blacks from the community to work as part-time employees.
The sports field outside of the recreation center was renamed in memory of a longtime black resident, and black seniors gathered at the picnic
tables on a daily basis. Black youth used the gym inside, black activists
organized and held meetings in and around the recreation center, and the
old library building was renamed the Vera Davis Center in memory of a
local black activist, becoming the home of several black-run, social service agencies.
    The increasing need for affordable housing and social services among
black residents pointed specifically to an internal community transition
along generational lines. Life for the older generation of Oakwood residents was marked by the pronounced culture of camaraderie and community that blurred the boundaries between public and private life. However, teenage pregnancy, drug use, street crime, gang proliferation, and

extended prison sentences (most significantly among men) became more pervasive issues in the younger generation, altering the community structure for both the older and younger generations.

The shift along generational (and to some extent gender) lines, however, was not simply due to the coupling of economic restrictions and/ or the reproduction of family values as many sociologists have documented.[16] Many who became involved in hustling, drug dealing, and gang activities as part of the Venice Shoreline Crips,[17] were children of working and married parents. Antoine Small, in his mid-thirties, explained that his gang participation, despite strong parental influence, was a result of peer group association:

> I was a gang member for the majority of my life, from elementary school all the way until I was adult. . . . [Starting] about the fourth or fifth grade, and that was just the culture when I was growing up. . . . And because I was the way that I was, it didn't have anything to do with my parents. My father was a community activist. . . . He worked for several agencies in this area providing services. So it wasn't that. It wasn't my father, and it wasn't my mother. She worked at GTE for over twenty years.

According to Andre Mott, a forty-year-old former black resident, there were significant changes—beginning with his generation that grew up during the 1970s—in community relations related to street culture, prison sentences, and a new family dynamic of single-parent households:[18]

> When I was growing up [in the 1970s], the majority of the families had mothers and fathers, a few of them didn't because the father was off in the army or got killed . . . but it wasn't like the father was walking off. See my father didn't go to jail. He worked. I went to jail. All my siblings went to jail. We chose street life. And now, ya know, you don't have no fathers hardly in the household. None whatsoever. Ya know, and it's not getting any better.

This intergenerational transition forced some long-standing African American families to seek to protect their property and community. James Thompson, in his eighties, and Myra Washington, in her late sixties, were both senior African American homeowners. They were unhappy about the community transition that forced the need to protect one's private interests, creating skepticism about their long-standing social bonds.

James: This area went down to nothing. All kinds of crime was going on right here. Why? They came into Oakwood with the drugs and the cocaine, and then if you remember, you could hardly go to a meeting at night, because your home might've been burglarized. At that time, it wasn't no Mexicans. It wasn't nothing but our own people.

Myra: Yeah, it was. It was black on black.

The fourteen housing projects and the overwhelming perceptions of poverty and crime in Oakwood became the life support for affordability in this beachfront neighborhood. As counterculture and housing activists from surrounding sections of Venice struggled to resist city- and state-led coastal improvement programs and economic development during the decades between the 1970s and 1990s, housing in the Oakwood area continued to remain affordable, well below the market rates in surrounding coastal districts. As a result, Oakwood was a magnet for low-income tenants, many of whom were Latino immigrants who had limited housing options and highly constrained economic opportunities.

The Evolution of Black/Brown Relations

The first wave of Venice Chicanos mostly arrived in the 1950s and early 1960s. Within this category, there were two distinct types of residents: new immigrants, and children and grandchildren of immigrants. Although the first-phase Latinos tended to develop a close attachment to the neighborhood and an association to black residents, the second wave of immigrants who arrived during the late 1960s and throughout the 1980s were fundamentally different from the first wave, and language barriers confined social contact. Despite blacks' marginalized status in relation to whites, second-phase Latino immigrants tended to view blacks as simply "Americans." Since they came to Venice from different places in Latin America, it created problems for building community ties with other Latino residents and made it difficult to establish social connections to the broader Oakwood community.

The second-wave Latinos established different boundaries between public and private life than did black families and first-wave Latinos. Instead of uniting across houses by blurring together public and private space, much of the activity occurred within the walls of their living spaces, which sometimes became complex social worlds unto themselves. In part, the "private" social life was a way to deal with the difficult conditions that undocumented immigrants confronted.

Some black residents who were unable to acquire stable employment during this time period developed a competitive attitude when confronted by unknown Latinos on the street, who regularly worked, albeit at below-minimum-wage standards. The outcome was a rise in street crime, which led new Latino residents to develop feelings of insecurity and a belief that some blacks were dangerous. Such constraints on public life led second-wave Latino residents to embrace a more private type of social life, which hindered the possibility of establishing closer ties with longer-standing black residents and Latinos who had been living in Oakwood for decades. During this period, African Americans were undergoing a bifurcation process in Oakwood, with some becoming engaged in street and gang activities, and others avoiding it. Due to intragroup transitions along generational lines, intergroup relations between black and brown also started to transform, creating a renewed conflict dynamic between the two groups. In the past, there had been some conflict, but it had slowed down over the years, only to re-emerge with the coming-of-age of the younger generation.

Although blacks and Latinos faced similar experiences outside of the neighborhood and similar economic conditions, they nonetheless established different historical connections to the social spaces of Oakwood. Latino residents who felt excluded by blacks from these social spaces and stood witness to re-occurring attacks against their parents took it upon themselves to come together and increase the protection of their family members. While the LAPD began to label this local competition over space as "gang-motivated behavior," those who grew up in Venice—blacks and Latinos—tended to see it as "family-motivated behavior."[19] Sal, a Latino man in his thirties who grew up in Venice, noted:

> When we would live on a daily basis here, we didn't understand the people that we lived around were gang bangers, in the sense that the city and the state defines it. We were just responding to immediate situations, ya know, the fact that we were being robbed, this is how we're going to do it.

Kin-based social dynamics mobilized to respond to the social, economic, and political conditions of the time, made the second-generation residents human capital for the expansion of the Venice 13 gang. At the level of gang participation, blacks and Latinos historically shared the space and respected the rights of others to use it for economic purposes, most significantly, for the dealing of drugs on the streets of Oakwood. If competition over space arose, members of one group commonly approached older members of the other group to quell any rise in hostility. For the most part, violence between members of these two gangs was minimal. Still, at certain moments, under stressed conditions, extreme levels of violence occurred.

Gang Impact on Daily Life

Although there were growing problems with crime between 1970 and 1990, property values continued to rise. One study[20] reports that from 1969 to 1989 the median household value in Oakwood increased from $90,000 to $280,000. Yet, as a group of middle-class residents began to find its way into Oakwood during the 1980s and early 1990s, a devastating gang war altered the trajectory of gentrification for several years and dramatically re-created the uses of social space in the neighborhood.

Prior to the gang war, although street crimes occurred, residents describe it as a comparatively safe time period. Many people, especially long-standing black residents, point to a history of peace between racially different groups, especially between Latinos and blacks.[21] Yet, even early white arrivals, mostly middle-class residents moving in during the 1980s, share this perspective about the community. Jerry Robinson, a white man in his fifties, says, "There was a lot of rampant drug dealing in the streets, but it was fairly peaceful. . . . And then there was the gang war."

During the 1990s, gang proliferation became a serious problem in Oakwood, and a war over turf rights pitted four distinct gangs against one another and forced people to take sides.[22] Despite efforts to work out the problems within the community, violence slowly emerged in Oakwood through interpersonal conflict between members of these rival groups, eventually intensifying into a full-fledged gang war. Some blacks believed Latinos, whose drug trade had expanded significantly in Los Angeles, also wanted to take over their control of the drug trade in Oakwood, while others pinned the hostility on individual characteristics of the shooters or those killed.[23] Despite the fact that the controversy started in the Mar Vista Gardens Projects over control of territory for the distribution of drugs, different groups of people started to interpret group oppositions by categorizing the enemy in Oakwood according to contrasting physical racial indicators—black or brown—rather than individual, group, or historical associations.

The traumatic gang war resulted in seventeen deaths and more than fifty injuries in a ten-month time span. The violence created an atmosphere of perpetual anxiety, as residents became wary of entering the public spaces around their homes. Individuals described to me how, during daylight hours, they were afraid to take their trash out to the curb, sit in their yards, or walk around the neighborhood. Some had awakened to dead bodies in their front yards and bullet holes in their houses, windows, and cars. One resident remembered waking up to ear-shattering screams of a mother who found her son dead in the street. Another, an anti-gang activist, put bars on his windows and placed chicken wire to block attempts of gang members who threw Molotov cocktails (or fire bombs) at his home. One man I encountered rearranged his house, so his and his wife's bed faced the backyard instead of the street, for fear of being hit by a stray bullet.

Even members of the Shoreline Crips and Venice 13 reorganized their understandings of public life. Gang members collectively arranged to protect the senior members of their community. They walked their grandparents to church on Sundays, and they monitored their houses and yards like the Secret Service. The rise of violence and fear temporarily "stalled" the gentrification process in Oakwood,[24] as the median household value dramatically decreased.[25] In 1997, for instance, three years after the gang war, the median price of houses sold in Oakwood was \$161,000,[26] more than \$100,000 less than eight years earlier in 1989. Long-standing residents became increasingly concerned not only about the new label of Oakwood as violent but also the traumatic effects of gang violence on the relationship between family, community, and individual identity.

The focus on the gang war as the central feature of Oakwood's local culture worked to overshadow the constellation of legal, economic, and political factors that had transformed the community. A series of factors related to a more intense phase of gentrification, development, political, and legal intrusions by agents of the City of Los Angeles, and the arrival of an additional cohort of immigrant residents in Oakwood, further transformed the uses and meanings of public space and community, and produced the social ecology evident in the early 2000s.

Gentrification City

Beginning in the late 1970s and early 1980s, middle-class whites, including artists being shut out of other parts of Venice, began to look for affordable locations to live by the beach. Many moved to Oakwood.

At about the same time, the Venice Family Clinic held its first Venice Art Walk in 1980. Founded in 1970 on Oakwood's northern border of Rose Avenue, the clinic eventually became the largest clinic in the United States to provide free health care, including services to local Venice artists and many residents living in Oakwood. The annual Venice Art Walk began as a form of payback by artists to the clinic, and it quickly became a famous Los Angeles institution and a key source of fundraising that allowed the clinic to expand its services.[27]

Longtime Oakwood residents expressed a sense of appreciation for the clinic's service to the community, but they had more critical opinions about the Art Walk, which brought wealthy white people in droves from other parts of Los Angeles and who paid to visit the artist studios in Venice, many of which were scattered throughout the Oakwood area. In numerous interviews, residents described the beginning of the Art Walk as the start of changes to their neighborhood. The invasion of voyeurs and their police escorts, who served the purpose of manufacturing a feeling of safety, was distinct from past social conditions when outsiders were unlikely to infringe on this neighborhood location. Dante Miller, a third-generation African American resident in his forties, expressed to me what his community was like before the Art Walk introduced Oakwood to whites:

> White people didn't come here. And police didn't either. We didn't see people like you [white people]. . . . White people think that we [referring to black people] exaggerate about the police, like the police don't really ignore our neighborhoods. But it's true! We [the Oakwood community] had all sorts of crime and things that we were dealing with, but the police wouldn't come out when we called. We had to take matters into our own hands a lot of the times.

The emergence of police presence after years of alleged harassment and avoidance of Oakwood was viewed by longtime residents with skepticism. Newcomers, primarily white, on the other hand, found ways to link their internal actions with formal routes into city bureaucracy, showing a willingness to work with and interact with city officials, including members of the LAPD. In her account of gang violence and police/community relations in Oakwood during the 1990s, Karen Umemoto explains how the expansion of the white population enabled greater access to political resources:

> New property owners and real estate interests exerted pressure on law enforcement officials to "clean up" Oakwood by eliminating the robberies, drug dealing, and vandalism occurring at purportedly higher rates than surrounding areas. . . . Some of them cooperated with police to videotape criminal activity from their homes at the risk of their personal safety.[28]

Newcomers established closer connections with city officials, whereas longtime residents remained suspicious. Steve Nelson, a white anti-gang/ anti-drug activist who moved to Oakwood in the 1980s, described the limited role people of color played in their organized neighborhood task force:

> Ya know we had a pretty strong neighborhood watch group, block captains, maybe twenty people that would come to regular meetings at the police station. And of course, there were *some* Latinos and *some* blacks involved but not many. Certainly, it was disproportionate to what the actual population was at the time

Notwithstanding their distrust of "official" avenues of political participation, black homeowners were very active in "cleaning up" the neighborhood but often differed from newcomers in their methods. They tended to work from the ground up to solve problems inside the community without assistance from external agencies and without any connection to incoming developers. At the center of the community, four churches in Oakwood became gathering places that brought many people together to address community issues. Yet, beyond the churches, local black activists also started a number of organizations to curb some of the immediate threats facing children and families and help to rebuild the community. Two black residents, for instance, started the Oakwood Beautification Committee to organize long-term Oakwood homeowners. According to one of the founders, John Wilbanks, "Once word went out . . . white people started calling and wanting to get involved. That hurt us. The whites and the developers just supported this whole conspiracy theory [that whites, police, and developers were in bed with one another]." In fact, at one point, police officers started coming to the meetings and black participants had to ask them to leave, because many black residents were skeptical about the role that police officers played in the process of gentrification.[29]

As gentrification and development became more prominent, black activists became increasingly vocal about the new relationships between incoming white residents with the LAPD and real estate developers. New residents and old-time activists had a similar aim—to see the end of the drug dealing and violence that threatened the stability of the community. However, many of the people selling drugs and involved in gang activities were members of the old-timers' families or kin to families they had known for decades, and they did not want to see these people suffer at the hands of LAPD officers who had had a long history of alleged abuse in Oakwood. Several black activists also began to look at these new residents as meddling into their internal family/community affairs, expressing the view that newcomers "should mind their own business."

Myra Washington, like many longtime residents, was confused about the role of increased police involvement in Oakwood. Although she saw the potential for positive outcomes, she recognized the possibility for targeting Oakwood as a "bad" part of town:

> I went to a meeting . . . and that's when they were talking about, "We're gonna call all this little section, Oakwood. And we're gonna have more police than ANY OTHER SECTION, ya know, in the neighborhood." And it sounded good. It sounded really good. But, in the back of my mind I'm thinking, is this good? Or is it going to be bad? Ya know. It actually turned out not to be good, because then we developed the reputation that this is the bad section. This is where the bad people live. And to me, I couldn't see dividing it like that. We always just said we lived in Venice. Now, all of a sudden we were Oakwood and Oakwood was a bad place.

Outside Forces and How They Shape Community

During the 1980s and 1990s, a constellation of factors that I call "external interventions" accumulated and overwhelmed the idea of Oakwood as simply a low-income community. As the surrounding districts of Venice were changing to include residents with greater levels of wealth, Oakwood remained the most visible standout location. Just as long-term residents watched white people disappear between the 1950s and 1970s in a process of white flight, during the late 1990s and early 2000s, individuals began to observe a reversal house-by-house and street-by-street.

External interventions such as legal, economic, police, and political influences gave rise to an improved sense of safety and facilitated a more rapid process of gentrification that long-standing residents acknowledged was more aggressive than the past phases, thus leading some to label it as "hypergentrification." Newcomers began to enter Oakwood at a rapid pace, and they established different connections to the neighborhood and distinct definitions of public and private space, leading to struggles over the meaning of community.

Although the gang war subsided in 1994 due to a truce between the different gangs, the memory of bloodshed and enduring drug sales in public spaces continued to reinforce the opinion that further intervention was necessary. Increased police presence in Oakwood, coupled with the gang injunction against members of both Venice gangs (Venice Shoreline Crips and Venice 13) and the Culver City gang (Culver City Boys), hindered their ability, not only to distribute drugs but also to participate with friends and relatives in public gatherings.

The gang injunction allowed the LAPD to build a case against particular individuals who they believed had gang affiliations. LAPD officials and Los Angeles Neighborhood Prosecutors[30] reinforced in public meetings that people were placed on the gang injunction due to accrued evidence of misconduct. The ten identifying criteria that provoked law enforcement officials to gather evidence about a suspected gang member were as follows: (1) admits gang membership or association; (2) is observed to associate on a regular basis with known gang members; (3) has tattoos indicating gang membership; (4) wears gang clothing, symbols, etc., to identify with a specific gang; (5) is in a photograph with known gang members and/or using gang-related hand signs; (6) name is on a gang document, hit list, or gang-related graffiti; (7) is identified as a gang member by a reliable source; (8) has been arrested in the company of identified gang members or associates; (9) corresponds with known gang members or writes and/or receives correspondence about gang activities; and (10) writes about gangs (graffiti) on walls, books, paper, etc.

In Oakwood, the blurred boundary between "street" and "decent" culture complicated the definition of "gang" and the impact of the gang injunction on this community.[31] The injunction provoked mixed reactions, with some people interpreting it as racist and an attack on low-income residents, while others put forth an argument about the right of all people —"even the poor"—to live in a safe environment. A series of public meetings, held in 2004 by the Los Angeles Human Relations Commission to address the relationship between the LAPD and the African American community, protested the function and ramifications of the gang injunction. Individuals also criticized the injunction for its inability to deal with one-time gang members who had turned their lives around. They also questioned the definition of a gang, as community members complained that relatives were placed on the injunction without actually participating in organized criminal activity, but rather by simply affiliating with known gang members.

An activist from the Youth Justice Coalition[32] pointed out:

> There are ten- and eleven-year-old kids who get on the database because of the way they are dressed, or they have an older brother. Well almost every black or brown kid fits that description. Does that mean that every black or brown kid is going to be on the gang database?

LAPD officers repeatedly responded with vague answers that they act "with compassion" and "sensitivity" when dealing with these matters. Other city officials readily responded by changing the topic to discuss the decreased crime rates in Oakwood and the goals of the LAPD gang unit. The audience of senior-citizen, black residents and Venice activists became frustrated with the LAPD officers, Los Angeles Human Relations officials, and Los Angeles Neighborhood Prosecutors who managed the meeting. The lack of clarity in the official responses was a sign that family members and friends might never escape this legal stronghold.

In addition to the gang injunction, which had a lasting effect on public participation, the city attorney's office and the city council used "nuisance abatement programs" to dislodge residents from their homes and to force homeowners to comply with new aesthetic standards. An example of this can be found in the case of the Safe Neighborhoods Division of the City Attorney's Criminal and Special Litigation Branch, which brought a suit against a family for purportedly distributing crack cocaine out of its house. In a seven-month period between May 2003 and June 2004, sixteen people were arrested at this property for drug-related crimes, including several members of the family. A Superior Court judge labeled the home as a "public nuisance" through a legally binding order, which prohibited four of the adult children from living in, or even entering, the property. As an outcome of the legal injunction, the judge required the homeowner to pay $140,000 in fines and penalties,[33] which eventually forced the family to sell the property in order to make the payments.

Legal injunctions against known criminals facilitated increased neighborhood safety by restricting drug sales and gang activities. Yet, other city programs unfairly targeted longtime homeowners with no positive outcomes. During the 1990s, representatives of the Los Angeles code enforcement agencies, Pro-Active Code Enforcement (PACE) and the Systematic Code Enforcement Program (SCEP), walked through the neighborhood looking for housing and apartment structures in need of repair. Longstanding residents and activists representing them from People Organized for Westside Renewal (POWER), a West Los Angeles–based activist organization, believed that these city agents targeted low-income homeowners and declared that these residents received tickets for minimal violations, many of which were aesthetic in nature (e.g., chipping paint, broken flower planters, mangled fences, and broken light bulbs). Many of the long-term homeowners were black senior citizens living on fixed incomes and who perceived such aesthetic matters as less of an economic priority than other compelling needs like mounting healthcare bills and continuing struggles to pay them. These violations forced senior citizens to pay the fines and invest in repairs. Longtime residents, regardless of race, seemed to be more likely to encounter the city agents because they lived in aging housing structures, which differed in size, landscape, aesthetic appearance, uses of the yard, size and types of fences surrounding the property, among other indicators. Agents used such property characteristics, which disproportionately led them to target longtime homeowners of a lower socioeconomic status.

Activists organized to stop the code enforcement agencies, believing they unjustly targeted long-term residents for aesthetic flaws, rather than problems oriented toward safety and protection. They forced then-councilwoman Ruth Galanter to eventually recall these random inspections. Although the city claimed they did not disproportionately inspect the houses of residents of particular racial, ethnic, or socioeconomic backgrounds, I could not find one new, white resident who lived in Oakwood at the time that faced this scrutiny. Although the code enforcement programs did not force people out of the neighborhood in large numbers, it had an emotional impact that vibrated throughout the community and further added fuel to the historic fire of distrust against the city.

Economic interventions through the actions of apartment management companies, developers, and real estate agents further contributed to a feeling among African American residents of being unwanted in their own neighborhood, an identity-shattering sentiment for those who had struggled for many years to uphold their family's place in Oakwood. As Sheila Stephens, the daughter of deceased African American activist Pearl White, told the *Los Angeles Times*, "It's very frustrating realizing that an area where I have roots will be taken away and we'll be pushed into other living conditions like rats. . . . It seems like a conspiratorial effort on the part of rich whites, developers, and police."[34]

During my field research, I encountered more than a dozen people who contended that landlords forced them, family members, or friends out of their apartments or tried to evict them through a variety of means. As long-term black families felt attacked by landlords and real estate agents, the black community once again organized around these issues. During the 1970s, the HUD "Holiday Venice" buildings transferred ownership between the nonprofit organization that ran it, Project Action, and a private owner who arbitrated a contract with HUD to sustain Holiday Venice as Project-Based Section 8 housing.[35] However, when the owner of the fourteen buildings decided to sell them in the 1990s, the new owners —NAMCO Capital Group, who changed the name of the buildings from the community-named "Holiday Venice" to the new name, "Breezes Del Mar"—decided in 2001 that they wanted to relinquish the Section 8 contracts by prepaying the HUD mortgage that included the project-based subsidies. If they succeeded, they could then evict 1,200 low-income tenants living in 248 affordable apartment units,[36] raise the rents to market rate, or even demolish the buildings and petition for new zoning, which would allow for condo-conversions or another form of housing.

The close ties between residents of the housing projects and long-term homeowners motivated the latter to action, regardless of the fact that they had no economic interest in the outcome. Mike Rivera, a community organizer whose agency works with the Holiday Venice tenants in Oakwood, explained: "What has kept them [the buildings] so important to the community, is the people who live in them have very deep roots to people in the community."

The Holiday Venice Tenant Action Committee (which kept its namesake despite the buildings' name change), along with the assistance of long-standing homeowners and community organizers from POWER, attempted to protect the buildings from this infringement by mobilizing more than two hundred people to protest against these changes. The organized struggle was somewhat successful, pressuring HUD to require the new landlord to uphold the contracts until they were due to expire in 2011 and 2015. An uncertain future for these low-income apartment structures haunted many long-term families and housing activists. With the recent demise of the nearby Lincoln Place Apartments, they interpreted their continuing resistance against development and real estate conversion as the last straw in maintaining any reminder of a history of housing affordability in Venice.

Every black homeowner I spoke with expressed a concern about constant harassment by real estate agents who pressured them to sell their properties. While unsolicited postcards and roving real estate agents had become commonplace throughout the neighborhood, longtime residents were unaware of this real estate trend and perceived it as a threat made specifically to their community longevity. Regina Stanton, explained:

> God, I get calls, five or six calls every day. I get mail. They say, "Why don't you want to sell? I could offer you this, that, or the other. You can be a millionaire." And I say, "Who the hell wants to be a millionaire?" You know, I say, "I'm not moving. That's up to my kids if they want to sell." I said, "Here I am, almost ninety. I'm not thinking about moving." I said, "Money don't excite me."

Real estate agents recognized the growing potential for profit. Aging residents worried that these agents targeted them and brokered deals with developers by using manipulative strategies to access properties for below-market rates. Lila Riley, a life-long resident expressed:

> A lot of people don't know what their houses are worth. You and me, we might think it's commonsense, but if you own a house, or it's been in your family for fifty, sixty years, and you haven't dealt with the market over that time, well you might not know.

Although activists commonly overlooked it, residents did acknowledge that part of the demographic transition also occurred through a natural economic process. Some people moved when crime started to increase, seniors decided to sell properties and retire to where they had family, or move to less expensive cities to improve their standards of living. In addition, when seniors passed away, they left their homes to their children and grandchildren, who then commonly sold the properties. Senior-citizen homeowners recognized the rights of fellow community members to sell inherited homes, but they expressed concern about some of the younger generation's search for quick money, which might lead them to sell homes below the market rate without thinking about the potential property value if they were to hold on to it.

Legal and economic interventions facilitated the emergence of new conditions that wealthier people viewed as more conducive to their lifestyles. With an improved sense of public safety, many new residents who opted to make Oakwood their home tore down houses, remodeled older ones, or moved into one of the many condo-conversions, in many cases next door to those with far lesser economic resources. The rise of a wealthier group of residents created a complex social environment that led some people to actively struggle over the changing boundaries between public and private space and the meaning of "community."

With new people moving into a neighborhood that has locals with strong historical ties, both new and old residents established reciprocal scripts about "unknown others." Residents merged together individual characteristics with collective histories and group identities, generating feelings of fear on one side and feelings of defensiveness on the other. These labeling actions gave rise to a tripartite political process between new arrivals with more private lifestyles, old residents who developed a feeling of lost community, and police and city officials operating under a new model of monitoring public spaces.

The LAPD temporarily positioned a mobile police station outside of the Oakwood Recreation Center in April 2004 to intimidate drug dealers and alleged gang members (see fig. 3.3), and its presence instantly created

Figure 3.3. Photographs of LAPD mobile substation at Oakwood Park. Photos courtesy of Andrew Deener.

a stir on the street with "new versus old" and "white versus black" dynamics.[37] In this situation, "white" translated as wealthy homeowners who supported increased police control, whereas "black" translated as resisting criminals opposed to police surveillance. I observed changes to the surveillance of public spaces viewed as both a welcome addition and a threat. My field notes describe the scene one day:

Across the street from the park, a mobile police substation is parked. About twenty or so African Americans, mostly young adults (twenties and thirties) and young teenagers (fourteen to fifteen), are outside the recreation center hanging out. Four police officers in uniform stand together near the police substation, two with dark black shades, waiting with their arms crossed. I follow a white couple walking hand in hand. The officers greet them and then they greet me as well. I stop to talk. I suggest to them that some people think their presence is intimidating. One officer responds by saying that they are not aiming to be intimidating at all. In fact, he feels as though he is protecting people, telling me that the homeowners in the neighborhood are unhappy with drug dealing, graffiti, and gang violence on the streets and they want to get rid of it. By his comments, it becomes clear he means new homeowners. "They pay a lot of money to own homes here," he says, "and they have a right to feel safe in their own neighborhood." As we are standing on the street, a white woman walks by with two dogs. As she approaches them she stops briefly and says, "I'm so happy that you guys are here."

Then the officer walks with me a few hundred feet up the sidewalk and points out a broken car antenna on the street that is snapped into a small handheld size. He picks it up and holds it out to me. "Handmade crack pipe. See the burnt tip?" A black woman and her son walk by us, and the child, no older than seven or eight, waves to the officers. The woman, who appears to be his mother or caretaker, scolds him: "Don't wave to those pigs. They're a bunch of muthafuckers." She walks off cursing and yelling at the officers. The one officer asks me, "Did you see that, did you see her give us the finger and curse at us?" I raise my eyebrows, uncertain how to act in this situation, not wanting to appear too close to the LAPD. Meanwhile, another kid yells out to the officers, "Suck my cock!" The officer yells back, "Do you even have one?" The kid pulls down his pants to show him. The officer turns to me and asks, "What are we supposed to do about that?"

The intermingling between those of different moral dynamics created the appearance to outsiders—who came to perceive differences through a stereotype that associates black with crime—of a cohesive community of criminals. As a result, some new white and Latino residents avoided walking around the park at certain hours, especially if it was crowded with African Americans. The targeting of black residents around this categorical cohesion often produced fear on one side and a defensive attitude about unjust harassment on the other.

According to local blacks, the answers to the public safety concerns are multifaceted. Lakesha Holt, a lifelong resident, discussed with me the mistakes the LAPD made by parking their mobile unit across from the park:

> The police just don't understand what this neighborhood is about. I mean, there are problems, I know that. I'm working on it. A lot of us are working on it. But this is not the right way to go about solving it. Standing around, on the opposite side of the street [from where African American youth are openly congregating by the dozens], with your arms crossed is no way of getting at the problem. If you want to work out the problem, you want to start to solve it, then cross the street and talk to these guys.

For Lakesha, organizing to create opportunities for youth followed a long tradition of Oakwood community activism, with residents engaging either the youth or the criminal element in their daily lives in order to bring an end to crime and gang association. As family members and close friends, they worked with a similar mind-set about familial/community conditions as former activists did in the 1970s, 1980s, and 1990s. By having close access to individuals, they continued to reinforce alternative life courses and possibilities for youth.

A number of activists took on this role as "community protector." Some residents, in addition to more spontaneous and everyday efforts, started nonprofit agencies, which directly served the people in the community. These proactive efforts pointed to the common interest between most neighborhood residents, the interest of achieving a safer place to live. Although the political contest between "unknown others" continued, residents of different racial, ethnic, and economic backgrounds, living within a one-square-mile area, often cooperated in their everyday lives. With changing property relations, the Oakwood culture increasingly became more private and segmented, and when residents did engage public spaces, they erected boundaries that facilitated a relatively peaceful, if not dramatically transformed, coexistence.

Coexistence vs. Community

For Oakwood residents, their complex social, cultural, and political lives created significant changes over time to intragroup and intergroup dynamics. One significant outcome of the transformation of the local culture is that many of the wealthier new residents had upbringings that prized private life. They had come to prioritize their personal lives, leisure activities, and complex careers in ways that kept them separate from the local ecology. Coupled with their perceptions of gang organization, drug dealing, and street crimes in public space, they created markedly different ways of living in Oakwood. Many manufactured tall fences that far exceeded the legal height limitation, as defined by the city, to surround their properties and block out any field of vision from public space into private space.[38]

Cynthia Dell, an eighty-year-old black woman who had lived in Oakwood since 1936, expressed a popular sentiment among long-term residents about the impact of gentrification on the social ties between neighbors:

> When the whites start moving back, they don't like some things. We're two different kinds of people. There are things we like to have, like yard parties and everything. And wherever there's a white family, they build that big high fence, and you just don't know who is in there. They don't socialize with the neighborhood. And the blacks and the Mexicans they all got together and socialized, but these whites, they don't. They don't want to socialize with nobody, not even the other white people in the neighborhood. They're very private.

New white residents, with a distinct cultural apparatus, often resented the public condemnation by black activists who challenged their rights to privacy and security. Jackson Norris, a two-year homeowner in his early forties, explained:

> I mean, it's like some people they think because they're here longer that their way of living is better, like better for the neighborhood. And that's

fine, I mean, people have a right to complain that I'm killing the neighborhood . . . that my fence has ruined their lives, or the size of my house goes against the idea of Venice [laughs].

Coexistence and community-building are two distinct social processes. Coexistence means that people are willing to tolerate differences between individuals who live nearby. They become accustomed to seeing people of different racial, ethnic, and economic backgrounds, and they learn to protect their own lifestyles by maintaining a culture of segmentation. As Darcy, a white resident for five years, expressed, "I've gotten used to it all. Even the drug dealers say hi to me now. They know who I am and I know who they are, and it's this mutual, 'Hey, how's it going' thing that we do." Although they lived close to one another and recognized each other as neighbors, they did not become intertwined in each other's personal lives.

Community, on the other hand, from the perspective of long-standing residents, implied an effort to establish common interest, mutual trust, and/or reciprocity between different people. It requires that people break down categorical distinctions by interacting, communicating, and engaging with one another as they share the local social space. As lifelong resident Lila Riley emphasized to me as we walked through the neighborhood, "These people just need to come out from behind their fences and talk to people. Get to know your neighbor. Hang out. This used to be a fun place to live."

For long-term residents used to a feeling of close-knit social bonds with neighbors, the idea of coexistence was a depressing fact of life in the new insular Oakwood culture, where those who moved in more recently appeared quite content with the idea of peaceful coexistence. The newcomers' own lifestyle preferences continued to alter the everyday patterns of Oakwood's social ecology, as they sought peaceful coexistence in a neighborhood within which residents historically sought to build community.

NOTES

1. Los Angeles is well known as a "fragmented city" due to the piecemeal development of neighborhoods during the late nineteenth and early twentieth centuries (Fogelson, *The Fragmented Metropolis*). It is also widely recognized by urban scholars as having a history of racial and socioeconomic segregation (e.g.,

Massey, and Denton, *American Apartheid*; Soja, *Postmetropolis*, 264–97; Beveridge, and Weber, "Race and Class in the Developing New York"; Halle, Gedeon, and Beveridge, "Residential Separation and Segregation").

2. Neighborhoods long thought to be "black neighborhoods" largely due to historical demographic composition and popular culture media expressions—the most famous of which is Watts in South Los Angeles—increasingly became reshaped by low-income Latino immigrants, who even made up a clear majority of South Los Angeles overall by the early 2000s. Massey and Denton (*American Apartheid*, 63) note that although Los Angeles seems to have experienced a decline in residential segregation by race between 1970 and 1980, stability of income separation remained.

3. Cunningham, "Venice, California"; Umemoto, *The Truce*.

4. Cunningham, "Venice, California," 173–74.

5. African Americans readily migrated from the South to urban centers during this time period as southern farms disappeared and black men and women sought out new lives (see Drake and Cayton, *Black Metropolis*; Stack, *All Our Kin*, 1). See chaps. 1 and 2 for the impact of this migration on Black Los Angeles.

6. Umemoto, *Truce*.

7. See chap. 2 for a discussion of the Santa Monica Freeway's impact on Black Los Angeles.

8. Names have been changed to protect the identity of interviewees.

9. It is important to call attention to the highly gendered experience in Oakwood, per this historical memory. There is a vast literature on the role that women play in African American communities. See Chapman, "I Am My Mother's Daughter"; P. Collins, "The Meaning of Black Motherhood" and *Black Feminist Thought*; A. Davis, "The Black Woman's Role"; Frazier, *The Negro Family in the United States*; Hooks, *Ain't I a Woman*; Stack, *All Our Kin*. Since the 1960s and 1970s, a number of distressing community situations led to the exaggeration of a matrifocal phenomenon that spread throughout black neighborhoods in the United States. Such factors contributing to this change were the lack of stable employment, increase in poverty conditions, increase in crime, drug use and distribution, and disproportionate prison sentences for black men. Women often took over as the center of the community as homeowners, activists, breadwinners, educators, and as agents of cultural and ritual reproduction.

10. Examples of streets in the area that were traditionally majority black.

11. Lakesha mentioned that you cannot see people in the neighborhood due to the high fences that barricade many of the properties.

12. This finding is consistent with Stack's study of "The Flats" (*All Our Kin*), a housing project in a midwestern city where black families band together because of the urgency of their needs and thus create a culture of extended households.

13. According to oral histories with longtime residents, when the housing on certain streets was not entirely made up of African Americans, their neighbors

were almost certainly Latinos. Combined, Latinos and African Americans made up more than 75 percent of the Oakwood population over a period of decades (according to census figures, which may undercount certain populations, especially undocumented immigrants, potentially making the actual numbers even higher), a surprising statistic given the proximity to the Pacific Ocean.

14. Wilson (*The Truly Disadvantaged; When Work Disappears*) argues that a shift in the structure of the national economy produced terrible consequences for African American urban communities across the country. Meaningful work opportunities rapidly disappeared in the second half of the twentieth century, underlining a profound explanatory twist from racism, which always existed, to a combination of historic patterns of racism and more current patterns of economic restructuring, the latter now becoming more significant.

15. Cunningham, "Venice, California."

16. This finding in Oakwood's black community is consistent with Pattillo-McCoy's (*Black Picket Fences*, 68) study of the black middle class in a Chicago community, an ethnographic response to Wilson's (*The Truly Disadvantaged*) economic isolation approach and O. Lewis's (*La Vida*) subculture of poverty explanation. Pattillo-McCoy argues that spatial context in reference to racial segregation can blur economic boundaries.

17. See chap. 5 for a history of street gangs in Black Los Angeles.

18. Although Andre described such changes as generational, some families in Oakwood still had the opportunity to improve their lives through the real estate wealth cultivated by their relatives. For example, one man, a one-time gang member, could give his daughter the opportunity to go to an expensive private college that others without these economic resources could not have possibly attained.

19. Katz ("Metropolitan Crime Myths") argues that in Los Angeles, organized public activity is often labeled as "gang-related," despite any clearly articulated definition of the term. My findings here further add to this claim, in that I argue that the meaning of gang has less to do with organized crime, and more to do with the internal naming of a group by individuals who participate.

20. Umemoto, *Truce*, 45.

21. Umemoto also expresses this in her account. Historically, political leaders made an effort to present a front of racial cooperation, despite the fact that the second cohort of Latino immigrants, in many cases, feared having to interact with African Americans in public spaces and warned their children about participating in the predominantly African American youth culture at the Oakwood Park.

22. Ibid, 85–118.

23. Ibid., 102.

24. B. Williams, *Upscaling Downtown*.

25. It should also be noted that the gang war coincided with repercussions from the Savings and Loan Scandal of the 1980s, felt in the real estate market at the national level during the 1990s.

26. Betsy Goldman, "Venice, California Real Estate Sales," http://www.betsy sellsvenice.com/Nav.aspx/Page=%2fPageManager%2fDefault.aspx%2fPageID%3d 182650 (accessed June 27, 2006).

27. The Art Walk, which attracted about 4,000 people annually, was a good source of fundraising, but was no longer the clinic's central resource. By the early 2000s, the clinic had a huge following of wealthy corporate donors that allowed it to sustain and expand its services well beyond its initial aims. For more information, see www.venicefamilyclinic.org.

28. Umemoto, *Truce*, 47.

29. Shawn Doherty, "Not Welcome," *Los Angeles Times*, March 5, 1992.

30. The Los Angeles Neighborhood Prosecutors is a program through the city attorney's office that began in 2001 and places a deputy city attorney in each of the LAPD's nineteen divisions (http://www.lacity.org/atty/Securing_Our_ Neighborhoods/NPP/attynpp.htm).

31. Anderson, *Code of the Street.*

32. The Youth Justice Coalition (YJC) began in 2002 as a youth-led movement that battles injustices and inequities in the Los Angeles County juvenile justice system. For more information, see http://youth4justice.org/blog/.

33. "Oakwood House Declared Public Nuisance; Owners Barred from Site," *Argonaut Newspaper*, January 28, 2006.

34. Shawn Doherty, "Not Welcome," *Los Angeles Times*, Mar 5, 1992, 1.

35. The difference between Project-Based and Tenant-Based Section 8 Housing is as follows: The first implies that the specific apartment in the complex is governed by the regulations of federally-funded Section 8 housing, where the voucher is attached to the building, and if a person moves from that building, they are no longer obliged to receive assistance unless they apply for a new tenant-based voucher; with a tenant-based voucher, commonly known as a "sticky voucher" because it sticks with the tenant, the tenant can leave a building and continue to have assistance from Section 8, as that person tries to secure another landlord that will accept this rental agreement. For more information, see: http://www.hud.gov/offices/pih/programs/hcv/project.cfm.

36. For more information see "POWER Tenants Save Affordable Housing" at http://www.disclosure-us.org. Also see James Allardice, "Venice Tenants Rally on Boardwalk to Protest Landlords' Eviction Plan," *Santa Monica Mirror*, August 29–September 4, 2001. For more information on POWER, see www.power-la.org.

37. I write "white versus black" because the presence of black leadership in local political efforts, despite a reduction in the percentage of the overall population, points to my earlier discussion about the rooted community presence of blacks, which contrasts with Latinos who had not developed that same rooted community identity.

38. Discussions of the "privatopia" and "fortress lifestyle" of protection and privacy in suburban life have become central to urban studies. See, for example,

M. Davis, *City of Quartz*; McKenzie, *Privatopia*; Soja and Scott, "Introduction to Los Angeles"; Blakeley and Snyder, *Fortress America*; Caldeira, *City of Walls*; and Low, *Behind the Gates*. Specifically related to this trend of privatizing wealthy spaces in proximity to lower-income surroundings, see Caldeira, *City of Walls*, 256–96. She describes the construction of enclosed "fortified enclaves" as a new pattern of separation between economic classes living in close proximity to one another in São Paulo.

Part 2

‖‖‖

People

If you want to get across an idea, wrap it up in a person.
—Ralph Bunche

You judge a society by how it treats its most vulnerable citizens.
—Karen Bass

Chapter 4

||||||||||||||||||||||||||||||||||||||||||||||||||||

"Blowing Up" at Project Blowed
Rap Dreams and Young Black Men

Jooyoung Lee

In 2009, Trenseta was a thirty-four-year-old African American male who stood around 6 feet and weighed close to 180 pounds. Despite being lean, he had a deceptively muscular build, which he credited to lifting weights and playing pickup basketball almost daily. A die-hard Los Angeles Lakers fan, he never missed televised games and made sure the game was always playing on the television at Crenshaw Faders, the local barbershop where he worked full time.

Trenseta spent ten years building a reputation for being one of the most respected rappers in South Central Los Angeles.[1] In the past few years, he had recorded songs with Jamie Foxx, The Game, and other major recording artists. Although many underground hip-hop fans knew him as the "King of Crenshaw," things were not always this way. As a teenager, Trenseta was a member of the Harlem Rollin' 30s, a Crip gang whose territory runs from the Crenshaw Corridor (see chap. 2) and into other neighboring communities. Trenseta remembered getting into fights with rival gang members and random strangers during his time in the Rollin' 30s. All that changed after the birth of his first daughter. He recalled:

> And then my baby mama got pregnant. Once she had my baby, you start taking it [life] serious, man. . . . Before, I was running around trying to break into something, trying to look for the next scheme, trying to get some cash. . . . So that's what really changed my mind over . . . having a daughter, you got to show some care in that, you know what I'm saying?

Trenseta also recalled how he came to a point in his life when he started maturing out of the gang and realized that he didn't want to head down that path. After a short stint in the county jail for his role in a nightclub fight, he began to devote his time and energy to "blowing up," a rapper's term for gaining notoriety and landing a record contract.

Despite juggling a full-time job and family duties, he still found time to mentor younger rappers each week at Project Blowed, a hip-hop "open mic" that served as a training ground for up-and-coming rappers. For example, on some nights, Trenseta cheered on younger rappers, urging them to take rapping at Project Blowed seriously; on other nights Trenseta led by example and performed on stage. My field notes reflect his charisma and energy as a performer:

> Trenseta walks to the front of the stage and points over to Big Flossy, his "hype man," who's rocking his body to the beat and says, "This is Big Flossy right here!" Flossy poses and sways to the beat looking up to the sky, "Uuuuuh!" Trenseta uses a couple more lines, then dives into his song, "Ya'll wanna hear me rap?! Ya'll gonna listen close!? Ya'll gonna listen close!?"
>
> Audience members are completely enthralled now; many are fully bobbing their heads and bodies to the beat, while others begin lightly cheering for Trenseta to start rapping.
>
> For the next three-and-a-half minutes, Trenseta holds the audience's attention. People cheer, wave their hands in the air, and do a variety of gestures to show that they are enjoying Trenseta's performance.

Trenseta's story highlights two key points I explore in this chapter. First, his story shows how participation in hip-hop positively shaped the lives of young black men in South Central Los Angeles in the early 2000s. This finding does not fit with contemporary stereotypes about how hip-hop consumption negatively shapes the lives of young men.[2] Indeed, although he was an active member in a street gang, it was his passion for rapping and "blowing up" that provided him with a creative outlet and alternative career outside of the gang life. This is a common story among many of the young black men who hung out and rapped at Project Blowed each week. Trenseta's story also demonstrates the importance of community organizations like Project Blowed in the lives of young black men. In addition to mentoring up-and-coming rappers about the technical aspects of rapping, older members in the scene, like Trenseta, used Project Blowed to socialize younger and less-experienced rappers into a local culture that encouraged creativity over violence.

"Blowing Up" in Leimert Park

Project Blowed is part of a larger history of black arts and cultural production within Leimert Park—a nearly all-black[3] area in South Central Los Angeles that filmmaker John Singleton[4] has called "The Black Greenwich Village." Leimert Park (see chap. 2) was the center of cultural production in Black Los Angeles from the 1960s through Trenseta's day. I started spending time in Leimert Park in the winter of 2004 and continued fieldwork in and around the area into the spring of 2009. Located along Crenshaw Boulevard, one of South Central Los Angeles's largest retail thoroughfares, Leimert Park is home to famous jazz clubs, black bookstores, beauty-supply stores, coffee houses, boutiques selling African art and jewelry, and soul food restaurants, all of which drew crowds to the area. For example, during my time in Leimert Park, jazz clubs like "Sonny's Spot" and "World Stage" provided a forum for jazz fans, which spanned working-class and middle-class black backgrounds. Meanwhile, at the northern end of Leimert Park, "M&Ms Soul Food" restaurant attracted patrons from all over Los Angeles who wanted to try the locally famous chicken, yams, and waffles. Leimert Park was always buzzing with activity. On the weekends, passersby were likely to check out a drum circle in the park or browse a farmer's market, which had vendors selling everything from bootlegged rap CDs to organic cookies. On weekdays, locals window-shopped and struck up conversations with the neighborhood merchants.

KAOS Network was the community center in Leimert Park that housed Project Blowed. Ben Caldwell, an independent filmmaker and community activist, started Kaos Network in 1990 as a community center for local youth in South Central Los Angeles.[5] Kaos Network ran a variety of after-school programs during the week, such as film-editing workshops, youth mentorship programs, and "capoeira"[6] practice, among other activities. Since 1995, Thursday nights at Kaotic Sounds were dedicated to Project Blowed, Los Angeles's longest running hip-hop open mic. Each week, regulars, most of whom are African American men between the ages of eighteen and thirty, traveled from different parts of Los Angeles to rap with each other. Many signed up on "The List," a piece of paper with the names of people who wanted to perform prewritten songs on a stage inside of Project Blowed. Others hung out on the corner outside of Project Blowed, rapping in what were locally known as "ciphers"[7] and "battles."[8] These street-corner rapping sessions often went into the early hours of the morning.

Leimert Park and the surrounding Crenshaw Corridor is a prime location for studying hip-hop. Despite its long history as a hub of hip-hop cultural production in Los Angeles, relatively little is known about the underground hip-hop scene in South Central Los Angeles. Instead, the Crenshaw Corridor is part of the popular imagery of West Coast "gangsta rap" in South Central Los Angeles. Gangsta rap pioneers like South Central Cartel, Kurupt, MC Eiht, and Ice Cube rapped about gang violence, police brutality, drugs, and other social problems along the Crenshaw Corridor, and have shaped how the mass public views South Central and the cultural production that comes from it.[9] At the same time, the Crenshaw Corridor is also the birthplace of a much less visible, but nonetheless important underground hip-hop scene. Groups like Freestyle Fellowship, Jurassic 5, and Hip-hop Clan, emerged as central figures in Los Angeles's "underground"[10] hip-hop scene during the early 1990s at "The Good Life"—an open mic hosted at a small organic food store[11] also located on Crenshaw Boulevard, which predated Project Blowed.

When I began my research, I was not aware of Leimert Park's history, its connections to black community life, and hip-hop culture more generally in South Central Los Angeles. I had come to Leimert Park almost by chance, when a friend mentioned an "open mic" night and suggested I check it out. I arrived on the scene eager to meet people and find out about their lives both in and out of the scene. Although I was able to make a few close contacts in the beginning, I—a second-generation, Korean American male—also experienced unique difficulties establishing a rapport with some of the older regulars who were skeptical of my participation in the scene. Indeed, there were occasions when I would realize that I was not as "in" as I would have liked. In the beginning, some of the regulars called me "Bruce" or "Jackie," in reference to martial arts icons Bruce Lee and Jackie Chan. These playful jokes continued for close to a year. However, once regulars realized that I knew how to "pop," a robotic funk-inspired dance associated with the streets of Los Angeles, many began to warm up to me. And after they saw me dancing with Tick-a-Lott —a forty-two-year-old African American male who sometimes danced while regulars performed on stage—I went from being an often-teased

Figure 4.1. Tick-a-Lott and Jooyoung Lee (chapter author) practicing a "tut-ting" routine. Also known as "Egyptian-style," tutting is a style of popping that involves angular arm bends and hand pointing, much like the figures commonly found in Egyptian hieroglyphics. Photo courtesy of Jooyoung Lee.

fringe member in the scene to an accepted member who was put on the guest list at hip-hop shows across town, invited to weekend get-togeth-ers, and included in other aspects of the rappers' lives outside of Project Blowed (see fig. 4.1).

Community within the Community

In important ways, Project Blowed was a community within the com-munity, where aspiring rappers developed performance skills that helped them further their rap career goals. Like the Groundlings improv theater on Los Angeles's Melrose Avenue, or acting schools throughout the nearby San Fernando Valley, Project Blowed was a training ground for aspiring rappers hoping to break into a competitive underground hip-hop market.

Each week, aspiring rappers came to the open mic room to practice performing their "writtens," insider-speak for prewritten songs. This was an important part of the rapper's career because many hoped to perform at different locales and in front of different people.

The host rapper played a big part in reframing the meanings associated with getting booed off stage. Many described how it was "part of the learning curve" at Project Blowed, much like falling down while learning to skateboard. Although many regulars in the audience were highly critical of poor performances, some used a less confrontational way of communicating their dissatisfaction with the performer. For example, audience members might pull the performer who just got booed off stage aside, offering side comments on things they noticed that the performer could improve upon. These interactions highlight one aspect of the local community life that emerged from interactions at Project Blowed. There was a shared feeling that "we're all in this together and trying to help each other get better." In short, interactions *inside* of Project Blowed's performance room and conversations *about* performances in that room opened a broader discussion on the types of skills rappers aimed to develop at Project Blowed, but also described part of the informal status system at Project Blowed.

The ciphers and battles on the street corner provided regulars with an opportunity to practice "freestyling"—an improvised style of rapping —and "battling"—a type of verbal duel in hip-hop culture.[12] While the open-mic room was a place where they got to practice "writtens" in front of a highly critical audience, the corner was a place where they got to sharpen their freestyling skills. These interactions also revealed intimate details about their experiences and relationships. In addition, ciphers are a routine activity in which regulars negotiated standards regarding what is and what is not "dope" rapping. So, in addition to defining a space in which artists honed and developed their freestyling abilities, ciphers provided a common interactional space for young black men with very different musical styles, identities, and career goals to get together and participate in a common activity.

Regulars did a lot of interactional work to manage how ciphers and battles unfolded on this corner. Local sociability on the corner was built around a shared understanding and respect for the corner as a place for rapping, not for gang-banging and other kinds of violent activity. Often, more seasoned members of the scene intervened in situations that appeared to be approaching violence. Regulars felt a sense of responsibility and gratitude toward the filmmaker/activist Ben Caldwell, who helped obtain permission from city officials and police to hold the open mic. They saw Caldwell as a role model and helped him to uphold standards of conduct at Project Blowed, which discouraged violence, public intoxication, and other signs of disorder.[13] Because regulars understood that the police and other outsiders viewed Project Blowed negatively, they made sure that no one gave these outsiders more reasons to want to shut Project Blowed down. For example, regulars discouraged public drinking of alcohol on the corner. Although a few regulars sometimes sipped on cans of beers or "40s" while hanging out in front of Project Blowed, others regulated this type of behavior in the area outside the community center. Trenseta, for example, had disciplined younger and less experienced rappers for treating Project Blowed as if it were a nightclub. On different occasions, he openly criticized younger rappers who showed up, half-drunk, sipping on beer cans because this behavior provided police and other outsiders with more reason to shut Project Blowed down.

Institutions like Project Blowed were, unfortunately, not very common in South Central Los Angeles during the research period. In addition to large cuts to after-school program budgets, inner-city Los Angeles had also lost considerable funding for the arts—a problem that Ben Caldwell dedicated his life to resolving. These creative programs were especially important because of the limited creative and positive outlets for youth living in and around the Crenshaw Corridor—an area that had an abundance of liquor stores (e.g., Liquor Bank) but relatively few playgrounds and community centers for youth.

My fieldwork clearly shows that institutions like Project Blowed made a positive difference in the lives of young black men. Many of the men in this study were former members of local gangs. Some of these men, like Trenseta, were once involved with youth who were into fighting, robbing, and other illicit street activities. Project Blowed provided a safe space for these at-risk men to explore their creative side and participate in a community that encouraged artistic expression over gang violence. It also provided them with an avenue for pursuing their hip-hop dreams.

Before rappers started performing at Project Blowed, recording songs, and trying to "make it" in the industry, they progressed through what appear to be rather distinct stages in the rap career.[14] The men in my study described how they started off as *fans* who only consumed hip-hop music. From there, they became *wannabes* who privately wrote and performed their own songs. Finally, they arrived at the point where they were confident enough to "go public" with their music and organize their lives around trying to "blow up" as a *rapper*.

Fans: Consuming the Music

The rappers I studied each vividly remembered how they first got into hip-hop. Regulars at Project Blowed talked about how they started listening to hip-hop music as children, while hanging out with family members and friends. Hip-hop, at this stage of their lives, was a type of "background noise" for their day-to-day activities. They couldn't help but become fans. CP was a twenty-two-year-old African American male, a regular at Project Blowed, who, with his light olive-brown complexion, bore a slight resemblance to mainstream rapper and movie star, Nick Cannon. When we first met, he was an avid car enthusiast and said he wanted to get into auto racing after his rapping days were over. He drove a Honda Civic with customized "Lamborghini doors" that lifted up and swung open like the wings on the Batmobile. In the summer of 2005, CP, his friend Peezy, and I were at his grandparent's house in Baldwin Hills. This affluent black neighborhood sat high on a hill overlooking Leimert Park and the heart of the Crenshaw Corridor (see Introduction). While we hung out, I asked CP about his first memory of hip-hop:

> I can even date back to the first rap song. My first actual tape was "Bone Thugs" (N Harmony), the one where they had "Crossroads" on it. That was like, my introduction to rap, to hip-hop. They were my favorite rappers; I used to love how they rapped fast and all that. That was my first introduction. I was pretty young. And my mom introduced me to it. She gave me the tape—cuz this was before people were buying CDs—and it said, "Bone Thugs" on it, and I popped it in and from then, just started listening to it. I think I was like 8 . . . it just hit me and I was like, "Dayum, these niggas are really spittin' [rapping well]!

Other rappers from Project Blowed remembered listening to hip-hop while riding with family members in the midst of everyday routines. Open Mike was a twenty-eight-year-old native Chicagoan who had moved to South Central in his early teens. He had neatly tied dreadlocks and was known on the corner for his uncanny freestyling abilities. An avid professional wrestling fan, Open Mike spent his free time catching up on wrestling and reading new-age philosophy books. In the spring of 2005, Open Mike and I met at one of the fast food joints in Leimert Park, and after grabbing a quick bite to eat, we headed over to Kaos Network. Open Mike recounted how his older sister introduced him to rap, how he first heard Eazy-E[15] while riding in the car with his mother:

> I just started listenin' to whatever [my sister] was listenin' to, hearing everything from Ice-T, to De La Soul, to Sir Mix-A-Lot . . . whatever she had was my original . . . and my moms used to listen to Eazy-E; I'll never forget that. The first time I ever heard Eazy-E was in my mom's car.

Other rappers remembered what it was like to be fans, but also recall how some of their parents did not like them listening to hip-hop. E.M.S. (short for El Haj Malik Shabazz)—a thirty-year-old African American male who played cornerback on his high school football team and worked as a full-time manager at a local Italian restaurant chain before returning to a local university to get a bachelor's degree—talked about how his mother didn't want him listening to hip-hop inside of the house, forbidding him from listening to gangsta rap altogether out of fear that he would become a gangsta. He understood why his mother didn't want him listening to the music, but explains how he enjoyed the poetics of gangsta rap without adopting the values or lifestyle promoted in the lyrics:

> Well, because of the content of the music (gangsta rap), my moms heard that one time and was like, 'Don't be playin' this in my crib!' So I took it out, ya know? But, ya know, it was DOOOPE, though!

Like E.M.S., many respondents remembered deciding that they didn't want to be in gangs long before listening to gangsta rap. Many described differentiating between consuming the music and acting out what is described in the music.

Although most aspiring rappers began as fans who consumed hip-hop *music*, at least one rapper described a deeper immersion and appreciation for hip-hop *culture* as a fan.[16] Aspect One was a twenty-eight-year-old black male who grew up in the Bronx, the birthplace of hip-hop culture.[17] Some regulars joked that Aspect One looked like a younger and more athletic version of Hollywood actor, Don Cheadle.[18] Aspect One was known among his peers for being a superb rapper, but also had gained a reputation for producing beats in a group called "Missing Page." Aspect

One's earliest memories of hip-hop consisted of a surprising and detailed account of growing up in the "Boogie Down" Bronx with his father, DJ Panama Red, a prominent hip-hop DJ who taught him how to "scratch"[19] at an early age:

> JL: What is your first memory of hip-hop?
> AO: I grew up, just born in it [hip-hop]. I swear, my pops was probably fucking my mom to some hip-hop. [Laughs] And you know, my sperm was just break-dancing all the way to her egg. I was just fertilized in a hip-hop zygote and shit!
>
> My dad, he pretty much grew up in hip-hop. He's from the Bronx, he knew Kool Herc, Grandmaster Flash, Melle Mel.[20] . . . I was into the whole culture as a kid.

Aspect One's account was not typical for a couple of reasons. First, he described growing up in a family and neighborhood (the Bronx) deeply embedded in hip-hop culture. Unlike other respondents, who first learned about hip-hop as a type of *music*, he remembered learning about hip-hop as a *culture* that included different elements: break-dancing, deejaying, graffiti, and rapping. Second, since his father had an established career as a hip-hop deejay, Aspect One was introduced to the godfathers of hip-hop culture, and his exposure to the culture was vastly different from fans who only consumed the music.

Fans remembered listening to music with overtly sexual and violent themes, but many, like Open Mike, apparently didn't internalize these values. They, like E.M.S., described being able to appreciate the poetics of rap music without adopting or acting out the content of the lyrics. These accounts revealed different ways aspiring rappers constructed the meanings of hip-hop fandom. At the same time, there was a common way in which family members—mothers, fathers, and older siblings—introduced the men in my study to hip-hop music. This appears to represent a striking departure from other studies of artistic careers, which show that parents often discouraged their children from getting involved in art.[21]

Wannabes: Flirting with the Dream

Wannabes went beyond hip-hop fans and actually tried their hand at writing songs and rapping. But they did so privately. Although they didn't (yet) have the confidence to perform in front of a live audience or to record and distribute their music publicly (both of which rappers do), wannabes began to flirt with the possibility of becoming a rapper someday.

Many of the men in this study described how they became wannabes after seeing other people rap. Pterradacto, a thirty-year-old African American male, began rapping at "The Good Life" as a teenager. The younger cousin to Rifleman—an underground legend in South Central Los Angeles's rap scene—Pterradacto was well connected with many of the older rappers in the Project Blowed community. He was about 5'10" and, despite being skinny (he also calls himself Skinny Swagga), he assured any doubters that he had "hands" and could hold his own in a fist fight. He was known around town for his ability to "chop," a local rap style in which rappers speed up their delivery to a point where their words are almost unintelligible. While hanging out in the parking lot behind Project Blowed, Pterradacto described an "instrumental moment" that inspired him to start rapping:

> Basically, my cousin—"Rifleman"—had a group, which I'm a part of now. And he had it goin' on since like '86. And even before that they had a group, L.A.P.D.—Los Angeles Poetry Dictators, or some crazy shit like that. I was a kid in LA at the time when gangbanging was very poppin' [popular]. And when I saw my cousins, dressin' hip-hop, you know they be all LL Cool J'd out [dressed like LL Cool J], and it was the coolest thing, and I knew that's what I wanted to do. So that's at least back as far as '86.

There were also other attractions to becoming a wannabe. For example, N/A ("No Alias") a twenty-six-year-old black rapper, also produced hip-hop beats. He was one half of "The Middlemen," with longtime friend E.M.S. Although he sampled from various genres of music, N/A preferred to sample from jazz and soul music, both of which he listened to with his mother while growing up. While hanging out at E.M.S's apartment, N/A explained how he got inspired to rap after seeing Kriss Kross—a popular youth rap group—make it in the music industry. "I decided, 'You know what? These little Kriss Kross kids can do this, so can I!' So that like started me actually trying to come with some rhymes. I wrote my first rap in sixth grade."

These accounts highlight key differences in how young black men become wannabes. In some instances, the men were mentored—whether formally or informally—by family members who were already rapping. Others, however, got inspiration from more indirect sources; like N/A, several men in my study expressed how seeing Kriss Kross, A.B.C., and other youth rappers' careers blossom actually encouraged them to try rapping.

Becoming a wannabe also shaped other aspects of the rapper's life. Because many of the regulars at Project Blowed grew up around gangs, their adolescent years were filled with peers who flirted with and eventually joined local gangs. Instead of falling into the gang world, however, rappers described how they began to devote more time to writing songs, rapping, and other creative activities as wannabes. In other words, the wannabe stage was often a turning point in the lives of at-risk youth who otherwise might have found themselves socialized into gangs. For example, Dibiase, a thirty-year-old African American rapper and producer from Watts, often sampled video game sounds in the beats he produced. He explained how he started making "mixtapes" (i.e., compilation tapes) around the same time that his friends joined the neighborhood street gang—the Grape Street Watts Crips.[22] Instead of joining the gang and getting into trouble, he stayed at his house to make mixtapes, which he then distributed at school and at summer camps. His peers didn't seem to mind that he had taken an interest in making mixtapes, and some encouraged him to pursue his musical interests outside of the gang and didn't pressure him to join the gang.

Dibiase's experience complicates a mainstream discourse that links the consumption of hip-hop music with deviant attitudes and behavior.[23] While these studies argue that *consumption* of hip-hop may lead to negative outcomes in a person's life, they don't explore how *production* of culture may have positive outcomes on the lives of those engaged in the pursuit of hip-hop dreams. Dibiase's story illustrates this point. According to his account, the time and energy Dibiase spent making mixtapes kept him away from local gangs. Like athletics, youth groups, and other extracurricular activities, music can provide an alternative social world for youth who are at risk for gang membership.

Other men remembered how they began to take an active interest in writing and rapping after getting into trouble. In these cases, becoming a wannabe deterred at-risk youth from getting into *more* trouble. For example, Flawliss was a twenty-six-year-old African American male from Northridge, California, who was unabashed about his weight problems (he weighed over 300 pounds and stood around 5'11"). He had a quick wit and a booming, distinctive voice that captured people's attention. Within moments of meeting him, you got the sense that he'd always been a bit of a "class clown" or "life of the party." He described how he wrote his first songs when he was in juvenile hall, detailing how his increased interests in writing rap songs helped him stay away from trouble while serving his time:

> I remember my rhyme, I was like, "My name is Dyno-mite and I strike with rhymes so tight / it'll take the jaws-of-life to dismantle my mic . . . I sting like killa bees with the most deadly disease / I rock the crowd mentally, physically, simultaneously /. . ." Most of the time, most of that shit, I really didn't know what it meant. Like "simultaneously." Shit at that time, I was just hearing words around me that my teachers were using. But yeah, that shit was really good for me to get stuff off my chest and stay outta trouble, cuz niggas in "juvie" was tryin' to come at you on some gangsta shit.

Writing, even when it "wasn't about anything serious," was a cathartic experience for Flawliss during a troubled part of his life. Although he wasn't a straight-A student, Flawliss and other rappers' stories complicate popular assumptions that link the consumption of hip-hop music to lowered academic expectations and achievement.[24] Instead, his story shows one way in which increased interest in hip-hop may encourage young men to work on their vocabulary and verbal dexterity, two skills important to academic achievement that aren't often associated in mainstream discourses with rapping or writing rap lyrics.

While most rappers in this study described how becoming a wannabe shaped their lives in positive ways, one rapper questioned whether hip-hop was the cause of these positive changes. Psychosiz, a twenty-three-year-old African American corner regular who collected comic books on the side and worked as a video game tester, talked at length about his experiences getting into rapping and becoming a member of the local rap group "Customer Service." He wasn't convinced when I described how several other rappers from Project Blowed linked their increased involvement in hip-hop to staying out of trouble. "Music hasn't kept me out of trouble," Psychosiz pointed out, "most people I know who do music, do drugs! I know a lot of people who do music, who gangbang, too, ya know?" Instead, Psychosiz argued that hip-hop *may* help redirect people's energies and time away from gangs, much like other recreational diversions:

I think people put too much emphasis on music being a crutch, or an inspiration, as opposed to their time is just devoted elsewhere. Maybe if, I mean, maybe you didn't join a gang because you were off doing music— So?! You wouldn't have joined that gang if you were off cleanin' dog shit! It's the same principle; it's not music per se. You wouldn't have joined the gang if you were at the movies that day, ya know?

With the exception of Psychosiz, the young men in my study described subtle ways in which becoming a wannabe steered their energies away from gangs and other deviance. For these men, becoming wannabes represented a critical first step into an alternative career outside of gangs that provided them with hope for a successful future.

Rappers: Going Public

All of the participants in my study self-identified as rappers. Although there are numerous definitions of what constitutes a rapper, I adopted a straightforward definition that emerged from my data: rappers are individuals who have gone public with their musical production, and who have professional aspirations for their music. The concept of "going public" includes many things, from performing regularly at weekly open mics like Project Blowed, to recording songs and producing demos that they sell on the streets or over the Internet.

Unlike wannabes who may have tried their hand at rapping and performing privately, rappers put themselves "out there" for public criticism and approval. These initial public performances were turning points in their careers. As opposed to those who rap "on the side" or "behind closed doors," the men in my study used these performances to feel more comfortable about the idea of going public with their musical aspirations. Some started performing at Project Blowed or other local open mics. These were relatively low-pressure settings in which aspiring rappers could work on their live performance. N/A described his first performance at Project Blowed as a rite of passage into becoming a rapper: "I just heard my name and was like, 'Hey, this is the moment of truth now.'"

Others started performing at local talent shows. Like the "open mic," the talent show was a relatively low pressure setting in which rappers remembered getting their first taste of performing. Still, these performances held special meanings for rappers, who remembered them as "turning points" marking their transition from wannabes to rappers. For example, Big Flossy was a twenty-five-year-old African American corner regular who stood about six feet tall and weighed close to 300 pounds. He often wore a large white T-shirt with his nickname, Floss Dogg, written in graffiti letters across the front. He described his first performance at a talent show as a pivotal moment in his career, a significant event that gave him the confidence to continue developing and "going public" as a rapper:

> To tell you the truth, I was a little surprised too, cuz up til then, rapping was just something that I did, it wasn't really nothin' I thought I could make money off of. I was like, "Damn, nigga, I can do it like this!?" That just inspired [me] to keep on and keep on.

Performing in public boosted Big Flossy's confidence as a performer and helped him realize that he could be successful as a rapper. Moreover, winning the talent show also changed Big Flossy's outlook on his music. After winning a small cash purse, he began to dream of making a long-term career out of rapping and took steps toward realizing this dream, such as making recordings.

Rappers also went public when they began to record their music. There was some variation in how they did this. Some rappers recorded in a friend's homemade garage studio, some saved up money and built their own mini-studio, while others, like Black Soultan, traveled great distances to record in professional studios after normal business hours. Black Soultan was a thirty-one-year-old African American male whose family was originally from the Bahamas. During 2006, he met Jeremy, a white sound engineer who worked at a small recording studio in Burbank, California. After some initial negotiations, Jeremy agreed to let Black Soultan record songs after normal hours for a small fee paid under the table. For nearly half a year, Black Soultan drove forty-five minutes to the studio and recorded songs for his "Demonstration" album.

Rappers also went public by distributing and selling their music. Many, for example, had MySpace Internet accounts and other social networking sites from which they sold and distributed songs. E.Crimsin, a twenty-five-year-old, self-described "Blaxican" (black and Latino) rapper, lived just minutes away from Project Blowed and worked full-time as a porter in the international terminal at Los Angeles International Airport. During the fall of 2007, he showed me his Musicplus TV account on his computer. Before it went out of business in 2007, Musicplus was a social networking site for musicians. E.Crimsin, proud of the fan base he'd recruited online, gloated at how many comments female fans had left him on his page that day:

> Shiit, the hoes love me on here, my nigga! I only been on this for a cool minute, imagine what it's gonna be like when I really get this shit crackin'.

Rappers also spent time distributing their music and networking with people "in the industry." Big Flossy, for example, started networking with people outside of his typical peer group as he pursued dreams of a rap career. Although most of his friends and family had lived their entire lives in "the 40s"—a local neighborhood near Leimert Park—he began to attend parties and mixers to recruit fans and find "rich white people" who had money to help fund a rap album he was producing with a cousin. During the spring of 2008, I hung out with Big Flossy and his cousin, Wildchild, outside of a small cell phone store along Vermont Avenue in South Central. I was surprised to see that he and his cousin were dressed in sport coats and collared shirts; this was much different than the typical baggy jeans and white T-shirts that they typically wore. Wildchild explained that they had met up with different artists and representatives from small clothing start-ups in Los Angeles and claimed they were heading to an industry mixer that night at a club in Hollywood. They planned to show up "wearing the business coat" to show people that they meant business.

These examples reveal different ways rappers went public with their music. Many remembered how a successful public performance was a turning point that encouraged them to pursue their dreams of "blowing up." From there, many began to record their songs in a studio, others distributed and sold their music, and some began networking with people in the music industry and related cultural industries. These processes were all distinct aspects of how young black men organized their day-to-day lives around trying to "blow up."

Getting Your "Bars Up"

The rap careers outlined in this study help contextualize the ways young black men used Project Blowed to advance their professional aspirations. Week in and week out, Project Blowed was a place where rappers went to "get their bars up"—that is, establish their reputation. In addition to

Figure 4.2. Trenseta and CP hanging out at "Crenshaw Faders." Photo courtesy of Kyle "Verbs" Guy.

learning how to "rock the mic," regulars also developed local reputations based on how well or poorly they performed on stage. Those who consistently "rocked the stage" or "bombed" developed reputations based on those performances. Indeed, getting asked to "Please, pass the mic" was embarrassing because it signaled to others in the scene that a rapper was not polished as a performer and still needed more training before he had a chance to "blow up." Many regulars concealed and downplayed past experiences in which they were asked to "Please, pass the mic!" Others made it a point to explicitly point out that they'd *never* been asked to "Please, pass the mic!"

Others, like CP (see fig. 4.2), claimed that they only had the mic passed on them once. Although CP admitted to the potentially embarrassing episode, he clarified that it was because people didn't like the beat, *not* because the audience didn't like his rapping:

> Yeah, I only been asked to pass the mic one time when I was at the Blowed, and it wasn't really cuz I was wack or nothing like that—like I didn't get asked to pass the mic because I wasn't comin' hard, or because I was weak. People told me afterwards that they passed the mic because they weren't really feelin' the beat.

Whatever the reason for being asked to "Please, pass the mic," the defensive posture taken by the men in my study reveals how important it was for these young black men to be seen as competent and proficient performers in the eyes of their peers. Lacking the material resources that middle-class and more well-to-do people use to garner respect from others and wider society, regulars came to see rapping as a form of symbolic capital from which they could build a local reputation.[25] Part of what distinguished a more accomplished rapper from a novice was the ability to stay on stage, engage the audience, and if they were really successful— "rock the mic."

By contrast, poor performances illustrated how devastating it could be for rappers who have so much invested—not only emotionally but also in terms of career aspirations—if they failed. In the spring of 2007, Trenseta hosted a performance at Project Blowed. He "opened the stage," allowing anyone from the audience to come up on stage and freestyle over a series of beats provided by the deejay. Although the first couple of rappers (Alpha MC and Lyraflip) had no trouble freestyling over a beat, the next guy, Tragic, had difficulty keeping the flow of his rap going. He paused at different points, reverting to a fairly simplistic and generic hook. Trenseta, watching in disbelief, hopped on stage and made a career recommendation to Tragic:

> C'mon dog, you can't come with that weak shit up here. If you gonna get on stage like all this (he starts marching around, parodying Tragic by puffing his chest out) then you gotta come with some fire and not practice yo hooks on stage!

Meanwhile, the audience (led by Flako in the back) began chanting, "Whatchu gonna do with that beat? Whatchu gonna do with that beat?" over and over. The chants coming from the audience almost drowned out the actual beat and Tragic's rapping. After a few chants, the audience began to settle down. Within a few lines, however, Tragic was stumbling over his words, eventually reverting back to the hook that he was previously using, and Tren interrupted Tragic for the second time, criticizing him and telling him to "Leave hip-hop alone, and go get you a job at International House of Pancakes or some shit, but leave this rappin' to some *real* rappers!"

The success or failure of a performance opens not only a broader discussion of the types of skills rappers tried to develop at Project Blowed but also raises the question of why rappers take rapping so seriously in the first place. For many rappers, rapping was a career that grew out of a lifelong commitment to chasing one's hip-hop dreams. Trenseta's comment that Tragic should leave rap and get a job at International House of Pancakes illustrates the differing values young black men placed on living the life of a struggling rap artist versus working at a minimum-wage job. Although one actually might have made more money at the minimum-wage job, the social status of that kind of work could be stigmatizing. Having rap dreams, on the other hand—while not as stable financially— at least provided young black men with an activity they cared about and for which they got to "call their own shots."

Rap Dreams and Opportunity in Los Angeles

Although Oscar Lewis[26] published his "culture of poverty" thesis nearly fifty years before my field research, themes from his work informed contemporary debates about hip-hop culture. Many scholars, policy-makers, and media personalities in the early 2000s had joined in a moral crusade against hip-hop. These critics claimed that the sometimes violent, sexist, and countercultural aspects of hip-hop lyrics discouraged behaviors closely linked with upward mobility.[27]

As images of black violence, misogyny, destitute urban neighborhoods, and drugs continued to saturate hip-hop media, it became more important to understand how these images shaped the ways society viewed urban black men and, conversely, how urban black men viewed their own life chances in society. For hip-hop critics, the mainstream hip-hop industry constructed negative stereotypes about the innercity and young black men. To them, popular mainstream films like *Boyz N the Hood*, *Colors*, and *Menace II Society* stereotyped young blacks in South Central Los Angeles as gangstas, pimps, and thugs.[28] They perceived the same meaning-making at work in gangsta rap, where artists like South Central Cartel, MC Eiht, and The Game rapped about robbing and killing other young black men in Los Angeles.

But what these accounts often missed is that hip-hop music had a very different meaning "on the ground" and in people's everyday lives. Despite the negative and often sensationalistic images associated with hip-hop lyrics, urban black youth typically consumed the music as part of the daily routines they shared with family members and friends. This consumption traversed class lines and, for most youth, was not a determining factor in the life-altering decisions they made. Moreover, the men in this study described how their increased interests in producing their own rap music actually helped to keep them out of gangs and other trouble as adolescents. This is especially pertinent in urban areas like South Central Los Angeles, which have a long history of neighborhood gangs and associated problems. Although it is difficult to isolate an increased interest in a rap career as *the* cause that kept some young black men away from gangs and other violence, it is equally difficult to pinpoint consuming hip-hop music as *the* cause for why other young men decided to join gangs, commit acts of violence, or lower their academic aspirations. A more grounded perspective on hip-hop moves away from the dominant discourse foregrounding the perils of hip-hop and looks at how real people experience, use, and make sense of hip-hop in the course of their lives.

Indeed, beyond the production of negative images in hip-hop, there are larger sociological questions that the hip-hop debate invokes. Specifically, this study raises questions about stereotypes linked with cultural production in South Central Los Angeles. Despite the controversy surrounding gangsta rap, which describes (and often sensationalizes) a particular social reality in South Central, most of the young black men in this study experienced rap as an alternative to careers in gangs and other street violence. Moreover, this study also raises questions about the ways in which young black men come to understand their prospects of achieving social mobility in a city and nation that seemed to offer few opportunities for them to do so. What does it say about America when young black men see hip-hop as a more attractive long-term career option than college or more traditional (and probably stable) career paths? While this chapter does not directly address this question, it does offer findings suggesting that many young black men in the city do not feel they have a tremendous number of opportunities for upward mobility and advancement in America. Rap dreams keep alive the idea that something better and more meaningful awaits those who may not have faced the most promising career options. Rap dreams, in the end, provide hope where little otherwise exists.

NOTES

1. Although the city council unanimously voted to change the name of the area to "South Los Angeles" in 2003, I use "South Central Los Angeles" because the men in my study and community members refer to it this way. For a more detailed discussion of the meanings associated with "South Central," see Dionne Bennett's discussion in chap. 8.

2. McWhorter (*Winning the Race*) and others have described various ways that listening to hip-hop negatively shapes adolescent views and practices. These studies show a negative correlation between consumption of hip-hop and educational aspirations (Cutler, "Yorkville Crossing"; Orlando Patterson, "A Poverty of the Mind," *New York Times*, March 26, 2006), and a positive correlation between consumption of hip-hop and violence (Miranda and Caels, "Rap Music Genres and Deviant Behaviors") and premarital sex (Wingood et al., "A Prospective Study of Exposure to Rap Music Videos.").

3. Ninety-three percent of the population in the Leimert Park census tract self-identify as "Black" or African American in 2000 (U.S. Census Bureau, "Census Data, Geographic Area: Census Tract 2343, Los Angeles County, California Census 2000, Summary File 1 (Sf 1)," 2000.).

4. Director John Singleton is perhaps best known for his Oscar-nominated 1991 film *Boyz N the Hood*, which starred Los Angeles-based rapper Ice Cube in a story about three black males coming of age in South Central.

5. See Caldwell, "Kaos at Ground Zero."

6. A Brazilian martial art/dance where participants look like they are fighting each other.

7. Ciphers are group rap sessions that usually include anywhere from three to eight people. Typically, participants stand around in a circle and take turns rapping with each other.

8. Battles are typically one-on-one verbal duels in which participants take turns exchanging ritual insults in front of their peers. Scholars in sociolinguistics and related disciplines have studied the long history of black oral traditions and verbal dueling in the inner city (see Abrahams, "Playing the Dozens" and *Deep Down in the Jungle*; Ayoub and Barnett, *Ritualized Verbal Insult*; Kochman, *Black and White Styles in Conflict*; Labov, *Sociolinguistic Patterns*; Mitchell-Kernan, "Language Behavior in a Black Urban Community" and "Signifying and Marking").

9. See chap. 8 for a deeper look at how South Central has been portrayed in popular media.

10. The term "underground" is often used in contrast to "mainstream." Within the hip-hop community, "underground" represented music that is not signed to a major record label. At the same time, "underground" rappers did various things to separate themselves from "mainstream" or "commercial" rappers. The main difference between underground and mainstream is that underground rappers claimed to be "in it" for the music and not the profits. Not surprisingly, underground rappers tended to have more control over their music.

11. This location was represented in the controversial and short-lived situation comedy about life in the area, *South Central*, which aired on Fox in 1994.

12. Jooyoung Lee ("Battlin' on the Corner") outlines the social meanings of street corner rap battling, and illustrates how regulars on this corner sustain the playfulness of battles that sometimes escalate into near conflict.

13. Elijah Anderson (*A Place on the Corner*) and Elliott Liebow (*Tally's Corner*) describe local kinds of sociability on urban street corners that help organize interactions among urban black men.

14. Everett Hughes ("Institutional Office and the Person," "Careers") was one of the earliest sociologists to study "careers" in the sense I mean here. He describes the career as a two-sided process involving change: On one hand, the concept of career involves how individuals acquire new statuses, ranks, and other objective measures of socioeconomic well-being over time; on the other hand, the career is a "moving perspective" on the role of work in a person's life. Howard Becker's (*Outsiders*) work on the careers of jazz musicians, and Erving Goffman's (*Asylums*) research on the moral career of mental patients are other sociological studies on careers that inspire this analysis.

15. Eazy-E was a rapper, producer, and record executive from Compton, California. He was the founder and a member of the pioneering gangsta rap group, N.W.A., and later achieved success as a solo artist. He died of AIDS at the age of thirty-one in 1995.

16. Although different people have different accounts of what constitutes hip-hop culture, many agree that it is a combination of (1) rapping; (2) deejaying; (3) bboying [break-dancing]; and (4) graffiti (Chang, *Can't Stop Won't Stop*).

17. Chang (*Can't Stop Won't Stop*) describes the historical process by which hip-hop emerged within the Bronx.

18. Don Cheadle is a celebrated black actor who played "Mouse Alexander" in the 1995 Hollywood adaptation of Walter Mosley's *Devil in a Blue Dress*—a mystery set in 1940s South Central Los Angeles.

19. "Scratchin'" or "turntablism" is the art of taking "samples" (sounds) and manipulating them over another hip-hop beat.

20. Kool Herc is long regarded as the original deejay in hip-hop culture (Chang, *Can't Stop Won't Stop*). Grandmaster Flash and Melle Mel also are considered by many as pioneering rappers in hip-hop (Chang, *Can't Stop Won't Stop*; Fricke and Ahearn, *Yes Yes Y'all*).

21. For example, Simpson (*Soho: The Artist in the City*) shows that many artists living in Soho—an artist community in New York City—remember how their middle-class parents often discouraged them from participating in the arts as children. Many parents were afraid that their children would turn into "starving artists" who missed opportunities associated with following more financially viable career paths in the professions.

22. For background on the infamous Crips and a historical overview of black Los Angeles street gangs, see chap. 5.

23. For example, see Barongan and Hall, "The Influence of Misogynous Rap Music"; J. Johnson, Jackson, and Gatto, "Violent Attitudes and Deferred Academic Aspirations"; J. Johnson et al., "Differential Gender Effects"; and Miranda and Caels, "Rap Music Genres and Deviant Behaviors."

24. For example, see McWhorter, *Winning the Race*, and Patterson, "A Poverty of the Mind."

25. Anderson, *Streetwise*, *Code of the Street*, describes how inner-city men use violence as a form of capital on the streets. Those who show that they have "nerve" win the respect of their peers for being ready to exact violence on others without hesitation.

26. O. Lewis, *Five Families.*

27. See McWhorter, *Winning the Race*, and Patterson, "A Poverty of the Mind."

28. For a more detailed discussion of these images and South Central, see chap. 8.

Chapter 5

|||||||||||||||||||||||||||||||||||||||||||||||||||||||||

Out of the Void

Street Gangs in Black Los Angeles

Alex Alonso

With the exception of a few studies,[1] what is most striking about the corpus of gang research is the lack of attention paid to how race, segregation, and discrimination worked together to create the communities that have spawned street gangs. These important factors certainly shaped the first clubs that later became street gangs in Black Los Angeles.

Los Angeles's notorious Bloods and Crips gangs can be traced back to the early 1970s, but the first major wave of black street gangs in the city actually developed decades before. As early as the 1930s, there were reports of a disproportionate amount of black juvenile delinquency related to street gang formation in Los Angeles.[2] These groups, however, lacked the durability to sustain themselves into the 1940s. During the 1940s, California received the largest decennial population increase, more than any other state in the nation's history. This population increase prompted a radical change and disorientation in neighborhoods and local institutions in Los Angeles[3] and may have contributed heavily to the subsequent increase in racial tension that prompted the need for gang formation and sustained gang behavior.

In the late 1940s, blacks formed the first durable clubs in the historic Central-Vernon community.[4] This community was part of the Central Avenue black center (see chap. 2), where blacks from the South migrated in large numbers during and following the post–World War II employment boom. By 1945 blacks had attempted to move to nearby Willowbrook with little success, prompting the development of ethnic and racial paranoia among white residents. Chronic overcrowding began to take a toll, and housing congestion became a serious problem, forcing blacks to live in substandard accommodations.[5] Neighborhoods outside of the Central Avenue community were covered by legally enforced, racially restrictive covenants that had been adapted by white homeowners in 1922 (see chaps. 1 and 2). The covenants were designed to maintain social and racial homogeneity of neighborhoods by denying non-whites access to property ownership.[6] In the surrounding communities of Huntington Park, South Gate, and Inglewood, white residents were developing a growing resentment toward the growing black population, particularly as black residents began to challenge the restrictive-covenant laws that prevented them from purchasing and renting property in other communities. These legal housing discrimination laws further exacerbated racial conflict between whites and blacks. It was within this environment that black street clubs developed as a defensive reaction.

During the late 1940s and 1950s, black teens organized to combat much of the white violence that had been plaguing the black community during this period. The Ku Klux Klan resurfaced during the 1940s, twenty years after their presence faded in the late 1920s,[7] and white youth formed street clubs to fight against integration of the community and schools by black residents. The Spook Hunters were a white teenage hate group that publicly expressed their animosity toward blacks by wearing club jackets displaying an animated black face with exaggerated facial features and a noose hanging around its neck. The club's name, "spook," demonstrated their racist attitude by the use of the derogatory term, and "hunters" highlighted their desire to fight integration and promote residential segregation by hunting and hurting blacks. The Spook Hunters were active predominately in the cities of Compton, Downey, Huntington Park, Lynwood and South Gate, trying to prevent the black population in the Central-Vernon community from moving into these white areas. They targeted blacks at public schools in South Los Angeles and attacked those seen outside of the original black settlement area, crudely bounded by Slauson to the south, Alameda Street to the east, and Main Street to the west.[8] As a defensive reaction, blacks formed social clubs that provided protection to black students who felt threatened by the white mob mentality.[9] Raymond "Suge" Wright, one of the founders of the Businessmen[10] described how "you couldn't pass Alameda [Street] because those white boys in South Gate would set you on fire."[11]

In 1941, white students at Fremont High School threatened blacks by effigy-burning and displaying posters with "We want no niggers at this school."[12] During the 1940s, there were also racial confrontations at Manual Arts High School and Adams High School.[13] White clubs in Inglewood, Gardena, and on the Westside engaged in similar acts, but the Spook Hunters were perhaps the most infamous. In East Los Angeles, black youths in Aliso Village, a public housing project, started a club called the Devil Hunters in direct response to the Spook Hunters. They used the term "devil" to describe white oppressors, a phrase commonly used in the early teachings of the Moorish Science Temple Movement, the predecessor of the Nation of Islam.[14] The Devil Hunters and other black residents fought back against white violence with their own forms of violence.

The formation of these clubs continued to expand during the 1950s,[15] in direct reaction to the growing violence by white gangs against black migration into white communities.[16] As the number of clubs increased the balance of power shifted, and black residents were no longer intimidated by white residents. Legal rulings also aided black migration, changing the racial landscape of Los Angeles (see chaps. 1 and 2). This impacted the development and growth of black street clubs.

From *Shelley v. Kraemer* in 1948, which increased housing opportunities and hastened black migration into white areas, to the *Brown v. Board of Education* decision in 1954, to California's Unruh Act in 1959, which outlawed discrimination for housing and employment, to the Rumford Act in 1963, which prohibited discriminatory real estate practices, the Los Angeles area became increasingly more attractive to black migrants. These legal developments accelerated the growth of black clubs, particularly in the new communities farther west, where blacks were now able to settle.

Even at this early stage, however, black-on-black violence between clubs was becoming a serious concern in Los Angeles. The Gladiators, whose turf was Fifty-fourth Street and Vermont Avenue, was the largest black club in the area. Between the late 1950s and 1960, intraracial violence between black clubs started to rise, with a rivalry developing between Eastside and Westside clubs.[17] Because gang disputes at the time were commonly handled with hand-to-hand combat or weapons such as tire irons and knives, murders were extremely rare. Indeed, there were only six gang-related murders reported in 1960, a number still considered high by previous standards.

On the surface, the rivalry between clubs was associated with altercations on the football field, disputes over girlfriends, and disagreements at parties. However, most clashes were actually rooted in socioeconomic differences between the two groups. Eastsiders resented the upwardly mobile

Westsiders, who came from families that were able to break out of the Central Avenue ghetto (see chap. 2). Westside youth wanted to prove their toughness even though they lived in communities comprised of single-family stucco homes and manicured lawns. In an effort to establish themselves as equally tough, Westside clubs regularly engaged in confrontations with Eastside clubs during the early 1960s. By that time, the three separate, previously black communities of Watts, Central Avenue, and West Adams had been amalgamated into one continuous black settlement area adjoining lower-, middle- and upper-class regions of blacks into one. It was during the early part of the 1960s that the conflict among black clubs took on the characteristics of street gang warfare.

Rebels with a Cause

While intraracial fighting among black clubs continued into the early 1960s, in 1965 the largest urban uprisings[18] to hit the United States in modern history struck Los Angeles and forever changed the course of development of those black clubs.

The Watts riots occurred as a result of a traffic stop of a black motorist and escalated into six days of fires and looting that left the city in disarray. On August 11, 1965, Lee Minikus, a white California Highway Patrol Officer (CHP) pulled over twenty-one-year-old Marquette Frye,[19] a black male, along with his older brother, twenty-two-year-old Ronald, two blocks from their home. The officer administered a sobriety test and placed Frye under arrest. As Frye was being taken into custody, his mother, Rena, approached the scene to retrieve the vehicle and confronted the police officers. Residents sitting on their porches observed the commotion, and a crowd slowly assembled as Marquette protested his arrest. The CHP refused to allow Rena to take the car, and she reportedly became agitated and jumped on the back of one of the police officers. In the course of arresting Frye and dealing with his mother, the officers reportedly resorted to an unnecessary level of force, which was witnessed by the crowd and enraged them. The CHP radioed the Los Angeles Police Department (LAPD) for assistance. When LAPD officers arrived, the crowd of discontented blacks numbered more than one thousand.[20]

By the time LAPD officers left the scene at 7:25 p.m., the spectators had transformed into a hostile mob. As the police cars departed, onlookers began to pelt the vehicles with rocks and bottles. They continued to

Figure 5.1. Aerial view of two buildings on fire on Avalon
Boulevard, between 107th and 108th Streets during Watts
Riots, August 15, 1965. Photo courtesy of *Los Angeles Times*
Photographic Archive, Department of Special Collections,
Charles E. Young Research Library, UCLA.

harass other traffic passing through the neighborhood. For a time, the police stayed outside the area and hoped that the situation would cool down;
but by midnight the hostile crowd grew to fifteen hundred. After a brief
lull in activity, a full-scale revolt broke out the following evening, covering a forty-six-square-mile area well beyond Watts. The uprisings lasted
for six days, during which thirty-four people were killed, eight hundred
wounded, and more than three thousand arrested. Damages amounted to
$40 million (see fig. 5.1).

The uprisings and the aftermath had a profound impact on Black Los
Angeles, especially on young black men involved in street gangs. After
Watts, street gang culture began to change. The Watts riots of 1965, considered "the Last Great Rumble," caused members of street clubs to dismiss old rivalries and collectively seek to challenge more important social

problems impacting their quality of life, specifically the practice of police brutality, which had increased under LAPD Chief William Parker.[21]

After Watts, a sense of cohesiveness began to form among the various clubs, with members expressing an increased sense of self-worth and positive identification as pride pervaded the black community.[22] The direct racial confrontations with white residents had nearly disappeared by 1965, but new problems emerged for black residents, and the men from the street clubs created new socially conscious organizations, which sought to politically mobilize for social change to address issues such as black-on-black crime, police brutality, and rising unemployment in the black community. As young black men from the streets grew more politically aware, they began to have a greater concern for the social problems that plagued their streets, helping to transform many into agents for social change during what became known as the Black Power movement.

Police abuses in Los Angeles had become a serious concern in the black community after William Parker's appointment to chief of the LAPD in 1950. Concerned only with maintaining order, Parker was not interested in appeasing the black community.[23] He often resorted to using illegal methods of police investigation, and he was severely criticized by Governor Edmund Brown and Los Angeles district attorney S. Ernest Roll for his entrapment and intimidation methods.[24]

Because of Parker's insensitivity toward minority groups and his attitude toward blacks during the 1950s and early 1960s, his actions alienated the community and contributed to tensions that led up to the Watts uprisings. Parker had a negative view of the civil rights movement, and ignored the fact that LAPD tactics contributed to a decline in race relations in the city.[25] The Seventy-seventh Division of the LAPD served a community that was 85 percent black, yet only five of the two hundred employees of that division were black.[26] Parker assumed no responsibility for the events that led to the outbreak of civil unrest in 1965, and was unapologetic at the McCone Commission hearings, placing blame on the CHP's handling of the arrest for sparking the revolt. Coming to Parker's defense, Los Angeles mayor Sam Yorty stated that he believed the revolt was the work of "subversive forces," which actually planned incidents to spark a riot, and that he was not aware of any case where a police officer was dismissed for brutality.[27] Throughout Parker's sixteen-year tenure, and until his death in 1966, no authority was able to control the actions of Parker and the LAPD.[28] As a result, relations between the LAPD and the black community became increasingly polarized.

In the post-1965 era, young black men began to challenge police practices. Alprentice "Bunchy" Carter, a well-respected member of the Slausons who had served time in prison, became a leader and advocate for the plight of Black Los Angeles. His goal was to transform the mind-set of young blacks into revolutionary soldiers against police brutality.[29] Carter became president of the Los Angeles–based, Southern California chapter of the Black Panther Party (BPP). Under his leadership, many former gang members were recruited, changing the personal and political agendas of these young black men.[30] In 1967 the BPP in Los Angeles helped organize black student unions on several high schools campuses and formed The Black Congress, a meeting place for black residents concerned about community issues on Florence and Broadway. Many street gang members also found themselves active in the popular Los Angeles–based, cultural-nationalist group, the US Organization,[31] headed by Ron (aka "Maluana") Karenga.[32] Working together, many gang members of the 1950s and early 1960s became agents for social change within South Los Angeles.

Throughout the country, and particularly in post-Watts Black Los Angeles, the Black Power movement was gaining strength. Groups that grew from the energies of former black gang members sought to provide political support to the Black Power effort and the idea of building organizations and institutions that were led by and entirely responsible to the black community.[33] The new activism offered black youth a vehicle for positive identification and self-affirmation, which occupied energies that might have been wasted on the streets. During that period, reports of declining black gang activity began to circulate,[34] and according to Sergeant Warren Johnson, "during the mid and late 1960s, juvenile gang activity in black neighborhoods was scarcely visible to the public at large and of minimal concern to South Central residents."[35] After the Watts uprisings, most black gangbanging stopped until the end of 1968.[36]

In the beginning, the BPP, US Organization, and the Student Nonviolent Coordinating Committee (SNCC) appeared united in their quest for self-determination and black unity.[37] As national civil rights leaders began challenging the establishment in the 1960s, all levels of government began paying attention to Black Power groups and their beliefs as they spoke on college campuses, protested police policies, and recruited young blacks into the movement. Mayor Yorty and Chief Parker characterized the Black Power organizations as racial-agitation organizations and communist sympathizers.[38] The emerging black consciousness that had redirected many black gang members was viewed as hostile, and the U.S. government, along with local law enforcement, began to target those groups, believing them to be a national threat.[39] The federal government began to pay close attention to groups they viewed as subversive and insurgent in their activities.[40] Leadership of the Black Power groups became targets of FBI's COINTELPRO,[41] which was used against black "extremist" groups from 1968 to 1971.[42] Because of their opposition to the Vietnam War, their respect for assassinated leader Malcolm X,[43] and their "radical or revolutionary rhetoric,"[44] the BPP and US Organization were prime targets of this program. FBI director J. Edgar Hoover led the charge with the LAPD against the groups—the two most recognized Black Power groups in Los Angeles.

In addition to protesting local issues, the US Organization, the BPP, and the Black Congress were antiwar and vocal in their opposition to the United States' presence in Vietnam. Members of the US Organization also inspired a group of black marines stationed in El Toro, California, to form an affiliate division in Vietnam.[45] Meanwhile, the FBI used counterintelligence measures to fragment and pit different organizations against each other. On August 25, 1967, Hoover wrote an internal memo to all FBI offices stating, "The purpose of this new counterintelligence endeavor is to expose, disrupt, misdirect, discredit or otherwise neutralize the activities of Black Nationalist hate-type organizations and groupings, their leadership, spokesmen, membership, and supporters."[46] The FBI successfully investigated and arrested many activists often on trumped-up charges in an effort to neutralize and incapacitate group efforts toward social change. The FBI and LAPD chief Thomas Reddin, who replaced Parker after he died suddenly of a heart attack in 1966, both worked to neutralize the black organizations. Reddin believed that the BPP represented a major threat to the safety of his officers and their authority on the streets,[47] and used the military model and police tactics that Parker had employed for sixteen years in his enforcement efforts. The FBI was responsible for the arrests of dozens of BPP members, who in most cases had their charges dropped, only to be rearrested on new charges. In 1969 law enforcement conducted approximately 101 arrests against BPP members in Los Angeles, which led to only six convictions, mostly for disorderly conduct and disturbing the peace.[48]

The local police also provoked physical confrontations with those considered radical members, often resulting in gun battles. One of the most severe assaults on the BPP occurred when the FBI, along with the LAPD, organized a four-hour police assault on the BPP office at 4115

Figure 5.2. Black Panthers press conference. January 21, 1969. Photo courtesy of Los Angeles Times Photographic Archive, Department of Special Collections, Charles E. Young Research Library, UCLA.

South Central Avenue on December 8, 1968.[49] Black political figures in Oakland, Chicago, Philadelphia, and other cities were also experiencing similar attacks by law enforcement during the same period. However, the incident that truly marked the beginning of the end of the BPP in Southern California was the murder of Los Angeles Panther leaders Alprentice "Bunchy" Carter (age 26), and John Huggins (age 23) at the University of California, Los Angeles's (UCLA) Campbell Hall on January 17, 1969.[50] Carter and Huggins—both of whom were also UCLA students at the time —were shot while attending a student meeting on campus to determine the direction of UCLA's recently announced Black Studies research center.[51] Figure 5.2 shows a BPP press conference that occurred after the shooting.

The incident at UCLA was the culmination of confrontations over a two-year period between the BPP and the US Organization. The FBI, aware of the fractious relationship between the two groups, actively worked to create more friction. On November 28, 1968, the FBI sent the following directive to its field offices:

[A] serious struggle is taking place between the BPP and the US organization. The struggle has reached such proportions that it is taking on the
aura of gang warfare with attendant threats of murder and reprisal. In
order to fully capitalize upon BPP and US differences . . . recipient offices
are instructed to submit imaginative, hard-hitting counterintelligence
measures aimed at crippling the BPP.[52]

Propaganda literature was distributed to encourage discord and violence between the groups, and ultimately this campaign helped escalate
tensions, resulting in the murder of Carter and Huggins. US members
George "Ali" Stiner, his brother Larry "Watani" Stiner, and Donald Hawkins were arrested and charged for the murders, but many former BPP
members and sympathizers believed that Carter and Huggins's assail-
ants were police infiltrators of the US Organization and that Karenga and
Tommy Jacquette, founder of SLANT (Self-Leadership for All Nationalities) were indirectly working for the police.[53] Countering that, members
of the US Organization claimed that allegations linking them to the FBI
were conjecture and that the root of the conflict was an ideological dis-
agreement that would not have been so pronounced if not for the dis-
ruptive activities of COINTELPRO.[54] Former FBI agent Wes Swearingen,
who was assigned to work the "racial squad" in Los Angeles at the time,
stated that George and Ali Stiner were FBI informers and that the assassinations of Carter and Huggins were partly organized by FBI agent Nick
Galt.[55] Shortly after the killings, the FBI assigned itself a measure of "good
credit" for the incident and recommended a new round of propaganda
cartoons be circulated.[56] Although George and Larry Stiner were convicted of conspiracy to commit murder and second-degree murder, and
sentenced to serve time in San Quentin, it has been speculated that actually US member Claude Hubert committed the murders,[57] a claim supported by J. Daniel Johnson,[58] a student at the time of the incident who
witnessed the shootings.[59]

The year 1969 marked the unofficial end of black cultural nationalist
groups in Los Angeles. After the UCLA murders, Walter Bremond, the
chairman of the Black Congress resigned.[60] US Organization founder
Ron Karenga, also a former UCLA student, was arrested in 1970 in an
unrelated case, convicted of felony assault and false imprisonment, and
sentenced to ten years in jail after an LAPD raid on the US headquarters.[61] Geronimo ji-Jaga Pratt, a BPP member, who despite being a Vietnam veteran with eighteen combat decorations, including the Silver Star,

Bronze Star for Valor, and the Purple Heart, quickly became a target for "neutralization" by the FBI. He was investigated, arrested, and indicted under COINTELPRO tactics,[62] and then was convicted of murder in 1970 and served twenty-seven years in a California prison, until a judge vacated his conviction in 1997.

The BPP and the US Organization was rendered ineffective by 1970, and according to author/journalist Lou Cannon, "the Panthers flashed across the western sky like a meteor; their own mistakes combined with repression meant that they were virtually extinct about five years after their 1966 founding."[63] By the end of the 1960s, after purportedly orchestrating the assassinations of twenty-nine BPP members nationwide, and the jailing of hundreds of others,[64] COINTELPRO proved to be successful in obliterating the Black Power movement in Los Angeles.

Filling the Void: The Crips and Bloods

The early 1970s represented a departure from the positive black identity that had diverted street conflict into positive social behavior in the 1960s. The Watts uprisings of 1965 had prompted Black Los Angeles leadership to form several political organizations that transformed the mind-set of the black community. They had been able to turn the energy and activities of black street gangs into positive political action, promoting black pride in Los Angeles, and consequently, causing a reduction in gang-related street crimes during that period. However, attacks on the black political leadership structure through the FBI's COINTELPRO led to the formation of a power vacuum as Black Power organizations folded. For black teens who saw their role models and leadership decimated and black identity groups rendered ineffective, a large void was created, which was soon filled by the resurgence of street gangs as black youths searched for a new identity and new purpose.

Raymond Washington, age fifteen, started his new street gang in late 1969, shortly after much of the BPP power base was eliminated and as other social and political groups became ineffective in Los Angeles. Washington, who was too young to participate in the Black Power movement during the 1960s, had absorbed much of the rhetoric of community control of neighborhoods.[65] He fashioned his street organization after the BPP militant style, sporting the popular black leather jackets of the time, clearly influenced by the slain BPP leader Bunchy Carter, who had lived on his street.[66] Washington also admired an older gang that was active throughout the late 1960s called the Avenues, led by brothers Craig and Robert Munson. When Washington was fourteen years old, he had joined them while a student at Edison Junior High School. The following year, Washington got into a fight with one of Munson's close friends and he split from the Avenues.

Washington, who was considered a fearless fighter who detested guns, gathered a few friends on the Eastside and started his new group on Seventy-sixth Street near Fremont High School and called them the Baby Avenues or Avenue Cribs[67] to represent a new generation of Munson's group. The name "Avenues" was dropped and eventually "Crib" morphed into the name "Crip,"[68] which became the common name in 1971.[69]

The initial goal of the Crips was to control and protect their neighborhood against other gangs. In 1969, however, the Crips were not the only ones organizing into gang units as many youth across the city in different neighborhoods organized along the same lines. The Black P Stones,[70] Brims, Piru Street Boys, Harlems,[71] LA Brims,[72] and others were all forming at about the same time. Washington branded his form of street-group formation with his philosophy of community protection. He and his group were successful in creating a citywide coalition of other Crips neighborhoods and spreading their influence; they were extremely effective at not allowing other gangs to intimidate members.[73] The Crips spread from the Eastside to Compton, to the Avalon Gardens, Inglewood, and the Westside.[74] As some resisted the movement of Crips into these areas, clashes occurred with other gangs in other neighborhoods that were known as anti-Crips. Unfortunately, as the group grew, the revolutionary ideology and spirit of organizing for change that were present in the group's formative years were quickly replaced by more destructive activities. Immaturity, lack of political leadership, and the power vacuum created in the post-1960s era were reasons why the younger generations of black teens were unable to advance their concept of community protection into a broader agenda for social change.[75]

In the early 1970s, the Hoover Groovers and Harlems turned Crip,[76] but the Crips were met with resistance from the Brims, Black P Stones, Van Ness Boys, and Denver Lanes, which maintained their own identities. In contrast, in 1971 the Piru Street Boys, led by Sylvester "Puddin" Scott and Vincent "Tam" Owens, joined with Washington and the East Side Crips and for a short period were known as the Piru Crips. However, Mac Thomas, one of the leaders of the Compton Crips immediately objected to the Piru alliance because of their ongoing rivalry. Any alliance with the Pirus would pit Crip against Crip; therefore the alliance between the East Side Crips and Pirus was short lived.[77] Later that year, the Pirus reverted back to their independent identity and continued their conflict against Mac Thomas and the Compton Crips.

When the Crips weren't expanding to other neighborhoods, they were robbing others for leather jackets made popular by the BPP style of the 1960s. According to Greg "Batman" Davis, an original Crip, "We wanted to be Black Panthers when we were young, we liked their style."[78] The acquisition of these leather jackets was accomplished through robbery and intimidation of vulnerable youth. Reporter Jerry Cohen described the early Crips as:

> A group of juveniles who committed extortion of merchandise, mugging the elderly, and ripping off weaker youths, particularly for leather jackets that have become a symbol of *Crip* identity.[79]

Ironically, the desire for leather jackets led to perhaps the first Crip murder—an important moment in Black Los Angeles history that exposed growing class tensions within the black community (see chap. 1). On March 21, 1972, shortly after a concert featuring Wilson Pickett and Curtis Mayfield, Robert Ballou Jr., sixteen, was attacked outside of the Hollywood Palladium by twenty youths who beat him to death after he refused to give up his leather jacket.[80] Ballou Jr., who was not a gang member, was the son of an attorney, a Westside resident who attended Los Angeles High School, and who played cornerback for the football team. According to the Los Angeles Police Department, the group that assaulted him fled the scene with five leather jackets and two wallets from Ballou Jr. and his friends. A few days later, nine youths were arrested for murder, including eighteen-year-old Ricardo "Bub" Sims, who was on the Washington High School track team and widely considered to be the city's best athlete. Others arrested were Conrad "Eric" Williams, eighteen, Erskine "Mad Dog" Jones, also eighteen, and James "Cuz" Cunningham, nineteen, all members of the Westside Crips.[81] The sensational media coverage of the murder, plus continued assaults by the Crips, increased their notoriety and popularity, attracting more alienated teens to join their ranks.[82] The Ballou murder put every neighborhood gang on notice—murder was now an option in gang warfare in Los Angeles.

Several non-Crip gangs that formed during this period were no match for the Crips, and they became concerned with escalating Crip attacks. The Pirus, Black P Stones, Athens Park Boys, and other gangs not aligned with the Crips, often clashed with both the Eastside and Westside Crips, the Compton Crips, and Inglewood Crips. On June 5, 1972, only three months after the Ballou murder, Frederick "Lil Country" Garrett, seventeen, from the Brims, was murdered by a Westside Crip. This marked the first Crip murder against another gang member and motivated non-Crip neighborhoods to align in retaliation against the growing Crips. Escalating the already heightened tensions between the Crips and non-Crip gangs, the Crips turned over the casket of Garrett at his wake. The Brims struck back on August 4, 1972, by murdering Thomas Ellis, an original Westside Crip. According to T. Rodgers, the founder of the Black P Stones, "We were out-numbered by the Crips, so we formed an alliance with the Brims, and eventually an alliance with other neighborhoods [that] felt threatened by the Crips."[83] By late 1972, the Pirus held a meeting in their neighborhood to discuss growing Crip pressure and intimidation, which by year's end resulted in a bloody death toll from gang warfare: 29 of the 501 homicides in Los Angeles, an additional 17 murders in unincorporated Los Angeles County, and nine in Compton.[84]

Several gangs that felt victimized by the Crips—including the Bishops, a Watts-based gang on Bandera Street, led by Bobby Lavender; the Bounty Hunters in the Nickerson Gardens Housing projects; and Jan Brewer and the Inglewood Families—joined with the Piru Street Boys to create a new federation of non-Crip neighborhoods.[85] This alliance would transform into the Bloods,[86] a group that would grow to be equally notorious as the Crips. Between 1972 and 1979, the rivalry between the Crips and the Bloods would grow, accounting for a majority of the approximately 450 gang-related murders in South Los Angeles.[87] When a split occurred among the Crips in 1979, gang warfare intensified even further.

On March 11, 1979, a member of the Westside Crips, Stanley Tookie Williams, was arrested for four murders, and then on August 8, 1979, Raymond Washington, the founder of the Crips, was gunned down. The Crips leadership had been dismantled, prompting Rollin' 60 Crips and Eight Tray Gangster Crips to wage full-scale war. Washington had been against Crip infighting, but with him gone, the East Coast Crips and the Hoover Crips severed their alliance, and by 1980 the Crips were in turmoil, warring with the Bloods and among each other. The original Crips and their concept as community protectors had drifted into a self-genocidal cycle over identities. The mentality of Crippin' gripped the community, and according to the Los Angeles historian Mike Davis, their early attempts to replace the fallen BPP dramatically evolved through the 1970s "into a hybrid of teen cult and proto-Mafia. At a time when economic opportunity was drawing away from South Central Los Angeles, the Crips were becoming the power resource of last resort for thousands of abandoned youth."[88]

In 1978 there were 45 black street gangs in Los Angeles. By 1982 conflict between gangs created more fragmenting, causing the number of reported black street gangs to rise as high as 151. From the 1940s and 1950s through to the 1970s, the establishment, growth, and evolution of these gangs can be directly linked to the feelings of self-worth, economic opportunity, and political involvement that engaged black youth. But the more distanced the young black men of Los Angeles became from the political consciousness of the 1960s, the more marginalized and destructive each generation became. The decade of the 1980s intensified the gang scene in Black Los Angeles as the infusion of crack and rock cocaine raised the stakes and turned already violent and murderous gangs into entrepreneurial drug traffickers. The introduction of drugs into the gang culture of Black Los Angeles heightened a bloody conflict of tribal gang warfare that would reach unbridled levels of violence for the remainder of the decade.

The Rock Cocaine Era

By the end of the 1970s, Los Angeles experienced an economic restructuring that caused more than half of the manufacturing jobs in the county to disappear.[89] Due in part to the relocation of businesses out of the area, there was a marked increase in unemployment, crime, and an emergent gang population in Black Los Angeles. The 45 black street gangs existing in 1978 grew to 151 by 1982.[90] Then, in 1982, "crack" or rock cocaine hit the streets of Los Angeles with a vengeance, profoundly transforming gangs and communities.

Initially introduced into Los Angeles as rock cocaine, the drug was a cocaine base, easily manufactured using powder cocaine. The powder, dissolved in a solution of sodium bicarbonate and water, was then boiled, resulting in a solid substance that separated from the boiling mixture and could be broken down into nuggets (hence the term "rock cocaine"), which could be smoked. The drug quickly became popular. It was easy to make, inexpensive to buy, and provided an immediate but short euphoric feeling after smoking it. When the drug first appeared in Los Angeles, street dealers were selling rock pieces for $25 dollars each, but as consumption increased, the price decreased to $10 and $5 per vial.

Although users of the drug were from all racial, ethnic, and socioeconomic backgrounds, the impact that crack cocaine had on South Los Angeles's black community was most recognizable. Los Angeles was the first city to produce kingpins out of gang dealers who peddled this new drug that had arrived in Los Angeles during the height of gang conflict. The combination of neighborhood conflict and drug trafficking in South Los Angeles resulted in a disastrous decade that left thousands dead.

By 1980 gang violence fueled by drugs had increased to the degree that the Los Angeles District Attorney's office created the Hard Core Gang Division to prosecute gang members,[91] and the LAPD established CRASH, Community Resources Against Street Hoodlums,[92] an anti-gang police unit trained to investigate gang-related crime. That year there were a record-high 1,028 murders in the city, a 51.6 percent increase from 1978 and the largest two-year gain in murders in Los Angeles history. During the summer of 1981, city officials characterized the violence in South Los Angeles as a "civil war," and the LAPD responded by raiding thirty separate locations in an effort to investigate fourteen shootings, which had left eight people dead.[93]

With the Olympic Games coming to Los Angeles in the summer of 1984, city officials grew nervous about the mounting gang conflict. Led by Los Angeles Summer Olympics Organizing Committee chairman Peter Ueberroth,[94] a concentrated effort was made to clear the streets and crack down on gang-related incidents. By 1984—just in time for the games— gang-related homicides dropped to 212 countywide, a 35 percent decrease from 1980. But after the games had concluded, in 1985, rock cocaine was again flooding the streets of Los Angeles.

The trafficking of rock cocaine in Los Angeles was in the early stages in 1982, when Nicaraguan-exile Danilo Blandon distributed cocaine through Freeway Ricky Ross.[95] Ross, who excelled in tennis at Dorsey High School and at Los Angeles Trade Tech College, stumbled into cocaine dealing as a way to make extra income in 1981. Because of his contacts and his entrepreneurial spirit, Ross appeared to Blandon as the ideal person to unload large quantities of cocaine. Ross lived in the Hoover Crips[96] neighborhood, and although he was never a gang member, he maintained relationships with gang members across the city. Unknown to Ross and other black cocaine distributors in Los Angeles and later nationwide, they were being used by the government to aid a Nicaraguan-based, right-wing guerilla campaign attempting to overthrow the left-wing Sandinista government that took power in 1979. The CIA backed the campaign and President Ronald Reagan described the guerillas as freedom fighters in the spirit of America's founding fathers.[97]

Although the *San Francisco Examiner* broke the story of several Nicaraguan Contra sympathizers arrested for drug smuggling in 1986, it would be ten more years before the Contra-drug-trafficking connection to Black Los Angeles would be fully exposed. The *Examiner's* story focused on men who claimed that drug profits from sales in the United States were sent to the Contras, marking the first time such allegations were supported by the accused.[98] In 1987 the Senate Committee on Narcotics and Terrorism investigated similar allegations that CIA-backed Nicaraguan Contras had been involved in drug trafficking in the United States and uncovered evidence that Panama's president, Manuel Noriega, had ties to Colombian drug traffickers.[99] However, the Justice Department under President Reagan seemed to stonewall the investigation.[100] Nearly ten years later, in 1996, *San Jose Mercury News* reporter Gary Webb began to investigate links between the Contras, drug smuggling, and the CIA. Other reporters uncovered connections as well,[101] but none was able to determine where the drugs ended up when they arrived in the United States. Webb tied the traffickers from Nicaragua to Los Angeles and directly to local traffickers like Ross in South Los Angeles. When Webb told his finding to his colleague Robert Parry, a reporter from the Associated Press also tracking the story, Parry warned Webb about the potential danger of publishing it. But according to friends, Webb would never listen to warnings or back down from a story.[102]

The fury of the crack cocaine epidemic began to wane by the 1990s, and in 1996 Webb's three-part story in the *San Jose Mercury News* shed new light on how the epidemic started. By this time, Ross had been convicted and sentenced to life in prison for attempting to purchase more than 100 kilograms of cocaine.[103] His former supplier, Nicaraguan exile Danilo Blandon, testified against him. Blandon was arrested too, but the Justice Department protected him, and he served only twenty months.[104] Ross's sentence was reduced from life to twenty years, and he was released on May 4, 2009. Webb's series of articles—which implied that the U.S. government was somehow involved in selling drugs in Black Los Angeles in order to finance Nicaraguan rebels—was initially ignored by the press.

But as black outrage over the allegations in the series grew, the *New York Times*, *Los Angeles Times*, and *Washington Post* eventually responded, all of them vilifying Webb. Perhaps the response was due in part to the editors of those newspapers feeling embarrassed by being upstaged on a big story by a small paper. Regardless, they all dismissed Webb's claims as conspiratorial, attacked erroneous allegations that Webb never made in his series, and belittled his claims. Jesse Katz, of the *Los Angeles Times*, who two years earlier had characterized Ross as "the king of crack,"[105] suddenly downplayed Webb's description of Ross as a cocaine trafficker.[106] Webb eventually left the *Mercury News* after being sent to the suburban beat, a demotion he felt was due to the heated response to the allegations in his series. Distraught over his inability to get another job at a major paper, Webb committed suicide in 2004.

Cracking Down on Crack

By 1984, as drug-related crime increased in Los Angeles, law enforcement began to take note of the young kingpins peddling rock cocaine across the city. By October of that year, two South Los Angeles drug organizations were blamed for twenty-five murders in a struggle over control of the rock cocaine market.[107] In an effort to crack down on the dealers, the LAPD deployed a battering ram in raids on suspected rock houses. Prior to that, only the Kansas City police had used an armored vehicle to breach a wall to apprehend a suspect.[108] But the raids were a controversial tactic that yielded few positive results.[109] Eventually, the LAPD idled the battering ram for nearly a year, using it only four times in 1985 but redeploying it in early 1986 when officers arrested several suspected drug dealers in two South Los Angeles raids. The battering ram would have little effect on cocaine sales in the city, as dealers responded by building fortified houses with steel doors and protected windows.

   Although Ricky Ross was one of the most active crack dealers in Los Angeles, at his height earning $1 million a day, there were several others who emerged in areas across the city.[110] When Ross and other dealers acquired large quantities of cocaine from Central American sources, gang members proved to be the best distribution leg of a vast network that delivered the drug to the end user. The street gangs had complete access to and control of neighborhoods stretching across South Los Angeles into Compton, Gardena, Inglewood, Long Beach, Lynwood, Pasadena,

Pomona, and West Covina. It was not long before gang members were earning significant sums in the crack cocaine business. As the crack cocaine trade flourished, gang conflict between new and splintering sets also grew. Their added mobility, aided by increased income, also allowed gang members from South Los Angeles to be more mobile and travel outside of their neighborhood turf, frequenting locations such as Magic Mountain, Disneyland, and the Santa Monica Pier. This mobility brought differing gangs into contact and increased the possibility for conflict. For the first time, gang violence began to regularly occur outside of South Los Angeles and brought national attention to Los Angeles's drug epidemic.[111]

By 1987 Los Angeles had seen a record high of 387 gang-related homicides, an 18 percent increase from 1986. The following year, 1988, set a new homicide record of 452. Los Angeles gang members were shooting it out over neighborhoods and identities, resulting in murders at the rate of more than one per day. Between 1979 and 1988, there were more than 2,994 gang-related murders in Los Angeles. This was part of the "murderous arc" of gang killings that began its biggest ascent in 1984.[112] The bloody gang disputes also had a profound impact on innocent bystanders, who accounted for about one-third of the gang-related homicide deaths.[113] In January 1988, twenty-seven-year-old Karen Toshima, an innocent bystander enjoying an evening out in Westwood Village, an area adjacent to UCLA, was struck in the head and killed by a stray bullet. In nearly two decades of gang conflict among the Bloods and Crips, this murder marked the first time an affluent white community like Westwood was the setting of a gang-related murder.

Toshima's murder ignited huge media coverage and immeasurably more attention from the LAPD than shooting deaths that occurred in the black community. The night of the shooting alone, members of LAPD's CRASH unit brought in forty people for questioning,[114] thirty officers were assigned to case, and Councilman Zev Yaroslavsky suggested that the city council offer a $25,000 reward for information leading to the killer's arrest.[115] Compared with how the LAPD responded to inner-city murders, where gang rivalry and territorial disputes had been part of the landscape for nearly twenty years, the attention this shooting received was unprecedented, and black residents were outraged by the double standard. Black Councilman Robert Farrell had this to say about the discrepancy in the police response between the two communities: "Unfortunately there is a perception that a life lost in South Los Angeles and East Los Angeles does not measure up to a life lost in [Westwood]."[116]

As gang violence increased, the LAPD implemented new strategies to deter gang activities. Immediately after the Westwood shooting, the LAPD assigned $6 million in emergency funds to anti-gang suppression programs and hired more than 650 police officers in the following months to help implement the new plans.[117] In April 1988, $2.5 million was approved by the city council[118] to assist Los Angeles police chief Daryl F. Gates in instituting citywide gang sweeps dubbed "Operation Hammer," an anti-gang suppression program designed to stop and question gang members loitering on the streets. In the early evening hours, up to 1,000 officers riding four deep in patrol cars would arrest and detain alleged gang members congregating in public places. During the first week of the operation, the LAPD stopped 2,466 individuals on the streets, but more than 1,000 of those stopped did not have gang affiliation.[119] One weekend, the LAPD arrested 1,453 people in gang sweeps, which leaders deemed "successful." The arrests included felons as well as those with minor infractions. Many who were picked up for minor violations were released the same night, and 45 percent of those arrested were non-gang members.[120]

As the operation continued, there were so many gang members to process that the parking lot of the Los Angeles Memorial Coliseum was used as an immediate booking and release center for the detainees.[121] The NAACP received hundreds of harassment complaints from black residents outraged about the police operation. But the sweeps continued throughout 1988, and the gang killings did not decrease. Despite the massive sweep efforts and arrests of thousands of gang members, by the end of 1988 there had been 3,065 gang-related crimes committed, 452 of those gang-related homicides.[122]

During the 1970s, there were approximately 451 gang-related murders in South Los Angeles, but in the 1980s, when gang membership jumped to 75,000, there were more than 3,272 gang-related murders countywide. Gang-related homicides in Los Angeles County reached epidemic proportions for black and Latino males, who together represented 93 percent of all gang-related homicide victims from 1979 to 1994.[123] From 1985 to 1992, gang-related homicides increased in each of the eight consecutive years. However, in 1993, the year following the 1992 Los Angeles uprisings, there was a 10 percent drop in homicides, the first reduction in gang-related homicides in Los Angeles since 1984. Some suggested that the drop in killings was the result of a gang truce organized in part by former gang member Tony Bogart and implemented by the four largest gangs in Watts, the Bounty Hunters, the Grape Streets, Hacienda Village Bloods and PJ

Watts Crips.[124] But a cease-fire was already in effect in Watts before the 1992 uprisings exploded on April 29. After the uprisings, a peace treaty was developed among the largest black gangs in Watts, and the LAPD started to credit the truce for the sharp drop in gang-related homicides.[125] The homicide rate remained relatively stable for the two years following 1993, and in 1996 there was a notable 25 percent drop in gang-related homicides from the previous year. By 1998 gang-related homicides in Los Angeles were at their lowest levels in more than ten years, despite the increasing number of gang members over the same period.

Understanding Gangs in Black Los Angeles

When the news media reported a gang-related crime by the Crips or the Bloods in South Los Angeles, those images likely shaped and manipulated the general public's perception of black street gangs and their members. The offenses these young black men committed were routinely described as "senseless" acts of violence. City officials typically referred to the troubled youth as "hoodlums," "terrorists," or "rotten little cowards,"[126] which did little to advance the understanding of gangs or to address the deepseated structural factors fueling their conflict. Meanwhile, the cycle of violence continued unabated, as the Los Angeles community, government officials, law enforcement, and activists exhibited little earnest desire to collectively join forces to understand and mitigate the conflict that was taking place. Rarely were the circumstances that led to the violence, the gang motivations at the core of the conflict, and the factors that had contributed to the formation of gangs examined in their proper context.

Between the 1970s and the first decade of the 2000s, law enforcement in Los Angeles focused on stigmatizing gang members, creating specialized units to police their activity, enhancing penalties for "gang-related" acts,[127] and imposing restraining orders on suspected members by filing gang injunctions covering over seventy-five square miles of Los Angeles.[128] All of this was part of an effort, according to city officials, to "end a reign of [gang] terror"[129] by using "highly effective tool[s]."[130] But these approaches actually did very little to hamper the growth and notoriety of gang culture in the city. In fact, Los Angeles gang culture was internationally recognized and emulated in Europe, Africa, Canada, Central America, and countries in South America during the early 2000s.

Examining the Black Los Angeles gang phenomenon from a historical perspective provides insights into the forces that contributed to the initial formation of black street gangs, as well as necessary conditions for reducing gang-related violence. At the core of early black gang formation was the desire of marginalized, low-income, young men to protect their neighborhoods and communities from the effects of racial oppression, disenfranchisement, and police brutality.[131] While black street gangs clearly took a nihilistic turn in the void left by the demise of the Black Power movement, these pressing community concerns still existed into the early 2000s.

NOTES

1. Vigil, "Cholos and Gangs," and Spergel, *Youth Gang Problem*.

2. Bond, "The Negro in Los Angeles," 270.

3. Horne, *Fire This Time*, 31.

4. Black youth from the 1940s, self-identified as clubs, rarely used the term "gang." Law enforcement called these clubs "gangs" from the onset, so the terms are used interchangeably in this chapter.

5. K. Collins, *Black Los Angeles*, 26.

6. Bond, "The Negro in Los Angeles"; M. Davis, *City of Quartz*, 161, 273; Dymski and Veitch, *Financing the Future*, 40.

7. Adler, "Watts: From Suburb to Black Ghetto"; K. Collins, *Black Los Angeles*.

8. Main Street bounded the Central Avenue community to the west, but eventually the boundary moved farther west. The move out of the ghetto occurred in a westerly direction, and eventually Broadway became the west boundary, followed by Vermont Avenue in a later period.

9. "Negro Student Attacked on Bus, Told Not Wanted," *California Eagle Newspaper*, September 25, 1947, 1.

10. The Businessmen was one of the first black clubs to form in South Los Angeles in 1947. Originally called the Boss Men, it was based in South Park in the Central-Vernon area of Los Angeles (Alonso, "Territoriality Among African American Street Gangs," 72–76). Grammy Award–winning singer Barry White (1944–2003) grew up among members of the Businessmen during the 1950s.

11. Alonso, "Territoriality Among African American Street Gangs," 75.

12. Bunch, "A Past Not Necessarily Prologue," 118.

13. M. Davis, *City of Quartz*, 293.

14. Asante and Mazama, *Encyclopedia of Black Studies*, 354.

15. New clubs included the Bartenders, Coachmen, Dartanians, Dog Town, Huns, Farmers, Gladiators, Low Riders, Outlaws, Pueblos, Rebel Rousers, Roman Pearls, Ross Snyder Boys, Sir Valients, Vineyard, and Voodoomen.

16. Alonso, "Territoriality Among African American Street Gangs," 76.

17. By 1960, though more than 50 percent of the gangs active in Los Angeles were Latino, black gangs represented a significant proportion of gang incidents that were rapidly increasing in numbers (Los Angeles County Probation Department and Youth Studies Center, *Study of Delinquent Gangs*, 1).

18. In 1863 the Draft Riots of New York City resulted in 104 deaths and was considered the bloodiest revolts in American history.

19. Marquette Frye was born in 1944 in Oklahoma and grew up in Hanna, Wyoming. He moved to Los Angeles in 1956 and got involved briefly with gangs. His arrest in August of 1965 sparked the deadly Watts riots. He died in 1986 from pneumonia at the age of forty-two as "Marquette Price," adopting his mother's maiden name in order to escape his troubled past with alcohol and his ties to the riots.

20. California Governor's Commission on the Los Angeles Riots, "Violence in the City."

21. D. Baker, *Crips: The Story of the L.A. Street Gang*, 28; M. Davis, *City of Quartz*, 297.

22. J. K. Obtala, "The Sons of Watts," *Los Angeles Times*, August 13, 1972, B6–9.

23. Bollens and Geyer, *Yorty: Politics of a Constant Candidate*, 131.

24. Tyler, *Black Radicalism in Southern California*, 124–38.

25. Cannon, *Official Negligence*, 69.

26. U.S. Congress, "Subversive Influences in Riots, Looting, and Burning, pt. 3."

27. Ibid., pt. 1.

28. Tyler, *Black Radicalism in Southern California*, 136.

29. Hilliard and Cole, *This Side of Glory*, 218.

30. Several locally based, grassroots organizations started by former gang members worked for social change during the post-1965 era, including the Community Action Patrol (CAP), Sons of Watts, Self-Leadership for All Nationalities Today, Malcolm X Foundation, Marxist Leninist Maoist, Student Non-Violent Coordinating Committee (SNCC), a national group that opened an office on Central Avenue, Watts Council for Equal Rights, Committee to End Legalized Murder by Cops, Afro-American Cultural Association, and Freedom Now Committee.

31. The US Organization was founded in February 1965.

32. Maluana Karenga was founder of the US Organization in 1965. A lifelong political activist, he is best known for founding Kwanzaa in 1966, a celebration of black heritage and culture held annually from December 26 until January 1. Karenga is an author and college professor who headed the California State University, Long Beach Black Studies Department from the late 1980s until 2002.

33. Bullock, *Watts: The Aftermath*.

34. Klein, *Street Gangs and Street Workers*, 22.

35. J. Cohen, "Theories Vary on the Rise of Black Youth Gangs," *Los Angeles Times*, March 19, 1972, B1–3.

36. Jah and Shah'Keyah, *Uprising: Crips and Bloods Tell the Story*, 121.

37. S. Brown, *Fighting for US*, 78.

38. U.S. Congress, "Subversive Influences in Riots, Looting, and Burning, pt. 3."

39. Federal Bureau of Investigations, partially redacted memo # LA 157-3436, investigative period May 6, 1969–June 21, 1970, June 26, 1970.

40. U.S. Congress, "Subversive Influences in Riots, Looting, and Burning, pt. 3."

41. In the 1950s, the FBI created a covert program to investigate "dissident" and "subversive" political organizations known as Counter Intelligence Program or more commonly referred to by its acronym COINTELPRO. Directives issued by FBI director J. Edgar Hoover used false claims and illegal surveillance to prevent groups from exercising their First Amendment rights (Blackstock, *COINTELPRO: The FBI's Secret War*).

42. U.S. Senate, "Supplementary Detailed Staff Reports on Intelligence Activities."

43. Malcolm X was assassinated on February 21, 1965, at the age of thirty-nine in Harlem, New York City.

44. U.S. Senate, "Supplementary Detailed Staff Reports on Intelligence Activities."

45. S. Brown, *Fighting for US*.

46. U.S. Senate, "Supplementary Detailed Staff Reports on Intelligence Activities."

47. Schiesl, "Behind the Badge," 168.

48. The arrests of BPP members in 1969 was determined by the print media reports of the *Los Angeles Times* and *Los Angeles Sentinel* newspapers that reported on their arrests and outcomes. This analysis identified 101 arrests on charges ranging from disorderly conduct to murder. There were six convictions, three acquittals, and ninety-two arrests that resulted in dismissals or charges dropped.

49. D. Torgerson, "Police Seize Panther Fortress in Gunfights," *Los Angeles Times*, December 9, 1969, A1.

50. William J. Drummond and Kenneth Reich, "Two Black Panthers Slain in UCLA Hall," *Los Angeles Times*, January 18, 1969, A1, 17.

51. This tragic event would pave the way for what eventually became the Ralph J. Bunche Center for African American Studies at UCLA.

52. U.S. Senate, "Supplementary Detailed Staff Reports on Intelligence Activities."

53. M. Davis, *City of Quartz*, 298; Churchill and Vander Wall, *Agents of Repression*, 42; Tyler, *Black Radicalism in Southern California*, 16.

54. Ngozi-Brown, "The US Organization."

55. Swearingen, *FBI Secrets: An Agent Exposé*, 82.

56. Churchill and Vander Wall, *Agents of Repression*, 42.

57. S. Brown, *Fighting for US*, 97.

58. In chap. 16, Ramón and Hunt interview Daniel Johnson, who was also a member of a community-based collaborative committed to providing more access for black students to UCLA in the first decade of the 2000s.

59. Bob Pool, "Witness to 1969 UCLA Shootings Speaks at Rally," *Los Angeles Times*, January 18, 2008, B1–7.

60. Joe Bingham, "Black Congress Chairman Quits," *Los Angeles Sentinel*, January 30, 1969, A1, 10.

61. Jim Cleaver, "L.A.P.D. Raids US Headquarters; Arrest Two," *Los Angeles Sentinel*, January 15, 1970, A1, D2.

62. Federal Bureau of Investigations partially redacted declassified memo # LA 157-3436, investigative period May 6, 1969–June 21, 1970, and June 26, 1970.

63. Cannon, *Official Negligence*, 197.

64. Robinson, *Black Movements in America*, 152.

65. D. Baker, *Crips: The Story of the L.A. Street Gang*, 28.

66. "Raymond Washington the Founder of the Crips," *Allhood Magazine*, vol. 3, no. 5, April 2008.

67. Greg "Batman" Davis, interview, *Lords of the Mafia* (directed by Dan Goldman, USA: Ampersand Media, Public Broadcasting Service [PBS], 2000).

68. Alonso, "Territoriality Among African American Street Gangs," 80.

69. S. Williams, *Blue Rage, Black Redemption*, 83.

70. Jah and Shah'Keyah, *Uprising: Crips and Bloods Tell the Story*, 203.

71. S. Williams, *Blue Rage, Black Redemption*, 108, 112.

72. Alex Alonso, "Blood Pressure Rising," *Source Magazine*, vol. 205, December 2006, 82–87.

73. Michael Krikorian, "Tookie's Mistaken Identity: On the Trail of the Real Founder of the Crips," *LA Weekly*, December 15, 2005, 16.

74. Some of the other original Westside Crips include Donald "Sweet Back" Archie, Melvin Hardy, Anthony Hatchett, Thomas "T-Bone" Ligon, and Curtis "Buddha" Morrow.

75. M. Davis, *City of Quartz*, 300.

76. "History of the Harlems," *Allhood Magazine*, vol. 2, no. 3, July 2007.

77. S. Williams, *Blue Rage, Black Redemption*, 81.

78. Greg "Batman" Davis, interview, *Lords of the Mafia*.

79. J. Cohen, "Theories Vary on the Rise of Black Youth Gangs," *Los Angeles Times*, March 19, 1972, C1–3.

80. "Gang of 20 Beats Youth, 16, to Death after Rock Concert," *Los Angeles Times*, March 22, 1972, 2, D1, 8.

81. David Rosenzweig, "Gang Violence Linked to Desire for Notoriety," *Los Angeles Times*, December 12, 1972, B1–3.

82. Ibid.

83. T. Rodgers, interview by author, November 11, 2006.

84. Rosenzweig, "Gang Violence Linked to Desire for Notoriety."

85. Twilight Bey, interview by author, November 10, 2006.

86. Some of the gangs that were part of this alliance in the 1970s included Athens Park Boys, Bishops, Black P Stones, Bounty Hunters, Brims, Denver Lanes, East Side Pirus, Fruit Town Brims, Fruit Town Pirus, Hoover Family, Inglewood Family, Lueders Park Pirus, Pain, Pueblo Bishops, Swans, and West Side Pirus.

87. The LAPD did not begin keeping complete statistics on gang-related crime until 1985; but throughout the 1970s gang related murders were being reported to the local newspapers by the Seventy-seventh, Southwest, Southeast, and Newton Divisions of the LAPD. Based on examining multiple reports, there were approximately 450 gang-related murders from 1972 to 1979 in South Los Angeles, with twenty-nine gang-related murders occurring in 1972 and eighty in 1979. During that period, gang-related murders accounted for 9 percent of the total murders in Los Angeles, but in 1985, the gang-related definition changed and gang-related murders from 1985 to 1989 accounted for 23.7 percent of all murders.

88. M. Davis, *City of Quartz*, 300.

89. Wolch, *Malign Neglect*, 52.

90. Alonso, "Territoriality Among African American Street Gangs."

91. Collier and Horowitz, "The Bandana Wars," 94.

92. CRASH was instituted in 1977 under LAPD Chief Daryl Gates in an effort to train officers in the suppression of gang activity. In 2000, CRASH units were officially disbanded following the LAPD Rampart Division police scandal where several CRASH officers were arrested and convicted of various criminal activities.

93. Bill Farr and Mark Landsbaum, "Crackdown in South L.A.'s 'Civil War' Area," *Los Angeles Times*, August 7, 1981, A3.

94. Cannon, *Official Negligence*, 360.

95. Schou, *Kill the Messenger*, 84; Webb, *Dark Alliance*, 142.

96. Hoover Crips are one of the oldest Westside Crip gangs in Los Angeles that started in the early 1970s as the Hoover Groovers. In the mid-1990s they dropped the Crip identity and became known as the Hoover Criminals, because of all their rivalries with other Crip neighborhoods.

97. Schou, *Kill the Messenger*, 68.

98. Leo Grande, "Did the Prestige Press Miss the Nicaraguan Drug Story?" 13.

99. Schou, *Kill the Messenger*, 71.

100. Streatfeild, *Cocaine: An Unauthorized Biography*, 335.

101. Brian Barger and Robert Parry, "Reports Link Nicaraguan Rebels to Cocaine Trafficking," *Associated Press*, December 20, 1985.

102. Schou, *Kill the Messenger*, 92.

103. Tony Perry, "Ross Gets Life," *Los Angeles Times*, November 20, 1996, 1, A1.

104. Webb, *Dark Alliance*, 432.

105. Jesse Katz, "Deposed King of Crack Now Free after 5 Years in Prison," *Los Angeles Times*, December 20, 1994, A20.

106. Jesse Katz, "Tracking the Genesis of the Crack Trade," *Los Angeles Times*, October 20, 1996, A1.

107. Andy Furillo, "Cocaine Syndicate War Blamed for 25 Murders," *Los Angeles Times*, October 20, 1984, A2.

108. Patricia Klein, "Rock Houses: Police Ram Opens Door to Debate," *Los Angeles Times*, June 4, 1985, pt. 2, A1.

109. John Nielsen, "Police Using Battering Ram Seize Cocaine, 1 Suspect," *Los Angeles Times*, March 25, 1985, pt. 3, A8.

110. Wayne Caffey, "Crips and Bloods," *The Deputy*, vol. 6, 2005, 42.

111. In chap. 8, Dionne Bennett dissects popular media representations of this epidemic.

112. M. Davis, *City of Quartz*, 270.

113. Hutson et al., "The Epidemic of Gang-Related Homicides," 1035.

114. Ann Wiener, "Woman Fatally Hit by Gang Gunfire in Westwood," *Los Angeles Times*, February 1, 1988, C1.

115. John M. Glionna, "The Murder That Woke up Los Angeles," *Los Angeles Times*, January 30, 1988, A1.

116. Carol McGraw, "Police Arrest Suspect, 19, in Westwood Gang Slaying," *Los Angeles Times*, February 2, 1988, pt. 2, 1.

117. Glionna, "The Murder That Woke up Los Angeles."

118. Harris, *Cholas: Latino Girls and Gangs*.

119. Paul Feldman, "Police Use a Wide Broom," *Los Angeles Times*, May 8, 1988, pt. 2, 1–2.

120. Bob Pool, "Police Call Gang Sweep a Success," *Los Angeles Times*, April 12, 1988, pt. 2, 1.

121. Located in the Exposition Park section of South Los Angeles, just north of Martin Luther King Jr. Boulevard and west of the Harbor Freeway, the Los Angeles Memorial Coliseum was home to the 1932 and 1984 Olympic Games.

122. Kristina Lindgren, "Tougher Drug War, More Jails Urged as Gang Violence Sours," *Los Angeles Times*, January 13, 1990, B3–4.

123. Hutson et al., "The Epidemic of Gang-Related Homicides."

124. Perry, *Original Gang Truce*, 24.

125. Leslie Berger, "Police Give Truce Credit for Drop in Gang Killings," *Los Angeles Times*, June 17, 1992, B1.

126. Mayor Tom Bradley often referred to gang members as terrorists during the late 1980s, and LAPD police chief Daryl Gates during several televised news conferences called gang members punks and cowards. See Feldman, "Police Use a Wide Broom."

127. In Los Angeles, "gang-related" activity, including crime, is defined by law enforcement as an action committed by a gang member regardless of the motivation of the crime. Nearly any crime a gang member commits, once identified as a gang member, will be classified as "gang-related," lending itself to heightened gang statistics. The implication for this overzealous identification process can have a gang member's sentence enhanced by five to ten years, even for a crime that carried no benefit for the gang. In Chicago, the definition follows strict criteria to where the crime has to be motivated by the gang identity to be classified as gang-related. See Decker and Curry, "Gangs, Gang Homicides, and Gang Loyalty"; and Maxson and Klein, "Defining Gang Homicide: An Updated Look at Member and Motive Approaches" for more detail on "gang-related" definitional issues.

128. "San Fer Injunction Approved," *Los Angeles Daily News*, June 25, 2008, A1.

129. District Attorney Gil Garcetti during a press conference announcing a gang injunction against the *18th Street* gang in the Pico-Union area of central Los Angeles southwest of downtown Los Angeles, August 4, 1997.

130. Patrick McGreevy, "Judge Grants an Injunction against L.A. Street Gang," *Los Angeles Times*, February 28, 2007, B3.

131. Although factors such as economic restructuring, deindustrialization, population shifts, and poverty are significant factors that have exacerbated more recent gang phenomena and have contributed to *gang maintenance* and *proliferation,* it is racial oppression that played a significant role in the early gang formation process in New York, Chicago, and Los Angeles.

Chapter 6

||||||||||||||||||||||||||||||||||||||||||||||||||

Imprisoning the Family
Incarceration in Black Los Angeles

M. Belinda Tucker, Neva Pemberton,
Mary Weaver, Gwendelyn Rivera,
and Carrie Petrucci

As co-investigators, we shared an academic interest in examining the impact of incarceration on families, but as we became better acquainted, we discovered that the topic had far more intimate significance for us. Some of us grew up in neighborhoods where incarceration was commonplace and access to the elements that allow for success were limited; we considered ourselves privileged to have obtained university educations. We shared personal experience with the incarceration of close family members, of being arrested, and of coping with the legal system. These were threads that bound us in a deep understanding and common commitment to our research.

In this chapter, we examine the rapid and disturbing escalation in the jailing and imprisonment of African Americans and its impact on families and close ties of inmates in Los Angeles County. We describe the national and local context of these trends and the factors associated with such a dramatic surge. We argue that a unique, complex set of variables made blacks in Los Angeles especially vulnerable to arrest, conviction, and long-term punishments. Using data from interviews with close relatives and partners of persons who have been imprisoned, we discuss perceptions of the criminal justice system as well as the multilayered consequences of incarceration for family and community functioning.

A Defining Moment

Over the last half-century, a central defining characteristic of the United States has been its unrelenting drive to incarcerate its citizens. Since the 1970s, the number of persons held in America's prisons has increased to five times the pre-1970s level,[1] with the United States leading all nations worldwide in this remarkable pursuit.[2] At the start of the twenty-first century, more than two million Americans, nearly 1 in every 100 adults, resided behind bars.[3] There are huge racial disparities in this trend, which reveals a virtual explosion in the jailing and imprisonment of persons of African descent. In 2006 male incarceration rates (defined as the number of inmates per 100,000 in the population) were 4,789 for blacks, 1,862 for Latinos, and 736 for non-Hispanic whites.[4] The rates for black, Latino, and non-Hispanic white females were 358, 152, and 94, respectively. By the middle of 2006 nearly 1 million (905,600) black men and women were serving time in state prisons, federal prisons, or local jails—representing more than 40 percent of the total inmate population in the United States.

By the end of the first decade of the 2000s, the vast majority of incarcerated persons in the United States, approximately 91 percent, were held in state or local rather than federal facilities,[5] and California housed the largest state prison population in the country. In 2008 California operated thirty-three state prisons, forty camps, twelve community correctional facilities, and five prison mother facilities, which held over 172,000 inmates.[6] The population residing in these facilities was 93.3 percent male, and the racial and ethnic makeup was 29 percent black, 39 percent Latino, and 26 percent non-Hispanic white.[7] Yet in 2006, the respective racial and ethnic breakdown for the total state population by race was 6.7 percent black, 43.1 percent Latino, and 35.9 percent non-Hispanic white,[8] demonstrating that the representation of African Americans in the state correctional facilities was far in excess of their population share. Despite the fact that Latino males were the largest incarcerated group in the state, blacks were far more likely than any other racial and ethnic group in California to reside behind bars. Notably, blacks were the only group incarcerated in state facilities at four times the rate that they were represented in the general population. In 2005 California ranked twelfth among the fifty states in the rate of incarcerations of blacks, but ranked only twentieth for whites.[9] Even more disturbing, in 2008 California had the greatest number of inmates under sentence of death, and of those 667 persons on death row, one-third were black.

Figure 6.1. Los Angeles County Men's Central Jail, with sheriff's detainee bus in foreground. Photo courtesy of Darnell
Hunt.

The California Three Strikes legislation, which mandated a sentence of
twenty-five years to life for persons with at least two previous convictions
for serious or violent felonies, was particularly hard on African Americans and contributed significantly to these rates. In 2005, 38 percent of all
persons incarcerated under the Three Strikes Statute were black.[10] Despite
studies demonstrating that increased imprisonment does not lead to a reduction in crime or an increase in public safety,[11] California remained determined to maintain its dubious leadership in this regard. Between July
1, 2005, and June 30, 2006, the state increased the number of inmates in
state and federal facilities by more than 20 percent.[12]

Los Angeles County was a central feeder of the California prison industry in the first decade of the twenty-first century, accounting for one-
third of all state inmates, closely approximating its proportion of the general population. However, due largely to increased admissions from the
San Joaquin Valley and the Inland Empire between 1990 and 2002, the
proportion of California state inmates coming from Los Angeles actually
declined from 39 percent to 26 percent.[13] Although figures on the prison
population by race and by county of admission were not available, since

40 percent of the black population in California resides in Los Angeles County,[14] it is likely that a large proportion of black state prisoners were drawn from this area.

Politics, Drugs, and Race

The dramatic increase in incarceration rates, particularly among black males in Los Angeles, was fueled in large part by the so-called "war on drugs" (see chap. 5). Starting in 1980, the incarceration rate of drug offenders increased by an astonishing 1,100 percent over the next two decades, resulting in just under a half million drug-war inmates by 2003.[15] A 2007 study by the Justice Policy Institute examined the differential application of drug laws among the 198 counties across the nation with populations of over one-quarter million people.[16] Despite the fact that whites were actually more likely than blacks to have used cocaine and equally likely to have used heroin,[17] in all but four of the 198 counties, blacks were incarcerated at greater rates than whites.[18] In that study, three counties in California placed in the top five nationally in the incarceration of blacks for drug offenses. Even though Los Angeles County ranked forty-third in the nation among the 198 counties, it was still in the top 25 percent, and blacks were seventeen times more likely than whites to be locked up for drug offenses in Los Angeles.[19]

In some ways, Los Angeles had become the epicenter in a maelstrom that combined drugs, politics, and race, resulting in unprecedented levels of jailing and imprisonment in African American communities. As documented in the Drug Enforcement Agency's own "history book," the early 1980s were characterized by what was widely referred to as the "crack cocaine epidemic"—a period that saw a great increase in the availability of low price, high purity cocaine.[20] Cocaine addiction spiraled to unheard of levels, becoming a drug of choice even among poor and working-class people, as the high-priced powder form of cocaine was used more widely in affluent neighborhoods. The battle for distribution rights and profits in Los Angeles spurred huge increases in black gang activity, drug-related homicides, and drive-by shootings (see chap. 5). Additionally, with new record levels of cocaine use by women, stories of abandoned and drug-addicted babies became staples of a sensationalized media firestorm. In many ways, Los Angeles became an iconic representation of this descent, as the carnage emanating from the drug-fueled warfare between the Crips and the Bloods, two notorious Los Angeles-based street gangs, could be viewed worldwide on CNN. In the early 1990s, this was poignantly demonstrated to one of the project's co-investigators when the young son of a visiting Jamaican scholar, given what he had seen at home on television,[21] expressed the fear of being killed by gang members if he visited Los Angeles.

By the mid-1980s, citizens demanded new efforts to address the untenable conflux of conditions that increasingly targeted African American communities. During this time, from 1985 to 1990, the Drug Enforcement Agency's budget was essentially doubled.[22] Under the Reagan administration, with the Anti-Drug Abuse Act of 1986 and a second version in 1988, Congress established mandatory minimum penalties for selected drug-related offenses. Since crack cocaine was viewed as being far more destructive than powder cocaine, the penalty for selling or possessing crack cocaine was set arbitrarily at 100 times the penalty for powder cocaine. Crack cocaine was seen as the scourge of many black communities, so many African American congressional representatives, including such stalwarts as Ronald Dellums (D-CA) and Cardiss Collins (D-IL), co-sponsored the act.[23] The penalty differences based on substance form unfairly targeted blacks, who were the primary users of the lesser-priced but more severely penalized crack cocaine. The full impact on Black Los Angeles of this focused assault on crack cocaine use and distribution was only later to be revealed. With more than 80 percent of those charged with crack-related violations being black, and the same percentage of powder-cocaine violators being white, in a few short years the proportion of blacks in the prison and jail populations swelled to record levels. Despite widespread recognition of these existing and increasing disparities, and intense lobbying by the Congressional Black Caucus and other interested parties, nearly twenty years passed before federal sentencing guidelines were revised to significantly reduce the penalty differences for crack- versus powder-cocaine violations.[24]

Human Costs

The impact of the extreme racialization of punishment and mass incarceration on African American families and communities, and the larger society more generally, has been well documented.[25] Studies have demonstrated the powerful negative effects of incarceration on personal, family, and community health,[26] the quality and nature of intimate relationships,[27] child well-being,[28] relationships with children,[29] family life,[30] the structure and well-being of neighborhoods and communities,[31] and even the state of our societal moral compass.[32] The scientific evidence is clear that the human costs of mass incarceration have been significant and enduring.

With funding from the UCLA Center for Community Partnerships,[33] we joined forces with the Ralph J. Bunche Center for African American Studies at UCLA and Friends Outside in Los Angeles County[34] to conduct research on the impact of incarceration on family and close ties of inmates in Los Angeles. Although there have been a number of excellent studies on the wider impact of incarceration on families and communities in other regions of the country, there has been a dearth of studies examining the consequences in the state that places more people behind bars than any other, and exhibits one of the highest rates of recidivism in the nation—with over 54 percent returning to prison within two years.[35] This investigation was designed as an initial exploratory study to examine the well-being of Los Angeles County–based families and close ties of incarcerated persons, their adaptive responses, their perceptions of and experiences with the criminal justice system, and other contextual factors that shaped these responses.

Respondents included twenty-five Los Angeles–based residents who had close ties with individuals in prison. The purposive sample was developed through social service agencies that addressed the needs of such populations and through snowball-sampling techniques. Friends Outside in Los Angeles County was a key initial recruitment site through the distribution of flyers and announcements at large events such as an annual holiday party. Participants were also sought through programs that provided transportation to local prisons for visitation, halfway houses, and word of mouth. There was an attempt to ensure diversity on the basis of race/ethnicity and sex of the inmate. However, as the vast majority of incarcerated persons were men, most of the focal inmates in our study are male and most of the key ties who were interviewed are female. The racial and ethnic and gender breakdown of our participants and incarcerated families members is presented in table 6.1. While some participants had been incarcerated only for a short period at the time of the study, two had been imprisoned since the early 1980s. We report only the responses of the nine African American study participants in this chapter.

From 2007 to 2008, in-depth interviews were conducted with one key

TABLE 6.1
Characteristics of Sample

	Participants			Incarcerated Family Members		
	African American	Latino	White	African American	Latino	White
Female	8	9	4	2	1	2
Male	1	2	1	7	10	3
Total	9	11	5	9	11	5

Source: Data from the study "Examining the Needs of Adult Family and Close Ties of Incarcerated Persons in Los Angeles County," University of California, Los Angeles, and Friends Outside in Los Angeles County.

family member or close tie of the incarcerated person, although in one case involving an incarcerated mother, other individuals provided supplemental interviews.[36] Interviews were conducted in a variety of locations, including the homes of the respondents, restaurants, parks, etc.[37] We present views and observations of the family members we spoke with on the following issues: perceptions of the criminal justice system; the deep impact of substance abuse on the criminal justice experiences of families; the role of environmental circumstances and social location, including the changing racial dynamics in Los Angeles; and the mobilization required from families to deal with incarceration, including the experience of a family member's imprisonment in the broader context of loss and trauma.

A "Criminal" Justice System

Relatives and close ties of African American prisoners were highly critical of the criminal justice system. This is not surprising, in part, because this study concerns only those persons convicted of a crime. Seven of the eight interviewees who responded to the question of satisfaction with the criminal justice system were either very dissatisfied (6) or somewhat dissatisfied (1) with the outcome of their family member's case. Most participants also believed that their loved ones did not have adequate legal representation. One young woman's observation of the attorney for her mother, a fifty-five-year-old woman who was imprisoned for five years and left five children to care for at home, was rather typical:

> *Respondent*: He [the lawyer] didn't do his job, like he was supposed to. He didn't even go visit my mom. He didn't want to talk over the phone

really about the case. My mom never seen him until she got to court. That was the only time my mom seen him.

Interviewer: What do you think he could have done to do a better job?

R: He could have went and found out about, like send out an investigation to get all the information that he needed to see that she can have a fair trial. He needed to go visit her, talk with her, get some consultation going, you know hearing two sides of the story. [W]e didn't have much money, that was a big case, so it was like we couldn't afford like the $5,000 to $10,000 lawyers. We had to scrape to get what we had then.

As has been commonly observed, without the means to hire highly skilled attorneys or fund a thorough investigation, justice is illusive. Even in cases where families spent huge sums of money for what they believed would be a high-quality defense, representation was perceived to be faulty. One participant concluded that attorneys were simply "a big rip-off." It is also of note that only one case came before a jury and that only one judge was African American. Our participants tended to view the judges as being either biased against their loved ones or lacking the information required to make an educated decision due to incompetent representation or the absence of investigatory findings. Notably, the one respondent who expressed some satisfaction with the outcome of her family member's court case had the African American judge, who appeared to take a direct hand in the conduct of the case.

Interviewer: Want to tell me why you were somewhat satisfied (with the outcome of your case)?

Respondent: He had a beautiful judge and a lousy attorney.

I: How come the attorney was so bad?

R: Because he never showed up on time. . . . But the judge . . . I'll never forget it, he was very nice, he dismissed the gun, which took two years away, and he didn't give my son the fifteen to life like they [the D.A.] said.

A number of our respondents believed that race was a key factor in their unfair treatment by a legal system that was especially biased against black men. Moreover, they were unanimous in the belief that racial and ethnic minority residents received worse service from the Los Angeles Police Department (LAPD) than did whites. Yet, despite that perception, they did not tend to see the police in their neighborhoods as uniformly or extraordinarily biased or unfair. This may stem in part from the emphasis in Los Angeles on community policing as well as the understanding —since many believed their neighborhoods to be unsafe—that the job of maintaining order was difficult and complex. One male participant who worked with the police as a community advocate and had a nephew serving a nearly twenty-year sentence observed:

> Okay, now I've been an advocate for almost ten years now, but I can't really speak for all police, because I haven't worked with all the police you know . . . but the people I deal with at the police department, I think they're really good people and I think they're really fair and actually some of them are really, really good people, really.

Obviously, these observations merely confirm what has typically been found in many other major urban environments. The residents are at once highly dependent upon, yet based on past experience, greatly distrustful of law enforcement.

The Impact of Drugs

In their accounts, our respondents confirmed the massive and dreadful impact of drug use, addiction, and sales on the lives of African Americans in Los Angeles. For four of the nine respondents, their loved one's incarceration was linked directly to cocaine use or distribution. A number of others were under the influence of drugs or alcohol when committing the crimes that led to their imprisonment. Moreover, those who were convicted of drug-related offenses were sentenced to extraordinarily lengthy terms, sometimes in distant facilities that taxed the ability of kin to maintain contact. Some study participants were negotiating their own substance-abuse challenges, and a number of them noted the peculiar confluence of forces that seemed to launch the epidemic that had marred their communities and stolen the best years of their own and their loved ones' lives. A forty-eight-year-old woman whose brother was serving an extremely long sentence reiterated the widely held belief that the federal government bears responsibility for the crack-cocaine epidemic in Los Angeles:

> *Interviewer*: Do you think he'll be there for all thirty-two years?
> *Respondent*: Honestly, I hope not, but the way the law is and the way that

went, that particular situation, you know he and a lot of other guys were put in this situation due to the CIA coming to the South Central. They came to South Central and they put drugs in our community. Really. I was there. I was on the drugs. And they made them very prevalent in our community.

In another instance, an uncle shared his observations about the forces that snared his nephew and his futile warnings about the severity of the consequences of drug involvement:

I grew up in Compton. It [drugs] was everywhere. So I knew everybody that was doing it, and I knew a lot of people, they were selling it and stuff. I told them you know y'all better be careful with those stuff because they givin' big time to people getting caught doing this stuff, I mean, really, really, really big time.

With the long sentences meted out under the drug statutes revised for the crack-cocaine era, we found individuals still incarcerated from that period and families with constant, never-ending concern for their welfare. A father fearing for his son's safety, expressed his understanding of the complex dance he was compelled to play out. What is most compelling about his account, though, was his desperate attempt to protect his son from the dreadful risks that existed inside the prison by offering paternal guidance and support. As a former felon himself, he said, knowingly:

[I'm fearful] . . . because he can hurt somebody or he can get hurt. No telling, because you know they got a lot of monitors and stuff, but you know, things happen, you know, and I've been telling him whatever you say and whatever you do up in here they're gonna send it back to the courtroom to the judge. I tell him that, so don't get all out of hand, and get to talking, you from here and all that stuff, you from a gang, because you're not even finished court yet, that can reflect back on you, partner. . . . You just got to chill and do your time and serve and stuff, and keep people out of your business. Don't be telling people your business.

A number of participants felt that encounters with law enforcement were largely a function of the trying circumstances in which they found themselves. Risk was ever present, in the form of intimidation by gang members, desperate economic conditions, lack of jobs, living in neighborhoods that generated fear, and the like. Several described the incident leading to incarceration as basically defensive. In recounting the situation that led to her mother's imprisonment, one young woman argued that it was merely a mother's effort to prevent gang members from harming her son. As the mother attempted to intervene in what she viewed as the gang members' intent to jump her son, battery acid was thrown on one of the girls in the crowd, which resulted in the mother being charged with aggravated mayhem, a charge that was later reduced. Though she denied any involvement, she believed that a previous conviction for assault hurt her chances in court.

> *Interviewer*: Why do you think she committed this crime?
> *Respondent*: Um, to protect her kids, basically for the safety of her and her kids based on the situation that went on. You know they had weapons; these are gang bangers that they didn't know. And the situation for where I come from on the streets, if you're a gang banger you're either with red or you're with the blue. So, if you are not with one side or the other, you end up getting hurt or killed.

In this case, we were able to talk with the mother herself, since she was released from prison during our study. Not surprisingly, the mother viewed the situation as inherently unjust:

> Why did I go to jail for doing what any mama would have did? Any mama would have gone over there and take her son out of the fight. I went to jail, and the gang bangers that was guilty is walking around free. . . . They were the ones that hurting my son. . . Now why did I have to suffer for that?

Shifting Racial Dynamics

These kinds of sentiments were what we might have expected to hear from African Americans in other large urban settings. However, one feature of the Los Angeles environment that was distinctive for blacks was the rapid demographic shift that occurred in areas where African Americans had been the majority for more than half a century and its relationship to the strains perceived that lead to incarceration.[38] The community of Watts in the 1960s, for example, had been emblematic of urban blacks in the West.

During the period of this study, however, Watts was predominantly Latino.[39] Our participants mentioned the tensions and resentments between
blacks and Latinos, and the impact on community relations, interpersonal
violence, prospects for incarceration, and even the prison experience itself. A woman, whose eighteen-year-old son had been locked up for a
year, attributed his problems, in part, to the ethnic-based gang conflict in
Compton:

> *Interviewer*: Why do you think black folks and brown folks, Latinos and
>   black folks, are fighting each other like this?
> *Respondent*: For one reason, it has always been like that. It's got something
>   to do with the prison population, between politics.
> *I*: Over what? Over drug distribution?
> *R*: About disrespect, [Latinos] want to run this, you know. It's like a, this is
>   your side. In prison, they really play it tough out there. And you know
>   by the immigration, being so overpopulated over here, that's what
>   makes it like that, too. Because all this back in the days was black dom-
>   inated. When I went to ——, it was all black, one Latino.

What concerned this woman was the sense of being an outsider in
communities where African Americans formerly had a sense of ownership and belonging, despite their problems. Tensions were especially evident in prisons, where turf issues were more salient. For years, California
had an official policy of segregating prisoners on the basis of race, but by
court order that policy ended in July of 2008, although members of rival
gangs were still not to be placed together.[40] Los Angeles County Sheriff
Lee Baca even suggested that what often appeared to be random shootings in local communities actually may have been racially motivated attacks ordered by incarcerated gang members.[41]

Family Costs

The family members and close ties who were imprisoned during this
study expressed varying degrees of engagement with family. Although we
do not have the space in this discussion to provide interview text for each
family type, they seemed to fall into several categories. Some incarcerated
persons were stalwart figures who maintained and supported their families and left gaping holes in the fabric of their social networks when they

left for prison. Others were more marginal figures who, since childhood, had been troubled. A number were addicted to substances and had not yet been driven to change their lives. Still others had been imprisoned so long that their roles in the family were ambiguous. They were so young when they left that they had not fully developed their central functions within a family context. The people left behind were often "doing time on the outside."[42]

One young participant had a reasonably good life before her mother's criminal justice encounter, including college, an apartment, and a job. Her mother's imprisonment meant that she would be responsible for the five children that were in her mother's care.

> *Interviewer*: How has your life changed since the incarceration?
> *Respondent*: Ooh, dramatically! From being a college student with two jobs and single. It was very hard. . . . I had to change my schedule. My classes, they decreased. I had to keep up with the kids' schedule, their schooling, their doctor, everything, it changed a whole lot, especially my sister having ADHD . . . I had to really like stay home and up at her school because she was acting up . . . you know, so it changed a whole lot. Becoming a single parent, I mean a single person with no kids, to being a single parent.
> *I*: Have your household tasks changed?
> *R*: Ooh, everything changed.
> *I*: And financial responsibilities, all that kind of stuff?
> *R*: Everything, it was hard. It was real hard. Working nights, going to school in the day, trying to be around to schedule with the kids, like when they're at home, I'm at school. When they come home, I go to work. When they're at home, I prepare the meals, clean up and everything. I had to go to work once they're in bed. Then I come home and be there in the morning to get them ready to go back to school, and I had to get myself to school. So, it was like I wasn't getting no sleep neither.

In another situation, a mother whose son was imprisoned twenty-five years earlier, described the personal impact of the loss of her son:

> *Interviewer*: How has your life changed since the incarceration?
> *Respondent*: Drastically. That is the one child that I could just count on taking care of things for me, doing what needed to be done, and I don't have to worry about it. He would just do it.

I: What kind of roles or responsibilities did he have?

R: Even though my health was pretty good back then [participant now has serious health problems], he was really overprotective of his sisters, and he helped there, because he made sure they were going to be in class—no classes or ditching of school. That was him. He did grocery shopping for me, paying bills, and when I needed to be somewhere, he always was there to take me, you know, doctor, some place, church, whatever it is I needed to do, he did it. When it comes to cooking, because I taught all my boys how to cook and clean. He cooked four-course meals.

Yet another participant in her forties, described the impact of her older brother's absence on the family when he was incarcerated twelve years earlier:

Well, there is a void. There is like a missing arm in my family. There is a piece of us that is no longer available. When we have family reunions and family functions, there is a gray cloud because someone is missing. Being an older brother, he kind of protected and oversaw us—my mother being gone—and he's no longer there. You know, he was always the exciting, smiling, and "pull-us-together" type of person. Family functions, we're always waiting for him to come. . . . He spent a lot of time with my children. He was a really good uncle to them, not just financially, mostly there for them. He would…take them places that I wasn't able to take them. They [would] go to his house to spend the weekend, sometimes summer.

In these cases, the missing family member played very critical roles in the family, most particularly with regard to the children. All were also financial contributors, but the loss in these cases was socio-emotional as well as instrumental. It is possible, that in the case of long-term absences, the family had romanticized the member's contributions. Even if this were the case, the void left by the family member's absence was palpable in our respondents' accounts.

Quite a few of our respondents reported extraordinary levels of loss that were quite separate from their incarceration episode. A participant whose thirty-year-old daughter had been in prison for eight years, explained that her coping with this situation had been made all the more difficult due to the deaths over the years of her uncle, brother, mother, husband, and older son. Another sample member's eighteen-year-old son

Figure 6.2. Two of the dozens of bail bonds businesses surrounding the Los Angeles County Jail. Photo Courtesy of
Darnell Hunt.

had been incarcerated for about a year, but during the same period, she
had experienced the loss of an estimated ten friends and family members.
She said, "Last year, I lost a sister, a brother, a niece, and a nephew . . . I
lose so many. I feel like so many people are just dying around me, it's piti-
ful." Another participant lost an aunt and two friends over the course of a
few months. One could theorize that these deaths could serve to contextualize the incarceration of a family member, making the loss occasioned
by imprisonment more tolerable. Yet, these respondents described the
compounding of loss, in addition to their loved one's absence, adding to a
weight that already seemed unbearable.

Loss appeared as one of several psychological issues associated with
incarceration from which both those outside and inside suffered. With
her son incarcerated since 2006 and facing a potential sentence of thirty
years to life, this woman described the psychological support she tried to
provide:

> Due to the nature of this crime . . . he's feeling depressed himself. He's
> feeling alone; he mentions this a lot to me. I've gotten several—I don't

want to say disturbing letters from him—but letters that I was very concerned about because he's feeling so alone. He says he has no one to talk to; that's why I try to talk to him as much as I can. I try to get in touch with the chaplain, so he can talk to him. But I feel sad for him, because he talks about how he wished he could be out going on with his life; how he wished he had listened more intensively to his parents, to me and my husband, and he just wishes he could be out. Especially since his dad passed away four months ago, he recalls a lot of the time that he spent, you know, with his dad and how things could have been different.

Freeing the Family

The findings and discussion in this chapter suggest a number of potential strategies for addressing the incarceration crisis confronting Black Los Angeles. First, in the first decade of the 2000s, efforts to eliminate the harsh and unfair penalties associated with infractions involving crack cocaine represented a major step toward remedying the conditions that resulted in the mass incarceration of African Americans. In November 2007, the U.S. Sentencing Commission reduced the penalties for most crack-cocaine offenses by two levels.[43] Perhaps more critically, in April 2009 the Obama administration urged Congress to eliminate disparities between sentencing for crack and powder cocaine.[44] However welcome these changes were, they couldn't undo the effects that two decades of the previous policies wrought. Individuals and families were scarred by both the criminal justice experience (including arrest, defense, time-served, family adaptation, re-entry) and the missed opportunities and years of life. It will likely take generations and a more formidable commitment of will and resources to even begin to address the disruptions that resulted.

Second, our interviews suggest that a more sensitive judiciary with greater representation by persons familiar with the conditions faced by African Americans could serve to counter other systemic failures. Judges are there not only to mete out justice but to monitor and prevent injustice. A more active mobilization of the public to elect judges who truly represent the interests of Black Los Angeles would also work to ameliorate the ills wrought by the system.

Third, the perspective of African Americans on the incarceration crisis is informed by a collective historical memory that contextualizes government authority, police power, and the criminal justice system. Native

American scholars have advanced the construct of "historical trauma" to describe the cumulative and enduring effects of generations of traumatic events on individuals, families, and communities.[45] We argue that this may be an appropriate vehicle to understand how African Americans experience and interpret the mass incarceration that has had such an extraordinary impact on families and communities.

Given the financial crisis of the early twenty-first century, the prospects for prioritizing the needs of families with incarcerated members appeared to be dim. In fact, the continued exploitation of "imprisoned" families was exemplified by the onerous prison communication system[46] that restricted inmates to making telephone calls using the operator-assisted collect service that included whopping surcharges.[47] Between 2005 and 2009, California placed more money from the general fund in corrections than in higher education.[48] Journalists questioned this calculation even before the budget megacrisis of 2009.[49] The state also limited admissions to the university system as well as the community colleges at the very moment when demand was highest due to the absence of jobs, the need to re-tool, and the inability of higher income families to afford private schooling.[50] It is hard to imagine that the state could continue to invest in a correctional system that by all scientific accounts does not reduce crime—particularly at the expense of higher education. What is perfectly clear is that significant segments of Black Los Angeles have been traumatized and permanently affected by the policies of the last quarter century.

This chapter has not addressed the specific social-service needs of the individuals and families who participated in this study. Nor have we focused on the many exceptional agencies and individuals who continued to work in the interests of both prisoners and families, despite dwindling resources and increased need. Still, despite the indiscretions of some, a generation of black Angelenos, most particularly young men, were effectively stripped of the means to function effectively in this society—even after they were released from prison. This was tragic for them and for the larger society; it reinforces the need to renounce the failed practices of the past and to forge a new community compact that recognizes the inherent worth and potential of every member.

NOTES

1. Mauer and King, *Uneven Justice.*

2. Wormley, *World Prison Population List.*

3. The PEW Center on the States, *One in 100.*

4. William J. Sabol and Paige M. Harrison, "Prison and Jail Inmates at Mid-year 2006, Bureau of Justice Statistics Bulletin, June, NCJ 217675," U.S. Bureau of Justice, 2006, http://www.ojp.usdoj.gov/bjs/pub/pdf/pjim06.pdf (accessed January 9, 2009).

5. Sourcebook on Criminal Justice Statistics Online, "Number and Rate (per 100,000 U.S. residents) of Persons in State and Federal Prisons and Local Jails, United States, 1985, 1990–2008," U.S. Bureau of Justice, 2009, http://www.albany.edu/sourcebook/tost_6.html#6_b (accessed September 21, 2009).

6. California Department of Corrections and Rehabilitation, "Third Quarter 2008 Facts and Figures," http://www.cdcr.ca.gov/Divisions_Boards/Adult_Operations/Facts_and_Figures.html (accessed December 22, 2008).

7. Ibid.

8. U.S. Census Bureau, "State and County Quick Facts (State of California)," http://quickfacts.census.gov/qfd/states/06000.html (accessed January 9, 2009).

9. Mauer and King, *Uneven Justice.*

10. Bailey and Hayes, *Who's in Prison.*

11. Clear, "The Impacts of Incarceration"; Mauer and King, *Uneven Justice*; The PEW Center on the States, *One in 100.*

12. Sabol and Harrison, "Prison and Jail Inmates."

13. Bailey and Hayes, *Who's in Prison.*

14. California Department of Finance, "Census 2000, SF1: Selected Racial Groups and Specific Origin of Hispanic or Latino (1-page) Profiles by Individual Counties," http://www.dof.ca.gov/HTML/DEMOGRAP/SDC/Profiles/SF2/SF2profiles.php (accessed January 24, 2009).

15. King, *Disparity by Geography.*

16. The Justice Policy Institute is a Washington, DC–based think tank committed to reducing society's reliance on incarceration.

17. United States Department of Health and Human Services, "National Survey on Drug Use and Health."

18. Beatty, Petteruti, and Ziedenberg, *Vortex.*

19. Ibid.

20. U.S. Department of Justice, "U.S. Drug Enforcement Administration: History 1985–1990," http://www.usdoj.gov/dea/pubs/history/1985-1990.html (accessed January 9, 2009).

21. For a more detailed examination of the media influence on images of Black Los Angeles, see chap. 8.

22. U.S. Department of Justice, "U.S. Drug Enforcement Administration."

23. Anti-Drug Abuse Act. H.R. 5484. 1986, 1988.

24. U.S. Sentencing Commission, "News Release: U.S. Sentencing Commission Votes Unanimously to Apply Amendment Retroactively for Crack Cocaine Offenses: Effective Date for Retroactivity Set for March 3, 2008," December 11, 2007, http://www.ussc.gov/press/rel121107.htm (accessed January 25, 2009).

25. Braman, *Doing Time on the Outside*; Garland, *Mass Imprisonment*; Pattillo, Weiman, and Western, eds., *Imprisoning America*; Travis and Waul, eds., *Prisoners Once Removed*.

26. Farmer, "The House of the Dead"; Massoglia, "Incarceration, Health, and Racial Disparities."

27. Comfort, "In the Tube at San Quentin"; Harman, Smith, Vernon, and Egan, "The Impact of Incarceration."

28. Hairston, *Focus on Children with Incarcerated Parents*.

29. Braman and Wood, "From One Generation to the Next"; Hairston, *Focus on Children with Incarcerated Parents*.

30. Braman, *Doing Time on the Outside*.

31. Western, *Punishment and Inequality*.

32. Brewer and Heitzeg, "The Racialization of Crime and Punishment"; Roberts, "The Social and Moral Cost of Mass Incarceration."

33. The Center for Community Partnerships promotes existing and new partnerships in research and teaching between UCLA and the community to develop new knowledge that improves the quality of life in Los Angeles.

34. Friends Outside is a social service organization addressing the needs of families and individuals involved in the criminal justice system.

35. California Department of Corrections and Rehabilitation, "One and Two Year Follow-up Recidivism Rates"; U.S. Department of Justice, "Recidivism of Prisoners."

36. Three sessions were conducted with each family member and ran from approximately forty-five minutes to several hours in length. A total of seventy-seven interviews, three for each family, plus two "bonus" interviews with an incarcerated family member after release, were used for the final study. Respondents were reimbursed for their time and effort with gift certificates to merchants of their choosing. Persons who completed the initial session were given a $25 gift certificate; $35 and $50 certificates were given for the second and third sessions, respectively.

37. Data were compiled in two ways. All quantitative information was entered into an SPSS data file. All open-ended qualitative responses were transcribed and entered into the EthnoNotes data system for coding and analysis. This initial reporting relies primarily on the rich qualitative material that was gathered; only descriptive quantitative data will be presented. Themes for qualitative analysis were developed in two ways. First, we examined responses to questions on key conceptual areas developed a priori when the project was conceived. Second,

we searched all transcripts for issues that were salient across families that had not been previously identified in the development phase. Two reviewers reached agreement on the categories that were finally selected for presentation.

38. See chap. 1 for a detailed account of the demographic shifts that have occurred in Black Los Angeles history.

39. U.S. Census Bureau, "State and County Quick Facts."

40. California Department of Corrections and Rehabilitation, "Integrated Housing, Recently Adopted Department Rules," http://www.cdcr.ca.gov/Regulations/Adult_Operations/New_Rules_Page.html (accessed January 27, 2009).

41. Lee Baca, "In L.A., Race Kills," *Los Angeles Times*, June 12, 2008, op ed.

42. Braman, *Doing Time on the Outside.*

43. U.S. Sentencing Commission, "News Release."

44. Josh Meyer, "Obama Administration Urges Equal Penalties for Crack, Powder Cocaine Dealers," *Los Angeles Times*, April 30, 2009, http://www.latimes.com/news/nationworld/nation/la-na-crack30-2009apr30,0,4286524,print.story (accessed on May 15, 2009).

45. Evans-Campbell, "Historical Trauma in American Indian/Native Alaska Communities."

46. Zimmerman and Flaherty, "Location Monopolies."

47. Telephone contact has become a significant barrier for communications between prisoners and loved ones (Travis, *But They All Come Back*). This bizarre system was popularized, perhaps not coincidentally, with the huge increase in the prison population occasioned by changes in the crack cocaine drug laws (Johnson-Mitchell, "When Is a Collect Call"). State correctional systems negotiate with telecommunications carriers for the contract that will pay the state prison systems the largest "site commissions" or kickbacks (Zimmerman and Flaherty, "Location Monopolies"). Clearly, the incentive to stick families and friends with higher and higher surcharges is great. The American Bar Association's Government Affairs Office (Cardman, "Letter to Federal Communications Commission") has objected to this practice and has called on the Federal Communications Commission to take "meaningful action to address excessive inmate phone service rates and ensure the broadest possible range of calling options."

48. California Legislative Analyst's Office, "California Spending Plan 2007–08"; RAND California Statistics, "State General Government Finances, Calculator Compared Grant Total, Higher Ed-UC, CSU, & Other, K–12," http://ca.rand.org/cgi-bin/annual.cgi (accessed February 8, 2009).

49. James Sterngold, "Prison Budget Trumps Colleges: No Other Big State Spends as Much to Incarcerate Compared with Higher Education Funding," *San Francisco Chronicle*, May 21, 2007, http://www.sfgate.com/cgi-bin/article.cgi?f=/c/a/2007/05/21/MNG4KPUKV51.DTL (accessed February 8, 2009).

50. Detailed examination of the university admissions system can be found in chap. 16.

Chapter 7

Black and Gay in L.A.

The Relationships Black Lesbians and Gay Men Have to Their Racial and Religious Communities

Mignon R. Moore

On November 4, 2008, California voters passed Proposition 8, an initiative on the state ballot that sought to eliminate the right of same-sex couples to marry. The proposition passed by a 52 to 48 percent margin, and the first exit polls conducted by the Associated Press reported that 70 percent of black voters backed the initiative, which effectively overturned the California Supreme Court's May 2008 decision that had allowed same-sex marriage.[1] Three weeks after the vote, the *Los Angeles Sentinel*[2] sponsored a town hall meeting[3] to allow black Angelenos to voice their opinions about the vote on Proposition 8 and to discuss their views on gay sexuality. Nevin Powell, an activist supporting the rights of lesbian, gay, bisexual, and transgender (LGBT) people, was on the panel and shared his experience talking about Proposition 8 with members of the black community.

Powell said that on the morning after the vote, he noticed a group of African Americans, mostly men, who had gathered at the Magic Johnson–owned Starbucks in Ladera Heights.[4] He overheard them talking about the news that overwhelming numbers of blacks in California had voted "yes" on Proposition 8, and that African Americans had played a significant role in getting the measure passed. They all said they had voted "yes" and agreed it was the right thing to do. Powell interjected and told them he had voted "no." He explained that he had been gay for many years and had a long-term partner that he wanted to marry. He told them how disappointed he was that he would no longer have that opportunity. He also told them he was a church-going man, believed in God, and believed that the government has no right to tell him what he should do in the privacy of his own home. Powell asked them two questions that he says resulted in a real turning point in the conversation: "Would you want me to marry your sister? Would you want me to marry your daughter?" By the end of his discussion, he believed he had convinced almost everyone to agree with his point of view. Some of the men said they had never thought about the issues that way but were persuaded by what he told them.

Powell's arguments were persuasive because they indirectly addressed a strong fear in black communities of "down low" men (men who have sex with other men while in heterosexual marriages and relationships). When Powell asked the men if they would want him to marry their sisters or daughters, he was indirectly saying that keeping gay people from the right to marry would result in more people hiding their homosexuality by using a facade of heterosexuality. He was insinuating that denying gay people the right to publicly enact a gay sexuality would result in greater deception within the racial community and leave more people, particularly black men, in the closet. The fear in black communities of "down low" men is a powerful one and a persuasive argument supporting same-sex marriage. Powell knew this and used it effectively in his discussion. Powell concluded his comments on the town hall panel by telling the audience he was glad he had decided to be open about his sexuality to these strangers, and wondered what would have happened had he and others done so before the election.

This chapter draws from ethnographic data I collected in the year prior to the November 2008 election and in the year immediately following the election to give voice to black lesbians and gay men in Los Angeles on gay rights issues, and more generally to consider their experiences as openly gay people living, worshiping, and socializing in African American communities.[5] I interviewed twenty-five black gay activists and everyday black gay and heterosexual Angelenos, visited churches and spiritual centers, engaged with black LGBT people from Los Angeles in online discussions, attended and participated in town hall meetings and community forums on Proposition 8, and analyzed news stories in the *Los Angeles Times*, the *Los Angeles Sentinel*, and other periodicals referencing African Americans and the vote on Proposition 8. This chapter examines the public debates over same-sex marriage as a representation of the move from private to public expressions of sexuality that take place not only in national and international arenas but, most importantly, affect life in the local, public and private spaces of church pulpits, coffee shops, bars, dinner tables, living room couches, and other social environments across America. It discusses the conditions under which black gays and lesbians are likely to garner support from black heterosexuals on gay rights issues, and analyzes some of the tactics black LGBT people use when negotiating multiple identity statuses based on race, gender, and sexuality to create a sense of belonging in black racial environments.

The 2000 U.S. Census counts roughly 85,000 black, same-sex couples in the United States. Some 14 percent of all same-sex couples who self-identified on the census are African American, roughly the same proportion of African Americans in the larger U.S. population.[6] Census and other survey data show that nationally, and within the state of California, the majority of black same-sex couples resides in cities, towns, and rural areas that are predominantly African American. They are more likely to live with other blacks in minority communities than to live with white homosexuals in cities and neighborhoods with high percentages of same-sex couples.[7]

In 2007, 4 percent of African American adults in Los Angeles County identified as lesbian, gay, or bisexual, compared to 5.1 percent of whites, 2.8 percent of Latinos, and 3.7 percent of all adults.[8] California ranked third in the United States for the number of black same-sex couples, after New York and Georgia, and the geographic distribution of non-white same-sex couples in the state also mirrored the respective distribution of minorities generally.[9] Seventy-one percent of black LGB people in Los Angeles County lived in the South (38 percent) or South Bay (33 percent) areas, communities with heavy concentrations of African Americans and Latinos. Less than 1 percent of gay blacks lived on the Westside of Los Angeles, which includes West Hollywood, the area of the city most known for gay social life.[10]

Although black gay people lived in predominantly black areas, they were not a visible group in neighborhoods like Carson and Ladera Heights, which are considered suburbs of Los Angeles. They tended not to post rainbow flags or have bumper stickers with gay-themed logos displayed in their neighborhoods,[11] and tended not to talk about gay sexuality or gay liberation politics with heterosexual neighbors and family members. More generally, there was very little public discussion between gay and heterosexual members of the larger racial community about what it meant to be a gay person of color. LGBT community centers tended not to be located in black neighborhoods, and gay- and lesbian-themed events taking place

Figure 7.1. Catch One nightclub on Pico Boulevard. Photo
Courtesy of Darnell Hunt.

in these areas were not publicized in a way that revealed their content
to outsiders.[12] Despite the Catch One nightclub (see fig. 7.1) and various
social events for Latino LGBT people that took place in other parts of
the city, the most visible gay community and representation of gay life in
Los Angeles was found in West Hollywood, a predominantly white, upper
middle-class neighborhood.

A national study published in 1995 found that the majority of African
Americans surveyed expressed homophobic attitudes about gay sexuality.
Herek and Capitanio reported that seven out of ten blacks agreed with
the statements: "Sex between two men is just plain wrong" (74 percent),

192 MIGNON R. MOORE

and "Sex between two women is just plain wrong" (72 percent). About six out of ten blacks agreed with the statements: "I think male homosexuals are disgusting," and "I think female homosexuals are disgusting" (57 percent).[13] While the proportion reporting disapproval was similar across race, the figures were particularly important for black LGBT people because they were more likely to live with other African Americans than were white gays to live with white heterosexuals.[14]

The persistent sense of disapproval of gay sexuality, combined with expectations by black lesbians and gays that they would be openly accepted as legitimate members of the racial group, created a cross-cutting issue within the black community. The political scientist Cathy Cohen defines cross-cutting issues as concerns "rooted in or built on the often hidden differences, cleavages, or fault lines of marginal communities." These issues are "perceived as being contained to identifiable subgroups in black communities, especially those segments of black communities which are the least empowered."[15] The contradictions within African American spaces between disapproving attitudes toward same-sex desire and support for basic civil rights for everyone, including gay people, have a particular impact on the lives of sexual minorities who also define themselves by their membership in this racial category, and who increasingly insist on having others in the racial group recognize and respect their sexuality.

Because of the black community's collective discomfort around sexuality, black gays and lesbians had not gained the political and social traction to be able to create many public, gay-friendly spaces *within* black communities that were comparable to the predominantly white, LGBT spaces that existed in many large urban areas. During the period of this research, several important social and political organizations existed for black LGBT people in Los Angeles, including Jeffrey King's In the Meantime Men's Group, the Barbara Jordan/Bayard Rustin Coalition, and United Lesbians of African Heritage. These groups usually met in the homes of individual members or at the Catch One center, and their focus was on self-empowerment as LGBT people rather than specifically on building relationships with heterosexual blacks. The lack of dialogue between black gays and heterosexuals hindered the transmission of information about black LGBT people and their place in the larger black community.

The Simultaneity of Black Racial Identity and Gay Sexuality

National public debates over the legalization of same-sex marriage and other related issues in the early 2000s brought the topic of gay sexuality more directly into the public life of black communities. In turn, this situation created the space for family members, neighbors, and others to be more up-front in their feelings and opinions about the visible enactment of same-sex desire expressed through such public pronouncements as weddings or gay-partner adoptions.[16] The process of incorporating homosexual behavior into everyday experiences and encouraging others to acknowledge this sexuality is what historians refer to as having a "modern gay identity."[17] But for many African American elders, both heterosexual and gay, native and foreign-born, the practice of moving same-sex desire and behavior into an identity category threatened the primacy of a preexisting group membership based on race and ethnicity.

These elders conceptualized black group membership as an identity status that must remain primary for the continued advancement of the race,[18] and many LGBT people who were entrenched in black communities agreed with this sentiment. They were raised with parents and grandparents who migrated from the South to build black communities in the West, and were subjected to discriminatory practices in employment[19] and housing that helped them cohere around a group identity.[20] This collective racial identity grew as civil rights issues began to take center stage in the 1950s and 1960s. This generation built churches, newspapers, social clubs, racial uplift groups, and various other political and social institutions that continued to serve as the foundation of black community life through the first decade of the 2000s. Those raised in and around these institutions or socialized by these elders have had a firm, taken-for-granted sense of themselves as members of black communities, maintaining the historical memory of these events and understanding the cultural symbols, subtle cues, and other interactional language that accompanied an insider status.

At the same time, those born in the late 1960s and early 1970s who came into a gay sexuality in late adolescence or early adulthood did so amid an emerging public discourse about the enactment of same-sex desire through the HIV/AIDS epidemic, depictions of gay people in film and on talk shows, news articles about gay rights issues, and dramatic increases in women and men choosing to lead openly gay lives. The socialization they received from African American elders helped cement a strong racial

group membership, and growing up in this contemporary historical period has encouraged the construction of a modern gay identity. Younger
black lesbians and gay men have tried to figure out for themselves how
to enact a modern gay identity within a particular cultural context. They
also have called on the racial group to take seriously the fact that group
members can have other salient identities that co-exist with and do not
threaten a strong racial identity and sense of linked fate.

When dealing with heterosexuals within the racial community, some
(mostly older) black gay people have experienced gay sexuality as a
stigma they had to endure throughout their adult lives. These women and
men entered adulthood in the 1950s through the early 1970s, during a
time of overt racial subordination, which required various types of support from the racial community to survive. Under these conditions, they
historically felt less free to violate community norms. They believed that
the open and public way of expressing gay sexuality through marriage
and other processes of family formation was slow to reach black communities. Further, until black heterosexuals gained a more full understanding
of black gay people, black gays chose not to add to their marked status by
embracing rainbow flags, "queer" language, and other indicators. Instead,
they created vibrant gay communities that were still in black neighborhoods, but kept these parts of their lives separate from other components
of black life.[21]

A gradual shift occurred from gay sexuality as behavior enacted in se-
crecy or with a "nod and a wink" but no direct acknowledgment, to a
public *identity* that existed alongside of a racial identity. The people I interviewed had an acute awareness that the social norms of the community
labeled gay sexuality as immoral and wrong, and experienced a resistance
from the heterosexual community toward their attempts to more publicly
express their sexuality. One gay woman remarked that while about 10 percent of black heterosexuals "want to beat you up and always say you're
going to hell," and another 5 or 10 percent "think everybody should be gay
like they are" [laughs], she estimates that the remaining 75–80 percent
have a "don't ask, don't tell" way of dealing with the issue. Her comments
imply that she believed very few blacks who are not gay are supportive of
gay people. Instead, she believed that the majority does not want to engage in discussions about it, even if they "give a dirty look" or, with their
body language, suggest that they do not actually approve.[22]

Younger, black LGBT people came of age during a time of greater access to resources and opportunities, and this caused some of them to rely

less stringently on the racial community as their only source of support. They felt more freedom to express their frustration with what they experienced as pressure to deemphasize a gay sexuality in black social environments. For example, the Reverend Dr. Cecil "Chip" Murray, former senior pastor at First AME Church—the oldest and one of the largest black congregations in Los Angeles—said that during his tenure from 1977 to 2004 he witnessed among black lesbians and gay men an increased willingness to express a gay sexuality in public spaces. In a published interview, he said:

> I have seen their emergence . . . from the closet. They feel less [of] a need to be apologetic than a need just to assert their is-ness. And it is up to others how they are received. They seem to have taken the initiative and are saying "I have the right to be who I am and you don't have the right to determine who I shall be. . . . I think there has been a decided change in those who were hidden and who are now revealed and are proud of the revelation.[23]

In January 2008 Jasmyne Cannick, a political organizer, co-sponsored a forum at the Lucy Florence Coffee House in Leimert Park, as part of a national series of meetings across the country to define and discuss a black gay political agenda.[24] Ronald Moore was present at the Los Angeles meeting. While he acknowledged the difficulty blacks had in discussing their sexuality with others in the racial group, he also verified the importance of race for their identities:

> Coming out [as black gay men and lesbians] is the most potent weapon we have, but that's still the hardest step to take. . . . We need more people of color to come out and we need more of the white LGBT organizations to understand we can't and will not leave our blackness at the door.

In an online discussion[25] among a group of black lesbians living in Los Angeles following the November 2008 election, Aaliyah Knowles,[26] who lived in the historic West Adams district near the University of Southern California, shared her frustration about the high proportion of African American votes to ban same-sex marriage. One participant asked Aaliyah if she was out to her neighbors, and her response suggested she was not. The group agreed that if black LGBT people wanted the black community to support gay rights, they had to be willing to reveal themselves to black heterosexuals because this would help the community understand their sexuality as part of their identity and not an illicit behavior they engaged in secretly.

But one problem in asserting a gay sexuality in black social contexts is the puzzle of how to reveal oneself as gay to the racial community in a culturally appropriate way. Those in the online discussion group agreed they had to navigate a fine line between making their gay relationships more identifiable to heterosexuals, and conforming to certain patterns of interaction they were expected to enact with others, particularly African American elders. Regardless of sexuality, they had learned that it was not polite to refer to a partner as a "lover" or to use terminology that approached anything sexual in nature when describing someone who was not a husband or wife. Most of their parents had migrated to Los Angeles from Louisiana, Texas, Mississippi, and other places in the South, and they had been raised with particular southern norms around polite language and appropriate topics for public discussion. Those norms called for a certain type of discretion when discussing intimate relationships. In short, they needed to figure out how to portray their gay sexuality as a status that co-existed with familiar black cultural norms.

Fear of Violence

A different concern in openly expressing a gay sexuality in predominantly black neighborhoods was the fear of violence and homophobia. Effeminate gay men and women with a masculine gender presentation were particularly vulnerable to danger. FBI statistics showed that from 2005 to 2006, anti-lesbian, gay, and bisexual hate crimes nationwide increased by 18 percent.[27] In Los Angeles as in other places, there was poor documentation of violence inflicted as a result of perceived gender identity and homosexuality, particularly within communities of color.[28] Research suggested that when individuals were attacked for having a perceived gay sexuality or an alternate gender identity, the violence was particularly brutal and accompanied by high levels of vocalized prejudices.[29]

Concerns about violence most consistently arose from non-gender-conforming women and men. While there was a wide range of gender presentations that were acceptable for women, people tended to react strongly and negatively to women with a specifically masculine gender presentation. For black men, there was a very narrow range in gender presentation that was accepted. Masculinity must be performed, and the consequences of disrupting this expectation were severe. Stacey Robinson,[30] a twenty-eight-year-old woman with a nonfeminine gender presentation, shared an experience that occurred in the early 2000s, when she and four friends were dressed in a non-gender-conforming way:

> Me and four other friends were coming from the Catch, the Catch One nightclub. Now at that time of night there aren't that many places open to eat, so we go to eat at Denny's over here on Crenshaw. It was about 2:30, 3 a.m. . . . As we're leaving, there are a group of dudes, about seven of them, they were young like us. They were hungry, too. It just so happens we were doing check out at the same time. One of them started saying, because one of us [the women in her group] presented more masculine, so he started saying "Y'all girls dress like boys. Y'all supposed to be ladies! Y'all need to put on y'all skirts. If I was y'all Daddies, I would beat you. Y'all obviously gay, you shouldn't be gay"—but he didn't say it in a nice way. He couldn't have been no older than mid-twenties. . . . He kept getting louder and was belligerent. He wasn't using cuss words, and he wasn't threatening us with violence. . . . We were leaving, so he was saying "Yea, that's right, y'all better get out of here." He was really attacking the gender expression in a loud, belligerent way. . . . Now, when they followed us out to the car, I did notice that none of the others in his group joined him in yelling at us, and some of his friends were just trying to get him into the car.[31]

I asked Stacey how she might react if the same thing were to happen today, and she replied:

> If that were to happen now, I was thinking I would ask him, "Do I look like the enemy? You don't look like the enemy to me. You look like my brother. You look like my cousin. Do I look like the enemy to you?" Then I would say, "Quit acting like the white man—this ain't slavery!" [Laughs]

Throughout the conflict, her antagonist drew on a variety of patriarchal understandings of women in his verbal assault. He chastised them for not looking more like "ladies." Despite being of a similar age as the women, he aligned himself with the role of father and said they should be "beat" [spanked] for dressing outside of what is expected for women. He linked their gender nonconformity to a gay sexuality and was disapproving of that as well. But throughout the interaction, there was something familial to the tone and arguments he used. Likewise, the response Stacey imagined she would give if the incident had taken place today, also suggests a familial relationship. She thought she could persuade him to back down or to redirect his anger by drawing on their racial connection, a shared history of racial oppression, and a joint sense of communalism, which is a tenet of black political ideology.[32]

Black LGBT Protest in Los Angeles

On Sunday, November 23, 2008, Yardenna Aaron and Latrice Dixon joined with "Love at Work," a small community association, to organize a protest march of black LGBT people and their non-black and heterosexual supporters in the city. The march took place along Crenshaw Boulevard between King Boulevard and Leimert Park, which is an important, historically black corridor in South Los Angeles (see chap. 2). Dixon and Aaron were seasoned organizers, though Aaron had never before applied her labor skills to the defense of LGBT issues. Aaron explained that the march was meant to "show their anger at the passage of [Proposition 8] and increase the visibility of black LGBT people in their own community." They marched at noon on Sunday to avoid the church-going population and were escorted by the police. The event was successful with more than two hundred marchers, and shortly afterwards the organizers thought they should name the group so that it did not disappear into obscurity. They worked with other LGBT activists to form the "Here to Stay Coalition." The mantra of the group would be, "We've been in the community, we're in the community, and we'll always be in the community. We're Here to Stay."

After the event, the majority of the crowd dispersed and the police left. About six protesters remained by the fountain in the park and were approached by a few men. Several of the marchers shared their version of what happened. Here is organizer Yardenna Aaron's version:

> It got hostile. One dude comes up [and says] "You're going to Hell."
> "You're an abomination." "You're not wanted here." Then about three
> more dudes come up, so they're starting a little mob thing. . . . He was on
> the phone and told us he had called the homies and they were on their

way. So he was pretty much threatening us with physical violence, like we fixin' to get beat up or killed.[33]

The man assumed they were outsiders to the community. At one point he told them, "Take that shit back to West Hollywood. Me and the homies, we're going to come up to where y'all stay and get you." Aaron, who owned a home in South Central, replied "West Hollywood? Man, we live right here. *This is* our community." She said that startled him a bit so he returned "to his God piece, saying 'God don't like this—y'all can't even make babies!' "

Aaron's more serious concern was that the onlookers and business owners bordering the fountain where the confrontation was taking place were not responding to the harassment. They were not moving forward to protect or defend the protesters, most of whom were women. The onlookers were just silently watching the scene unfold. She recalls:

> The way I describe it, the community was setting itself up to "Hear no evil, see no evil," because people had come out of their shops, people were just watching! So I felt if something happened, there would be a great silence. No one would ever *really* know what happened. 'Cause if they're not stopping these guys, they're having complacent silence. So they could beat us, rape us, kill us and the police would *never* get a straight story. Our families would never get a straight story. 'Cause when the community cares about something, they speak out against it.

Aaron's concern was similar to the one expressed by Stacey in the aforementioned Denny's incident. When trying to decide how open to be about their sexuality, black LGBT people often fear the community's apathy toward the threats they face. They are uncertain of whether the racial group, who can be counted on to come to their defense in times of racial strife, will also be there to help when the threat centers on an issue that does not have consensus or unanimous support.

The Here to Stay Coalition partnered with the Jordan/Rustin Coalition, a black LGBT organization in Greater Los Angeles, to march in the Martin Luther King Day (MLK) Parade, on Monday, January 19, 2009. The parade route went through several black and Latino neighborhoods south of the I-10 Freeway, and the coalition organizers told me this would be the first time an openly gay African American group marched in the MLK parade with a sign that was specifically about black homosexuality.

Figure 7.2. Here to Stay Coalition and Jordan/Rustin Coalition marching at the MLK Parade in Los Angeles on January 19, 2009. Photo courtesy of Mignon Moore.

Given the events surrounding the 2008 California state election, the organizers thought it was very important that the group march with a clear banner. They chose "Black, Gay, and Here to Stay" as the main slogan and "We Are Your Family" as the secondary heading. The sign was written in plain, large lettering on top of a white background with the word "Gay" in lavender, and the words "Here to Stay" in the black nationalist colors of green, red, and black (see fig. 7.2).

Aaron commented that this was a critical moment to have something about gay sexuality so visible in the community, given the forums and discussions about Proposition 8 that had been taking place. In one of the planning sessions before the march, coalition members talked about the intense fear they had in walking with an openly gay banner, expressing concern over what they might encounter in some of the tougher neighborhoods. Some were also worried about seeing neighbors or former church members in the community while marching under the "gay label."

They were instructed to wear white because "it is the color of peace" and to respond to any heckling by returning positive affirmations like "Love!" and "Unity!"[34] In the planning sessions, one of the lead organizers predicted that the experience would be a positive one because of the communal nature of the racial group. In addition to marching as a group, the coalition had allies walking along the parade route who could hear and respond directly to the crowd. As they marched they could see the onlookers reading their signs and either clapping wildly in support, nodding as if they understood but perhaps not clapping, or just watching silently. They thought all of these responses were respectful and consistent with their goal of creating awareness in the community.

At the debriefing session immediately following the march, all of the participants reported that the positive responses by the crowd outweighed the negative reactions by ten to one, and that the strongest negative responses did not come as they walked through the rougher parts of town but when they reached some of the more middle-class areas. At one point a few onlookers in Leimert Park tried to rouse the crowd against the group, but were drowned out by the majority around them who said things like "Not today, man. Forget that. We're here together today." Aaron said she was happy with the love they received and grateful that "[i]t was not us having to control the crowd but the community itself, saying 'Peace out on that homophobia today.' So that was very powerful for us to hear."

The timing of the MLK Parade was important to the coalition's success. The mostly African American crowd was jubilant about the 2008 Obama presidential victory. Many were preparing to go or had already left for the Inauguration festivities in Washington, DC, and there was a spirit of anticipation, happiness, and togetherness in the community that day. The black LGBT community was elated and felt especially powerful and hopeful that by accomplishing this political act they were moving the racial group forward toward greater acceptance of them.

Reconciling with the Black Church

I'm going to teach today [congregant shouts "Come on, come on"] a brief message that will make it very clear about God's purpose for us, and for marriage, and for family. And how gay marriage would *disrupt* what God is doing [congregation responds "Yes, yes"]. Even though people may not do it intentionally, they don't know it will be used in that way. At the

202 MIGNON R. MOORE

meeting they said "No, it won't impact the schools, it won't impact religious freedom," but we see it is [sic] already. So it may not be the person who's saying it won't impact it but somebody's out there who really wants to push that agenda to the next level. And it won't stay in somebody's closet.[35]

Religious organizations are the moral, social, and political authority in black communities, and an understanding of this helps explain the African American vote on Proposition 8. Statistical analyses of a more comprehensive set of data suggest that the higher rate of "yes" votes among blacks relative to whites was due to the greater religious involvement of blacks. Egan and Sherrill analyzed data from a survey of 1,066 respondents selected at random from state voter registration lists.[36] Table 7.1 (reproduced from their study) presents the vote on Proposition 8 by race/ethnicity and by attendance of religious services. It shows that blacks were more likely to vote yes on Proposition 8 than whites and Asians, but in similar proportions to Latinos.

But it should be noted that 57 percent of blacks attended religious services at least once a week, compared to only 45 percent of all Californians.[37] Among Californians who attended religious services at least weekly, there was uniform support for Proposition 8—regardless of race or ethnicity. In other words, the table clearly shows that *religious* views on gay sexuality factored significantly in the voting patterns on the same-sex ballot measure.

TABLE 7.1
Egan and Sherrill's Report of the Vote on Proposition 8

	% of voters	% voting Yes on Proposition 8
Total		52
Race/Ethnicity		
White	68	49
African American	7	58
Latino/Hispanic	14	59
Asian	7	48
Attendance of Religious Services		
Weekly	45	70
Monthly	12	48
Holidays and special occasions	14	44
Hardly ever	29	30

Source: David Binder Research Survey of California Voters for Equality California, November 6–16, 2008, reported in Patrick J. Egan and Kenneth Sherrill, "California's Proposition 8: What Happened, and What Does the Future Hold?" Commissioned by the Evelyn & Walter Haas Jr. Fund in San Francisco, released by the National Gay and Lesbian Task Force Policy Institute, 2009, table 1, 3.

Religious institutions both react to and shape local sexual attitudes and behavior.[38] This was particularly the case in African American communities like the ones studied in Los Angeles. There were very few mainline black Christian denominations that supported marriage equality for lesbian and gay couples. The move from private to public presentation of gay sexuality had also influenced a contradiction among black lesbians and gay men between black churches' use of religion to constrain gay behavior, and the use of religion and spirituality by many gay people to support and validate their identities as same-gender-loving people who are black. Many black churches participated in public rule enforcement and policing of parishioners' behaviors, and some openly condemned behaviors deemed to fall outside of the church's teachings. Elders, deacons, even church mothers had the authority to confront individual congregants whom they suspected of engaging in activities that were antithetical to the rules of the church (i.e., wearing clothes that are inappropriate, engaging in nonmarital sex), and to sanction them for their behavior. This type of policing was framed around an interest in saving one's soul or helping people (usually young people) resist temptation.

LGBT people raised in most forms of black Christianity could not openly and proudly embrace a gay sexuality at the same time they were participating as congregants and leaders in the church, and this was the dilemma for those who wanted to practice their faith without being in the closet. Awareness and self-acknowledgment of same-sex attraction resulted in a line being drawn in the sand—either suppress or hide same-sex desires from others, act on those desires in a context of guilt and shame, or freely enact a gay sexuality while stepping down from leadership activity and organized involvement in the church or leaving organized religion completely.

In my research, LGBT respondents who worshiped at traditional, mainline denominations were able to actively participate in the church by entering what Griffin refers to as "an unspoken covenant of silence and restriction about their sexual identity."[39] They remained silent about the existence of their partners or were dishonest about the gender of their partners. They were also often vague or deceptive when pressed by older congregants about future prospects for marriage. In these ways they "passed" as heterosexual, all the while receiving spiritual guidance and prayer in a context where an important aspect of their lives was considered sinful.

Closeted gay people have always participated in the church. However, the majority of gay men have remained silent about their private lives, and as long as their sexuality remained within the private realm they could continue to be active in the church. For example, West Angeles Church of God in Christ is a large, black, middle-class church in Los Angeles whose doctrine holds that homosexuality and engagement in gay relationships are sinful. Nevertheless, many of the people who worshiped there during the research period were gay, and some may also have agreed with the theology that the enactment of same-sex desire is a sin. They participated in what Griffin defines as "guilty passing," or the act of indulging in their same-sex desires while feeling sinful and deserving of the rage and condemnation of church members.

Issues about how to balance respectability with same-sex desire are complicated ones, particularly for individuals who regularly attend religious services or take on leadership roles in traditional mainline black churches. For example, James Randall[40] was a thirty-five-year-old minister and head of the youth ministry in a large Pentecostal church in Los Angeles. The church leaders were outspoken in their disapproval of homosexuality, yet James spent ten years of his life living with a male partner. From time to time, church members would spend time at his house for barbecues and Bible studies. From the way the bedrooms and other areas of the house were configured and organized, it was easy to see that he and his partner were not just roommates. But the nature of their relationship was never made explicit. They never named their union or showed affection in public. Both the members of their families and the people in the church were satisfied with this arrangement, and James remained an integral part of the church's leadership. His partner felt welcomed at family functions, and the couple even hosted family events at James's home. His experience shows how effective a "Don't ask, Don't tell" approach to gay sexuality can be.

The racial community's acceptance of James's gay relationship so long as it remained *unnamed* reveals some of the alternative strategies many have used to enact a gay identity within particular cultural contexts. Many LGBT people have adopted a variety of ways to live a gay life that do not involve the public pronouncement of gay sexuality as an identity status, and have accepted this alternative way of incorporating a gay sexuality into their predominantly heterosexual social world. Not only were some heterosexuals not inclined to see a public pronouncement of gay sexuality as necessary, but even some black gay people also, perhaps begrudgingly, accepted this way of having relationships without naming them. For these people, the public pronouncement of gay sexuality as an identity status went against too many of the social norms and religious values that are part of the black culture they had felt relatively comfortable with for so long. The reluctance of some same-gender-loving people to openly define their relationships made it more difficult for heterosexuals to see the act of naming gay sexuality as an important one.

Even though some Christian churches have begun to question traditional teachings criticizing homosexuality, evangelical black churches in particular have been slow to modify their stance on this issue. They have held fast to Biblical scriptures that regulate all behaviors, particularly sexuality. And because so many African Americans have been raised and socialized with these religious teachings, many continue to use them as an anchor for their belief systems, holding tenaciously to the teachings as a moral guide, even when they do not actually practice what is preached.

Black Gay Angelenos and New Thought Religion

As the first decade of the 2000s drew to a close, more and more gay, black Christians were refusing to choose between silence and shame when enacting a same-sex desire. Some experienced difficulty reconciling the homophobic tendencies of many traditional black churches with their desire to live an openly gay life, and sought out alternative places to worship that combined elements of black evangelical traditions with more contemporary religious ideologies that did not condemn homosexual practices. In Los Angeles, I found strong support among middle-class black lesbians and gay men for African American Religious Science, a denomination within New Thought religion that embodied an African American worship environment while simultaneously modeling the tenets of a historically white New Age/New Thought religious practice.[41] Religious Science shares many of the symbols and scriptures of Christianity, emphasizing a diversity of religious thought, while also incorporating other liberal religious traditions such as Transcendentalism, writings of ancient and contemporary mystics, philosophers, and other various sacred texts.

Located in Culver City—a couple of miles from the Baldwin Hills communities discussed in the Introduction—is Agape International Spiritual Center (see fig. 7.3), a Religious Science congregation led by a dreadlocked African American man, Dr. Michael Beckwith. Agape teaches Religious Science and defines itself as a "trans-denominational spiritual community

Figure 7.3. Agape International Spiritual Center in Culver City, a couple of miles from Baldwin Hills. Photo courtesy of Darnell Hunt.

whose doors are open to all seekers in search of authentic spirituality, personal transformation and selfless service to humankind."[42] Dale Trenton,[43] a forty-nine-year-old black, gay woman who began attending Agape in the early 2000s, said that it appealed to her as a place of worship because of the empowerment she felt through the ministry. The people I spoke with who practiced this faith said their primary attraction to African American Religious Science is that the spiritual leader and the practice as a whole accepts their "full selves," including their gay sexuality. Similar to Darnise Martin's study of an African American Religious Science church in Oakland, California,[44] I found that blacks' attraction to the Religious Science practiced at Agape comes from a sense of familiarity with the style of ser-

mons and other performed aspects of African American cultural elements
in the service, the content of the sermons and self-determination that is
taught, the cultural politics of difference embodied by the congregation,
and the feeling of full acceptance no matter what one looked like, how
one dressed, or one's race/ethnicity.

Historically, Pentecostal and other traditional African American religions have embraced or are consistent with many New Thought principles
including self-determination, affirmative prayer (faith), spiritual healing,
and prosperity. Traditional religion has ensconced these tenets within the
more familiar Christian prayers and scriptures, shaping them to fit the
needs of blacks. Early black religious leaders who specifically incorporated
New Thought principles into their practices include Father Hurley, Father
Divine, Reverend Ike, and Daddy Grace,[45] although these ministries were
described as sects or cults and often discredited by traditional black religions.[46] Traditional and New Thought religion shares common ground in
"affirming the power of individuals to direct their own circumstances by
the power of their thoughts and the performance of specified actions."[47]
I asked Yandi Morrison,[48] a gay woman raised in the AME Zion church
and a satisfied parishioner at Agape, how she thought African American
Religious Science differed from traditional religion. She described the
draw of this philosophy in the following way:

> Well first, the message is coming without condemnation from an African
> American man, with dreadlocks—he is validating our identity as LGBT
> people. . . . It's an environment that calls you out in a positive way. . . .
> Because if you have a ministry, a place of worship that says LGBT people
> are welcome and there's support groups for you, when I speak from the
> pulpit I'm going to be inclusive of your experience, I'm going to make
> sure that our church shows up at Gay Pride Day, that we have a booth
> or whatever, people get the word and want to be a part of it. It's not to
> say that there are not a lot of LGBT people at Faithful Central or West
> Angeles on Crenshaw—you know they are there and they're closeted,
> and I don't know how they do that. I don't know how their souls are fed
> and uplifted when probably several times a year the person that you have
> chosen to be your spiritual leader is condemning you. I don't know how
> they do that but I know that they're there.

Having a place where the spiritual leader has a similar racial and cultural background, yet embraces the congregation as a whole and does

not offer condemnation, is something many looking for spiritual guidance thirsted for. The focus in New Thought religion on the strength and power within the individual, in tandem with a higher power, is important as well. Here there was a distinction between New Thought and more traditional black religions, where God is the ultimate Higher Power and operates at a higher status than the individual. There was more agency within the self in New Thought religion, and this was a significant attraction to many as well.

Insiders and Outsiders Within

The relationships the black LGBT informants in my study had with their religious and racial communities cannot be explained in a linear, uniform way. There were times when lesbians and gay men experienced support from the racial community, and times when they were disappointed with the lack of progress in their struggle for acceptance. Some in the community were becoming more supportive of gay sexuality as an identity status that could exist alongside a strong racial group affinity. Others were holding fast to religious and cultural ideologies that reduced gay sexuality to an immoral behavior and thus not a valid identity status. Some LGBT people responded to the inconsistencies and occasional rejection by physically distancing themselves from the racial community. Others exited a "gay" life and retreated to a primary heterosexual identity while continuing to have same-sex intimate relationships in secret.

However, despite the disapproving attitudes and religious condemnation that appeared from time to time, the majority of black LGBT people I studied remained in predominantly black neighborhoods and social contexts, and negotiated daily with family and community. Those who remained, particularly those with the resources to leave if they chose, said the support of and membership in the larger black community was important to them. They remained because they trusted in racial solidarity and racial group membership. They also remained because they had less confidence that they would ever be fully accepted as members of other identity groups such as those based solely on sexuality. Nevertheless, by the end of the first decade of the 2000s, they were increasingly willing to test the support of the black community by making their gay identities more public and asserting their interest in being involved and taking on leadership roles in black social environments.

But the move from gay sexuality as a primarily private activity or be-havior, to the open expression and insistence on acknowledgment of it from family, community residents, and even church parishioners, often comes at a price. Openly gay people might have to temporarily forego full acceptance from family and friends. This is a price many are willing to pay in order to nurture their racial group affiliation. To be a participat-ing member of the black racial community involves periodic engagement over debate and the negotiation and reconciliation that follows.[49]

The black LGBT Angelenos in my study remained in their racial com-munities, despite the conflicts over acceptance of their sexuality, because those conflicts were part and parcel of the sense of community and be-longing. The struggle over power and having one's voice heard were all part of the social organization of black communities. Group membership was not about sameness or having one voice but about sharing a com-monality, a perceived link that connected its members, regardless of other differences that also might have existed. This work offers an understand-ing of how black gay people in Los Angeles embarked on the maintenance of group affiliation and "insider" status around a racial identity, despite the cross-cutting issues around the public enactment of homosexuality that threatened to separate them from strong and positive affiliations with the racial group.

NOTES

1. Shelby Grad, "70% of African Americans Backed Prop. 8, Exit Poll Finds," *Los Angeles Times*, November 5, 2008, http://latimesblogs.latimes.com/lanow/2008/11/70-of-african-a.html (accessed February 13, 2009). More careful estimates later found that the proportion of blacks voting yes was more moderate than first assumed, though still higher than the yes votes by whites. See Egan and Sherrill, "California Proposition 8."

2. A black newspaper founded in 1934, the *Los Angeles Sentinel* is a key gate-way for news in the black community.

3. The meeting, "In the Aftermath of Proposition 8," was held on November 22, 2008.

4. The Magic Johnson–owned franchises were important social outlets in Black Los Angeles. This particular Starbucks was adjacent to the Johnson-owned TGI Friday's Restaurant. The *Los Angeles Times* described this area as "part com-munity center, part social club," and wrote "the scene around Friday's and Star-bucks has indeed become the place to be for the upwardly mobile buppies and

other working stiffs from the surrounding areas of Mid-Wilshire, Crenshaw, Leimert Park, Baldwin Hills, Ladera Heights, Inglewood, Westchester, and Culver City" (Janice R. Littlejohn, "Magic Johnson's Starbucks, Review," *Los Angeles Times*, special to the edition, January 8, 2004, http://www.calendarlive.com/nightlife/clubs/99640,2,3729448.location (accessed March 1, 2009). I spent time observing the social interactions at this Starbucks and the TGI Friday's next door, and found the area to be a major public space to meet and talk with others in the community. The atmosphere was friendly, and it was quite easy to sit down and strike up a conversation with strangers or join a discussion overheard at another table. The café was a place where individuals go to "see and be seen."

5. This research was supported by the Ralph J. Bunche Center for African American Studies at UCLA, UCLA Resource Center for Minority Aging Research/Center for Health Improvement of Minority Ederly (RCMAR/CHIME) at the David Geffen School for Medicine under NIH/NIA Grant P30AG021684. I thank Walter Tucker for his research assistance on the project and Yardenna Aaron for sharing her insights on the black LGBT community in Los Angeles.

6. Dang and Frazer, "Black Same-Sex Households in the United States."

7. Gates, Lau, and Sears, "Race and Ethnicity of Same-Sex Couples"; Dang and Frazer, "Black Same-Sex Households in the United States."

8. Gary Gates, unpublished raw data from the 2007 California Health Interview Survey (CHIS) tabulated on March 23, 2009.

9. Gates, Lau, and Sears, "Race and Ethnicity of Same-Sex Couples."

10. Gates, unpublished raw data, March 23, 2009.

11. In parking lots at venues for black lesbian-themed events, I have seen the occasional rainbow lei hung around the rearview mirror of women's cars, or stuffed animals in the colors of the rainbow displayed along back windshields.

12. The Catch One nightclub and related businesses owned by Jewel Thais-Williams were important exceptions. The Catch opened in 1972 as the country's first black lesbian and gay disco. At the time of this study, it was much more than a nightclub. With its three levels and various enclosed spaces, it was the primary center of black gay community activism and social life in Los Angeles. Thais-Williams regularly allowed local black gay community groups to use the space for meetings and events, and also housed HIV and peer counseling services, poetry readings, discussion groups, dependency groups (like Alcoholics Anonymous), and other programs and services with no or minimal charge.

13. In Herek and Capitanio's study ("Black Heterosexuals' Attitudes"), whites held similarly negative attitudes toward gay sexuality as their black counterparts. Sixty-nine and 65 percent of whites, respectively, agreed with these two statements.

14. Gates, Lau, and Sears, "Race and Ethnicity of Same-Sex Couples."

15. Cohen, *The Boundaries of Blackness*, 9.

16. Moore, "Invisible Families."

17. D'Emilio, *Sexual Politics, Sexual Communities.*

18. Dawson, *Black Visions.*

19. See chap. 15 for a detailed account of employment discrimination against blacks in Los Angeles.

20. Tolnay and Eichenlaub, "Inequality in the West"; D. Johnson and Campbell, *Black Migration in America.*

21. Moore, "Invisible Families."

22. Interview by author, Los Angeles, Calif., December 3, 2008.

23. Comstock, *A Whosoever Church*, 76.

24. The forum was called "It's a Black Thang: The Black LGBT Vote '08."

25. Posting to discussion forum, November 7, 2008, http://www.facebook.com.

26. Pseudonym.

27. This figure is lower than the number of incidents reported by the National Coalition of Anti-Violence Programs ("Anti-Lesbian, Gay, Bisexual and Transgender Violence").

28. Stotzer, "Gender Identity and Hate Crimes."

29. See Stotzer, "Gender Identity and Hate Crimes" and National Coalition of Anti-Violence Programs, "Anti-Lesbian, Gay, Bisexual and Transgender Violence."

30. Pseudonym.

31. Interview by author, Los Angeles, Calif., January 23, 2009.

32. Dawson, *Black Visions.*

33. Interview by author, Los Angeles, Calif., January 25, 2009.

34. McQueeney's ("'We Are God's Children, Y'all'") study of gay and lesbian participation in a southern black church uses the concept of "oppositional identity work" to explain how its research participants managed to maintain Christian identities while simultaneously having openly gay identities in the South. They were able to successfully challenge homosexual stigma while creating strong identities around their Christianity by "transforming discrediting identities into crediting ones and redefining those identities so they can be seen as indexes of noble rather than flawed character"(152). They moralized sexuality to challenge homophobia. This practice was carried out in the Los Angeles march.

35. Pastor Edward Smith of the Zoe Christian Fellowship Church, Whittier, California. An excerpt from his sermon regarding Proposition 8 before the election, October 26, 2008.

36. The study oversampled black, Latino, and Asian American voters. The survey was limited to those who reported voting in the November 4 general election, and the data were weighted to represent the characteristics of California voters.

37. Egan and Sherrill, "California's Proposition 8," 11.

38. Ellingson, Tebbe, Van Haitsma, and Laumann, "Religion and the Politics of Sexuality."

39. Griffin, *Their Own Receive Them Not*, 145.

40. Pseudonym.

41. Martin, *Beyond Christianity*.

42. Agape International Spiritual Center, "Welcome to Agape Live," http://www.agapelive.com.

43. Pseudonym.

44. Martin, *Beyond Christianity*.

45. I do not know whether these early leaders directly embraced openly gay people in their ministries.

46. Washington, *Black Sects and Cults*; Baer and Singer, *African-American Religion in the Twentieth Century*.

47. Martin, *Beyond Christianity*, 45.

48. Pseudonym.

49. Pattillo, *Black on the Block*.

Part 3

||||||||||||||||||||||||||||||||||||||||||||||||||

Image

Sometimes I get bored riding down the beautiful streets of L.A. I know it sounds crazy, but I just want to go to New York and see people suffer.

—Donna Summers

Relative calm is expected in South Central Los Angeles for the next several weeks, as looters stay home and try to program their new VCRs.

—*Saturday Night Live,* "Weekend Update"

Chapter 8

||||||||||||||||||||||||||||||||||||||||||||||||||||||

Looking for the 'Hood and Finding Community
South Central, Race, and Media

Dionne Bennett

"This is the worst neighborhood in Los Angeles?!" my friend shouted as we drove through Watts. In the mid-1990s, I took a visiting friend on my own political tour to show her some of the race and class segregation that quietly divides Los Angeles. We began in Bel Air and ended in Watts. She had seen John Singleton's *Boyz N the Hood*[1] (see fig. 8.1) and other films that claimed to authentically represent blacks in South Central Los Angeles.

As we traveled through the area, I reminded her that Watts was considered by many to be one of the worst neighborhoods in the country. When we arrived in Watts, she laughed, noting how lovely the houses were. We watched elderly black men and women tend small but well-kept gardens and black children play on their bicycles. I explained that we were looking at black- and Latino-owned homes that in many cases belonged to families who had resided in the community for decades. Watts looked not just normal but attractive and intimate, the kind of black community for which privileged blacks of our generation often longed. I was relieved that an outsider confirmed my long-held, positive view of the undervalued area.

We did not miss the challenges facing Watts. We discussed the complex history of the area, the disturbing signs of economic neglect, the drugs and gang violence. We noted that all neighborhoods, especially economically distressed ones, take on a different character at night. We addressed the ugly race and class politics of American cities and how South Central

Figure 8.1. *Boyz N the Hood* movie poster. (*Boyz N the Hood* © 1991, 1992. Columbia Pictures Industries, Inc., All Rights Reserved, Courtesy of Columbia Pictures.)

had not been spared. Yet, we witnessed cultural beauty in South Central that should not be ignored or abandoned.

South Central: From Space to Stereotype

Media representations of South Central have exaggerated, racialized, and distorted the social ills of the area and constructed Black Los Angeles as a site of grotesque cultural pathology.[2] These representations have simultaneously erased the overall cultural complexity and diversity of South Central in terms of race, ethnicity, class, gender, and age so that South Central becomes stereotyped as poor, male, young, and black, when the reality tells a richer, more complex story.

South Central has never merely existed; it has been invented and imagined, erased and resurrected through an intersection of competing names, narratives, images, and geographic spaces, some real and some merely represented. While there are various versions of how the term "South Central" came to describe the region,[3] the term was officially used in the McCone Commission Report, a document that has been criticized for its superficial discussion of the complex events that shaped the Watts riots of 1965.[4] The McCone Commission was formed by California governor Edmund Brown after the uprisings to analyze the event and make recommendations to the government. South Los Angeles residents who resided in the area prior to Watts have noted that the term "South Central" was not used in popular discourse until after the riots.[5]

The 1992 uprisings served as another significant event in the reputation of South Central, which branded the area and subsequently, because of the media coverage of the event, blacks in general.[6] The uprisings occurred in response to the acquittal of four Los Angeles police officers accused in the violent beating of motorist Rodney King after a traffic stop.[7] On the first day, April 29, 1992, conflict erupted at the intersection of Florence Avenue and Normandie Avenue, located in the South Central area, and included an infamous attack by black men on white motorist Reginald Denny. Even though Denny was rescued by black bystanders, their heroic role in the incident is rarely reported. South Central in general, and Florence and Normandie in particular, became indelibly associated with black violence. Although looting, arson, violence, and destruction of property occurred in various parts of the city and involved people of diverse ethnicities, news media overwhelmingly characterized the participants as blacks and referred to the location of the uprisings as South Central Los Angeles.[8] By the end of the twentieth century, South Central was used in such a relentlessly racialized manner that, in defiance of conventional spatial logic, it ultimately came to apply to any place in the city where blacks resided in significant numbers.[9]

Media images of South Central inspire particularly intense forms of interpretive ambivalence for black audiences, as these images carry the added cultural burden of often representing not only South Central Los Angeles but all of Black America. The geographic proximity of South Los

Angeles to the entertainment industries based in the other parts of the city have made South Los Angeles an accessible and relatively inexpensive symbol, or stand-in, for urban black communities nationwide. Many media projects featuring black artists operate on small budgets, so the financial expediency of the South Los Angeles location, its nearness to the talent, financing, and production resources of one the world's largest entertainment centers cannot be overstated. This geographic coincidence has combined with the global audience's cultural, political, and historical fascination with South Central Los Angeles—one that was initiated by the Watts riots, sustained by the 1992 Los Angeles uprisings and the Los Angeles–based hip-hop culture, and exploited by various mass media—to turn South Central into one of the entertainment industry's favorite and most frequently portrayed spatial characters.

Media representations of South Central engage in the rhetoric of social realism and urban authenticity that has, to some degree, been an enduring characteristic of national black cultural production for centuries.[10] Scholars of black history and culture have examined and named this phenomenon a "rhetoric of the 'real thing,'"[11] or "the problem of authenticity."[12] These conceptions and their creators all explore the degree to which black representations, from eighteenth-century slave narratives to twenty-first-century music videos, have been measured primarily by the degree to which they can successfully claim to be "authentic" or "real" representations of black experience. Indeed, in the 1980s Robert Townsend's comedy *Hollywood Shuffle*[13] examined the stereotypes black actors are compelled to embody in an effort to represent "authentic" black characters (see chap. 9).

Authenticity claims can be powerful and compelling. Authors of slave narratives, for example, depended on claims of realism, often endorsed by white abolitionists, in order to present their narratives as representative of the brutal dehumanization of the institution of slavery and as justification for social and legal action.[14] Contemporary claims of authenticity, however, often lack the moral motivations of these earlier expressions.

The construction of "authentic blackness" in American popular culture is the result of a complex negotiation of contemptuous, stereotyping representations and compelling cultural recognition.[15] The authenticity of black images is often evaluated as much in terms of how *places* are represented as how *people* are represented. "Authentic" black characters in a narrative film, television program, or book must symbolize entire communities rather than individual identities. In order to do this, these "authentic" blacks must be observed in equally "authentic" places and contexts, often designated as urban and described in terms such as "the 'hood," "the ghetto," the "inner city." For example, employing the term "urban" to describe lucrative and segregated media markets—as in "urban cinema," "urban music," and "urban fiction"—is much more than a neutral designation of space. Instead, it constitutes a racial euphemism for the place where blacks can be found in their "real," "authentic," or "natural" environments, even when those environments have usually been carefully constructed by the media through very "unnatural" means. It is within this complex discourse of the recognizable and the sometimes reprehensible pantheon of representations, that we find media images of South Central.

Sweet South Central's Baadasssss Images

Media images of South Central Los Angeles are numerous, diverse, and ultimately complex. However, many of the images can be analyzed in terms of how they represent and perpetuate at least two prevailing discourses about South Central. One is that of South Central as "glamorous ghetto," a dangerous urban jungle, which is frightening and fascinating, pathological but preternaturally cool. The other is that of South Central as "hilarious home-place," a close-knit, black, working-class community where economic and social challenges can be cheerfully confronted with a combination of jokes and high jinks.

Both discourses intersect with discourses of authentic blackness. Both are presented as providing a rare window on the dangers and delights of "real" black urban life, and both sustain political ideologies that ultimately undermine blacks. The "glamorous ghetto" perpetuates the ideology that scary black people are solely responsible for their terrible social troubles. Therefore, the social, political, and economic challenges of the blacks who are *not* on television or in films need not be addressed in a serious manner. Images of the "hilarious home-place" perpetuate the ideology that black life is one big party, that black people are tons of fun, and their social troubles aren't so terrible after all—in fact "they" are just like "us" except for the racism, the poverty, the substandard schools, the disappearing jobs, and the decaying social infrastructure of their communities. Again, this creates the belief that the social, political, and economic challenges of the blacks who are *not* on television or in films need not be addressed in a serious manner.[16]

In the 1970s, the image of South Central as "hilarious home-place" was featured primarily in television programs such as *Sanford and Son*[17] and *What's Happening.*[18] *Sanford and Son* (see fig. 8.2) was based on a British comedy but owed as much to the *Amos 'n' Andy* radio and television programs as its official source material. It featured one of the world's bluest comedians, Redd Foxx as Fred Sanford, a harmless curmudgeon facing the challenges of being a father to his adult son and running a junk business in Watts.

Inspired by the film *Cooley High,*[19] *What's Happening* (see fig. 8.3) was South Central's answer to the television show *Good Times,*[20] which was set in the Chicago projects. *What's Happening* was the story of three black high school students who had fun and got into innocent trouble. The only family consistently portrayed was that of the character Roger, who along with his sassy younger sister, Dee, was being raised by a single mother.

The South Central of *Sanford and Son* and *What's Happening* is full of silly but sweet characters whose problems could all be resolved in thirty minutes. The South Central of these 1970s situation comedies is a racially segregated community: white people may visit the characters, but the

Figure 8.2. *Sanford and Son* (Season 1), Redd Foxx (Fred G. Sanford) on left and Demond Wilson (Lamont Grady Sanford) on right. (*Sanford and Son* © ELP Communications, Inc., courtesy Sony Pictures Television.)

Figure 8.3. *What's Happening!* (Season 1), Fred Berry
(Fred "Rerun" Stubbs), Ernest Thomas (Roger "Raj"
Thomas), Haywood Nelson (Dwayne Nelson) (from left
to right). ("What's Happening! © ELP Communications,
Inc., courtesy Sony Pictures Television.)

characters rarely leave South Central to visit them. This South Central is
nonthreatening, racially isolated, and relentlessly charming.

In the 1990s, one television program that attempted to represent working-class people in South Central named itself after the area that it struggled to depict in a complex and compassionate manner. The short-lived
sitcom *South Central*[21] featured a working-class family and attempted to
balance a comedic tone with a thoughtful engagement of complex social
issues like gangs and violence. The program lasted only one season, and
most future sitcoms in the area focused on more privileged families and
less serious themes.[22]

The creator of *South Central*, Ralph R. Farquhar, based his next situation comedy, *Moesha*[23] in Leimert Park—a location often described as being in South Central that had become the cultural center of Black Los Angeles by the end of the twentieth century (see chap. 2). *Moesha* focused on the family of a middle-class black teen girl and inspired the spin-off *The Parkers*.[24] In 2007 the Nickelodeon program *Just Jordan*[25] featured a teenage boy who moves to South Central Los Angeles from Arkansas. Claiming that Jordan is "dreamin' and schemin' and payin' the price," the program attempted to benefit from the multiracial and cross-class impact of hip-hop culture.

It should be noted that in the late 1990s and early twenty-first century, a number of black sitcoms emerged that were set in Black Los Angeles communities, but they rarely associated their narratives with South Central.[26] Most of the characters were middle-class blacks who lived in Los Angeles communities that were often undefined or did not play a meaningful role in their narratives. Relationships outside of family were defined by work, school, leisure, and romance, rather than connections to a space-based community. *The Fresh Prince of Bel Air*,[27] one of the most successful sitcoms ever made about blacks in Los Angeles, ignored South Central almost completely, basing its action in a wealthy white suburb and exploring class conflicts within a household of elite blacks and their working-class Philadelphia-born cousin. When viewed alongside mediated images of South Central, these shows—like the juxtaposition of Baldwin Hills and "The Jungle" in the Introduction (see chaps. 6 and 7)—became exceptions that proved the racial rule.

Several films of the 1990s and early twenty-first century continued to depict South Central Los Angeles as a warm and "hilarious home-place." However, these films, like the television programs of the period, increasingly focused on black middle-class areas within or near South Central and on personal rather than political issues. Meanwhile, other films like *Friday*,[28] featuring rapper Ice Cube and comedian Chris Tucker, would resurrect some aspects of the South Central witnessed in the harmless sitcoms. But the South Central of these films was ultimately a different South Central from the former one. It was a South Central filled with the urban dangers that continued to dominate media representations of the area—despite the humorous situations characters got themselves into there. The problematic ease with which media discourses uncritically shifted back and forth between the history and the fantasy of South Central can be seen in this article from the *New York Times,* which reports on the renaming of the area:[29]

> The council voted unanimously today [April 9, 2003] to rename this 16-square-mile district South Los Angeles as part of an effort to erase the image of South-Central as the scene of race riots in 1965 and 1992 and the setting for films featuring gangs and drug dealers like *"Training Day,"* *"Colors"* and *"Boyz N the Hood."*[30]

At no point in the article does the author seriously distinguish the reality of the uprisings afflicting the area from the *fictional* films mentioned.

The historical events that took place and the fictional narratives that have been set in South Central are engaged in a dynamic but unresolved critical dialogue that represents conflicting and competing ideologies about blacks and how they are and should be represented in the mass media. The failure to recognize that these discourses were in conflict, that a week of civil unrest is not the equivalent of a two-hour film about a sociopath, mutes the complexity of this instructive dialogue about how black-lived experiences can either be revealed or repressed by the mass media's rhetoric of urban realism.

In 1971 Melvin Van Peebles's *Sweet Sweetback's Baadasssss Song*[31] would both redefine black popular culture and the future of racially diverse American urban cinema.[32] The film presented black urban spaces as "glamorous ghettos" but did so to pursue a very different agenda. *Sweetback* was at the vanguard of black cinema: it initiated the blaxploitation film genre and contributed to a global avant-garde film movement that fully engaged the political and cultural spirit of a generation of young activists and moviegoers.

Sweetback also shaped representations of South Central in enduring and sometimes problematic ways. The independent film featured a predominantly black cast, a production team made up of people of color, and was dedicated to "Brothers and Sisters who have had enough of the Man." Melvin Van Peebles directed, wrote, produced, edited, scored, and starred in the film, which he made for an estimated $500,000, including a $50,000 loan from black actor Bill Cosby. The film grossed more than $10 million and the next year became the top-grossing independent film of 1972.

Sweetback engaged the same themes of police brutality and political resistance that had shaped the Watts riots of 1965. The character Sweetback, named for his extraordinary lovemaking skills, is a black pimp and sex performer at a South Central brothel, where he was raised by prostitutes. When Sweetback is arrested on false charges and witnesses two police officers brutally attacking a young black male revolutionary, he becomes radicalized. He beats—and kills—the cops. When he is captured, he breaks free during a riot that references Watts. With the help of various members of the black South Central community, white Hell's Angels, and generous women sex partners of all races, Sweetback ultimately crosses the border to Mexico and to freedom. At the end of the film, the words appear "A baadasssss nigger is coming to collect some dues," indicating that Sweetback plans to return to Los Angeles someday to continue ruling his kingdom of the streets.

Sweetback earned its reputation for its realism. Van Peebles performed real sex scenes in the film, contracted gonorrhea, filed for health benefits from the directors guild, and used the money to help finance finishing the picture. Van Peebles, unable to afford a stunt double, performed his own difficult stunts, although he had not been trained to do so. And in a case of life imitating art, production crew members were harassed and arrested by the police, and Van Peebles got into an armed confrontation with a real Hell's Angel who had grown tired of shooting his scenes. The Black Panther Party made the film required viewing for all members,[33] and Huey Newton declared it a "great revolutionary document."[34]

Despite the film's hard-earned authenticity credentials, Van Peebles, who was a trained avant-garde narrative filmmaker, recognized it as cultural and political fantasy and described it as such when it was released:

> All the films about black people up to now have been told through the eyes of the Anglo Saxon majority—in their rhythm, and speech and pace. . . . I want white people to approach *Sweetback* the way they do an Italian or Japanese film. They have to understand *our* culture. . . . In my film, the black audience finally gets to see some of their fantasies acted out.[35]

Van Peebles consciously constructed the film as representative of black cultural fantasies and political desires rather than as a document of their sociopolitical realities.

Despite the film's problematic elements, young black audiences responded to the avant-garde film style, the hypermasculine performance of action and violence, the sexual charisma and conquests of the black folk hero, the political themes of the film, and the idea that, at least in fictional films, a brother could beat "the man." Sweetback's Los Angeles may have been an urban jungle, but Sweetback was the undisputed king. Issues that confronted South Central—such as police brutality, racial conflict, economic exploitation, poverty, and the demand for an alternate economy in the absence of other opportunities—were woven into the film's narrative and presented as legitimate everyday social concerns for blacks, even if they were engaged by a fantastical urban superhero.

Unfortunately, many of the urban films inspired by *Sweetback's* success retained only the graphic sex, sexism, and violence along with the urban setting. Collectively labeled as blaxploitation films, many were produced by Hollywood studios and by individuals of various backgrounds who wanted *Sweetback's* success without the responsibilities of its social message. Thus, many abandoned the themes of political resistance and cultural authority that made *Sweetback* so inspiring to black audiences.

The politics of place were a central feature of the blaxploitation films. Many of the films were set in unnamed urban locations but were clearly shot on the streets of South Central Los Angeles. In this way, the specific culture and history of South Central was erased, and South Central was transformed into the "generic ghetto" of Black America. *Sweetback* did not merely serve as a foundation for characters, themes, and plots; it also helped turn South Central into one of the most significant settings in American cinema.

Many of the blaxploitation films of the era were produced by Los Angeles–based companies, distributed by major studios, and used South Central as both an urban setting and a plot device. *Black Gunn*,[36] starring Jim Brown, was released by Columbia Pictures and was set in Los Angeles. It featured infighting between black revolutionaries that was inspired by the American government's COINTELPRO operation. This was an apparent reference to COINTELPRO's national assault on black activists, but also may have been invoking the 1969 murders of Los Angeles Black Panther Party members Bunchy Carter and John Huggins on the University of California, Los Angeles (UCLA) campus, which many believed occurred under similar circumstances.[37]

Sweetback glorified the very black men—pimps and drug dealers— who had been most demonized in mainstream American discourse.[38] The adulation of these characters in this and other blaxploitation films of the era was based in large part on the films' ability to both defy the racist dehumanization of white society and to master black urban territories. Yet, the driving goal of blaxploitation heroes often was to leave "the world of the ghetto" behind. It is this theme of "escape from the ghetto," along with the character of the glamorous urban outlaw, which we see resurrected in the urban dramas of the 1990s.

Media Menace to South Central

When the formal Black Power movement of the 1960s and 1970s was dissolved, or some would argue destroyed,[39] the black film movement that had been inspired by it was also diminished. In the 1980s only a handful of black-themed films were produced, many by New York–based filmmaker Spike Lee. By the 1990s, however, there was a new wave of black filmmaking, as more than twenty films were released by black filmmakers in 1991 alone—an unprecedented number in film history.

Of the many black-directed films set in South Central in the 1990s, few became as symbolic of the area in the popular imagination as *Boyz N the Hood* and *Menace II Society*.[40] John Singleton's *Boyz* presented itself as a black coming-of-age tale in the spirit of a Los Angeles–based *Cooley High*. *Menace II Society*, produced by Allen and Albert Hughes, reproduced many of the themes of *Boyz N the Hood*—black masculinity, violence, revenge, and the desire to escape from South Central, once and for all. *Menace* shunned fictional pretensions, asserting as many authenticity claims as possible. Indeed, the promotional poster for the film stated, "This is the truth. This is what's real," above the film's title.

Demonstrating its reality claim, the first scene of *Menace* is an inversion of a tragic, historic South Central event. In *Menace*, a sixteen-year-old black male character named O-Dog gets into an argument with a Korean American grocer over a bottle of malt liquor. The scene ends with O-Dog shooting the grocer and his wife. In 1991 Latasha Harlins, a fifteen-year-old black girl was shot and killed by Soon Ja Du, an adult Korean American woman. Du had shot Harlins in a dispute over a bottle of orange juice that Harlins was attempting to purchase from the small grocery store owned by Du. Although Du claimed that Harlins was stealing the juice, Harlins had already left the juice on the counter and was leaving the store when she was killed, the money for the juice still in her hand. The Rodney King beating verdict is widely identified as the most immediate catalyst for the Los Angeles uprisings of 1992. However, the shooting of Harlins, and Du's relatively light sentence, were often cited as another factor for the anger and violence that erupted during the uprisings.[41] Du's store was destroyed during the 1992 unrest.

Just as *Sweetback* was, in some ways, a response to the Watts uprisings of 1965, *Menace* was a response to the Los Angeles uprisings of 1992. But while *Sweetback* engaged in a considered, albeit sensationalized, critique of the political circumstances that led to Watts, *Menace,* clinging to its claim that it was *representing* reality, often failed to critique it. *Menace's* authenticity claims constructed a problematic image of South Central and its inhabitants. The character of O-Dog has all of the characteristics of a sociopath, and the South Central neighborhoods the young characters inhabit constitute a nihilistic nightmare. These images are rarely relieved by redeeming qualities, nor is the context in which the characters and the neighborhoods are situated, as they are explained or explored. This is not, in and of itself, unusual or even problematic for a fictional film attempting to create an imagined world. However, by constructing these deeply pathologizing images of young black men and their South Central neighborhoods as "true" and "real," *Menace* argues that young black men and South Central Los Angeles are truly pathological—people and places for whom rational and thoughtful behavior is not merely difficult but, in fact, impossible. This leaves viewers of the film with the belief that South Central cannot be understood or restored; it must be abandoned.

Menace's version of South Central ignores the complexity of the area and negates the range of possible experiences blacks may have there. The movie *Training Day*[42] like *Boyz,* received multiple Academy Award nominations, earning Denzel Washington a Best Actor Oscar award for playing a sociopath, crack-head cop who turns South Central into his psychotic playground.

Training Day's success inspired more films about troubled cops and the people and politics of South Central. *Dark Blue*[43] examined the Los Angeles uprisings from the perspectives of white police officers. *Crash,*[44] which won the Academy Award for Best Film in 2004, was lauded for examining race relations in Los Angeles from diverse perspectives, with South Central serving as an important setting for tensions between characters and their confrontations with the law.

Street Kings[45] was directed by the white male screenwriter of *Training Day* who, like John Singleton, claimed to have spent his youth on the streets of South Central. *Street Kings* also explored the area as racialized criminal territory, similar to the television drama *Southland,*[46] and the film *Life is Hot in Cracktown*,[47] which examined the notorious South Central drug trade (see chap. 5).

This menacing model of South Central is the one most consistently reproduced in urban cinema of the 1990s and the early twenty-first century, spilling over into other forms of media representations. The image of South Central as a dangerous but glamorous ghetto had long since shifted from the large screen to the small, in the form of music videos. As urban films set in South Central were distributed throughout the world, they were joined by another cultural phenomenon that was associated with South Central: gangsta rap, which became one of the most popular music genres of the 1990s. Although the hip-hop music that emerged from Los Angeles during the period was significantly more critical and complex than the news media revealed, the music videos that accompanied the songs sustained the image of South Central as a menacing urban wasteland.[48]

The blaxploitation films of the 1970s were often derided for their violent and sexualized images of South Central Los Angeles and other black communities, while the urban film dramas of the 1990s were often critically acclaimed for their "authentic" portrayal of the area. However, films from both periods were cinematic constructions, rather than authentic representations of black life in South Central. Nonetheless, for much of the world the urban dramas of the 1990s, which displayed some of the most nightmarish and dehumanizing images of the area, were indelibly marked in the cultural imagination as the "real" South Central.

In the early twenty-first century, media images of South Central Los Angeles continued to label and limit African Americans. They were typically presented as authentic portrayals of Black Los Angeles, and were generalized to represent all black people in any urban place where blacks resided. These images usually omitted the educational, social, and economic diversity of blacks not only in South Central, but throughout Black Los Angeles and ultimately Black America. In film and television, countless "real," complex, and diverse stories of Black Los Angeles have yet to be told.

NOTES

1. Directed by John Singleton (USA: Both Inc., Columbia Pictures Corporation, 1991). The film was also written by Singleton as a semi-autobiographical

story of a young man and his life in South Central. Singleton was nominated for an Academy Award for both Best Director and Best Original Screenplay, the youngest person ever nominated for Best Director and the first African American nominated for that award.

2. Kelley, *Yo' Mama's Disfunktional!*; Lott, *The Invention of Race.*

3. For example, one version maintains that "South Central" acquired its name from the black communities along South Central Avenue (see chap. 2).

4. California Governor's Commission on the Los Angeles Riots, "Violence in the City."

5. Jackson-Brown, "Media Coverage of South Central Los Angeles."

6. See Hunt (*Screening the Los Angeles "Riots"*) for a discussion of this media practice.

7. Ibid.

8. Ibid.

9. Although commonly referenced and depicted as a physical location in Los Angeles, South Central never had formalized, geographic boundaries.

10. For a more detailed discussion of urban authenticity, see chap. 9.

11. Lubiano, "'But Compared to What?'"

12. Kelley, *Yo' Mama's Disfunktional!*

13. Directed by Robert Townsend (USA: Goldwyn Entertainment Company, Conquering Unicorn Productions, 1987).

14. Foley, "History, Fiction, and the Ground Between."

15. Black stereotypes in contemporary media are often updated incarnations of centuries-old images of blacks. The "thug" is the urbanized version of the violent, hypersexual but seductively masculine "plantation buck," and the "ho" is the urbanized version of the evil, oversexed, treacherous but irresistibly desirable plantation Jezebel. The "buck," "Jezebel," "coon," "mammy," "ambitious mulatto," and the "white-identified tom" were immortalized in early American films like D. W. Griffith's film *The Birth of a Nation* (directed by D. W. Griffith, USA: Epoch Producing Corporation, David W. Griffith Corporation, 1915), but inhabited the American cultural imagination long before the age of cinema (Bogle, *Toms, Coons, Mulattoes, Mammies, and Bucks*).

16. See Hunt (*Channeling Blackness*) for a discussion of how these types of narratives have been used in popular media to reaffirm the reality of race in colorblind times.

17. NBC, 1972–77.

18. ABC, 1976–79.

19. Directed by Michael Schultz (USA: Cooley High Service Company, 1975). *Cooley High* was a comedy written by Eric Monte, a black sitcom writer, who based the script on his own teen experiences. The movie focuses on a group of black male friends during the end of their senior year in 1964 Chicago. It was included as one of the most important films on race by *TIME* film critic, Richard

Corliss ("The 25 Most Important Films on Race," *TIME*, February 4, 2008, http://www.time.com/time/specials/2007/article/0,28804,1709148_1709143_1709658,00.html (accessed April 27, 2009)).

20. CBS, 1974–79.

21. Fox, 1994.

22. Gray, *Watching Race*.

23. UPN, 1996–2001.

24. UPN, 1999–2004.

25. Nickelodeon, 2007, on air at time of printing.

26. Shows about blacks in Los Angeles included *Out All Night* (NBC, 1990–92), *In the House* (NBC and UPN, 1995–99), *The Jamie Foxx Show* (WB Network, 1996–2001), *The Bernie Mac Show* (Fox, 2001–06), *Girlfriends* (UPN and the CW, 2001–08), and the gay-themed *Noah's Arc* (Logo, 2004–06).

27. NBC, 1990–96.

28. Directed by F. Gary Gray (USA: Priority Films, New Line Cinema, Ghetto Bird Productions, 1995).

29. Increasingly disturbed by the negative associations inspired by the label "South Central," residents lobbied the city council to rename the area "South Los Angeles."

30. Calvin Sims, "In Los Angeles, It's South-Central No More," *New York Times*, April 10, 2003, New York ed., A18.

31. Directed by Melvin Van Peebles (USA: Yeah Inc., 1971).

32. *Shaft* (directed by Gordon Parks Jr., USA: Metro-Goldwyn-Mayer, Shaft Productions, 1971) and *Super Fly* (directed by Gordon Parks Jr., USA: Warner Bros., 1972) were also profoundly influenced by the success of *Sweet Sweetback's Baadasssss Song* and equally influential in shaping the blaxploitation film aesthetic. However, because these films were set in New York City, this chapter will remain focused on Van Peebles's film.

33. For further discussion on the Black Panthers in Los Angeles, see chap. 5.

34. Bogle, *Blacks in American Films and Television*, 212.

35. "Sweet Song of Success," *Newsweek*, June 21, 1971, 89, quoted in Jon Hartmann, "The Trope of Blaxploitation in Critical Responses to 'Sweetback'" *Film History* 6, no. 3 (Autumn 1994): 382–404.

36. Directed by Robert Hartford-Davis (Great Britain, USA: World Film Services Ltd., World Arts Media Group, Champion Production Company, Columbia Pictures Corporation, 1972).

37. Alex Alonso discusses the significance of COINTELPRO and the Campbell Hall shootings in chap. 5.

38. Critics of the blaxploitation genre cite the sexual objectification and marginalization of black women as problematic and enduring. In the media, South Central Los Angeles is a world frequently devoid of women unless being depicted

as having sex. This media depiction of women in South Central Los Angeles has continued long after the blaxploitation era ended.

39. See chap. 5 for Alonso's theory of planned government assault on the Black Power movement.

40. Directed by Albert Hughes and Allen Hughes (USA: New Line Cinema, 1993).

41. Hunt, *Screening the Los Angeles "Riots."*

42. Directed by Antoine Fuqua (USA, Australia: Warner Bros., Village Road-show Pictures, NPV Entertainment, Outlaw Productions, 2001).

43. Directed by Ron Shelton (United Germany, Great Britain, USA: IM Film-produktion und Vertriebs GmbH and Co KG, InterMedia Film Equities, United Artists, Alphaville Productions, Cosmic Pictures, 2002).

44. Directed by Paul Haggis (United Germany, USA, Australia: ApolloPro-Screen GmbH & Co. Filmproduktion KG, BlackFriar's Bridge, Harris Company, ApolloProScreen, Bull's Eye Entertainment, Arclight Films International Pty Ltd, Paul Haggis Productions, 2004).

45. Directed by David Ayer (USA: Twentieth Century Fox Film Corporation, Regency Entertainment (USA), Inc, Dune Entertainment III LLC, Monarchy En-terprises S.A.R.L., TCF Hungary Film Rights Exploitation Limited, 3 Arts Enter-tainment, Fox Searchlight Pictures, Regency Enterprises, Dune Entertainment III LLC, 2008).

46. NBC, 2009, on air at time of printing.

47. Directed by Buddy Giovinazzo (USA: Karmic Productions, Lodestar En-tertainment, Lightning Media (II), 2009).

48. Quinn, *Nuthin' but a "G" Thang.*

Chapter 9

||||||||||||||||||||||||||||||||||||||||||||||||||||||||

Playing "Ghetto"
Black Actors, Stereotypes, and Authenticity

Nancy Wang Yuen

As I sit across from a beautiful black woman with long, flowing hair, I feel like I am in the presence of a movie star. Although she is not a recognizable celebrity, Vivian's melodious voice and elegant movements underscore her background as a dancer and actor. Donning a red cashmere sweater, she tells me how her privileged upbringing has shaped her acting sensibilities despite the stereotyped, "South Central ghetto" roles she is typically offered to play. Vivian is one of many black actors in Los Angeles whose life experience bears no resemblance to the South Central stereotyped roles typically available to black actors. Vivian, like most black actors, prefers not to play such roles, distancing herself from these roles and challenging them whenever possible, while also struggling to make a decent living as a working black actor in Hollywood.

Vivian, like many of the thousands of other African American union actors in Los Angeles in the early 2000s, often found herself defined by and confined to an exceedingly narrow image of blackness. Mainstream media reinforced this image by exploiting the periodic violence and socioeconomic struggles in the region and using them to paint a picture of South Central as the prototypical "ghetto,"[1] conflating the real and the fictional (see chap. 8).

In standard usage, the term "ghetto" refers to "a quarter of a city in which members of a minority group live especially because of social, legal, or economic pressure."[2] But in common parlance, the term has come to signify something more: it has come to define a group of people and how they behave. That is, the term has been ascribed to lower- and underclass blacks, the people popularly associated with prototypical ghettos like South Central Los Angeles. Ironically, the South Central of the 1940s was comparable to the Harlem of 1920s and '30s, during the renaissance period—an epicenter of arts and culture for Black Los Angeles (see chap. 2).[3] But in the 1950s and '60s, with the emigration of more affluent blacks from the area and a general malaise followed by uprisings and gang proliferation, the name "South Central" became associated with poverty-stricken and violent black urban life.[4] The negative connotations associated with South Central persisted into the 1990s, amplified by the 1992 Los Angeles "riots." One Seattle newspaper went as far as personifying South Central as a violent being, describing it as "[h]aving torn itself apart in an agony of looting and burning, South-Central Los Angeles was a place of anger, sadness and futility."[5] With few alternative images to counterbalance "ghetto" portrayals of blacks, South Central became anywhere that significant numbers of black people lived, obliterating diversity in class, culture, and ethnicity within black communities.

Film and television usage of South Central as a backdrop for popular urban black comedies and dramas such as *Boyz N the Hood*, *Friday*, and *Training Day* further established the area as *the* setting for black urban malaise within the popular imagination (see chap. 8). Such images not only affect blacks living in Los Angeles but also those throughout the United States and beyond.[6] The idea of South Central became the lens through which much of the outside world understood blackness in the late twentieth and early twenty-first century. And this development became a source of ongoing personal struggle for black actors hoping to work in Hollywood.

For black professional actors, the reality of everyday life in Los Angeles intersected with fictionalized portraits of Black Los Angeles in contradictory and complex ways. Professionally, black actors were often typecast into "ghetto" roles set in South Central. Such roles were characterized by alternative speech patterns and slang associated with "Ebonics" (a stereotyped form of speech attributed to "ghetto" blacks), poverty, hypersexuality, and bouts of unpredictable violence and anger. For black men, this often took the form of gangbanger and drug-user roles. Indeed, one of the black male actors I interviewed described being typecast as a "crack head" and the "angry black man" with "weapons." Black female actors faced similar typecasting, as epitomized by the "no-nonsense black woman" role with her pseudo-masculine, overbearing attitude or the silly, dimwitted but eternally reliable "mammy" role. This latter role, of course, in 1940 won Hattie McDaniel the first ever Oscar awarded to a black actor for her part in *Gone with the Wind*;[7] it also relegated her to a lifetime of playing such roles.

In my work to discover how South Central "ghetto" behavior became the standard for the African American experience in television and film, I interviewed thirty black actors,[8] who consistently pointed to the profound degree of racial segregation in Los Angeles, both in and out of the entertainment industry, as a key factor that explained why the images were so distorted. I secured my sample through a variety of channels—from industry personnel I met while working on previous projects, personal networks, and snowball sampling to obtain the remaining informants. The single-session interviews lasted between forty-five minutes and two hours. These interviews demonstrate that the persistent stereotyping black actors faced not only hampered their ability to work but also forced them to accept, adapt to, or challenge the stereotypes while still confronting the real-life need to earn a living and achieve artistic and career goals. Meanwhile, my informants not only defied the ghetto stereotype as individuals but also as a collective—representing a diverse group with different class, ethnicity, and personal history backgrounds.

Racial Segregation and Images of Blackness

In the first decade of the 2000s, many black professional actors living in Los Angeles drew a link between the lack of authentic black characters in Hollywood and racial segregation in the Greater Los Angeles region. They cited how white writers, who dominate Hollywood, created black characters that are inauthentic. In 2005 blacks accounted for only 4.4 percent of all employed Writers Guild of America (WGA) writers, while whites made up 91.8 percent of the total.[9] With the limited number of people of color hired to write for film and television in Hollywood, white writers, particularly males, were responsible for most of the Hollywood images in circulation invoking blackness. These writers, who lived and wrote geographically and experientially far from Black Los Angeles, routinely fell back on the stereotypes learned from watching other film and television portrayals of blacks, most typically those originating in preconceived notions about South Central.

For example, Suzanne, a black female actor in her fifties, ascribed the stereotyping of black women in film and television to racial segregation in Los Angeles:

> Most of the people creating in LA don't go out of their bubbles. That's why they want the "no-nonsense black woman." It's because they have not gotten around to see—they've not had the conversations on the phone that I have with my [black] girlfriends. . . . They don't know what we are like because they live in a bubble in a segregated city.

In this study, it appeared to be a principal belief among black actors like Suzanne that white writers do not have the ability to write authentic black characters due to lack of contact and exposure, and most cited the lack of contact between racial groups within segregated Los Angeles. Similarly, Cassie, a forty-five-year-old black female actor, attributed the overrepresentation of white roles and under-representation of black ones to white writers' lack of exposure to and consequent knowledge about blacks:

> Well, the white actors get more [roles], because there's white writers writing it. See, you can't say they're prejudiced or nothing because they're white—white to white people. They're white, that's what they know . . . I mean, how many producers know black people, really? They don't hang out on Crenshaw.

Cassie believed two problems lead to fewer roles written for black actors—the "lopsided" preference of white writers over black writers in Hollywood and the lack of knowledge surrounding black people among "white producers" who "don't hang out on Crenshaw."[10] This perspective is corroborated by black screenwriters such as Teri Brown-Jackson, who pointed out a double standard limited the employment opportunities of black writers in Hollywood:

> There is an assumption that African American writers have too narrow a voice and can't reach a broad audience . . . non-black writers are hired for shows across the board, including African American shows.[11]

One black writer, Kenneth Rance, who co-wrote *New in Town*,[12] a 2009 film starring Renee Zellweger that had a predominately white cast in a non-urban setting, described how producers often pigeonhole black writers because they believe black writers can only write stories having to do with "the hood":

> [O]ur lives and our stories don't just deal with hip-hop, rap music, the hood . . . gotta make that money, son. Dope, drugs. Those stories are so negative and so tragic! . . . [T]here's a stigmatism that we can't write and that our stories aren't as good . . . but we have the same amount of talent and ability to excel and achieve if we're afforded that opportunity.[13]

Consequently, most in my study felt that racial barriers for black writers created a situation where black characters routinely were written by white writers in a city where there is little meaningful contact between blacks and whites. This situation constrained the quantity and quality of roles written for and available to black actors. As a result, the stereotypes portrayed on screen often become solidified in the minds of viewers as truth—especially when the viewers' only contact with blacks was through film and television.

Justifying Ghetto

With limited role options for struggling actors, few actors had the luxury to simply pass up ghetto roles. As a result, many justified portraying such roles on the basis of personal and professional considerations. One actor, "Marlon," age thirty-eight, cited his personal biography:

> I tend to play a lot of broken—broken people you know and my first movie, I played a crackhead. After playing that character, many in the black community said that was degrading. You know "How can you do that?" But you know the Caucasians and others like, "Oh my god, you are a great actor." But people didn't really realize that my mother was on crack. I like playing gritty characters, I like showing the people reality. And sometimes the reality isn't pretty.

Although ghetto roles were often more fiction than fact, some actors infused such roles with personal authenticity based on their life experiences. As a result, these actors provided multi-dimensional images of South Central "ghetto" life based not on stereotypes but on their lived realities. Thus, in the face of critique from the "black community" for portraying a "degrading" "crackhead" character, Marlon justified his portrayal as a reflection of his very real, personal life. Other actors justified portraying a "ghetto" role on the basis of the degree of the stereotype and/ or on the target audience. Sheila, a black female actor in her forties, described what she felt was the difference between a "tastefully" done and not "tastefully" done ghetto role:

> I think it's just that each job is so much different, and you're dealing with different people, their different perceptions of how ghetto and how not-ghetto. . . . I think that there are some ways that it's done tastefully and some ways that it's not done tastefully. . . . I guess maybe for a show that is kind of in an urban setting, and all the characters are kind of, you know, more hip-hop, and it's geared towards a specific audience, then I can understand why we would have to come in and audition that way. But if it's like something where the character is being made fun of, and it's kind of a joke, and so they want you to be really over the top, because in the actual project, a group of kids are making fun of this girl . . . then for me that's kind of a little different. . . . You just have to take it one by one.

Given the prevalence of "ghetto" roles in Hollywood, actors had to sift through the good and bad roles if they wanted to work. For Shelia, what she considered a "tastefully done" hip-hop role may be set in an urban setting and geared toward a "specific audience" (presumably black); by contrast, a "non-tastefully done" role might be one in which the character is made fun of and is exaggerated in terms of stereotyped behavior. Many of the informants in the study felt that while some movies allowed for more nuanced and subversive interpretations of traditional black stereotypes (e.g., *Hollywood Shuffle*,[14] and *Bamboozled*[15]), others tended to perpetuate them (e.g., *Soul Plane*[16] and *Hustle and Flow*[17]).

Distancing Ghetto

The blanket stereotyping of blacks in fictional Hollywood effectively erased class diversity—and arguable ethnic diversity—within black communities. Though black actors came from different backgrounds—some had immigrant parents from African countries, island nations, and Latin American countries, while others came from all different regions in the

United States—Hollywood rarely created black characters that encompassed those variations. As a result, the black actors in my study experienced a great tension between their personal identities and the South Central "ghetto" type they were expected to play, which was typically based on a stereotype-ridden, lower-class urban myth. To deal with this tension, some black actors distanced their personal identities from the roles they played, from audition to final portrayal. For example, Vivian, contrasted her real-life, middle-class identity from the ghetto role for which she auditioned:

> I remember I auditioned for a movie that took place in the 'hood. And my acting, my audition was beautiful. But I didn't get it. I said, "I want to know why I didn't get a call back." . . . They said, "Tell Vivian that when she comes back in she's got to be ghetto. Extremely ghetto, organically ghetto, can't see that she is putting it on." . . . I thought that she was trying to say that there was an innate sophistication and elegance about me, that's not associated with the 'hood. . . . That's just me, you know. I grew up in a black sophisticated, middle-class family. And I went to boarding school. And I went to college. And I was around beautiful things.

Even when actors portrayed "ghetto" roles, they continued to distance their real-life personas from that of their characters. Henry—a thin, mild-mannered, forty-seven-year-old man with wire-rimmed glasses and wearing a baby-blue, short-sleeved dress shirt—described how he and another "non-urban" black actor found themselves portraying gang members and the personal tension it caused:

> There was a riot scene where a black guy got shot and the neighborhood comes out and they're protesting in front of the precinct and they put me and this other guy in the front of the crowd. We didn't have any lines. She [the director] said, "Just yell out whatever you wanna yell out." And I remember at that time I went and put on my best 'hood clothes, you know, and I had my cap turned around backwards, and this guy that was standing next to me, I can't remember his real name, but it was like Aristotle. . . . And we were just joking about the fact that the two of us, the most non-urban guys that they could find, you know, besides the extras around us. We were scared of these guys, because I think they had real gang members doing the extras. And here we are out in front. . . . Yeah, that was hysterical.

The black actors I interviewed coped with the inundation of ghetto roles in Hollywood by distancing their lived experience from the fictional ghetto roles in Hollywood. They discussed their middle-class upbringing, labeled themselves as "non-urban" or "suburban," and contrasted themselves with actors or actual gang members, whom they thought were better suited to portray ghetto roles. These methods of distancing helped black actors to maintain a more authentic identity separate from the black stereotypes proliferating in Hollywood and society.

Challenging Ghetto

From time to time, black actors also challenged the stereotypical portrayals of "ghetto" roles in their performances. They did so by altering the behavior and speech patterns of the characters, and even by venturing outside of Hollywood to secure non-stereotyped roles. Ed, a sixty-five-year-old actor, described how he attempted to challenge one specific "ghetto" role, that of the black "pimp."

> I didn't play the "pimp" thing. . . . It wasn't necessary to go to that stereotypical—put your hand behind your back and hump your shoulders and wear the big hat and go through the whole, you know, slang thing—to pull this off. So the director allowed me to not go there. Not do that . . . to do it my way.

Similarly, Reyna, a fifty-eight-year-old actor, described how she challenged the "ghetto" dialect on set:

> I was a bank manager and they have this character saying "ain't," no final G's on her words and what have you. And I'm like, "Wait a minute. She's a bank manager." So I just went through the script and I changed all the "ain'ts" to "aren'ts" and put final G's on . . . and I was getting away with it until the director said, "Wait a minute. You left out a section there." And I said, "Yes, I don't believe the character would say that." And at that moment, [the star] happened to be passing by and she said, "Is there a problem?" and I shared with her what it was, and she said, "Ah, too street." I said, "Exactly." She said, "Oh, we'll change it." And the director stood there, and there was nothing he could do, because she was the star of the show, so he had to allow me to do that.

Shirelle, a thirty-two-year-old actor, described how she changed a "street hoochy momma" role into a more "down-home girl:"

> The role was hoochy momma. . . . But you read the script and it was more a script about stereotypes and relinquishing them. And though she was a hoochy momma, I played her as this woman that has her own business, she's running things, and she's very aware of her body and herself and very in tune to her surroundings. Instead of the street hoochy momma . . . in the script, I brought a more classier, down-home girl thing to the role, which I thought worked.

Besides changing roles through their performances on set, many actors attempted to escape the stereotyped casting practices by venturing outside Hollywood into theatre and independent films. Queena, a thirty-five-year-old actor, described how being typed as "tough" and "street" had driven her to seek non-traditional roles outside of Hollywood:

> You walk into a room, and the first thing an agent or a cast director sees is the color of your skin. And right away, they want to sort of put you in a box. And I had an experience where I had a meeting with an agent. I haven't been in the office for even a minute. . . He didn't see me beyond stereotyped roles . . . the tough street type . . . He didn't know that I had actually played leading lady roles. . . . So then I realized that I have to write my own roles, or get into student films, or theater where I'm allowed to play a non-traditional stereotypical role—so that I'm an actor, and not just a black actress that plays black roles.

In my study, the black actors came from a variety of backgrounds —most middle-class, some with immigrant parents, and all would have preferred to avoid playing stereotyped ghetto roles. However, financial constraints often necessitated taking roles that went against the actor's desire to play them. This created an ongoing tension between the need to work for financial reasons and one's self-esteem. Consistently having to play Hollywood roles that might induce shame and other feelings of guilt as a result caused some of the black actors in my study to draw strict distinctions between the ghetto stereotypes they have to audition for and portray and who they are outside of Hollywood. To salvage their everyday lived identities, the black actors in the study developed creative coping strategies that distanced, challenged and avoided stereotyped ghetto roles. As one fifty-eight-year-old male actor described the conflict:

> I work in television . . . a lot of times it's for roof money, to fix my roof on my house, right? What I do, I don't care if anybody sees it. It's not something I'm proud of. It's not something I'm ashamed of. But it's not something that I'm gonna call my mom up and my dad and all my friends and say, "I'm on television. This is really good. You should watch it." Not really. If they see it, fine. But mostly it's in this [theater], I call people up and I say, "Come see this. This is good. The play is hot."

Struggling Against Type

In the early 2000s, black roles in Hollywood were synonymous with "ghetto," with South Central the fictional epicenter of the black experience. Actors living in Los Angeles cited the racial segregation between blacks and whites as a major factor explaining why black roles, typically written by whites, were scarce and often stereotypical. Rather than serving as an urban backdrop of a variety of urban lifestyles, early twenty-first century Los Angeles was a segregated world that allowed whites to perpetuate fictionalized, one-dimensional stereotypes of blacks through the use of film and television.

But black actors were not mere puppets in Hollywood, mindlessly conforming in their performances to the expected stereotypes. Rather, as my informants reveal, they developed a variety of coping strategies to negotiate such roles and strived to make small, but meaningful, steps toward changing the popular image that blackness begins and ends with "the 'hood."

NOTES

1. Estrada and Sensiper, "Mending the Politics of Division, " 124.

2. "Ghetto," *Merriam-Webster Online Dictionary*, 2009, http://www.merriam-webster.com/dictionary/ghetto (accessed December 12, 2008).

3. Smith, *Great Black Way*.

4. Jill Leovy, "Community Struggles in Anonymity," *Los Angeles Times*, July 7, 2008, B1.

5. "Where Hopelessness and Danger Collide," *Seattle Post-Intelligencer*, May 2, 1992, P-I News Services.

6. Even news coverage of young blacks in France describes one as "[a] large black kid who looks as if he would be more at home in South Central LA than in this cold, bleak stadium at the heart of one of the most bourgeois districts in Paris" (Hussey, "Le Temps Modernes"). This demonstrates the power of South Central's myth to spread beyond the U.S. borders to encompass black people globally.

7. Directed by Victor Fleming (USA: Selznick International Pictures, Metro-Goldwyn-Mayer, Loew's Incorporated, 1939).

8. The quotes and excerpts presented in this chapter were taken from the author's in-depth interviews with fifteen male and fifteen female black actors in the Los Angeles area from 2005 to 2007.

9. See *2007 Hollywood Writers Report*, http://www.wga.org/uploadedFiles/who_we_are/HWR07_tables.pdf.

10. See chap. 2 for a discussion of Crenshaw Boulevard's significance in Black Los Angeles.

11. Phyllis Banks, "Spotlight on Teri Brown-Jackson," 7.

12. Directed by Jonas Elmer (USA, Canada: Gold Circle Films, Epidemic Pictures, Edmonds Entertainment, Safran Company, Lionsgate, Gold Circle Films, 2009).

13. Tara Harris, "New in Town—an Interview with Screenwriter Kenneth Rance: Rance Speaks About Writing the Film and Being a Black Writer in the Business," January 22, 2009, http://www.blackfilm.com/20090122/features/kenrance .shtml (accessed January 26, 2009).

14. Directed by Robert Townsend (USA: Goldwyn Entertainment Company, Conquering Unicorn Productions, 1987).

15. Directed by Spike Lee (USA: 40 Acres and a Mule Filmworks, New Line Cinema, Step'n Fetchit Picture Company, 2000).

16. Directed by Jessy Terrero (USA: Metro-Goldwyn-Mayer Pictures Inc, Metro-Goldwyn-Mayer Pictures Inc, 2004).

17. Directed by Craig Brewer (USA: Crunk Pictures, Homegrown Pictures, Paramount Classics, MTV Films, New Deal Entertainment, Rockefeller Media Arts Fellowship, 2004).

Chapter 10

||||||||||||||||||||||||||||||||||||||||||||||||||||

Before and After Watts
Black Art in Los Angeles

Paul Von Blum

In 1929, the California Art Club hosted the first recorded black art show in Los Angeles. The exhibit was brought to California from Chicago and did not feature local artists. Only at the request of the club were three local black artists included. Unfortunately, the exhibit was not warmly received by Arthur Miller, the leading art critic of the period for the *Los Angeles Times*, who lambasted the exhibit for not possessing enough "Negro naïveté" and "Negro warmth." He suggested that white artists would do a better job re-creating black images than the "Cultivated Negro working in a purely European tradition."[1] Over the years, the demeaning and racist tone of the review, although presented in much more subtle ways later in the century, would become typical of the dominant white art community in Los Angeles. Mainstream Los Angeles art critics would either not review exhibits of local black artists at all (while still reviewing black artists from other regions), or their reviews would be filtered through a critical analysis of black art using the lens of elitist standards of artistic quality. This European-focused perspective usually raised questions about the competency of black artists and the validity of black art as a legitimate art form.[2]

In this chapter, I review different historical periods in the evolution of the black arts movement in Los Angeles, paying particular attention to developments following the 1965 Watts Riots. This era saw a shift in tone not only of the artistic themes presented, but in the way in which black artists and art administrators, organized, presented, and created venues for black art. Black Los Angeles artists have engaged and challenged audiences of all backgrounds to reflect on the social issues confronting Black

Los Angeles, including race, civil rights, homelessness, police brutality, drugs, gender discrimination, and AIDS. This chapter chronicles this vibrant artistic tradition, as well as the methods black artists in the city employed to overcome efforts aimed at limiting their advancement.

Before Watts

The 1940s and 1950s saw an influx of black artists to Los Angeles, fleeing restrictions and humiliations of the racially segregated South.[3] They migrated to Southern California in search of personal and professional success. Yet upon arrival, they were confronted with the discriminatory practices of the white art world that regularly victimized artists of color, even in an increasingly multicultural city like Los Angeles. Like other black migrants, artists encountered a huge gap between American ideals of justice and equality, and the extensive racist realities on the ground. Still, their hopes and expectations were similar to other California migrants who believed that in the new postwar world, Los Angeles would provide relative freedoms and opportunities for blacks that were unavailable anywhere else in America.

In the early 1950s, Walt Walker, an artist who migrated to Los Angeles from Detroit in 1948, opened LeJan Gallery, the first black art gallery in Los Angeles. Walker opened his space after walking down La Cienega Boulevard in West Hollywood, an area dotted with art galleries, and being frustrated by not finding one image painted by a black artist.[4] Walker's gallery, located in the heart of the black community on Crenshaw Boulevard and Forty-eighth Street, became a nucleus of the nascent black arts movement in Los Angeles. The gallery provided black artists in the 1950s a venue in which to exhibit their art and seek possible critical attention and financial rewards for their work, two elements that black artists in Los Angeles have historically found elusive.[5] But the 1950s were to see an improvement in conditions for black artists in Los Angeles as they came together and found unique ways to support the production, collection, and sale of their work. As the historian Daniel Widener has noted, "The early 1950s were times of increasing visibility for black visual artists working in Southern California."[6]

In 1957 the artist William Pajaud found employment at the Golden State Mutual Life Insurance Company as an art director in the public relations department. At that time, Golden State was one of the largest black-owned insurance firms in the United States. Pajaud spent almost thirty years working a traditional eight-hour day at the Golden State building, which was designed by renowned black architect Paul Williams. The building was located in the West Adams District, a historic, predominantly black area with a rich cultural, architectural, and artistic tradition. At night and on weekends, Pajaud produced his own paintings and prints, creating a significant body of work. But his most enduring achievement was amassing a company collection of black art, which became one of the most remarkable repositories of original black art in Los Angeles.

Early on, Golden State had already made a commitment to artistic exhibition and preservation. In 1949 the company commissioned two oil-on-canvas murals for its lobby from two major black artists, Charles Alston and Hale Woodruff, that chronicled "The Negro in California History."[7] Alston painted the first panel, titled *Exploration*.[8] This effort depicts influential blacks in California's early years, such as former slave Biddy Mason, who journeyed to Los Angeles and became America's first black millionaire businesswoman and philanthropist.[9] Woodruff painted the second panel, *Settlement and Development*,[10] which depicted ordinary black workers from 1850 to 1949, whose efforts were instrumental in the economic growth of California.

In 1965, after trying for several years to convince the Golden State executives of the value of developing a significant collection of black art that could be made accessible to the community, William Pajaud commenced his curatorial efforts. The first work he obtained was the majestic ink drawing of Harriet Tubman by Charles White, titled *General Moses*[11] (see fig. 10.1). This massive piece hung below the Woodruff mural in the company lobby and was available for public viewing until 2007. Throughout his tenure at Golden State, Pajaud worked with a minuscule budget for art purchases, often trading his own artwork with other black artists to acquire new works. The Golden State collection included art by Henry O. Tanner, Richmond Barthe, Hughie Lee-Smith, James Van Der Zee, John Biggers, Elizabeth Catlett, Jacob Lawrence, Romare Bearden, Kofi Bailey, Beulah Woodard, P'lla Mills, Charles White, Samella Lewis, Betye Saar, Varnette Honeywood, Ian White, Noni Olabisi, Alonzo Davis, John Riddle, David Hammons, Richard Wyatt, Dan Concholar, Willie Middlebrook, and many others.

In 2007 Golden State, under financial duress, unfortunately placed most of its masterpieces up for auction with the Swann Auction Galleries in New York City. As the artist and art historian Samella Lewis lamented,

Figure 10.1. Charles White, *General Moses* (*Harriet Tubman*).
Courtesy of © 1965 Charles White Archives.

"It's going to be a great loss to California if it [the collection] leaves because we need that information."[12] The Swann Galleries sold off ninety-
four works of art from the Golden State collection, bringing in $1.54 mil-
lion dollars and achieving thirty-one artist price records. Amid local outcry over the impending sale, the auction house sought to find a single
buyer for the collection, a museum or comparable institution to purchase
the Golden State artworks, but the effort proved frustratingly unsuccessful. The reasons behind the sale appeared to be purely mercenary, causing
even more outrage in the Black Los Angeles art community. "Obviously,
it's a financial decision," said Nigel Freeman, head of Swann's African
American art department. "There are people who will be disappointed . . .
it's [the collection's] being broken up and leaving California. But the decision to sell it has been made, and Swann will make the most of the opportunity."[13] The loss of the collection was indeed a setback to the progress
made by early pioneers of the Black Los Angeles arts movement. Golden
State Mutual was indeed seized by state regulators in September 2009, another corporate victim of the 2008–9 financial collapse.[14]

As the early 1960s unfolded, the artist Ruth Waddy was compelled to
organize Art West Associated (AWA) in 1962, a black arts group that pro-

moted cultural discussion, organized educational programs, and agitated for recognition and participation in mainstream art institutions in the Los Angeles art world. Renowned Black Los Angeles artists such as Raymond Lark, Samella Lewis, John Riddle, and Alonzo Davis participated in AWA activities, which included sponsoring community and youth activities to educate Los Angeles about black art and advocating for black artists who could not get their work into the city's mainstream museums.[15] The early efforts of AWA set the stage for further cultural and political activities affecting black visual art in Los Angeles.

Benjamin Horowitz was another pioneer in the early days of the Los Angeles black arts movement. When he opened the Heritage Gallery on La Cienega Boulevard in 1961, Horowitz became the first of two mainstream, white, commercial gallery owners to break the artistic color line in the city. The Heritage Gallery gave black artists a premier setting in Los Angeles in an era when their efforts were regarded as primitive curiosities, merely "folk art," far beyond the canon of artistic "excellence." Horowitz's Jewish background and his political consciousness led him to feature black artists whose works combined outstanding artistic technique with trenchant social commentary and criticism.[16] His role as president of the Art Dealers Association of California gave him a level of clout that allowed him to dare to transcend art-world racial barriers. Horowitz included black artists for political and moral reasons; economic considerations were less relevant to him, although over the years he sold many works of art by black luminaries such as Charles White, William Pajaud, and Ernie Barnes. Horowitz played an especially significant role in advancing the artistic career of Ernie Barnes (see cover art). Horowitz encouraged Barnes, who transitioned into art from a career as an NFL football player with the San Diego Chargers and Denver Broncos, to go beyond his early sports-themed efforts and paint more general, humanist subject matter relating to his life in Black Los Angeles and the traditions of the African American community (see fig. 10.2).

Heritage Gallery's major Black Los Angeles artist was Charles White, whose paintings highlighted the dignity of African American culture while serving as a biting critique of American racism. In 1967 Horowitz himself wrote the commentary for *Images of Dignity: The Drawings of Charles White*.[17] Horowitz's efforts propelled White to critical visibility both in the United States and abroad, something that was almost unheard of for a Black Los Angeles artist in the mid-twentieth century.

Figure 10.2. Ernie Barnes, *Olympic Neighborhood Games*. Courtesy of © 1984 Ernie Barnes.

After Watts: 1965–1976

In the aftermath of the 1965 Watts uprisings, both the social and artistic scene in Black Los Angeles underwent rapid change.[18] Nationally, the violent events of the riots awakened the country to the persistence of racism in all aspects of American life and the need for institutional change to redress two hundred years of wrongs. Locally, the aftermath of Watts catalyzed substantial government and private action, compelling public officials and the media to begin to respond to the legitimate grievances of black citizens.[19] Numerous social programs emerged, as did serious public dialogue about race. Blackness was on the front burner, and the dominant institutions in America began to realize, at least theoretically, that the Watts uprisings could happen again unless immediate and durable steps were taken to ameliorate conditions. Despite formidable barriers prior to Watts, Black Los Angeles artists had made significant advances. However, the riots profoundly accelerated the development of the black art movement in the city. It forced government agencies to provide funding for social, artistic, and cultural programming in black communities. It put pressure on mainstream art institutions to exhibit the work of Black Los Angeles artists. It also increased the political consciousness of Black Los Angeles artists themselves and spurred a self-empowerment and self-determination that accelerated the growth of viable, black-owned, alternative institutional spaces, where black artists, shut out of mainstream venues, could showcase their work.

During this period, the Los Angeles County Museum of Art (LACMA) was *the* major regional art museum. It was founded in 1910 and was formerly part of the Los Angeles Museum of History, Science, and Art in Exposition Park. But as the residential area turned increasingly black, the museum moved to its mid-Wilshire Boulevard campus, located in a predominately white, Jewish, upper-class neighborhood, as an independent entity in 1965. It became one of the largest new museums built in the United States in the twentieth century.

Except for a 1935 exhibition of Beulah Woodard, one of the few major black artists in Los Angeles to achieve critical recognition in the pre–World War II era,[20] LACMA ignored both national and local traditions of black art. In addition, blacks who worked at LACMA appeared confined to menial custodial and staff positions where there were no prospects for serious occupational mobility. LACMA's discriminatory exhibition and hiring practices made it a main target for local cultural activism in the highly charged post-Watts era.[21] Many black artists and their supporters justifiably demanded that this publicly funded institution be responsive to *all* the region's citizens, not merely to the privileged white artists, collectors, and museum visitors it had served throughout its history. Both AWA and the Black Arts Council (BAC), which formed in 1967, worked tirelessly to address the practices at LACMA and force inclusion for Black Los Angeles artists.

BAC was co-founded by artists Claude Booker and Cecil Fergerson, employees of LACMA, who saw the irrelevance of the institution to the lives and interests of Black Los Angeles, and they used BAC to promote reforms for local black artists. Claude Booker's untimely death in 1974 at the age of thirty-six cut short an already remarkable career of cultural activism. Fergerson, affectionately known as the "Community Curator," began working at LACMA as a janitor in 1948, later becoming one of the few blacks to move into professional positions in that institution. He became a preparator and later a curatorial assistant, a junior role with some input and participation in public programming and exhibitions. Throughout his life, Fergerson, together with Booker, played a large role in unifying the black artistic community. The famous artist John Outterbridge frequently described Booker and Fergerson's organization, BAC, as the art world's version of the civil rights movement.[22]

The Ankrum Gallery was the other mainstream institution that showcased black works in the period immediately following Watts. Joan Ankrum, an actress as well as the director and proprietor of the Ankrum Gallery, was a social progressive who showcased black artists early on, even before the concerted political drive to bring black art into the mainstream. Ankrum Gallery represented another former NFL player-turned-actor-and-artist, Bernie Casey, as well as visual artist Dan Concholar, and painters Suzanne Jackson and Samella Lewis. During its existence from 1966 to 1990, the Ankrum Gallery presented both group and solo shows, and enabled major black artists in Los Angeles to sell their works and, equally important, achieve similar recognition to that of established white artists.

In 1967 Alonzo and Dale Davis, artists and brothers, founded the Brockman Art Gallery, adjacent to the Crenshaw District in Leimert Park, an area considered the center of black art and culture in Los Angeles.[23] Opening with shows of their own work, the Davis brothers went on to showcase the efforts of black artists in Los Angeles and elsewhere, organizing at least ten exhibitions a year, raising public awareness, and inviting critical discourse about West Coast African American artists. A unique component of Brockman's programming was organizing exhibitions in other venues in an effort to promote black artistic visibility in a mainstream Los Angeles setting.

Throughout its existence, the Brockman Gallery functioned as a commercial gallery, selling numerous prints, paintings, and sculptures from such luminaries as John Riddle, Varnette Honeywood, Marion Epting, Tim Washington, and others. But like many small businesses, particularly in the arts, its financial rewards were sporadic. Still, the gallery's community impact far transcended its limited economic success. In 1973 the Davis brothers established Brockman Productions, a nonprofit organization that attracted public funds and grants from the National Endowment for the Arts, the Los Angeles Cultural Affairs Department, and the Comprehensive Employment and Training Act (CETA), a federal training program. The infusion of grant funds alleviated some of Brockman's financial pressures, allowing its nonprofit entity to host the community art exhibition, Art in the Park, public concerts like the Watts Towers Jazz Festival, and various mural projects.

The legacy of the Brockman Gallery is significant, demonstrating how the social activism of the post-Watts era stimulated a deeper intellectual consciousness about black art and solidified the growing solidarity and networking among Los Angeles–area black artists. Brockman attracted visitors and artists from other ethnic and racial communities, promoting multiculturalism long before the term entered public and academic discourse. Brockman, which lasted until 1990, was the most influential and durable private space providing a major venue for exhibiting the creative efforts of black artists in Los Angeles and helped to generate a black artistic renaissance in the late 1960s. As John Outterbridge perceptively noted in 2008, the Brockman Gallery was, "The museum before the museum,"[24] referring to the later creation of the California African American Museum in Exposition Park in the late 1970s.

Jewish organizations also took a leading role in the post-Watts era in providing Black Los Angeles artists with exhibition space; they have continued this artistic/activist partnership into the twenty-first century. The Westside Jewish Community Center (WJCC), located near the mid-Wilshire area, exemplifies this type of collaboration. Through its cultural outreach activities, the center partnered with black artists/gallery owners Alonzo and Dale Davis and their Brockman Gallery to host satellite exhibitions at the center. These shows featured the work of black artists, particularly with paintings highlighting Jewish themes, like Pajaud's watercolor of children lighting Hanukah candles or Ernie Barnes's *Sam and Sidney*,[25] which depicts two Jewish men walking arm-in-arm through a Jewish neighborhood in Los Angeles (see fig. 10.3).

During the 1960s and 1970s, another Jewish organization that promoted black artists was the longtime progressive group, the National Council of Jewish Women (NCJW). Located in the historically Jewish Fairfax district of Los Angeles, NCJW organized art shows that included prominent local

Figure 10.3. Ernie Barnes, *Sam & Sidney*. Courtesy of
© 1988 Ernie Barnes.

black artists. In 1993 the NCJW, with financial backing from the Social
and Public Art Resource Center, arranged for a local black artist to paint
a large mural on its exterior wall. Titled *Not Somewhere Else, But Here*,[26]
this vibrant multicultural mural by Daryl Wells highlighted seven prominent Jewish women from different fields, major female activists from the
Chicano and black communities, as well as women from Burma and Gua-
temala (see fig. 10.4).

The other major art gallery serving black artists in the post-Watts era
was Gallery 32, founded in 1968 by the dancer and visual artist Suzanne
Jackson. With strong artistic training that included drawing classes at the
Otis College of Art and Design with the celebrated painter Charles White,
Jackson swiftly met most of the other major black artists who played
enormous roles in shaping the Los Angeles black arts movement. Jackson
ran Gallery 32 with minimal monetary support and largely through her
personal energy and labor. The operation was different from Brockman in

its focus and ethos. Alonzo and Dale Davis tended to exhibit artists with more formal credentials, while Jackson often attracted younger, experimental practitioners. However, some of Gallery 32's best-known artists, such as Betye Saar, Yvonne Cole Meo, and Timothy Washington, went on to develop regional and national reputations. The rivalry between Brockman and Gallery 32 was friendly, and many local black artists maintained close relationships and exhibited with both institutions. Gallery 32 and Brockman attracted artists and others interested in vigorous discussion and debate about art, politics, black history, and culture.

Gallery 32's 1969 exhibition of Emory Douglas, artist and the Black Panther Party minister of culture, was one of the most dramatic showings in the brief two-year existence of the gallery. This controversial show was well attended, most likely including representatives of local and federal police and investigative agencies concerned with Black Panther and other Black Nationalist activity.[27] As Jackson recalled, "when the Panther exhibition was at the gallery, tons of people came to see it because in a sense, it was—I guess you could call it a safe place for anybody in the community to come and find out what the Panthers were about."[28] Although Emory Douglas was a California artist and activist from the Bay Area, the infusion of a militant black artistic perspective in a local gallery reflected the growing linkage of art and politics in Black Los Angeles, particularly among its artists. Many of the works of local black artists at the time reflected a political edge that had pervaded black art since its inception and grown in the aftermath of Watts.

Figure 10.4. Daryl E. Wells mural, *Not Somewhere Else, But Here.* Fairfax and Clinton Avenue. National Council of Jewish Women, Los Angeles Section building. Courtesy of S.P.A.R.C. Archives.

The turbulent 1960s also led to the development of training facilities to nurture young black artistic talent, which further strengthened the infrastructure of the black visual art movement in Los Angeles. Charles White's mentorship activity at Otis College played a seminal role in the shaping of black art in the city. White, who also served on its faculty, directed the school in its support of black artists who lived in and depicted black Los Angeles in their work. For many years White held Saturday sessions at Otis, mentoring aspiring young black artists.

In 1969 the Communicative Arts Academy in Compton also added to these early training efforts. Compton, then a predominately poor, black community which in the late twentieth century turned increasingly black *and* Latino,[29] seemed an unlikely venue for a black arts training academy. Artists John Outterbridge (see fig. 10.5) and Judson Powell co-founded the space as an artistic alternative for young blacks who might otherwise have been attracted to gang life, giving them the opportunity to develop in music, dance, photography, and other visual arts. The academy became a serious community arts facility with galleries, classrooms, exhibits, and booths. Until it ceased operations in 1975, the Compton Communicative Arts Academy contributed enormously to the rich tapestry of black arts in Southern California.

Another iconic institution serving primarily the black and Latino communities also began in 1969. The still-thriving St. Elmo's Village is a residential arts organization located in mid-city Los Angeles, dedicated to the vision that participation in the arts promotes pride, self-reliance, and confidence, especially in young people. In the mid-1960s Roderick Sykes, a painter and muralist, and his artist uncle, Rozell Sykes, rented a group of houses on St. Elmo Drive, an area beset with high poverty and other urban problems, and co-founded St. Elmo's Village. By 1971, with Roderick Sykes as director and his wife, the artist Jacqueline Alexander-Sykes, as administrator, St. Elmo's Village was incorporated as a nonprofit organization and commenced art activities serving the community. Since that time, it has sponsored art workshops and classes, art and music festivals, art book launches and signings, hosted field trips from local schools, and numerous related programs encouraging black and Latino group involvement in creative activities. Over the years St. Elmo's Village has been a key gathering place for both established and emerging artists, adding a dynamic venue in the broader constellation of multicultural arts institutions and teaching facilities in the Los Angeles area.

Despite these promising developments, the mainstream art world was

Figure 10.5. John Outterbridge (b. 1933), *REVIEW/54—Outhouse, 2003*. Los Angeles, California. Mixed media assemblage construction, 84 × 32 W × 40 in. "Outterbridge constructed an outhouse . . . for viewers to read text on the walls, ceiling and floor. . . . [It] represents the disparity between those who are outside the power structure and those who make the rules for everyone else to live by. The wheels . . . are a symbol of mobilization and the potential to move forward." Courtesy of the California African American Museum, permanent collection. Gift of the artist.

still reluctant to embrace local black artists. In the early 1970s, BAC mounted a protest that included a letter-writing campaign, picketing, and other agitation techniques to pressure LACMA to showcase black artists. In response, LACMA held three exhibitions of black art. The first involved the 1971 show of three prominent black artists who had attracted regional and national critical attention—painters Charles White, David Hammons, and Timothy Washington. This exhibition generated controversy because it included only a small number of the area's black artists. Many black activists and artists sought a more extensive exhibit and again picketed in protest. The following year, LACMA offered the exhibition "Los Angeles 1972: A Panorama of Black Artists." These modest artistic advancements would not have occurred without organized black pressure and protest.

In 1976, again responding to growing regional and national demands to include blacks in all parts of American life, LACMA mounted a comprehensive exhibition of black art—the first and largest historical survey of that tradition. David Driskell, an artist and art historian who was then chair of the Art Department at Fisk University, was the curator for the

"Two Centuries of Black American Art" exhibition. The only artists from the Los Angeles area included in the exhibit were Richmond Barthe, who was not exemplary of the Black Los Angeles art community (having spent most of his time elsewhere), and Charles White. For the exhibit, Driskell assembled a huge array of paintings, drawings, prints, and sculptures from private collections, galleries, and museums throughout the United States. With the assistance of Leonard Simon, an early local supporter of black art, Driskell created a major catalogue that made a profound contribution to the extant scholarship on black art, although it did little, unfortunately, to showcase the work of Black Los Angeles artisans.

The seeds of change, however, had been planted when Dr. Samella Lewis moved to Los Angeles in 1964. Shortly thereafter she began an amazing array of artistic activities, such as creating gallery space for black artists. Perhaps more importantly, Lewis was instrumental in elevating the critical study of black art history in the eyes of the mainstream art establishment through the publication of scholarly books and journals on Los Angeles black art. In the 1970s Lewis wrote *African American Art and Artists*[30] and *African American Art for Young People*,[31] and in 1976 founded *The International Review of African American Art* journal. Initially working at LACMA as an educational coordinator in a position created as a result of the political efforts of AWA and BAC, Lewis soon returned to teaching at Scripps College until her retirement in 1984. Along with artist Bernie Casey, Lewis established the Contemporary Crafts Gallery, popularly known as The Gallery, on Pico Boulevard, located adjacent to a predominately black neighborhood. The major focus of The Gallery was to produce inexpensive prints of originals in order to encourage the purchase of black art by blacks and the general community. The goal was to begin to foster a culture of art collection in the black community.

In addition to The Gallery and her publications, in 1976 Lewis founded the Museum of African American Art in Los Angeles. Located in a major department store in the Crenshaw District,[32] the museum showcased Los Angeles black artists in a venue conveniently accessible to the large black population of South Los Angeles. The museum also sponsored symposia and other programs, regularly hosted visitors from schools and colleges throughout the region, and was dedicated to the interpretation, promotion, and preservation of art by people of African descent.

The impact of Charles White, Samella Lewis, the Davis brothers, Benjamin Horowitz, John Outterbridge, and other pioneers at mainstream institutions, galleries, and religious centers, cannot be overstated. These figures ventured beyond the accepted notions of the established art community in the post-Watts era in order to support black artists. They represented a powerful force in the historical development of the black arts tradition in Los Angeles. The creation and development of independent black cultural institutions by black artists, gallery owners, and arts administrators —which grew out of the political turmoil of the period—was crucial to creating a viable and thriving black artistic tradition in Los Angeles.

Art in the City: 1976–1999

The impact of the Watts riots more than a decade earlier, the growing political consciousness of local African Americans, and undoubtedly the growing influence in Los Angeles of the Black Panther Party and Maulana Karenga's US Organization,[33] had some effect, if indirectly, on the political impetus for government support of the creation of black-controlled venues promoting black art in the city. The Watts Tower Center, the California African American Museum (CAAM), and the William Grant Still Art Center are three examples of art in the city that grew from the ashes of the agitational, even angry spirit of a volatile time.

Responding to the political pressure of the civil rights era, the City of Los Angeles realized that it had to provide institutional opportunities for its increasingly diverse population, including its artists from many communities. In 1976 the Los Angeles Municipal Arts Department (later renamed the Cultural Affairs Department) assumed control over the Watts Towers Arts Center and organized numerous community events, including the Watts Summer Festival, a major public venue for local black artists, the Watts Jazz Festival, and the Day of the Drum Festival. The center also provided continuing art classes for young people and held regular exhibitions featuring many local black artists. It is the site of renowned murals by black artists Alonzo Davis, Elliot Pinkney, and Richard Wyatt, including Wyatt's iconic homage to the community curator Cecil Fergerson. The Watts Towers[34] Arts Center was one of the earliest venues that responded to the needs of black artists in the city (see fig. 10.6). The center was formed both to restore and preserve the magnificent folk art towers of Italian immigrant Simon Rodia and to promote the cultural life of the surrounding, majority African American community that had been at the center of the massive civil unrest of 1965. As Sarah Schrank, associate professor of history at California State University, Long Beach, noted about

Figure 10.6. John Outterbridge, director of Watts Towers Arts Center, Calif., June 5, 1977. Photo courtesy of Los Angeles Times Photographic Archive, Department of Special Collections, Charles E. Young Research Library, UCLA.

the towers, their resurrection had a profound impact on the economically depressed black community in which they were built:

> This presumably vanished artwork proceeded to morph over fifty years from an Italian immigrant's backyard fantasy to an iconic symbol of American blackness and a politically fraught civic landmark. In the struggle to render them visible to a local as well as an international public, the towers have become an important tool in understanding Los Angeles's conflict over civic identity, the city's politics of race and representation, and the significance of art in an often-avoided neighborhood.[35]

The California African American Museum (CAAM) was founded in 1977 as a public institution chartered by the state of California to bolster and ensure the future of black visual art in Los Angeles. Located in Exposition Park near the heart of downtown Los Angeles (see fig. 10.7), CAAM was chartered by the state with the mission to research, collect, preserve, and interpret the history, art, and culture of African Americans, with a particular emphasis on exhibiting the work of Los Angeles–area black artists and showing the impact of their art in the region and beyond. Originally housed in the adjacent California Museum of Science and Industry, CAAM (established as the California Museum of Afro-American History and Culture) moved into its spacious building in 1984 and has grown substantially since that time. In addition to hosting exhibitions, CAAM engaged in restorative and corrective activity that has been a staple of post–civil rights movement black cultural and intellectual life. In 1981, local curators Mary Jane Hewitt and Samella Lewis organized an inaugural show and catalogue of ten California artists, including some of the iconic figures in Los Angeles black art history.

Throughout the years, the museum continued this focus. In 1989 it offered an exhibition titled "19 Sixties: A Cultural Awakening," which included dramatic examples of the assemblage and collage movement of the period. Its focus on artists David Hammons, Alonzo Davis, Noah Purifoy, John Riddle, John Outterbridge, Betye Saar, Charles White, Suzanne Jackson, and Timothy Washington allowed viewers a six-month glimpse at the work of artists who were instrumental in the birth and development of the Los Angeles black arts movement. CAAM also used exhibition space to

Figure 10.7. Exterior of California African American Museum in Exposition Park. Photo courtesy of Darnell Hunt.

respond to urgent public events. In 1993, CAAM curator Lizzetta Lefalle-Collins organized a show titled "No Justice, No Peace? Resolutions . . ." to address the aftermath of the 1992 uprisings, which had been sparked by the acquittal of the four police officers in the infamous Rodney King beating case. The exhibition and its accompanying catalogue demonstrated how the King case echoed the same racist elements underlying the explosion in Watts almost thirty years earlier.[36] The artworks also validated the prophecies of those who predicted a repeat of Watts unless drastic political and economic changes occurred.

Exhibitions of CAAM's new acquisitions and the permanent collection highlighted Los Angeles-area artists and provided a valuable model for the deeper objective of artistic respect and preservation of black art, while also simultaneously encouraging a culture of collection. CAAM also regularly published catalogues, sponsored forums and symposia about black art, and frequently offered school outreach programs and presentations from recognized scholars in black art, history, and culture. CAAM's activities worked to reinforce the institutional foundation of black art in the region and ensure a viable, if still peripheral presence for this visual tradition.

The William Grant Still Community Art Center, established in 1978 in the historic West Adams area,[37] is a Cultural Affairs Department entity devoted to black artists. In the early twenty-first century West Adams, like many other districts in Los Angeles, became increasingly Latino and Asian, even while retaining a substantial black population. The center regularly featured the artistic efforts of the black community, especially younger black artists. Each year, free of charge, it showcased an exhibition of black dolls, offering another neglected genre of black art to public audiences. The center also featured *Troubled Island*,[38] a stunning mural by local black artist Noni Olabisi, which highlights the 1791 slave rebellion in Haiti and inspired the famous William Grant Still's opera of the same name. The mural, like many murals throughout the city, expresses the historical and political themes that pervade black art.

In 1984 another critical institutional development took place in the Los Angeles black arts movement when the photographer Roland Charles, founder and first director of the Black Photographers of California, opened the Black Gallery in the Crenshaw District. Whereas The Gallery, Brockman Gallery, and Gallery 32 showcased black imaginative art, the Black Gallery promoted black photographic art. The Black Gallery became a springboard for numerous black photographers, enabling them to

Figure 10.8. Cover art for the book, *Life in a Day of Black L.A.: The Way We See It*, edited by Roland Charles and Toyomi Igus. Photo courtesy of CAAS Publications.

exhibit and sell their works; it also augmented the public's understanding of the medium as a major fine arts enterprise and put Los Angeles on the map for black photographic excellence.[39] Charles sponsored six exhibitions each year and offered numerous workshops and seminars. Like the other black-owned-and-operated galleries, the Black Gallery was intricately connected to the larger black community. Among the many notable accomplishments of the Black Gallery, which closed in 1998, was the book and accompanying exhibition highlighting the lives of blacks in the region, *Life in a Day of Black L.A: The Way We See It*[40] (see fig. 10.8).

In the early 1990s, LACMA mounted a small but well-received Jacob Lawrence[41] exhibition and a more comprehensive show of the art of the Harlem Renaissance, again, two exhibits that did not respond to community interest in Black Los Angeles art. As the Los Angeles black arts movement matured and more alternative, smaller venues and state- or city-sponsored venues became available for Black Los Angeles artists to show their work, mainstream venues in the city no longer felt pressured by protests to include black artists in individual and group shows, or to include blacks in the institutional management process. Even into the early twenty-first century, LACMA, a publicly funded museum, still had no blacks on its board of directors.[42] As Samella Lewis explained when asked about the black artist's struggle for inclusion at mainstream, area art venues, "I don't pay too much attention to these museums anymore. I just try to do what I can do."[43] Despite the efforts of those in the Los Angeles black arts movement to push for representation and inclusion, there remained a sense of futility in the effort, along with a commitment to continue to create their own opportunities.

Founded in 1998, the M. Hanks Gallery served in the early 2000s as a key Los Angeles–area art gallery devoted exclusively to black art. Although located in Santa Monica, far from the geographical center of gravity of Black Los Angeles,[44] this gallery became a contemporary successor to the Brockman Gallery. Eric Hanks, the founder and proprietor, positioned the institution to occupy a central role in regional black cultural life. Its multifaceted program of exhibitions and educational programs encouraged a culture of collection among experienced and novice collectors alike.[45] The exhibitions at M. Hanks augmented black art museum shows in both local black and mainstream venues, reinforcing the impact of the region's black art and artists while, like CAAM and other black art venues, seeking to foster a tradition of artistic respect and consumption, particularly within the Los Angeles black community.

The M. Hanks Gallery exhibitions alone would have made it a central institution in the world of Los Angeles black art. But M. Hanks also made a commitment to a broader educational vision. Throughout the early 2000s, the gallery held low-cost art appreciation classes, which provided a valuable knowledge base for potential collectors and interested residents. The gallery routinely sponsored guest lectures about black art, poetry readings, and book signings on topics relevant to the broad theme of black art and culture. It also encouraged classes from local colleges and universities to visit the gallery to see original artwork and regularly had students spend academic terms as interns. The sheer breadth of cultural activities, along with its comparative longevity, distinguish the M. Hanks Gallery from commercial galleries in other cities with substantial black populations. By replicating the earlier Brockman model, and by engaging comprehensively with Black Los Angeles, the gallery added a powerful dimension to the development of black art in the city.

The image of the Black Los Angeles art scene is now a far cry from the one portrayed by my opening discussion of the 1929 California Art Club show. Seeded by migration to the city during the 1940s and 1950s, and inspired by Watts, Los Angeles–area black artists have exhibited their work throughout the nation and the world, including elite art venues in New York, Chicago, Philadelphia, San Francisco, Washington, DC, Paris, Amsterdam, São Paulo, and elsewhere. Meanwhile, legions of younger black artists and others have been influenced by both the form and content of this work. The continued growth of the arts movement in Black Los Angeles demonstrates how black resistance, persistence, and institution-building in the face of mainstream discrimination and indifference could create and sustain a viable artistic tradition. The proliferation of black cultural and educational venues, along with increasing scholarly documentation and critical review, encourages many black artists to remain in or relocate to the Los Angeles area, making it arguably "a major center for contemporary artistic production."[46]

NOTES

1. Schrank, *Art and the City*.

2. McEvilley, *Art & Otherness*.

3. See chaps. 1 and 2 for discussions of this period of great migration to Black Los Angeles.

4. "Walt Walker, Artist," http://www.waltwalker.com/about1waltwalker.htm (accessed April 2, 2009).

5. Susan Anderson, "The Artistic Void in the Collections of L.A.'s Museums," *Los Angeles Times*, December 19, 1999, op ed., http://articles.latimes.com/1999/dec/19/opinion/op-45400 (accessed March 16, 2009).

6. Widener, *Black Arts West*, 57.

7. Charles Alston and Hale Woodruff, *The Negro in California History*, Golden State Mutual Life Building, Los Angeles, California, 1949.

8. Ibid.

9. See chap. 1 for a detailed history of Biddy Mason in Los Angeles.

10. Charles Alston and Hale Woodruff, *Settlement and Development*, second panel of *The Negro in California History* mural, Golden State Mutual Life Building, Los Angeles, California, 1949.

11. Charles White, *General Moses*, Golden State Mutual Life Building, Los Angeles, California, 1965.

12. Lindsay Pollack, "Historians Angered by Auction of Black Art," *Los Angeles Times*, August 17, 2007, E-2.

13. Ibid.

14. Marc Lifgher, "Golden State Mutual Seized," *Los Angeles Times*, October 1, 2009, B1.

15. Lark, "Drawings and Paintings by an Afro-American Artist."

16. See Deriane, "Benjamin Horowitz," for a fuller account of Horowitz's life and commitment to black artists based on his vision of a shared but different heritage of racial and religious oppression.

17. White and Horowitz, *Images of Dignity*.

18. See chaps. 1, 5, 8, 10, and 12 for further discussion of the Watts riots and its aftermath.

19. California Governor's Commission on the Los Angeles Riots, "Violence in the City."

20. Riggs, *St. James Guide to Black Artists*.

21. Cecil Fergerson was promoted to curatorial assistant after filing a discrimination suit against LACMA (Cecil Fergerson, interview conducted in 1991 by Karen Anne Mason, Center for Oral History Research, Young Research Library, University of California, Los Angeles. Audio recording, tape no. 6, side 2; transcript, 260).

22. John Outterbridge, interview by author, July 11, 2008.

23. See chap. 2 for a detailed history of the Leimert Park area.

24. John Outterbridge, interview by author, July 11, 2008.

25. Ernie Barnes, *Sam and Sidney* (Los Angeles: The Art Department, 2004).

26. Daryl Wells, *Not Somewhere Else, But Here*, National Council of Jewish Women Building wall mural, Los Angeles, California, 1993.

27. See chap. 5 for a discussion of the role of the Black Panther Party in Black Los Angeles.

28. Suzanne Jackson, interview conducted in 1998 by Karen Anne Mason, Center for Oral History Research, Young Research Library, University of California, Los Angeles. Audio recording, tape no. 4, side 1; transcript, 128.

29. See chap. 1 for an overview of the black presence in different areas of Los Angeles.

30. Samella Lewis, *African American Art and Artists*.

31. Samella Lewis, *African American Art for Young People*.

32. The Museum of African American Art is located in the Baldwin Hills Crenshaw Plaza, the commercial and cultural hub of the community. The plaza hosts the annual Pan African Film Festival, one of the largest of its kind in the nation. See chap. 2 for a discussion of the Crenshaw District.

33. See chap. 5 for more detailed information on the US Organization.

34. Sam Rodia, *Watts Towers*, Watts Towers Arts Center, Los Angeles, California, 1921–1955.

35. Schrank, *Art and the City*.

36. See chaps. 1, 2, and 5 for more extensive discussions of the 1992 Los Angeles uprisings.

37. See chap. 2 for a discussion of the West Adams area.

38. The mural, completed in 2003, depicts the story of the 1791 slave rebellion in Haiti that inspired the Still's opera, *Troubled Island*. "The viewer experiences,

dramatically, the pain and suffering of the slaves and the rise to power of Jean-Jacques Dessalines, leader of the slave revolt. In the center of the pictorial saga is William Grant Still, with his spiritual 'eye' depicted in the middle of his forehead, conducting his powerful operatic score which expresses the need for a new era of interracial understanding, loving-kindness and God-consciousness on the earth" ("William Grant Still Art Center and Mural," *William Grant Still Music*, http://www.troubledisland.com/wgsartcenter).

39. Willis, *Reflections in Black*.

40. Charles, Igus, and Bellamy, *Life in a Day of Black L.A.* The book was published by the UCLA Center for Afro-American Studies (which later became the Bunche Center), and an accompanying traveling exhibit toured throughout the Southern California region, as well as to New York and other cities.

41. Lawrence is an African American artist best known for the *Migration of the Negro*, "an epic narrative series of sixty paintings that he completed in 1941 at the age of twenty-four" ("Biography of Jacob Lawrence: Art and Life," The Jacob and Gwen Knight Lawrence Virtual Resource Center, http://www.jacobandgwen lawrence.org/artandlife01.html).

42. Christopher Reynolds, "The Board Game," *Los Angeles Times*, April 27, 2003, arts section, http://articles.latimes.com/2003/apr/27/entertainment/ca-reynolds27 (accessed April 15, 2009).

43. Samella Lewis, interview conducted in 1995 by Karen Anne Mason, Center for Oral History Research, Young Research Library, University of California, Los Angeles. Audio recording, tape no. 2, side 2; transcript, 74.

44. See chaps. 1 and 2 for geographical renderings of Black Los Angeles.

45. Eric Hanks, interview by author, 2008.

46. Thomas Lawson, "Los Angeles 1955–1985: The Birth of an Artistic Capital," *ArtForum*, September 2006, http://findarticles.com/p/articles/mi_m0268/is_1_45/ai_n19492579 (accessed April 15, 2009).

Chapter 11

|||||||||||||||||||||||||||||||||||||||||||||||||||||||||

SOLAR

The History of the Sound of Los Angeles Records

Scot Brown

SOLAR (Sound of Los Angeles Records) was the most dominant, black-owned record label from the late 1970s through the 1980s.[1] SOLAR, known as the Motown of the 1980s, dominated R&B and pop music with a run of hits from a large roster of artists, including The Whispers, Shalamar, Lakeside, Midnight Star, Klymaxx, Carrie Lucas, The Deele, Calloway, and Babyface. SOLAR flourished in the midst of a major transformation in the history of American and African American music—large entertainment conglomerates took a serious interest in gaining a stronghold in black music consumer markets. This change corresponded with a trend toward globalization and corporate consolidation in the music industry at large, leading to the virtual eradication of any significant market share on the part of independent labels.[2] The drift toward consolidation and usurpation accelerated in the decades to follow, thereby generating new competitive challenges for the survival of black-owned record companies.

The late 1970s was not necessarily an opportune time for a start-up black record label, as major companies had established "black music divisions" aimed at gaining a foothold in African American music consumer markets. Larkin Arnold (Capitol), LaBaron Taylor (CBS), and Tom Draper (Warner Bros.) were among a slew of talented black executives who redesigned artist recruitment and product marketing practices to fit the distinctiveness of the African American music market—business strategies that had been, prior to the 1970s, the domains of black-owned and small "boutique" labels.[3] Though Motown Records (which had moved to Los Angeles in 1972) continued to reign as one of the most powerful African American enterprises, its commanding position vis-à-vis popular music

was steadily declining amid increased competition from larger corporations—a glaring symbol to this effect being the steady flight of its top artists and producers to other labels, such as The Jackson 5 (Epic), Four Tops
(ABC), Gladys Knight and the Pips (Buddha Records), Temptations (At-
lantic), and Marvin Gaye (Columbia).[4]

Two other prominent black labels—Stax and Philadelphia International
Records—each of which had their own controversial business relationship
with CBS records—were unable to endure these difficult times. Stax Records was sold in 1977, and by the early 1980s Philadelphia International
had already seen its most successful days. In 1997 the pop music historian
David Sanjek observed that SOLAR had distinguished itself from other recently established black labels: "[o]ne can point to such recent enterprises
as Sylvia and Joe Robinson's Sugar Hill Records, Dick Griffey's Solar Records, or Paisley Park Records . . . all, with the exception of Solar Records,
are no longer labels in the commercial spotlight."[5] This chapter chronicles
how the unique setting of Black Los Angeles gave rise to SOLAR, a black-
owned label that would define a decade of popular black music.

Dick Griffey: Road to Economic Nationalism

By the time SOLAR was launched, Dick Griffey had amassed decades of
experience in multiple facets of the music business. He learned to play the
drums at an early age, having grown up in a musical household in Nashville, Tennessee. His mother, Juanita Hines, was a gospel vocalist and key-
boardist for the National Baptist Convention. In the early 1950s, Griffey
attended Pearl High School in Nashville, studying with the formidable
music educator and band conductor, Marcus Gunter. The trumpeter Way-
mon Reed (who went on to play in Count Basie's band and who was married to Sarah Vaughn) played with Griffey in a jazz band during their high
school years. In 1957, after spending a year at Tennessee State University
on a music scholarship and playing with the university marching band,
Griffey served in the U.S. Navy as a medic and relocated to San Diego.[6]
After his discharge in 1961, he settled in the West Adams/West Jefferson
section of Los Angeles and worked as a certified private-duty nurse.

A few years later, Griffey's Tennessee State schoolmate and basketball
player, Dick Barnett, moved to California to play for the Los Angeles Lakers. The two opened the Guys & Dolls club, located at 3617 S. Crenshaw
Boulevard at a time when an increasing number of African American

residents and businesses were moving west of the city's historic Central Avenue district—a trend that continued to accelerate after the U.S. Supreme Court's ban on discriminatory restrictions in housing in 1948.[7]

Griffey booked top-performing acts at Guys & Dolls, regularly bringing in artists such as the Impressions, Temptations, Four Tops, Jackie Wilson, and Johnny "Guitar" Watson. Living up to its advertising slogan, "The Haven for the Greatest Athletes and Celebrities,"[8] the nightclub was a natural path toward Griffey's career as a concert promoter. Initially booking acts in Los Angeles venues such as the Adams West Theater, he went on to become one of the leading promoters of R&B and Soul concerts through the mid 1970s, handling the performances of Al Green, the Temptations, Aretha Franklin, as well as the international tours of The Jacksons, and Stevie Wonder.[9]

While among a small clique of black promoters of national stature in 1973, Griffey raised the issue of racism in the music industry and the need for African American empowerment—recurring concerns that would shape his entrepreneurial efforts. Noting the widespread exclusion of black promoters from large national venues, he stated in 1973 that "[t]here are a lot of capable black promoters all over the country who deserve a shot at some of these major concerts." In keeping with the popularity of economic nationalism throughout the Black Power years of the late 1960s and early 1970s, Griffey asserted that blacks themselves held the power to transform this problematic relationship to capital by way of their own cooperative efforts: "Black artists should be pressing their agents and managers to deal with some of these black promoters. . . . [They] have the power to do something about this bad situation, but they have been lax and indifferent."[10]

From Soul Train to SOLAR

Don Cornelius, the former Chicago newscaster for WCIU-TV and host/ executive producer of the black music variety show *Soul Train*, also considered his show as part of the ongoing struggle for black economic power. While the show's programming was centered on black music, Cornelius was interested in expanding African American leadership in the television industry beyond the entertainment level, arguing that "there is a place in television for blacks who don't sing, dance or tell jokes." "This is," he continued, "what I set out to prove with *Soul Train*."[11] Within two years of *Soul Train*'s debut in 1970 as a Chicago weekday program, the show emerged as a syndicated weekly program spanning media markets throughout the nation. The capacity for black financial cooperation to impact and potentially transform racially exclusionary segments of the American popular culture industry was perhaps best exemplified in *Soul Train*'s co-sponsorship by Johnson Products, one of the largest African American businesses and manufacturers of black hair care and cosmetics.[12] After *Soul Train* moved to Los Angeles in 1971, Griffey joined forces with Cornelius as the talent coordinator for the show. In 1975 they formed Soul Train Records, which featured a roster of artists that included The Soul Train Gang, The Whispers, Carrie Lucas, Shalamar, and Sunbear.

In late 1977, after Cornelius left Soul Train Records, came the label's name change to SOLAR, with Griffey as the head of the company.[13] The label experienced immediate commercial success with a string of hits on both the R&B and pop charts. Like Motown, Stax, and Philadelphia International, SOLAR's success was tied to its ability to translate local urban culture into a consumer product. Los Angeles's position as the nation's media and entertainment center, however, blurred traditional distinctions between "local" and national black cultural trends. *Soul Train* was as much a part of the Black Los Angeles public sphere as it was an iconic black cultural institution. The prize of appearing on *Soul Train* invigorated dance competitions in nightclubs, public schools, and neighborhoods throughout Los Angeles. Furthermore, the dances, fashions, and hairstyles popularized by the show were a reflection of the styles and tastes of African American youth in Los Angeles and of those transported westward by the steady migration of black artists from other cities (see fig. 11.1).

Temille Porter, a John Muir High School student, and her dance partner, Charlie Allen, received an honorary mention at the radio station KDAY's "Ultra Sheen, Afro Sheen, 7-Up Dance Contest," held at the Whiskey a-Go-Go club on Sunset Boulevard in June 1975. The prize for placing was an audition for *Soul Train* at the KTTV Studios. Two months later, the two of them—donning matching tropical print outfits, made by her mother, Mazree Porter—strolled gallantly down the *Soul Train* line.[14]

One of SOLAR's first top-selling groups, Shalamar, was a direct product of *Soul Train*. Two vocalists in the group, Jeffrey Daniel and Jody Whatley, were both dancers on the show and contributed to the growth of numerous dance styles seen by national audiences on *Soul Train*—for example, waacking, popping, robotics, and backsliding (popularized by Michael Jackson as moon-walking). SOLAR's promotion of the Shalamar

Figure 11.1. Jocelyn Banks and Fred Camble on *Soul Train* television program, Calif., August 27, 1975. Photo courtesy of Los Angeles Times Photographic Archive, Department of Special Collections, Charles E. Young Research Library, UCLA.

Disco Garden LP (1978) made use of national networks with radio stations and record stores through dance contests: "Radio personalities in all tour cities are being invited to host the contests held in each area's prominent disco," the *Los Angeles Sentinel* reported, "with entry blanks being distributed through record stores."[15] Clearly these events furthered Shalamar's status as a competitive vocal group affiliated with the disco craze, complementing the marketing niche of the label's dance music diva, Carrie Lucas

("I Got to Keep Dancin" [1977] and "Dance With You" [1979]). In 1978 the Shalamar vocalist Gerald Brown was replaced by Howard Hewitt. This lineup's dazzling stage performances and consistent hit records from 1979 through 1983 ensured Shalamar's passage from the last gasps of disco to early '80s R&B and pop music: "Second Time Around" (1979); "Right in the Socket" (1980); "Full of Fire" (1980); "Make That Move" (1981); "This Is for the Lover in You" (1981); "I Can Make You Feel Good" (1982); "A Night to Remember" (1982); and "Dead Giveaway" (1983).

Unlike Shalamar, The Whispers, a doo-wop styled vocal group from Watts, had been a staple in the Los Angeles music scene for more than a decade before SOLAR was formed. Described in the *Los Angles Sentinel* in 1970 as "the most popular vocal group in the Los Angeles area," the group comprised of twin brothers Walter and Wallace Scott, Nicholas Caldwell, Marcus Hutson and Gordy Harmon (all of whom attended Jordan High School)—began singing together in the early 1960s. In 1971 Harmon left, after which Leaveil Degree, formerly of The Friends of Distinction, joined the group. The Whispers had recorded on a number of smaller labels prior to signing with *Soul Train* and SOLAR Records.[16] Their final album with Janus Records, *Whispers Getting Louder*, was released in 1974 after which Griffey, then manager of the group, purchased its contract from the Chess Records subsidiary.[17] By 1979, when many Motown-styled vocal groups were facing challenges due to the popularity of self-contained funk bands and the mainstream dominance of disco, the Whispers had demonstrated the continued commercial viability of their style with the dance classic "And the Beat Goes On."[18]

The success of Shalamar and the Whispers notwithstanding, SOLAR embraced the trend toward self-contained bands in black music. One of the early SOLAR hit singles was "It's All the Way Live" (1979) by Lakeside, a nine-member band from Dayton, Ohio (Fred Alexander, Norman Beavers, Marvin Craig, Fred Lewis, Tiemeyer McCain, Thomas Shelby, Stephen Shockley, Otis Stokes, and Mark Wood). Formed in 1969 as the Nomads and Young Underground, Lakeside was a product of the rich live-music tradition in Dayton that gave birth to a host of self-contained funk and R&B bands, such as Ohio Players, Sun, Heatwave, Slave, Zapp (Roger Troutman), and several others. Dayton's African American public sphere was a virtual training ground for bands in the craft of live stage performance with its numerous nightclubs and talent show competitions. Mark Wood described the city's "battle of the bands" ethic as "sportsman-like." "When it came to the stage," he noted, "it was all about how the audience reacted and you had to do something to top the other guy's ability to get that instant impact out of the crowd."[19]

In 1972 Lakeside arrived in Los Angeles, due to the unintended consequence of a gig gone sour in Oklahoma. Armed with the sole resource of their performance skills, the nine-member band scrambled to find work in Los Angeles's nightclub scene. The band scored a major coup by impressing John Daniels, the famed owner of The Maverick's Flat on Crenshaw Boulevard, and thereby securing regular appearances at one of the most important Los Angeles venues for major black acts.[20] Lakeside's show, described as "Sexy Soul Unlimited," blended the choreographed, Motown-era style of vocal groups like the Temptations with the raw self-contained musical energy of their Dayton mentors, the Ohio Players. The group generated a big local following and regularly attracted, as Norman Beavers recalled, "a line of people halfway around the block coming to see us every night. We [were] like the thing in Los Angeles," he continued, and "[t]hey started having radio advertisements, 'Come see them, the panty snatchers, come see Lakeside!'"[21]

Within a few years, Lakeside surpassed local notoriety as a performing act and recorded their first album on ABC Records under the direction of Frank Wilson, former Motown producer/songwriter. Even though *Lakeside Express* was released in 1977, the LP did not fare well, given the acquisition of the label by MCA Records. Soon thereafter Lakeside signed with SOLAR. Griffey, who had managed the band, offered extensive artistic freedom and opportunities for songwriting and publishing. Their first two albums, *A Shot of Love* (1978) and *Rough Riders* (1979), were co-produced by Leon Sylvers III (the producer/songwriter behind SOLAR's initial success), but the largest commercial success occurred with the self-produced *Fantastic Voyage* in 1980.

Admittedly, Lakeside's members learned a great deal from the production expertise of Leon Sylvers. Leon was the second oldest in a musical family of nine children and had been involved in music for many years before he began working with SOLAR artists. As a youngster growing up in the Nickerson Gardens public housing complex in Watts, he—along with two of his sisters, Olympia-Ann and Charmaine, and his brother James —comprised a vocal group called The Little Angels. The group appeared on numerous television variety shows in the late 1950s and early 1960s, such as Art Linkletter's *House Party*, *The Groucho Show*, *The Spike Jones Show*, *The Dinah Shore Show*, and *The Danny Thomas Show*.[22] Leon and his siblings also competed at numerous talent shows through the 1960s, including one at his high school, Verbum Dei, where they placed second behind another family group called Johnson Three Plus One (Tommy, George, and Louis Johnson, and Alex Weir). George and Louis Johnson went on to become the sensational funk duo, The Brothers Johnson.[23]

In the early 1970s, the family group The Sylvers, which grew to include Edmund, Joseph, Angelia, Patricia, and Foster, recorded with MGM and then Capitol Records. Leon, a multi-instrumentalist (bass, guitar, and keyboards) and serious student of the Motown sound, learned recording skills from Freddie Perren, who had previously worked with the Motown production team known as The Corporation before producing The Sylvers and delivering the hits "Boogie Fever" (1975) and "Hotline" (1976).[24] This background gave Sylvers a unique penchant for arranging and recording complex harmonies alongside tight, up-tempo grooves, which became a trademark of dance hits by Shalamar, The Whispers, and Carrie Lucas.[25] Sylvers's musical voice resounds clearly in the compositions of his own group, Dynasty. In this group, he, along with Linda Carrier, William Shelby, Kevin Spencer, and Nidra Beard, as well as band members Wayne Milstein, Wardell Potts Jr., Richard Randolph, Ernest "Pepper" Reed, and Ricky Smith crafted a series of club classics, including the infectious "I've Just Begun to Love You" (1980). Summing up Sylvers's impact, Virgil Roberts, former president and general counsel for SOLAR, mused: "if you were doing a family tree probably all of the great producers from the last twenty-five years came from Leon."[26]

The 1980s SOLAR Sound

By 1981, SOLAR was a recognized force in the music industry, noted for being part of the revival of "spirited '[b]lack pop.'" Some music critics wondered if the label's late 1970s run would continue into the new decade.[27] The issue was certainly valid from a sonic standpoint. The pop and R&B music of the 1980s faced the displacement of strings, horns, guitars, congas, and timbales by the synthesizer and drum machine. Sylvers continued to produce Shalamar and The Whispers, as well as a host of artists on other labels (for example, Gladys Knight, The Brothers Johnson, Glenn Jones, Evelyn "Champagne" King, Blackstreet and Guy) but members from the self-contained bands Midnight Star and The Deele added significantly to the company's songwriting and producing resources during the period.

Figure 11.2. SOLAR act Midnight Star. Photo courtesy of
Vincent Calloway.

The Cincinnati-based Midnight Star released their initial SOLAR album in 1980 and, similar to Lakeside, began to self-produce by their
third LP *Victory* (1982) (see fig. 11.2). The group of highly trained musicians—Reginald Calloway, Vincent Calloway, Kenneth Gant, Melvin
Gentry, Belinda Lipscomb, Jeffrey Cooper, Bobby Lovelace, William Simmons, and Bo Watson (many of whom attended Kentucky State University)—developed a formula that worked for the changing times on the
No Parking on the Dance Floor LP, released in 1983. Produced by band
leader Reggie Calloway, the group blended 1980s electronic sound tech-
nologies with sophisticated musical and lyrical arrangements. Virtually
every member of Midnight Star played numerous instruments and possessed great songwriting skills. This facilitated its ability to change toward

a synthesizer-driven sound, as an accompaniment to the rich vocals of Melvin Gentry, Belinda Lipscomb, and Bo Watson.

Three years before *No Parking on the Dance Floor* reached the airwaves, another Ohio funk artist, Roger Troutman (leader of the group Zapp), transformed the range and melodic possibilities of the talk box or voice box, a device that allows an artist to fuse vocal patterns with the sound emitted by electronic instruments and thus mimic speech. "More Bounce to the Ounce," the first single released from Zapp's eponymous Warner Bros. LP, stood as a declaration of sonic progress—the fattened Mini Moog Bass line offered much more bounce than the standard four-string bass guitar. Troutman described the voice of the talk box on "More Bounce" with the imagery of science fiction film and television: "I consider the voice box . . . like an African robot. . . . It says logical things that a computer says, but instead of saying them very drab and disgusting as a robot would say, . . . I can sound computerized and I can also sound real funky."[28]

Even more robotic in tone, the device known as the vocoder closely linked the synthesizer with vocals and conveyed a sci-fi aesthetic in '80s dance music (for example, Kano's "I'm Ready" [1980], Kraftwerk's "Numbers" [1981], Earth, Wind & Fire's "Let's Groove" [1981], Afrika Bambaataa's "Planet Rock" [1982], and The Jonzun's Crew's "Pack Jam" [1982]). Reggie Calloway, ever-conscious of music as a gateway to a danceable futurism, conceptualized Midnight Star's first vocoder-laden single, "Freak-A-Zoid" as "already ahead of its time." He continued, "you're taking a word like freak which is old as dirt and then 'zoid' which is now until tomorrow and people will always deal with the freaky side of things and the whole computer age will continue and never die."[29] His brother Vincent's vocoder voice on other releases (e.g., "No Parking on the Dance Floor" [1983], "Electricity" [1983], and "Operator" [1984]) ensured Midnight Star's standing as innovative artists within this trend.

Beyond electro-dance and funk, Midnight Star introduced Kenny "Babyface" Edmonds as a co-writer on the ballad "Slow Jam" (1983). The same year Reggie Calloway produced the debut of The Deele—of which Edmonds and L.A. Reid were members—on SOLAR records with the LP *Streetbeat*. Furthermore, Midnight Star and The Deele provided a host of songwriter/producers—the Calloway brothers, Bo Watson, Babyface, and L.A. Reid—who worked on projects for other SOLAR artists (The Whispers, Klymaxx, Babyface, and Calloway), creating an identifiable 1980s SOLAR sound.

The all-women's R&B/funk band Klymaxx, also came of age as a SOLAR act as the label entered the era of Reagan, MTV, and Michael Jackson. Black women instrumental musicians in blues, jazz, rock, and other genres have a long history of subverting gendered notions of propriety in their mastery of instruments not deemed "feminine."[30] Just a few years prior to Klymaxx's first LP in 1981, Janice Marie Johnson and Hazel Payne, the vocal, bass, and guitar duo, had blazed a trail for women musicians as front persons for the Los Angeles band A Taste of Honey, which scored the iconic disco hit "Boogie Oogie Oogie" (1978). Though the disco era has been noted for offering an alternative to the masculine ethos celebrated in rock, funk and R&B, the notion of women as electric guitarists was (and remains) a novelty in American pop music.

Klymaxx, comprised of Bernadette Cooper (drums and vocals), Lorena Porter (lead vocals), Joyce "Fenderella" Irby (bass), Cheryl Cooley (guitar), and Lynn Malsby (keyboards) and Robbin Grider (keyboards and vocals), was a living testimony to their first album *Never Underestimate the Power of a Woman* (1981). The musical arrangement of the title track, with its hard-driving groove, many time-signature changes, crescendos, and modulations, and its defiant lyrics, posed a direct challenge to conceptions of the "band" as an exclusive male province. Unlike A Taste of Honey, Klymaxx—buoyed by collaborations with independent (newly minted Terry Lewis and Jimmy Jam)[31] and in-house producers (such as the Calloway brothers, Steve Shockley, and Bo Watson)—thrived through most of the 1980s with dance hits such as "Heartbreaker" (1982), "The Men All Pause" (1984), "Meeting in the Ladies Room" (1984), as well as classic ballads "I Miss You" (1984) and "I'd Still Say Yes" (1986).

Klymaxx emerged as the top-selling act on Constellation Records, a SOLAR subsidiary established after a contractual renegotiation with its distributor Elektra/Asylum following the replacement of CEO Joe Smith with Bob Krasnow in 1983.[32] Intent on cutting back Elektra's expenses, Krasnow moved to reduce SOLAR's artist roster and number of releases, which reportedly amounted to "about 12 albums and 25 singles per year."[33] Virgil Roberts explained that SOLAR "negotiated a reduction in the artist roster, but we also made it non-exclusive so we could take those artists and make another deal."[34] Subsequently, Constellation was formed and "the artists that we took off of the Elektra label [Klymaxx, Carrie Lucas, and Collage]," he continued, "we put on Constellation and made a distribution deal with MCA."[35]

The formation of Constellation occurred after SOLAR had already re-located to one of the lasting symbols of its 1980s prowess, its own multi-story building at 1635 N. Cahuenga Boulevard in Hollywood, which housed its own recording studio, executive offices, rehearsal hall, showcase rooms, and auxiliary businesses (see fig. 11.3). Griffey's economic empowerment agenda was evident in the effort to include as many African Americans as possible in the construction process. After securing financing for the build-ing project on the lot previously occupied by game show producer Chuck Barris, SOLAR employed real estate agent Vanessa Jollivette, daughter of Bettye Jollivette (the former deputy real estate commissioner for the state of California), as the developer and construction manager for the project. Jollivette hired Ray Dones, founding member of the National Association of Minority Contractors, as part of the general contractor team, and Ma-mie Johnson as the interior contractor.[36] "We knew," Jollivette recalled, "that we were embarking upon new territory that could instill entrepreneurial 'can do' attitudes in . . . not just the local community, [but also] the African American community throughout the United States."[37]

Pan-Africanism and Transitions

Griffey's focus on economic empowerment was tied to a spirited Pan-Africanist perspective. Unlike Philadelphia International or even Motown during the 1970s, SOLAR Records did not musically convey a strong iden-tification or affiliation with black social and political movements. Strategi-cally, Griffey tended to keep the world of selling records and liberation politics in different spheres. Prior to founding SOLAR in 1973, he had promoted a concert, co-sponsored by the Los Angeles Pan-African Law Center to assist in raising funds for FRELIMO (Liberation Front of Mo-zambique). Griffey became more fully engaged with Africa in 1980, when he along with activist Ayuko Babu, Rep. Maxine Waters (D-Los Angeles), and others mobilized to bring the Guinean dance troupe, Les Ballet Afric-ains, to perform at the city's bicentennial celebration. In making arrange-ments for the event Griffey traveled to Guinea with the delegation and met President Sékou Touré.[38]

Politically, thereafter, Griffey formed the Coalition for a Free Africa and became heavily involved in the U.S. anti-apartheid movement, work-ing closely with Rev. Jesse Jackson and PUSH/Rainbow Coalition, the NAACP, Artists and Athletes Against Apartheid, and other activists. Los

Figure 11.3. SOLAR building in Hollywood. Photo courtesy of Darnell Hunt.

Angeles, as the global media/entertainment center, became a major staging ground for anti-apartheid activism where the cause achieved heightened status, given the frequent publicity accorded by high-profile celebrity support.[39]

In 1986 Griffey, Jesse Jackson, and a large group of civic and business leaders embarked on a seventeen-day "fact-finding" trip to eight African nations: Nigeria, Congo, Angola, Botswana, Mozambique, Zambia, Tanzania, and Zimbabwe. The trip spurred closer bonds between the antiapartheid movement and liberation support of neighboring "frontline" African states.[40] The campaign to divest from the apartheid regime and pressure the U.S. government to withdraw support of South African–backed rebels in Angola and Mozambique was, from Griffey's standpoint, part and parcel of a vision for developing black economic solidarity.[41] While continuing to lobby for U.S. policy changes in respect to a number of political issues facing the African continent, Griffey was working steadfastly to create business relationships between SOLAR and African markets for black music.[42] He concluded that opportunities for international trade with African countries could generate an alternative to the inevitable pattern of large corporate interests overtaking the independence of smaller black-owned boutique record labels, such as SOLAR.[43]

By the 1990s, it became clear that the SOLAR CEO's Pan-Africanism framed his criticism and self-criticism of the music industry and broader obstacles to black economic empowerment. Looking at the history of his label, Griffey conceded that power ultimately rested with the conglomerates that controlled venues for market access to musical products. "Distributors have the best of everything," he asserted, "[i]t is not necessary for them to be very talented, since they have an infrastructure that says, 'If you want to get your product to the marketplace, you have to come through me.'"[44] Griffey stated that even SOLAR had "been dependent in that way: my record company and my music company were always distributed by RCA or Warner or MCA or Capitol or Lasky or through a joint venture with Sony."[45] He eventually started the African Development Public Investment Corporation, which specialized in investment and trade in the continent's vast mineral wealth. Moving in a new direction, Griffey declared, "I feel strongly that we Africans need to do something for ourselves that can stand on its own, where we do not need those [corporate] intermediaries."[46] In 1992 SOLAR released its last major recording, the soundtrack to the film *Deep Cover*, highlighted by the introduction of would-be West Coast hip-hop icons Dr. Dre and Snoop Dogg on the LP's title track. Griffey was instrumental in the subsequent creation of Death Row Records but eventually went on to focus primarily on his businesses in Africa.

Legacies

SOLAR (as an institution and sound) had deep roots in the Los Angeles African American public sphere, but it also benefited from the city's position as a global entertainment magnet that attracted multitudinous waves of black artists, cultural workers, political activists, and entrepreneurs from all over the United States and beyond. The label was a catalyst for a Los Angeles 1980s R&B sound characterized by polished melodic vocals, thick bass synthesizer lines, analogue and digital keyboard chords, steady drum machine beats, and lyrical themes centering primarily on love and celebrating life, as opposed to explicit confrontations with social and political issues. SOLAR's musical formula and commercial success from the late 1970s through the 1980s energized other black-owned labels based in Los Angeles during this period: Clarence Avant's Tabu Records (S.O.S. band, Alexander O'Neal, Cherelle), Lonnie Smith's Total Experience

Records (The Gap Band, Yarbrough and Peoples, and Goodie), and Otis Smith's Beverly Glen Music (Chapter 8, Anita Baker, and Bobby Womack).

Like so many black-owned record labels that preceded it (Vee-Jay Records, Motown, Stax, and Philadelphia International), SOLAR not only identified African American talent, but tended to stay with and develop artists in ways that were often not the case with major labels. Griffey, summarizing the success of black-owned labels in recent history, noted that the "majority of the majors . . . have money, they have financing, and they have the infrastructure but they really don't have the Berry Gordys, the Kenny Gambles or the Al Bells," who can see potential beyond quick profits. "When you're looking at the diamond in the rough," he concluded, "most people don't know if it's just a rock . . . Everybody can recognize something once it's already cut and polished."[47] By the close of the 1990s, the SOLAR Towers building was sold to one of the label's former artists, Kenny "Babyface" Edmonds, who along with L.A. Reid had established their own LA/Face Records. The structure stands as evidence of the institutional fortitude of SOLAR Records and the perpetuation of a black cultural and entrepreneurial legacy in Los Angeles.

NOTES

1. The author is grateful for critical assistance from Virgil Roberts in research for this chapter.

2. Kennedy and Mcnutt, *Little Labels—Big Sound*; Burnett, *Global Jukebox*.

3. Person-Lynn, "Insider Perspectives"; "Black Executives in the Record Business," *Los Angeles Sentinel*, December 29, 1977, 7, 15, 31; George, *Death of Rhythm & Blues*.

4. Posner, *Motown: Music, Money, Sex, and Power*.

5. Sanjek, "One Size Does Not Fit All," 555.

6. Dick Griffey, "Interview with the Author: Transcript" (University of California at Los Angeles, 2008).

7. *Westwood One: Special Edition LP [Solar Records]* (Culver City, CA: Westwood One, 1983), Sound Recording; "Guys & Dolls Host Jim Brown Night," *Los Angeles Sentinel*, December 31, 1964, B4; Griffey, "Interview with the Author: Transcript." See also chaps. 1 and 2 for a discussion of this trend.

8. "Guys & Dolls Host Jim Brown Night," B4.

9. Griffey, "Interview with the Author: Transcript"; Myers, "An Afternoon with Dick Griffey," 341.

10. Dennis Hunt, "Griffey: Kingpin of Soul Promoters," *Los Angeles Times*, August 9, 1973, C24.

11. "Don Cornelius Is Guest on WBEE's 'Minority Forum,'" *Daily Defender*, October 17, 1974, 15.

12. "Soul Train Hit with Teens," *Daily Defender*, September 21, 1970, 13; "'Soul Train' Back for 2nd Season TV Series," *Daily Defender*, September 20, 1972, 12; Walker, *History of Black Business in America*, 303–09.

13. "Dick Griffey Concerts," *Los Angeles Sentinel*, July 21, 1983, B8.

14. "Jim Maddox, KDAY Program Director, and Jean Tillman, KDAY Community Relations Director to Temille Porter, June 20, 1975" (Personal Files of Temille Porter, Los Angeles, CA); "Pam Brown, Soul Train Teen Coordinator to Temille Porter, August 1975" (Los Angeles: Personal Files of Temille Porter, Los Angeles, CA).

15. "SOLAR Launches National Dance Contest," *Los Angeles Sentinel*, November 16, 1978, B1A.

16. *The Whispers Bio*, http://thewhispers.com/BIO/BIO.html. (accessed March 18 2009); "May Day with Major Lance," *Los Angeles Sentinel* June, 3 1965, C10. "L.A. Twins Score Big with the Whispers Five," *Los Angeles Sentinel*, December 3, 1970, B.

17. Dick Griffey, "Interview with the Author: Transcript" (Los Angeles, 2009), 1.

18. "The Whispers Say: And Beat Goes On," *Los Angeles Sentinel*, April 24, 1980, B.

19. Mark Wood, "Interview with the Author: Transcript" (University of California at Los Angeles, 2007), 6.

20. For an insightful firsthand account of the black music scene in Los Angeles in the early 1970s, see Patryce Banks, *A "Choc' Let" State of Mind*, 56–87.

21. Norman Beavers, "Interview with the Author: Transcript" (University of California at Los Angeles, 2007), 11.

22. Leon Sylvers III, "Interview with the Author: Notes" (University of California at Los Angeles, 2009).

23. Ibid.

24. "Interview Transcript: Leon Sylvers III" (Karen Shearer Collection, Archives of African American Music and Culture, Indiana University, 1982).

25. Leon Sylvers III, "Interview with the Author: Notes"; "Interview Transcript: Leon Sylvers III." Sylvers often collaborated with individual members of different SOLAR groups and his own team of writers and musicians, including Vincent Brantley, Marcus Hare, Dana Myers, Wardell Potts, Ernest "Pepper" Reed, William Shelby, Ricky Smith, Kevin Spencer, and William Zimmerman.

26. Virgil Roberts, "Interview with the Author: Transcript" (University of California at Los Angeles, 2008). Indeed, Sylvers helped launch the careers of Terry Lewis and Jimmy Jam as independent producers.

27. Gene Sculatti, "'Home Runs, No Bunts'—Solar Power on the Rise," *Los Angeles Times*, December 6 1981, 82.

28. "Interview Transcript: Zapp (Roger Troutman)" (Karen Shearer Collection, Archives of African American Music and Culture, Indiana University, 1982), 2.

29. "Interview Transcript: Midnight Star (Reggie Calloway)" (Karen Shearer Collection, Archives of African American Music and Culture, Indiana University, 1984), 6.

30. See M. Johnson ("Black Women Electric Guitarists") and Porter (*What Is This Thing Called Jazz?*) for a discussion of black women blues guitarists such as Memphis Minnie, Rosetta Tharpe, Beverly "Guitar" Watkins, Barbara Lynn, Deborah Coleman, and B. B. Queen. Similar challenges face women instrumentalists in jazz, rock and other genres (Tucker, *Swing Shift*; Porter, *What Is This Thing Called Jazz?*; Mahon, "Race, Gender and Genre").

31. Terry Lewis and Jimmy Jam (James Harris III) secured initial production work for Tabu Records through their manager, SOLAR executive Dina Andrews.

32. "Warner Names Head of Elektra Record Unit," *New York Times*, January 12, 1983, D2.

33. "Dick Griffey/Solar Records Pact," *Los Angeles Sentinel*, June 4, 1981, B9.

34. Roberts, "Interview with the Author: Transcript," 18.

35. Ibid.

36. Ibid

37. Vanessa Jollivette, "Interview with the Author: Audio Recording" (University of California Los Angeles, 2009).

38. Ayuko Babu, "Interview with the Author: Transcript," (2008), 7, 27–31; Griffey, "Interview with the Author: Transcript," 15–26.

39. "ANC Mothers Inaugural Banquet," *Los Angeles Sentinel*, May 1, 1986; "Anti-Apartheid Telethon on Drawing Board," *Los Angeles Sentinel*, April 17, 1986, A1.

40. Stanford, *Beyond the Boundaries*, 149.

41. "Tutu's U.S. Visit Stirs New Anti-Apartheid Awareness," *Los Angeles Sentinel*, January 30, 1986, A16; "SOLAR Chief Keynotes Ebonics Awards," *Los Angeles Sentinel*, June 19, 1986, A3.

42. *Westwood One: Special Edition LP* [Solar Records].

43. For a debate on the usurpation of black companies such as Motown and Johnson Products by large corporations, see Rhonda Reynolds, "Must Black Firms Stay in Black Hands?" *Black Enterprise* 26, no. 1 (1995): 191–92, 194, 198; "Big Music Beef at Home Why Funk African Gestapo," *New York Amsterdam News*, July 28, 1984.

44. Myers, "An Afternoon with Dick Griffey" 342–44.

45. Ibid.

46. Ibid.

47. Griffey, "Interview with the Author: Transcript," 26–37.

Chapter 12

‖‖

Killing "Killer King"
The Los Angeles Times *and a*
"Troubled" Hospital in the 'Hood

Darnell Hunt and Ana-Christina Ramón

Awarded to the *Los Angeles Times* for its courageous, exhaustively researched series exposing deadly medical problems and racial injustice at
a major public hospital.[1]

The above quote, which comes from an overview of the 2005 Pulitzer Prize
winners for Public Service, is as familiar as it is ambiguous. The "courageous, exhaustively researched series"[2] referred to in the quote is based
on the investigative work of a team of white *Los Angeles Times* reporters.[3] Celebrated by American journalism's highest award, this work documented startling cases of incompetence and fraud at Martin Luther King
Jr./Charles Drew Medical Center[4]—a county-run hospital that served one
of Los Angeles's poorest minority communities. "[I]t became clear to us
that King/Drew rated poorly on practically all statistical measures," wrote
lead reporter Charles Ornstein, in an interview with his alma mater's
newspaper.[5] "As we investigated further, we concluded that the hospital
was far more dangerous than the public knew."

Poor medical care for the poor, unfortunately, was all too familiar in
early-2000s America. What's ambiguous about the quote is its conception of "racial injustice," which can be read a number of different ways.
One of these readings reverses the traditional American pattern: the implied villains here are minorities, as opposed to members of the majority. Throughout its thirty-four-year history, King/Drew was known as a
hospital staffed mostly by black administrators, doctors, and nurses. The
Los Angeles Times series charged that too many of these staff members

—enabled by a pathological hospital culture and timid county oversight —pursued their own interests over those of their patients. "[T]hey kind of saw it as, they were entitled to their jobs," said Ornstein in another interview.[6] "Not that they owed their jobs to the people that came into the hospital." The result, the award-winning series argues, was a shamefully low standard of care for the surrounding community. "[A]lmost immediately, it started to get a reputation and it was called 'Killer King,'" noted Tracy Weber, the other lead reporter.[7] "And things happened there that shouldn't happen there."

How Martin Luther King Jr./Charles R. Drew Medical Center became known as "Killer King," it seems, is a telling cautionary tale. Envisioned as a model medical facility for Los Angeles's poor black community, and opened as a symbol of black pride and empowerment, King/Drew soon came to represent black failure. This chapter aims to make sense of this dramatic rise and fall within the broader context of Black Los Angeles and, ultimately, race in America. The case of King/Drew, we argue, is emblematic of both the promise and the pitfalls facing African Americans who seek to control their own institutions in a society structured to undermine black control. At the core of our analysis is coverage of King/Drew in Los Angeles's major newspaper, the *Los Angeles Times*, from the period leading up to the hospital's celebrated opening in 1972 to its controversial closure in 2007. Through a detailed analysis of articles from the *Times* and other newspapers, historical documents, and personal interviews, we attempt to flesh out in this chapter the subtle and not-so-subtle ways in which racial framing worked to divert attention away from other important determinants of the hospital's performance, thereby sealing its fate. This racial framing, to be sure, is rooted in political struggles associated with the earliest days of the hospital.

Rising Out of the Ashes

The "riots" in Watts that started on August 11, 1965, are discussed extensively throughout this book (e.g., see especially chap. 5). The point to be underscored here is that these uprisings constituted a defining moment in American race relations, a precursor to an explosion of unrest that would plague American cities throughout the summer of 1967. Indeed, the national crisis had prompted President Johnson's Kerner Commission to proclaim in 1968 that America was "moving toward two societies, one

Figure 12.1. King/Drew Medical Center near Watts. Photo courtesy of Darnell Hunt.

black, one white—separate and unequal."[8] The Watts uprisings, in many respects, signaled the end of the civil rights era of nonviolent racial protest and the rise of the by-any-means-necessary doctrine of "Black Power."[9]

A year after Watts, in 1966, the Black Power movement was in full swing, marked by the founding of the militant Black Panther Party for Self-Defense in Oakland, California. The Black Panthers, who would establish a formidable branch in Los Angeles,[10] issued a "Ten Point Plan" that identified "free health care for all black and oppressed people" as one of its core objectives.[11] The movement was further codified in 1967, when the activist Stokeley Carmichael and the political scientist Charles V. Hamilton published *Black Power: The Politics of Liberation*, which boldly made the case for community control of institutions affecting the lives of black people.

It is impossible to understand the rise of Martin Luther King Jr./ Charles R. Drew Medical Center without considering the significance of this moment. For much of white America, Watts and the urban rebellions that followed revealed an underside to society that was hidden in plain view. While the relationship between white power and racial inequality in America was no great secret in the mid-1960s, it was as if the explosions of anger that appeared across America between the summer of 1965 and 1967 had caught whites by surprise. California's governor, Edmund G.

"Pat" Brown, charged the McCone Commission with studying the causes of the Watts uprisings, which seemed rather obvious to those living in the ghetto.[12] Although the commission found that Los Angeles could still be considered a Promised Land for blacks compared to other cities, it theorized that the recently passed 1964 Civil Rights Act and 1965 Voting Rights Acts had set up unrealistically high expectations among blacks for progressive change.

Indeed, despite the apparent progress represented by new civil rights laws at the federal level, California continued to wrestle with its own racial demons. The California legislature had passed the Rumford Fair Housing Act in 1963 to end discrimination by landlords who refused to rent or sell their property to "colored" persons.[13] But just a year later, in 1964, two-thirds of California voters repealed the act with the passage of Proposition 14. The McCone Commission acknowledged that this defiant reassertion of white power by the largely white electorate affronted blacks, who in turn became increasingly frustrated and disillusioned. At the time, it's worth noting, 88.6 percent of the black population in Los Angeles lived in highly segregated communities.

While some criticized the McCone Commission for blaming the people of Watts for their own plight,[14] the commission nonetheless managed to offer several high-profile recommendations that went to the heart of conditions in the ghetto. Among them were the need to create jobs for blacks, an emergency program for raising the scholastic achievement of black children, and—of most importance to us in this chapter—the need to create a "new, comprehensively equipped hospital" near Watts that would serve the largely black and impoverished community in the area.[15] In its discussion of this last recommendation, the commission noted that there were only 106 physicians for the 252,000 people in the area, a ratio that was only a third of the overall county ratio. The commission also pointed out that the other major public hospitals, County General and Harbor General, "are distant and difficult to reach," particularly given the degree to which the Watts area was underserved by public transportation.[16] These county facilities, especially County General, also had reputations for providing less-than-desirable service to poor patients.[17]

The McCone Commission was unequivocal in its recommendation for the new hospital, urging that authorities give it "immediate and favorable consideration."[18] The recommendation proved to be just the catalyst needed to jumpstart long-standing, largely futile efforts to build such a hospital in the community. It was a recommendation grounded in black protest and white appeasement, offered on the eve of the Black Power era, which would lead to an altogether new vision for a community hospital.

Envisioning a Model Hospital for the 'Hood

There had been a number of attempts over the years to establish a hospital to serve the largely black and poor ghetto in the Watts area. Wells Ford, a local black physician, had joined with a group of citizens from Watts in the 1950s in an unsuccessful bid to obtain state funding for a hospital. The prizefighter Joe Louis had also participated in a failed attempt. In 1964 another black physician, Sol White Jr., unsuccessfully petitioned the State Advisory Hospital Council to erect a hospital near Watts. He tried again in the immediate aftermath of the uprisings, this time with the aid of nationwide attention focused on Watts and the McCone Commission recommendation.[19]

Following the recommendation of the McCone Commission, the Los Angeles County Board of Supervisors—the powerful elected body that oversees public services in one of the nation's largest counties—voted 3 to 2 in February 1966 to approve a $21 million county medical facility for the Southeast area of the county.[20] The proposal had been championed by one of the five white supervisors, Kenneth Hahn, whose district included the largely black area that would be served by the new facility, originally named Southeast General Hospital. But after only 64 percent of voters supported a bond issue to support the new hospital (a two-thirds vote was needed), the supervisors were forced to seek funding elsewhere.[21] California governor Ronald Reagan, like many of the voters who rejected the bond issue, was reluctant to support the plan for the hospital because he felt it rewarded those who had taken to the streets during the Watts uprisings. Hahn, nonetheless, was able to convince Reagan to support the plan, which eventually led to the procurement of sufficient state funds to initiate the project.[22] In a gesture to the largely black community the hospital would serve, the Board of Supervisors voted to rename the facility in honor of Martin Luther King Jr., just days after the civil rights icon was assassinated on April 4, 1968. Groundbreaking for the first phase of the facility followed shortly, on April 10, 1968 (see fig. 12.2),[23] and attracted a large delegation of dignitaries and more than 3,500 onlookers.[24] The

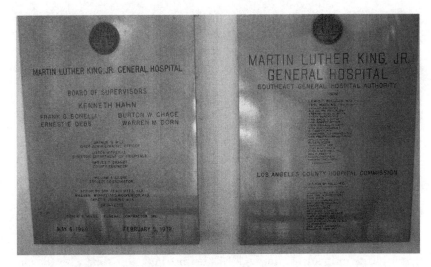

Figure 12.2. King/Drew Dedication Plaque. Photo courtesy of Darnell Hunt.

twenty-six-acre site in Willowbrook, an unincorporated area of Los Angeles County near Watts, was owned by the Public Housing Authority and sold to the county for $100,000.[25]

Prior to the civil rights movement, most black doctors were trained in hospitals founded by black physicians, fraternal organizations, and/or churches. These hospitals also served the lion's share of America's black patients. Indeed, there were 118 black-controlled hospitals throughout the nation in 1919, medical facilities that served a population often neglected by mainstream hospitals in a racially segregated America. As the civil rights movement slowly eroded the rigidity of segregation, however, mainstream hospitals became more accessible to both black patients and interns, which had the effect of offsetting at least some of the need for black-controlled hospitals. Between 1919 and 1993, the number of black-controlled hospitals declined by 93.2 percent, from 118 to just 8.[26]

But in 1968, when plans were taking shape for the new hospital named after Martin Luther King, more than half of all black medical students still attended a handful of black medical schools, and all of these schools were east of the Mississippi.[27] So it was in keeping with the times that the Charles R. Drew Medical Society—a Los Angeles–based organization of black doctors named after the famed black pioneer in blood storage techniques[28]—was selected as one of the entities that would direct the new hospital. The plan called for Drew Medical Society to be joined by the county's Department of Hospitals, as well as the medical schools at the University of California, Los Angeles[29] (UCLA) and the University of Southern California (USC).

Drew Medical Society was the key service provider in this shared-governance scheme. In conjunction with plans for the hospital, Drew Medical Society and its partners established the first black medical school west of the Mississippi in 1966,[30] which would train doctors interning at the new hospital and oversee the facility's medical staffing. Interns would provide most of the patient care, under the supervision of faculty from the Charles R. Drew Postgraduate Medical School and other hospital staff. The county would be responsible for administering the staffing of the hospital—which included hiring, performance evaluations, promotions, and paying Drew faculty members who provided services to the hospital.[31] This "teaching hospital" approach, in theory, constituted a cost-effective mechanism for providing care to indigent patients, who otherwise couldn't afford to pay and would include a significant portion of King/Drew's patients. The Drew-King linkage also would facilitate efforts to encourage Watts-area students to become healthcare workers, creating much-needed job opportunities in the area and addressing the critical shortage of medical staff willing and able to work in the ghetto-based facility.[32] The proposed 464-bed[33] general hospital would become the ninth hospital in the county's Department of Hospital system and only the third teaching-general hospital.[34]

In terms of geography, Los Angeles County was one of the nation's largest, its more than 4,000 square miles approximating the size of the state of Connecticut. The King Hospital Service Area comprised nine zip codes in the sprawling county[35]—a largely poor and black area in which most residents had experienced real declines in income between 1960 and 1965. Mervyn M. Dymally, a shrewd black politician who was elected to the California State Assembly in 1963 and the State Senate in 1967, represented these residents in Sacramento and was a staunch advocate for the proposed hospital.[36] As an early review of plans for the hospital pointed out, the facility's "strategic" location was carefully selected to maximize utility for area residents who were burdened by Watts's distance from other county hospitals.[37]

The new hospital was envisioned as a model facility for the community. Early plans identified six construction phases that would result in a comprehensive hospital providing an array of services not seen in most inner-city communities (or most hospitals, for that matter). As the hospital's first administrator noted prior to the facility's opening, these ambitious plans were aimed at setting a new standard for medical service delivery to the urban poor:

> In our opinion, it is this peripheral activity that is representative of the real excitement and hope of the Martin Luther King, Jr. General Hospital project. If our projections are correct, the project should serve as an example to the world of a sound treatment approach to all of the illnesses and disease which are bred of poverty and deprivation in ghettos around the world.[38]

And consistent with the ethos of the time, a moment informed by the Watts uprisings and key tenets of the doctrine of Black Power, those served by the hospital would play an active role in shaping its direction:

> The Martin Luther King, Jr. General is dedicated to community services and has adopted the philosophy that such service is possible only through a program of affirmative community involvement. Accordingly, all staff members regularly attend various community meetings as representatives of the hospital, and the community was invited to and has participated in the development of plans for the operation of the hospital.[39]

An editorial in the region's largest black newspaper, the *Los Angeles Sentinel*,[40] lauded the idea that the hospital would be "community-oriented" at its core and predicted that "[t]he eyes of the nation will be on this bold experiment."[41] For other observers—including the *Los Angeles Times* reporters who won a Pulitzer Prize in 2005 for exposing the hospital's fatal shortcomings—this noble idea marked both the hospital's creation and undoing.

Covering King/Drew (and Uncovering "Killer King")

Los Angeles's paper of record, the *Los Angeles Times*, had a complicated, forty-year relationship with Martin Luther King Jr./Charles Drew Medical Center. An early supporter of the Watts-area hospital project, the newspaper produced hundreds of articles and editorials focusing on the facility between the mid-1960s and 2007.[42] These offerings moved between the following foci: praising early plans to build the facility, chronicling how high hopes of improved medical care for the area's ghetto poor morphed into troubling concerns, and blaming hospital workers and Los Angeles politicians for shortcomings that resulted in tragic patient deaths and, ultimately, the facility's demise.

To be sure, mainstream news media like the *Times* typically serve as the "managers of public opinion" by emphasizing voices newsworkers believe should be heard, "while muffling or silencing others."[43] The *Times*— like most large metropolitan newspapers—enjoyed a symbiotic relationship with the local power structure, which more often than not motivated its newsworkers to toe the official line on the major issues of the day.[44]

In examining the distribution of *Los Angeles Times* news articles about King/Drew between the mid-1960s and the first decade of the 2000s, we found that nearly 70 percent of the 463 articles—282 articles—appeared between 2000 and 2006, when revelations of incompetence, fraud, and political compromise related to the facility reached a startling crescendo in the pages of the newspaper. By contrast, the amount of coverage in earlier decades was more modest, with just eight articles appearing in the 1960s, after the initial 1966 article on plans for the new hospital; 54 in the 1970s; 74 in the 1980s; and 45 in the 1990s. Our analysis of headlines from these articles uncovered five recurring themes that *Times* editors used to shape how readers approached the articles: hope, race, incompetence, fraud, and politics.[45] Embedded in the articles' headlines, these unifying ideas worked to establish preferred lenses through which readers might make sense of the otherwise, rather complex news narratives.[46]

In the following sections we delve beneath the headlines into the news narratives themselves, exploring how specific details embedded in each article work to "manage public opinion,"[47] to orient readers toward a particular understanding of the problems at King/Drew. In order to consider the implications of this "framing,"[48] we also consider many of the editorials, op-ed pieces, and letters to the editor presented in the *Los Angeles Times* over the decades, as well as articles from the major black newspaper in Los Angeles, the *Los Angeles Sentinel*, and interviews with key figures associated with the hospital.

The 1970s: Hope Gives Way to Concerns

The Martin Luther King Jr. General Hospital opened its doors on March 27, 1972, amid high hopes and great expectations. Early coverage in the

Figure 12.3. Coretta Scott King speaking to crowd at dedication of Martin Luther King Jr. Hospital, Watts-Willowbrook, Calif., May 17, 1972. Photo courtesy of *Los Angeles Times* Photographic Archive, Department of Special Collections, Charles E. Young Research Library, UCLA.

Los Angeles Times reflected this optimism, chronicling an impressive array of dignitaries who visited the facility, singing its praises. In May 1972, for example, the newspaper published a picture of Coretta Scott King, "speaking to [the] crowd during her first visit to the general hospital in Willowbrook that was named for her late husband, Martin Luther King." The image depicts King, flanked by other dignitaries, and surrounded by hundreds of black spectators on the grounds of the hospital (see fig. 12.3).[49] This "special occasion," as the *Times* noted in the photo's caption, included a hospital breakfast for King that was attended by local leaders. Community involvement at King/Drew was no small matter, particularly for black Angelenos predisposed to distrusting white-controlled institutions. The hospital's first year, it's important to note, was marked by the stunning revelation of the Tuskegee Experiment—a forty-year, secret government program in which treatment was withheld from black syphilis patients in order to study the effects of the disease.[50] Surely a community-oriented King/Drew could be trusted.

Later in the hospital's inaugural year, the *Times* covered a visit to King/
Drew by Dr. Merlin DuVal, assistant secretary for health and scientific
affairs in the U.S. Department of Health, Education, and Welfare. Com-
menting on King/Drew's community orientation, DuVal noted that the
hospital "started from scratch and it had broad interest from the community. It's a prototype because it brought in the community early on."[51]
DuVal's tour of the facility had clearly impressed him. "What a model!"
he remarked to the *Times* reporter covering his visit. To be sure, King/
Drew was widely seen as an exciting experiment, one that attracted some
of the nation's top black physicians to the Watts area.

But just three years after King/Drew's opening, the hope theme was
beginning to fade in *Times* headlines about the facility, giving ground to
the politics, incompetence, and fraud themes. Indeed, the newspaper published a lengthy feature article in March 1975 questioning whether King/
Drew was really up to the task of solving the problems it had been envisioned to address.[52] "How much of an impact can a modern medical
center have on the health care problems of an urban ghetto?" the reporter
asks in the opening paragraph. The answer is set up four paragraphs later,
when he lays out indicators of success by which one might judge the hospital's impact:

> Some thought King and its sister facility, the Charles R. Drew Postgradu-
> ate Medical School, would magically cut death rates, end unemployment,
> uplift the educational level of the community by training paraprofession-
> als and, in general, be all things to all people—poor people, politicians,
> physicians, academicians and health planners.

In the very next paragraph, he concludes, "Things have not turned out
quite that rosy."

The article goes on to review a litany of concerns that appeared to be
threatening King/Drew's ability to live up to its mission—"horror stories
implying neglect and incompetence" among staff, especially nurses; local doctors' dissatisfaction with the county's billing system; insufficient
waiting-room space for the large daily influx of clinic patients; a shortage
of registered nurses at the facility, which had prevented the opening of
a much-needed intensive-care unit;[53] financial problems at existing University of California medical schools, which undermined hopes of converting Drew into a four-year medical school; the fact that most jobs at
the hospital required technical skills, which disqualified most of the large

number of Watts-area residents seeking work there;[54] and the realization that Drew's training programs were unable to make a serious dent in the Southeast region's shortage of 689 physicians (relative to other areas of the county).

In 1975 disgruntled doctors went on strike at King/Drew, demanding that county officials increase their pay and provide the resources necessary for better patient care. Invoking the race theme, a *Times* article on the strike reports that "[m]ost of the striking interns and residents are black."[55] Among their demands, it's worth noting, were additional electrocardiograph machines and the hiring of additional staff for the hospital's blood bank. A few months later, Drew announced a new doctor training program designed to increase the number of minority medical students, students who would pledge to work in low-income areas for at least five years after graduation. "[A]lthough blacks make up 11 [percent] of the nation's population," the article points out, "they account for less than 2 [percent] of its doctors."[56]

The issue of patient care and working conditions arose again in 1976, as doctors went on strike, this time at each of the county's three teaching hospitals. A *Times* article on the strike reported that doctors, some of whom were "on duty for 100 hours a week or more," demanded that the county hire more nurses so that the doctors could reduce their hours.[57] In early 1978, the *Times* invoked the fraud theme in the headline of an article about the manager of a federally funded training program[58] at the hospital who embezzled "more than $100,000" from the program, for which he "supervised the work of a large number of orderlies, clerks and nurse's aides."[59] The use of funds at the hospital would become an increasingly contentious political issue. The county, which relied heavily on property tax revenues, had its coffers significantly reduced later in the year, when 65 percent of voters in the state passed California Proposition 13. This "political earthquake,"[60] reduced property tax revenues by 57 percent and put even greater pressure on Los Angeles County supervisors to ration funding to public services like healthcare.

By the end of the decade, it had become clear that the state's poor faced a serious healthcare crisis. The *Times*, in a 1979 article,[61] reported on a new study noting that "[o]nly one new hospital has been built in a poverty area of Los Angeles in the past 20 years—Martin Luther King Jr. Hospital, built by the county after the 1965 Watts riots." Echoing the language of the previous decade's Kerner Commission report, the study critiqued a "separate" and "unequal" health care system in which "[t]he vast majority of California physicians and hospitals often refuse to treat the poor and near poor, even in life-threatening situations." Public funding, or the lack thereof, had assumed center stage in a defining political moment for access to healthcare in Los Angeles.

The 1980s: Starvation

On August 17, 1980, the *Los Angeles Times* published the fourth article in a front-page series commemorating the fifteenth anniversary of the Watts uprisings. The lengthy, 140-paragraph feature story—which covered a typical, bloody day in the emergency room of King/Drew hospital—is notable because, for the first time in our sample, in the article's tenth paragraph, the hospital is referred to as "Killer King."[62]

"Killer King" is a particularly potent term, one loaded with irony and multiple meanings. On a very basic level, it takes the black icon of the nonviolent civil rights movement and pairs his last name with the idea of killing. More specifically, it associates the pride of Black America, as embodied by King, with a hospital that apparently fails to do what competent hospitals do—save lives.

This said, the article in which the term appears, on balance, actually makes a strong case for viewing the hospital in a positive manner, as "a lighted ship on a dark ocean." King/Drew often was "dismissed as Killer King" unfairly, the article explains, due to the "battle zone" of a neighborhood that surrounded it, which resulted in emergency room doctors confronting an inordinate number of life-threatening injuries in any given day:

> About 3,600 patients a month pass through the emergency room at MLK, among them battered and bloodied victims of urban warfare; in one month, 90 gunshot wounds, 70 stab wounds, 125 traumas (beating, etc.), 70 assaults.[63]

Indeed, the article goes on to point out that 95 percent of the emergency room patients at King/Drew were "real emergencies," compared to just 20 percent in emergency rooms nationwide. As the reporter put it: "Dying is a fundamental truth in any emergency room, but the nature of the community MLK serves makes death a more visible presence. An average of 10 people a month die in E.R."[64] A doctor interviewed in the article identified yet another reason for the high death rate at King/Drew. He charged that private hospitals in the area routinely dumped indigent patients on King/Drew, in some cases near death, thereby raising the hospital's death statistics: "They keep them for five or six hours, discover they've got no cash or insurance, then dump them on us. By then, it may be too late . . . and we get the reputation as Killer King."[65]

In a time when King/Drew was acquiring the reputation as "Killer King," it's important to note, Los Angeles politics were taking a significant turn to the right. The Los Angeles County Board of Supervisors, on the coattails of Ronald Reagan's 1980 election to the White House, became Republican-controlled for the first time in years. The election resulted in pro-business supervisors Michael D. Antonovich and Deane Dana joining incumbent supervisor Peter F. Schabarum to form a 3–2 conservative majority on the board. In a fiscal environment constrained by reduced property tax revenues (recall that voters had approved California Proposition 13 in 1978), the new board quickly went to work to cut funding to as many public services as possible, ration funding to others, and privatize whatever remained. The county's healthcare system—one of the largest in America—was a convenient target, and King/Drew received more than its fair share of the attention.

Throughout the early 1980s, the *Times* ran a series of articles and editorials highlighting how "the conservative-dominated Board of Supervisors balanced its tight budget by cutting into health services and other social programs."[66] A *Times* editorial from July 8, 1981, for example, chastised the board for cutting "gaping holes" in the "safety net," noting that King/Drew—because of its perceived shortcomings in "administrative efficiency"—had received the largest share of the $13.6 million cut from spending on the three county hospitals.[67] A *Times* article from October 29, 1981, reported that because of "the continuing squeeze on county services caused by Proposition 13 and other ballot measures" the board was considering privatizing the emergency rooms at King/Drew and Harbor/UCLA, as well as the laboratories at King/Drew and two other facilities.[68] At the same time that the board rationed resources to the major county hospitals, 43,000 needy patients who had been treated at private hospitals were cut from Medi-Cal, forcing them to seek treatment at the county facilities. Meanwhile, the combination of the extraordinary amount of violence in the King/Drew service area and county cost-cutting pressed the hospital into the radical practice of sending gun-shot victims home after treatment, *without* admission to the hospital:

At the busy King emergency room, said Ordog [a doctor who conducted a study of the practice], sending gunshot wound victims home is a practice rooted in financial constraints, overcrowding and the hospital's unique role and experience.[69]

It was in the midst of these difficult financial times that Charles R. Drew Medical School—the teaching unit associated with the hospital —welcomed its first class, a diverse group of twenty-one students. The school had received 500 applications for the class but ultimately selected a "very nice mix" of students who were committed to working in "primary care" and to spending "their professional lives helping the medically underserved."[70] An August 1981 *Times* article presented Drew—the nation's second-smallest medical school, and the first black-run medical school west of the Mississippi—as something of a gamble:

The hypothesis is this: That, despite a predicted glut of doctors in the United States by 1990, a small, black-operated, minority-oriented medical school that answers almost directly to the Watts-Compton community in which it is located can produce physicians who will spend their professional lives helping the medically underserved.

The article goes on to explain that because Drew was associated with the University of California, the students, who also had offers from other medical schools, "had to meet the same admissions criteria as UCLA's first-year class." The students would take their first two years of classes at UCLA, before returning to the makeshift Watts campus[71] (see fig. 12.4) in order to finish up with practical clinical instruction across the street at Martin Luther King Jr. Hospital. (The complex became known officially as Martin Luther King Jr./Charles Drew Medical Center in May 1982.[72])

The article also notes that Drew was "controversial"[73] because some outside observers believed existing area medical schools—particularly USC's or UCLA's—were better equipped to train the medical students and residents serving the hospital and its surrounding community. These same observers, no doubt, resented the fact that "the community around King has demanded a voice in the Drew operation," which resulted, as the article put it, in "a process that has at times been tortuously slow." But community involvement, of course, was at the core of the original vision for the hospital and affiliated medical school.

As the 1980s wound down, the incompetence and fraud themes became

Figure 12.4. Charles Drew University Trailer, across the street from the hospital. Photo courtesy of Darnell Hunt.

more prominent in *Times* headlines about King/Drew. More often than not, however, the idea of insufficient funding loomed in the background of this coverage. An October 13, 1988 article, for example, reported on a county audit concluding that "poor fiscal controls" and "lax computer security" at the hospital "jeopardized the collection of millions of dollars."[74] Compared to other public hospitals, the audit charged, "King's revenue operation 'is on the bottom.'" The audit also criticized the hospital for a "serious shortage of trained staff and capable leadership."

In September 1989, the *Times* covered the removal of the hospital's administrator, William Delgardo, who claimed he had prepared a plan for "correcting scores of hospital deficiencies cited recently by state health inspectors."[75] Delgardo, the newspaper reported, maintained that the deficiencies found at the hospital "exist at other county hospitals and that King has been unfairly singled out for criticism." Moreover, he claimed, "the hospital lacks sufficient funding and staffing to handle its heavy caseload."

Finally, a *Times* editorial published on September 15, 1989, boldly underscored the links between poor patient care and inadequate funding that had been drawn in the pages of the newspaper throughout the 1980s. The editorial acknowledged that the growing list of "shocking disclosures" about the quality of patient care and management at King/Drew actually "stemmed from inadequate funding and staffing."[76] Over the course of the next decade, however, the newspaper would effectively bury the link between King/Drew's problems and the matter of resources.

The 1990s: The Politics of Incompetence

During the 1990s, the incompetence theme increased in prominence in *Los Angeles Times* headlines about King/Drew, raising pressing questions about the management and staffing of the medical complex. Although the race theme accounted for only about 5 percent of all themes in the newspaper's headlines during this period, the newspaper's sporadic invocations of the hospital's Watts-uprisings origins farther down in the texts of articles worked to (re)connect the facility's increasingly alarming shortcomings with black control. These practices, of course, resonated nicely with the "colorblind" politics of the 1990s. A period marked by the neo-liberal, class-over-race policies of the Clinton Administration, the 1990s constituted a time in which race was officially characterized as something of a non-issue in American politics. Yet, just beneath the surface of public discourses about the controversial social developments of the day, race frequently loomed large in the commonsense explanations embraced by most Americans. In the case of King/Drew, the *Times*'s gradual abandonment of the "insufficient funding" idea of the 1980s—and the concurrent rise of the incompetence theme in its coverage—left few reasonable explanations for the hospital's stunning failures other than the capabilities of the (black) people running it.

Indeed, the decade of the 1990s also saw the retirement of the white "father" of the hospital, County Supervisor Kenneth Hahn. Yvonne Brathwaite Burke, the board's first black elected member, replaced Hahn in 1992 and assumed primary responsibility for King/Drew. Burke was a woman of firsts: She was the first black woman elected to the California State Assembly in 1966; she was the first black woman elected to Congress from the western United States in 1972; she was featured on the cover of the March 1974 issue of *Ebony* after becoming the first sitting member of Congress to give birth; and she was the first black *or* woman elected to the Los Angeles County Board of Supervisors.[77] As supervisor for the Second District,[78] Burke would find herself on the hot seat with each new *Times* revelation about the "troubled" hospital near Watts, a facility popularly understood as black-controlled.

The early 1990s marked a turning point in how the issue of funding was treated in *Los Angeles Times* stories about King/Drew. An article from 1992, for example, still relied heavily on the idea of inadequate funding to account for at least some of the problems associated with the hospital.[79] It reported that paramedics frequently complained of excessive delays in unloading sick and injured patients at King/Drew, waits that sometimes lasted up to six hours. "It's not just that they don't have enough gurneys," explained one interviewee. "'They could buy a bunch of gurneys, but that wouldn't help solve the problem' of inadequate staffing and space." Similar resource-related problems, the article noted, recently had been disclosed at one of the other three county general hospitals, County-USC Medical Center.

As the remainder of the 1990s unfolded, however, the incompetence and fraud themes rose in prominence in *Times* coverage, while the matter of inadequate funding largely faded from view. An article from 1994, for example, suggested that a white physician working at King/Drew—"an internationally renowned pioneer in the field of intensive care"—might have been the victim of reverse discrimination when he was ordered to resign as chairman of the emergency department.[80] According to the article, Dr. William Shoemaker, 70, charged that he was fired because of racial and age bias, as well as in retaliation for "his apparent whistle-blowing" in the death of a sheriff's deputy treated for gunshot wounds at the hospital. But Dr. Reed Tuckson, the black president of Drew University, disputed the charge, telling the reporter that Shoemaker was reassigned because he was not a board-certified emergency specialist and it was this fact that had threatened the emergency program's accreditation.

Much of the article, nonetheless, painted a poignant picture of a respected white doctor once "summoned to care for King" who is later forced to resign from a hospital named after the civil rights leader. To be sure, the charge was particularly potent because King/Drew was commonly seen as a black hospital, one that, as the reporter put it, "had struggled to attract good doctors." While two other articles in our sample similarly bestow praise on a white doctor working at King/Drew, this time for his humanitarian deeds,[81] most of the articles questioned the competence and/or commitment of a medical staff that is routinely rendered in black.

A *Times* article from December 1995, for example, reported that hospital administrators had "tried to rein in" a prominent infectious disease specialist who directed the complex's AIDS clinic because of "the extraordinary amount of independence and lack of accountability he has had there."[82] According to the article, Dr. Wilbert C. Jordan—who recently had been a guest of President Clinton at the first White House conference on AIDS—pled guilty in 1987 to federal misdemeanor fraud charges in connection with $250,000 of questionable Medi-Cal billing at his private practice.

Another *Times* article from late 1995 reported that Supervisor Burke called for "an immediate and sweeping reorganization" of King/Drew due to "widespread problems" at the facility, including mix-ups at the blood bank that led to a woman receiving HIV-infected blood.[83] Because of recent *Times* stories about problems at the complex, the article noted, Burke said she was "concerned that 'people are afraid to go to the hospital.'" The supervisor, the article reported, had been "unaware of the depth of many of the hospital's problems until she read about them in the newspaper."[84]

A *Times* article from early 1996 again raised the specter of racial bias at King/Drew, this time reporting that the Civil Service Commission found that "the hospital and the affiliated Drew School of Medicine had an 'unwritten policy of maintaining itself as a black institution and of placing black candidates in positions of leadership . . . to the exclusion of non-blacks.'"[85] At issue this time was a Civil Service proceeding initiated by Dr. Subramaniam Balasubramaniam, who charged that "black hospital administrators" refused to reinstate him as head of the emergency room —he was acting head from 1979 to 1986—"because he is Indian." (Yvonne Brathwaite Burke—supervisor at the time over the district where King/Drew was located—coincidentally served as Dr. Balasubramaniam's attorney when he first leveled the charges in 1985.[86]) The article also reported that the county was considering privatizing the emergency room and that many of the doctors working in it were under investigation for "excessive moonlighting."

Finally, a 1998 *Times* article revealed that a King/Drew patient died from drinking a deadly mixture of preservatives "left on her night stand by an inexperienced medical resident."[87] According to the article, an unnamed "top hospital administrator" was angered by what he considered unfair efforts to blame the hospital for the woman's death: "It's like if I parked my car outside and you ran into it and killed yourself, or I left a knife out and you killed yourself. Why is that my fault?" The incident, the article concluded, "is sure to raise more questions about the quality of care at the troubled public hospital," particularly about the "inadequate supervision of residents."

By the end of the 1990s, Martin Luther King Jr./Charles Drew Medical

Center had clearly lived up to its reputation as "Killer King" in the pages of the *Los Angeles Times*. Something was deadly wrong with the hospital, and a significant portion of the blame seemed to rest with black administrators who were hell-bent on keeping King/Drew a black-controlled institution—even if it meant incompetent staffing, rampant fraud, and needless patient deaths. This seemed particularly problematic because the community surrounding King/Drew was no longer majority black, and this fact was reflected in the hospital's predominantly Latino patient population.[88] Los Angeles's paper of record, however, would not stand for the subordination of quality healthcare to racial politics. In its role as "manager of public opinion," the *Times* was poised to expose the hospital's fatal flaws once and for all.

The 2000s: Times Crusade

In the midst of the *Los Angeles Times*'s increasing scrutiny of King/Drew, CBS debuted in January 2000 what has been described as "network television's first predominantly black medical drama," a show centered "around the professional and personal lives of the doctors and nurses at Los Angeles's Angels of Mercy Hospital."[89] *City of Angels*[90] was created by a powerful, white executive producer and his well-known black collaborator, and featured several popular black actors of the day.[91] Undoubtedly inspired by King/Drew's prominence in the news, the groundbreaking drama aired for twenty-four episodes before being canceled after its final episode of December 21, 2000.

The *Times* published an article prior to the show's debut, which anticipated controversies arising from its comparisons to King/Drew.[92] After an advance screening of the show for a group of black professionals at the Magic Johnson Theaters in Los Angeles's Crenshaw District, the article reported, the medical director at King/Drew "raised concerns about the show's authenticity" and expressed "fears that viewers might confuse his facility with the fictional hospital." What the medical director couldn't know at the time, however, was that the problems depicted at the fictional Angels of Mercy Hospital paled in comparison to those the *Times* would soon expose at King/Drew.

Referencing a story on racial bias it published in 1996, the *Times* reported in February 2000 that a Los Angeles County panel recommended settlement of a case in which two doctors "allege that they were discriminated against because they are white."[93] Jonathan Wasserberger and Gary Ordog (see n. 69), the article noted, "filed more than 140 employment grievances before alleging in a pair of 1998 lawsuits that the African Americans who headed emergency medicine at the hospital south of Watts subjected them to harassment and threats because of their race." But County Supervisor Burke, whose district contained King/Drew, questioned the charges. The hospital, she told the reporter, "has the most diverse group of department heads in the county." In an attempt to undermine her credibility on this point, however, the article had noted in the prior paragraph (paragraph 6 out of 22) that Burke was the attorney for a Sri Lankan plaintiff (the earlier-mentioned Dr. Balasubramaniam) alleging similar discrimination by black administrators at King/Drew in the mid-1980s.

In November 2003, the *Times* published an article about a state report concluding that nurses and other staff at King/Drew "botched the care of two women who died there this summer."[94] The report found that nurses "failed to adequately examine the patients and that some apparently had never been taught to use new bedside monitors at the hospital." In one of the cases, the article reported, nurses failed to notice that the patient's heart "had slowed and stopped over 45 minutes." The state report also revealed that a nurse lied about performing a crucial test ordered by a doctor.

A month later, another *Times* article reported that state inspectors—alerted by the two women's deaths—found King/Drew nurses lax in providing basic care at the hospital. The article announced that Dr. Thomas Garthwaite, who provided oversight for the hospital in his role as county health director, had lost confidence in King/Drew:

> Previously, Garthwaite has defended the quality of care provided at King/Drew, saying that it was comparable to other county hospitals. But in an interview Monday, he said he could no longer provide that assurance.[95]

Garthwaite, the article noted, indicated that it might be time for the hospital to cut back on many of the specialty services it offered—services otherwise unavailable in the Watts area—in order to focus on basic care.

County supervisor Zev Yaroslavsky was more blunt in his criticism of the facility. "King/Drew," the article quoted him as saying, "has been a bottomless pit of problems that have in large measure been inadequately addressed. And now the cumulative effect of this decades-long neglect is that the whole institution is threatened." Yaroslavsky, the article later noted, said it might be time for the county to end its relationship with Charles R. Drew University of Medicine and Science, the black-run medical school across the street that administered the doctor training programs at the hospital.

It's worth noting that toward the end of the article (paragraphs 24 and 25 of 28), the reporter quotes a critical-care nurse who blamed some of the problems on nursing cuts. "At times we have to assist with basic care, do the bedpans and also give our medications. . . . We are working very hard," she said. The "insufficient funding" idea so prevalent in the 1980s and early 1990s thus resurfaced in the article, if only for the moment.

Times coverage of problems at King/Drew reached a feverish pitch in 2004. Shortly after New Years, the newspaper reported that the president of Charles R. Drew University of Medicine and Science was placed on paid administrative leave "after a national task force questioned his leadership skills and called for his ouster."[96] Toward the end of January, the *Times* reported on a rally led by Rep. Maxine Waters (D-Los Angeles) to protest what community members feared were county plans to close King/Drew after supervisors moved to downgrade the facility's neonatal unit.[97] But Supervisor Burke, the article noted, quickly introduced a motion in which the board reaffirmed its commitment to "correct the problems at King/Drew."

In March, the *Times* reported that King/Drew was in danger of losing federal funding because of "serious flaws in the way prescription drugs are managed."[98] The article noted that the hospital already faced the possible loss of funding for Medicare and Medi-Cal patients "because of unfavorable inspections in other areas."

In May, the *Times* reported that King/Drew would lose its third doctor training program, this time when a national accrediting group refused to pass its neonatology program.[99] Previously, the article noted, the Accreditation Council on Graduate Medical Education had decided to shut down the facility's surgery and radiology training programs and place its anesthesia, family practice, and internal medicine programs on probation. "The hospital's oversight of its entire graduate medical education program," the reporter wrote, "has been deemed substandard by the council."

In June, the *Times* reported that a federal health official praised King/Drew for its response to "patient-care lapses uncovered by inspectors over the last six months at the hospital."[100] At a meeting hosted by Rep. Juanita Millender-McDonald (D-Carson) and attended by "about 200 King/Drew

staff members and supporters," the article pointed out, the congresswoman and others blamed county supervisors for underfunding and "not
really paying attention to this hospital." Consistent with the newspaper's
rejection of the "insufficient funding" explanation, however, the article
concluded with an interview of county health director Dr. Thomas Garthwaite, who "disputed the characterization that King/Drew was underfunded, pointing to [unnamed] data and studies showing otherwise."

In July, the *Times* reported that—in "hundreds of surgeries"—operating staff at King/Drew "sewed up patients without checking whether instruments were left inside them."[101] The article pointed out that studies
suggest such mistakes are generally uncommon, occurring "in as few as
one in 1,500 abdominal surgeries."

In October, the *Times* reported that the county planned to give control of King/Drew to a private consulting firm that specialized in turning
troubled hospitals around.[102] Navigant Consulting would be paid up to
$13.25 million to "take over from current county managers for at least a
year and complete a top-to-bottom review of how the facility operates."
(The firm would eventually be hired, and in January of 2005 it identified
more than 1,000 steps that needed to be taken to fix the hospital, asking
for an additional $3.4 million for its services.[103])

In early December, the *Times* reported that a federal judge denied a
temporary restraining order sought by a group of doctors and residents
committed to keeping King/Drew's trauma center open.[104] One of only
about a dozen trauma centers in the county, and the only one in the Watts
area, the hospital's trauma center was generally perceived as a solid operation, one where military doctors often interned because of the unit's huge
influx of gun-shot victims. County supervisors and department of health
officials planned to phase out the costly unit, the article reported, in order
"to save the rest of the troubled hospital."

Of course, *Times* coverage of the hospital's problems in 2004 would cli-
max with publication of "The Troubles at King/Drew," the five-part series
for which the newspaper won the coveted Pulitzer Prize for Public Service. The first installment of the series was published on December 5 and
presented chilling vignettes of "the lost and the bereaved," the ordeals of
patients who had met untimely deaths at King/Drew, and the grief of the
family and friends left behind.[105] It also set up the basic argument of the
series: the hospital's promise was betrayed by unnecessary and deadly errors, which could have been corrected had it not been for racial politics.

Whereas the *Times* had generally relegated the "insufficient funding" explanation for the hospital's failures to the distant background during the early 2000s, the second installment in the series aggressively presented the idea as a myth. The hospital, the installment maintained, had "squandered" ample resources through inefficient operations, excessive legal settlements, and widespread employee fraud.[106] The third installment chronicled the medical errors committed by several King/Drew doctors, focusing in on one particular doctor who had a "long trail of dangerous mistakes."[107]

The fourth installment went beyond the mistakes of individuals at King/Drew to cover what was described as a dysfunctional culture at the medical complex; this culture, the article argued, accounted for "how whole departments fail a hospital's patients."[108]

The final installment reviewed the roots of King/Drew in the Watts uprisings of 1965 and argued that county supervisors let "deadly problems slide" at the hospital because they were "fearful of provoking black protests." Instead of "imposing tough remedies on inept administrators," the article charged, county supervisors "took the easy way out" and let King/Drew lapse into "one of the worst" hospitals in the nation.[109]

Throughout the series, the *Times* repeatedly recognized itself for uncovering facts about shameful lapses in patient care at King/Drew that were largely unknown prior to disclosures in the newspaper's pages. Three *Times* editorials accompanying the series similarly worked to highlight the newspaper's prominent role in bringing the problems at King/Drew to light; they also tied up any loose ends that may have remained regarding the newspaper's position on exactly what went wrong at the hospital. The first editorial (December 5, 2004) lashed out at black leaders who challenged the *Times*'s assessment of the King/Drew situation.[110] Critics who accused the newspaper of "exaggerating run-of-the-mill problems that wouldn't get so much attention in a white-run hospital," the editorial charged, cared "more about symbols than reality." The second editorial (December 7, 2004) underscored the *Times*'s position that King/Drew's problems had nothing to do with insufficient funding.[111] "Despite receiving its fair share of taxpayer dollars and then some," the editorial maintained, "King/Drew is today the worst hospital in L.A. County and among the worst in the nation." In a reference to Dr. Martin Luther King Jr.'s famous speech, the final editorial (December 12, 2004) argued that King/Drew fulfilled "the wrong dream" because it "was conceived as much to create jobs as to heal patients." County supervisors, the editorial concluded, "averted their eyes" to the problems at King/Drew "rather than take on this public works project and risk being called racially insensitive."[112]

In a final article considered by the Pulitzer Prize jury, the *Times* argued that the board of supervisors must give up control of King/Drew if it "is to survive, let alone thrive."[113] The front-page article also explored calls to "root out incompetent workers," to associate the hospital with a different medical school, and to establish a politically independent health authority that would manage the county's five general hospitals.

The inevitable fallout from "The Troubles at King/Drew" series was diligently covered in the pages of the *Times*. An article from January 2005 reported that, at a public forum in Watts, hospital faculty and community representatives criticized the newspaper's coverage for not placing "enough of the fault for the hospital's woes with the county Department of Health Services."[114] A vocal critic of the *Times*'s coverage, Rep. Maxine Waters correctly anticipated what was at stake for the newspaper and hospital, even if she got the timing wrong: "The *L.A. Times* thinks it's going to get a Pulitzer Prize on our backs. . . . Part of their trying to get a Pulitzer Prize is they've got to see to it that the hospital is closed."

Less than three weeks later, the *Times* reported that King/Drew was in jeopardy of losing $200 million a year in payments from Medi-Cal and Medicare public health insurance programs unless it passed an upcoming federal inspection.[115] The article pointed out that loss of the funds "would make it extremely difficult [for supervisors] to keep the hospital open." A hospital accrediting organization, the article noted, had already recently "revoked its seal of approval for King/Drew."

While followers of the King/Drew saga awaited final word on the hospital's fate, the *Times* continued to cover alleged instances of fraud and incompetence at the medical complex. An article from April 2005 reported that King/Drew paid a radiologist who was under contract to the hospital "$1.3 million over the last year"; incredibly, he claimed to have worked "on average 20 hours a day, seven days a week, during one recent six-month stretch."[116] An article from August 2005 covered the administrative hearing of an ex-King/Drew pathologist whose "trail of alleged misdiagnoses was detailed in a *Times* story in December."[117] The doctor admitted to the mistakes, the article reported, but "contends that the hospital's deficiencies set him up for failure."

In September 2006, the *Times* reported that King/Drew had failed its final inspection and would lose federal funding by the end of the year.[118] Federal regulators, the article noted, "identified problems in nursing, pharmacy, infection control, surgical services, rehabilitation services, quality control, patient's rights, and the hospital's governing body and physical plant." Indeed, the article reported that inspectors found more problems at the "supposedly reformed King/Drew than they had at any time in the last three years." On the heels of the news about the loss of federal funds, the *Times* reported in October 2006 that the county planned to transfer King/Drew patients to other county and private hospitals as the doomed facility awaited downsizing or closing.[119] A *Times* article from November 2006 reported that Drew University "took the first step Wednesday toward closing its long-standing residency program," which had placed county-paid residents at the hospital for decades. According to the article, county supervisor Zev Yaroslavsky said the county was "concerned" about the black medical school but that its "responsibility is to our hospital system first and foremost."[120]

A Set-Up for Black Failure?

King/Drew was clearly envisioned as a "black institution," one that would serve an impoverished, predominantly black community that gained national attention in the aftermath of a signature black rebellion of the 1960s. Universally understood as redress of sorts for the Watts uprisings, the comprehensive medical facility would not only provide an underserved community with much-needed, first-rate healthcare, but it also would create thousands of new jobs for area residents locked in a cycle of underemployment and despair. Moreover, the community would have a meaningful say in determining how all of this would work—how it would be served—and black administrators, doctors, nurses, and other employees committed to the community would provide the lion's share of the service. For early supporters, this was undoubtedly a noble experiment in black community self-determination—one that could provide a model for replication in other sectors of public life and in other local contexts, possibly even providing a way out of the double bind so often associated in Black America with high need and low expectations.

But hindsight, of course, is 20/20. Looking back on the history of King/Drew, some had compellingly argued that the institution—in its basic design—was set up for failure. Charles Drew University of Medicine and Science never enjoyed the resources or influence that USC and UCLA used to manage problems at the county's other two teaching hospitals.[121]

Instead, the only black medical school west of the Mississippi relied upon what amounted to a subsistence contract with the county to compensate its employees, who understood themselves as primarily accountable to the county (if accountable at all). Because the county's Department of Health Services (DHS) hired, compensated, evaluated, and fired these employees, Drew University and hospital administrators had little leverage for rewarding good performance or sanctioning poor performance.[122] To be sure, *Times* articles over the decades reported numerous cases of underperforming employees (or worse) being allowed to continue working at King/Drew because of the county's convoluted employment bureaucracy, despite complaints from within the facility itself. Some even charged that King/Drew became a dumping ground for the DHS's least desirable workers, which they say only worked to reinforce the image of the facility as a cesspool of incompetence when problems arose.

There was also ample reason to question the commonsense notion that King/Drew was ever really a "black institution." The black administrators identified as running the facility throughout most of its history, critics charge, actually had little to no control over its budget or workforce due to what amounted to a "colonial" oversight arrangement with the county.[123] For example, the nursing shortages documented in early *Times* coverage —shortages associated with unusually long nursing shifts and, in later coverage, with woefully inadequate patient monitoring and care—were the direct result of county cost-cutting measures over which black administrators had no control. Not only were there significant questions about the degree to which King/Drew's administrative shortcomings should be attributed to black leadership lapses, but the popular image of the facility's workforce as "black" was hardly accurate. Indeed, periodic *Times* coverage of controversies involving several non-black doctors at the facility seemed to support Yvonne Brathwaite Burke's claim that King/Drew had the most diverse staff in the county system.

Dr. Richard Baker[124] became dean of Drew University's School of Medicine in 2007, after the hospital was shuttered. In a compelling presentation, he contended there was a plot to bring down King/Drew, one in which the DHS essentially "attacked a politically powerless community" in order to manage mounting county budget deficits.[125] The DHS, he charged, systematically undermined King/Drew's ability to function, thereby creating the self-fulfilling prophecy that the hospital was so beset with problems the only option was to close it down. Moreover, he noted, "[p]eople would actually believe [King/Drew] was inferior because it was perceived as black," which conveniently worked to divert attention away from the DHS's dollar-driven plot. The plot was consummated, of course, when the hospital failed a final inspection in 2006 and soon thereafter lost its federal funding. This outcome, he noted, occurred only after the county "took over" the facility in 2004.

Whether or not Dr. Baker was 100 percent correct in his explanation for the fall of King/Drew, one thing seemed clear: King/Drew became the antithesis of its originating vision. Not only did it fail to deliver on its decades-old promise of first-rate healthcare for the poor, good jobs for area residents, and community self-determination, but it also became popularly understood as a model *not* to be replicated, an experiment whose findings work to prove the futility of these noble goals.[126]

The Benefits of Attacking an Easy Target

Since at least the middle of the twentieth century, when it became the highest circulation newspaper in Los Angeles, the *Los Angeles Times* clearly was the most influential newspaper in the region. By the last two decades of the century, the newspaper had also gained recognition as one of the four or five most important newspapers in America. Daily circulation for the *Times* peaked at about 1.2 million in 1990, making it the largest daily metropolitan newspaper in the nation at the time. Competition from the nascent Internet and other media outlets, however, led to a continual decline in the newspaper's daily circulation, which had dropped to just about 740,000 by 2008. Family-owned since its founding in 1881, the *Times* was sold to the Tribune Company media conglomerate in 2000.[127] Thus began a period of restructuring, layoffs, and other cost-cutting moves at the newspaper geared toward increasing profits.[128]

In the *Times*'s 119 years between 1881 and 2000, the newspaper was recognized exactly four times with the prestigious Pulitzer Prize in Public Service.[129] The newspaper, of course, would win the coveted gold medal for a fifth time in 2005, when it was lauded for its series exposing "deadly medical problems and racial injustice" at Martin Luther King Jr./Charles Drew Medical Center. This series, to be sure, punctuated a clear and relentless campaign on the part of the newspaper to decisively explain the problems at the medical complex in terms of racial politics, fraud, and, of course, incompetence.[130]

Not only did the newspaper's coverage of King/Drew explode during the early 2000s,[131] but the incompetence theme was most prominent in headlines about the medical complex during this period as well. The latest revelations about the substandard patient care and other problems at the facility routinely hit the pages of the *Times* before county supervisors, the public officials ultimately responsible for the facility, even got word.[132] Some maintained that this was because the DHS—in an effort to build a budget-balancing case against King/Drew—secretly fed the *Times* the latest damning information on a regular basis.[133] In a classic example of the symbiotic relationship that typically exists between journalists and official sources,[134] this theory holds, the *Times* dutifully reported facts supporting the position that the hospital was irredeemable, while withholding other facts supporting its normative performance and critical value to the community. In fact, evidence ignored by the *Times* suggests that as late as 1998, King/Drew was on par with, if not better than, the county's other general teaching hospitals.[135]

Indeed, it is important to note that during this period—for the first time in our sample—the *Times* also began to explicitly and consistently debunk the "insufficient funding" theme. That is, whereas the *Times* had treated insufficient resources as an important cause of the hospital's troubles throughout the 1980s and into the early 1990s, by early 2000s the idea that the hospital was underfunded was aggressively dismissed as a "myth" in the pages of the newspaper. Surely, funding to the complex was not increased between the decades to the point where it suddenly became a non-issue. It was not farfetched to imagine here that the *Times* may have singled out King/Drew for special criticism because of its image as a "black institution," despite the fact that it was embedded in a larger county system that was similarly underfunded and equally inadequate.[136] The *Times*, after all, wasn't known for its flattering portrayals of Black Los Angeles.[137]

Even if *Times* coverage of King/Drew—in the end—was not just a "smear" campaign designed to increase the newspaper's distinction (and circulation) in difficult financial times, as some alleged,[138] it undoubtedly invoked the age-old myth of black incompetence to explain and justify the closure of a sorely needed hospital in the 'hood. The *Times* vehemently denied that anything other than a commitment to the truth motivated its crusade against King/Drew. It accused those who suggested otherwise of being, at best, out of touch with reality, and at worst, motivated by racial politics. Nonetheless, the newspaper unabashedly promoted its campaign against the "troubled" hospital, freely referencing the nameplate and its reports about the facility in a string of successive *Times* reports. The *Times*, of course, won a Pulitzer Prize for its work as "manager of public opinion" on the King/Drew matter. Shortly thereafter, a Watt-uprisings-era dream of black self-determination died on the vine.

NOTES

1. Columbia University, "The 2005 Pulitzer Prize Winners, Public Service: Citation," *The Pulitzer Prizes*, http://www.pulitzer.org/citation/2005-Public-Service.

2. The five-part series, "The Troubles at King/Drew," ran from December 5, 2004, to December 9, 2004. The newspaper was also recognized for related pieces, including editorials, which appeared between February 26, 2004, and December 23, 2004. See Columbia University, "The 2005 Pulitzer Prize Winners, Public Service: Works," *The Pulitzer Prizes*, http://www.pulitzer.org/works/2005-Public -Service.

3. The team consisted of lead reporters Charles Ornstein and Tracy Weber, two other white reporters, and one black reporter who left the *Times* for *Newsweek* "midway through the project" (Tracy Weber and Charles Ornstein, interview by Brian Lamb, *C-SPAN Q&A*, transcript, July 17, 2005, http://qanda.org/Transcript/?ProgramID=1030).

4. In this chapter, we refer to the facility primarily as "King/Drew," although its name changed several times over the course of its nearly forty-year history.

5. Charles Ornstein, interview by Jordana Horn Marinoff, "Alumni Profiles: Eye on the Prize," *Pennsylvania Gazette*, August 25, 2005, http://www.upenn.edu/gazette/0905/0905pro04.html.

6. Weber and Ornstein, interview by Lamb, *C-SPAN Q&A*, transcript, July 17, 2005.

7. Ibid.

8. National Advisory Commission on Civil Disorders, *Report of the National Advisory Commission*, 1.

9. Horne, *Fire This Time*.

10. For an account of Panther activities in Los Angeles, see E. Brown, *Taste of Power*.

11. Dr. Huey P. Newton Foundation, "The Ten Point Plan," *The Black Panther Party*, http://www.blackpanther.org/TenPoint.htm.

12. See Bullock, *Watts: The Aftermath*. The folk wisdom of Watts-area residents concerning American race relations clearly emerges from the interviews presented in the book.

13. Ibid.

14. Dissenting remarks by Commissioner Rev. James Edward Jones, California Governor's Commission on the Los Angeles Riots, "Violence in the City."

15. California Governor's Commission on the Los Angeles Riots, "Violence in the City," 74.

16. Ibid.

17. Bullock, *Watts: The Aftermath.*

18. California Governor's Commission on the Los Angeles Riots, "Violence in the City," 74.

19. Sandra Lewis, "Background Information."

20. Ibid.

21. Windsor, "A Summary of the History and Plan for Development."

22. The *Los Angeles Times* described Reagan's support as "crucial though clandestine" ("Hahn Starts Record 25th Year in Office," *Los Angeles Times*, December 8, 1976, OC2).

23. Windsor, "A Summary of the History and Plan for Development."

24. "Ground-Breaking Ceremonies For Hospital Draws Crowd," *Los Angeles Sentinel*, May 9, 1968, A2.

25. Ibid.

26. Gamblo, *Making a Place for Ourselves.*

27. Ibid. By 1993, only about 16 percent of black medical students were enrolled in black medical schools.

28. The Charles R. Drew Medical Society was the Los Angeles branch of the National Medical Association, a nationwide, professional organization for black doctors.

29. See chap. 16 for our discussion of the history of UCLA in Black Los Angeles.

30. Sandra Lewis, "Background Information."

31. Note that the county cut the paychecks, which differed from the arrangement at County/USC and Harbor/UCLA. According to a front-page *Los Angeles Times* article, the original contract between the county and Drew University amounted to $900,000 for 22,500 hours of physicians' services to the hospital (about $40/hour). Medicare and Medi-Cal and patients fees were expected to pay for a little over a third of the contract amount, while the rest would come from county funds. See "Medical School, King Ties Proposed," *Los Angeles Times*, July 11, 1971, A5.

32. "Program Seeks Health Workers in Watts Area: Goal Is to Motivate Minority-Group Students to Enter Medical Profession," *Los Angeles Times*, June 14, 1970, G5.

33. The number of beds at the proposed hospital, it should be noted, changed throughout the facility's history.

34. Windsor, "A Summary of the History and Plan for Development."

35. These zip codes include 90001, 90002, 90003, 90011, 90037, 90059, 90061, 90220, and 90222.

36. Sandra Lewis, "Background Information."

37. Ibid., 46.

38. Windsor, "A Summary of the History and Plan for Development," 7.

39. Ibid., 3.

40. See chap. 2 for a more detailed discussion of the newspaper.

41. "Bold New Experiment," *Los Angeles Sentinel*, February 27, 1969, B6.

42. This analysis is based on a random sample of 100 news articles about the hospital (out of 463) that appeared in the *Los Angeles Times* between April 17, 1968, and November 2, 2006. It is also based on the entire population of 88 *Times* editorials, op-ed pieces, and letters to the editor mentioning the hospital that appeared between March 15, 1966, and August 18, 2007.

43. Van Dijk, *Elite Discourse and Racism*, 281.

44. For example, see Hunt, *O. J. Simpson Facts and Fictions*; and Domanick, *To Protect and to Serve*.

45. We reviewed the complete list of article headlines for distinctive themes, narrowing them down to the five identified here (plus a residual "none of the above/unclear" category).

46. According to the "inverted pyramid" convention governing the structure of the standard print news narrative, the importance of information presented generally declines as one delves deeper into the narrative. In other words, the essential news is summarized in the headline, with the most important facts about the news stated in the first (or "lead") paragraph. Subsequent paragraphs merely complement or provide alternative takes on the news summarized in the headline and lead. Feature stories often depart from this convention, and may exhibit narratives with more conventional beginnings, middles, and ends. See Schudson, *Power of News*.

47. van Dijk, *Elite Discourse and Racism*, 281.

48. See Richardson and Lancendorfer, "Framing Affirmative Action," 75. The authors define "frames" as consisting of "a theme, story line, or label suggesting a preferred interpretation of some policy question." Their analysis of affirmative-action framing convincingly demonstrates both how media frames "reflect larger public discourse" on an issue and can also work to "influence public opinion."

49. From "Changing Times: Los Angeles in Photographs, 1920–1990," *Los Angeles Times* photographic archive, UCLA Library.

50. See NPR Online, "Remembering Tuskegee: Syphilis Study Still Provokes Disbelief, Sadness," *Morning Edition*, July 25, 2002, http://www.npr.org/programs/morning/features/2002/jul/tuskegee/.

51. "An Approach to Health Care for 'Consumers,'" *Los Angeles Times*, November 23, 1972, E1.

52. "King Hospital: Optimism Amid the Headaches," *Los Angeles Times*, March 23, 1975, B2.

53. The article notes that 104 of 239 registered nurse slots at King/Drew were unfilled. The shortage of nurses at King/Drew, as we shall see, was an issue throughout the facility's history.

54. The article notes that the hospital had recently received 2,000 applications for 29 food service jobs and 6,000 applications for 40 attendant openings.

55. "Hospital Doctors' Strike Ends; New Walkout Slated: Long Beach Area Anesthesiologists to Halt Work Monday to Protest Malpractice Insurance Rates," *Los Angeles Times*, May 14, 1975, B1.

56. "Minority Doctor Program Unveiled at King Hospital," *Los Angeles Times*, September 9, 1975, A3.

57. "Strike Disrupts Care at 3 County Hospitals: USC Facility Is Hardest Hit by Doctors' Walkout; Emergency Aid Still Provided," *Los Angeles Times*, April 22, 1976, B1.

58. The Comprehensive Employment Training Act (CETA) was a federal program initiated in 1973 to train workers and provide them with jobs in public service.

59. "Ex-Hospital Training Chief Pleads No Contest in Embezzlement Case," *Los Angeles Times*, January 7, 1978, A27.

60. PBS Online, "First to Worst: The Special Challenge of Prop 13," *Merrow Report*, 2004, http://www.pbs.org/merrow/tv/ftw/prop13.html.

61. "Health Care for Poor 'Separate, Unequal,'" *Los Angeles Times*, August 5, 1979, A3.

62. "For the Fallen: King Hospital: Succor in the War of Watts," *Los Angeles Times*, August 17, 1980, 1.

63. Paragraph 11 out of 140.

64. Paragraph 97 out of 140.

65. Paragraph 70 out of 140.

66. "County Jumps Gun on Deadline for Cuts, Shuts 8 Health Centers," *Los Angeles Times*, July 29, 1981, D1.

67. "Holes in the Safety Net," *Los Angeles Times*, July 8, 1981, C4.

68. "Who Will Run Emergency Rooms at County Hospitals," *Los Angeles Times*, October 29, 1981, 11.

69. "Hospital's First-Aid Method Sends Many Gunshot Victims Home," *Los Angeles Times*, August 12, 1983, C17.

70. "First Class at Drew Medical School: Institution Readies Doctors to Aid the Medically Underserved," *Los Angeles Times*, August 27, 1981, 11.

71. At the time, the campus consisted of "an assembly of house trailers parked near the corner of 120th Street and Compton Avenue."

72. "History of King/Drew Medical Center," *Los Angeles Sentinel*, December 16, 2004, A1.

73. A follow-up article published on January 15, 1985 ("Dr. King Legacy Lives On at Drew Medical School," F1) refers to the program as "a still controversial experiment aimed at trying to increase the supply of doctors committed to fill the unmet primary heal needs of the poor."

74. "King Hospital Billing Foul-Ups Reportedly Cost Millions," *Los Angeles Times*, October 13, 1988, Metro, 1.

75. "Delgardo Calls Removal Unfair, Says He Had Plan," *Los Angeles Times*, September 29, 1989, Metro, 1.

76. "Even Worse Than We Knew," *Los Angeles Times*, September 15, 1989, 6.

77. See "Asked & Answered: Yvonne Brathwaite Burke: Exit Interview," *Los Angeles Wave*, November 27, 2008, A1. Also see "Yvonne Brathwaite Burke: California's First Black Congresswoman Has Never Forgotten The Lessons of Her Youth," *Los Angeles Times*, February 24, 1974, M26.

78. King/Drew was housed squarely within the 158 square miles comprising the Second District, which included Watts, Crenshaw, Baldwin Hills, View Park, Ladera Heights, and Culver City as well as dozens of other cities and unincorporated areas in Los Angeles County.

79. "Paramedics Cite King Hospital's Long Delays," *Los Angeles Times*, February 8, 1992, B1.

80. "Doctor Files Bias Suit Over Losing Key King Hospital Job," *Los Angeles Times*, January, 28, 1994, B1.

81. The *Los Angeles Times* published at least two feature stories on Dr. Peter Meade, a white King/Drew surgeon who volunteered for the Nobel Prize–winning humanitarian organization, Doctors Without Borders. See also, "He Follows His Heart to the Front Lines," *Los Angeles Times*, October 19, 1999, E1.

82. "Battling Over Control of AIDS Clinic," *Los Angeles Times*, December 10, 1995, B1.

83. "Supervisor Urges Sweeping Hospital Overhaul," *Los Angeles Times*, December 23, 1995, B1.

84. Herb Wesson, who was Speaker of the California Assembly between 2002 and 2004, earlier served as chief of staff for Supervisor Burke in the early 1990s. He acknowledged that supervisors frequently learned of problems with King/Drew from *Times* stories (Wesson, interview by one of the authors, November 17, 2008).

85. "Panel Finds Bias at Hospital but Declines to Act," *Los Angeles Times*, January 18, 1996, B1.

86. "Settlement of Hospital Bias Suits Urged," *Los Angeles Times*, February 10, 2000, B1.

87. "Patient Killed by Poison, Tests Find," *Los Angeles Times*, March 5, 1998, B1.

88. Indeed, rumors circulated during this period that the hospital would be renamed after the Mexican American labor leader, Cesar Chavez.

89. See CBS Interactive, "City of Angels: Show Summary," TV.com, http://www.tv.com/city-of-angels/show/243/summary.html.

90. CBS, 2000.

91. Steven Bochco and Kevin Hooks were executive producers on the show, which was created by Bochco and Paris Barclay, the show's co-executive producer and an Emmy Award–winning director. Actors Blair Underwood, Vivica A. Fox, Gabrielle Union, and Hill Harper were featured in prominent roles.

92. "Anticipating 'City of Angels,'" *Los Angeles Times*, January 13, 2000, Calendar, 58.

93. "Settlement of Hospital Bias Suits Urged," *Los Angeles Times*, February 10, 2000, B1.

94. "Hospital Blamed in 2 Deaths," *Los Angeles Times*, November 8, 2003, B1.

95. "Inspectors Rebuke King/Drew," *Los Angeles Times*, December 9, 2003, B1.

96. "Medical School Ousts Chief," *Los Angeles Times*, January 3, 2004, B1.

97. "L.A. County Says It Has No Plans to Close King/Drew," *Los Angeles Times*, January 28, 2004, B1.

98. "King/Drew Is Again Assailed Over Prescription Drug Flaws," *Los Angeles Times*, March 5, 2004, B1.

99. "King/Drew to Lose 3rd Program," *Los Angeles Times*, May 6, 2004, B1.

100. "King/Drew Praised for Response to Lapses," *Los Angeles Times*, June 29, 2004, B1.

101. "King/Drew Ignored Surgical Safety Checks," *Los Angeles Times*, July 29, 2004, B1.

102. "County May Hand Control of King/Drew to Private Firm," *Los Angeles Times*, October 14, 2004, A1.

103. "A Mounting Tab to Fix King/Drew," *Los Angeles Times,* March 21, 2005, B1.

104. "Judge Denies Bid to Halt Trauma Unit's Closure," *Los Angeles Times*, December 3, 2004, B8.

105. "The Troubles at King/Drew: The Lost and the Bereaved: A Damaged Boy; A Struggling Girl; A Brother Gone; A Family Broken," *Los Angeles Times*, December 5, 2004, A29.

106. "The Troubles at King/Drew: Underfunding Is a Myth, but the Squandering Is Real. Series: Second of Five Parts," *Los Angeles Times*, December 6, 2004, A1.

107. "The Troubles at King/Drew: One Doctor's Long Trail of Dangerous Mistakes. Series: Third of Five Parts," *Los Angeles Times*, December 7, 2004, A1.

108. "The Troubles at King/Drew: How Whole Departments Fail a Hospital's Patients. Series: Fourth of Five Parts," *Los Angeles Times*, December 8, 2004, A1.

109. "The Troubles at King/Drew: Why Supervisors Let Deadly Problems Slide. Series: Last of Five Parts," *Los Angeles Times*, December 9, 2004, A1.

110. "King/Drew Fatal Neglect; Eyes Averted," *Los Angeles Times*, December 5, 2004, M4.

111. "Perilous Chairs," *Los Angeles Times*, December 7, 2004, B12.

112. "Fulfilling the Wrong Dream, King/Drew Fatal Neglect," *Los Angeles Times*, December 12, 2004, M4.

113. "The Troubles at King/Drew: The Search for Answers," *Los Angeles Times*, December 23, 2004, A1.

114. "King/Drew Supporters Blast Hospital's Critics," *Los Angeles Times*, January 16, 2005, B3.

115. "Hospital Faces Loss of Funding," *Los Angeles Times*, February 3, 2005, B1.

116. "Doctor's Marathon Shifts in Question," *Los Angeles Times*, April 26, 2004, A1.

117. "Ex-King/Drew Doctor Admits Misdiagnosis," *Los Angeles Times*, August 26, 2005, B10.

118. "King/Drew Fails Final U.S. Test," *Los Angeles Times*, September 23, 2006, A1.

119. "Proposal Calls for Patient Transfers," *Los Angeles Times*, October 17, 2006, B1.

120. "Medical School Plans to Curtail Training," *Los Angeles Times*, November 2, 2006, B1.

121. Despite being the nation's second-smallest medical school, Drew University nonetheless excelled in NIH-funded research, traditionally an indicator of quality. The school ranked 87th in NIH funding among the nation's 125 medical schools in 2003, despite its relatively small size. See California State Assembly, "A Status Report on the King/Drew Medical Center."

122. On this matter, a California Assembly report on King/Drew quoted Assemblymember Mervin Dymally as follows: "The contractual relationship between the Drew University and the LACDHS is a one-sided proposition that must become more equitable. Drew University has the *responsibilities* while Los Angeles County has the *authority* [emphasis original]." See California State Assembly, "A Status Report on the King/Drew Medical Center."

123. Dr. Richard S. Baker, interview by one of the authors, November 26, 2008.

124. Ibid. According to the website for UCLA's David Geffen School of Medicine, where he was also an associate professor in Ophthalmology, Dr. Baker specializes in the field of ophthalmic epidemiology and is credited with initiating "an ongoing collaborative effort with the epidemiology group of Charles R. Drew University" (http://dgsom.healthsciences.ucla.edu/).

125. For a critical discussion of how DHS budget woes undermined equal access to healthcare in Los Angeles, see Behzad Raghian, "LA County's Sick Health Care System," SocialistWorker.org, October 8, 2004, http://socialistworker .org/2004-2/515/515_02_LAHealthCare.shtml.

126. The King/Drew debacle was covered widely in media throughout the nation. Many of the stories framed the hospital's rise and fall in terms of its Watts-uprisings origins, effectively presenting the facility as a failed social experiment. See for example, "In South Central L.A., a Hospital Fights for Its Life, *Washington Post*, August 26, 2006, A3; "South-Central L.A. Hospital in Critical Condition," *Washington Post*, October 4, 2006, A11; "L.A.'s Beleaguered King-Drew Awaiting Its Fate," BlackAmericaWeb.com, January 6, 2005, http://www.blackamericaweb .com.

127. See *Los Angeles Times* Online, "Historical Milestones," *Media Center*, http:// www.latimes.com/services/newspaper/mediacenter/la-mediacenter-milestones ,0,117814.story.

128. It should be noted that during this turbulent period (in 2000) the *Times* hired its first black managing editor, Dean Baquet, who was promoted to editor of the newspaper in 2005. He left in late 2006 in response to a cost-cutting dispute with the Tribune Company.

129. Previous gold medal awards for *The Times* were bestowed in 1942, 1960, 1969, and 1984. See Columbia University, "Past Winners and Finalists by Category," *The Pulitzer Prizes*, http://www.pulitzer.org/bycat.

130. In early 2009, Rep. Maxine Waters (D-Los Angeles) during a panel discussion charged that the *Los Angeles Times* "targeted Martin Luther King in the name of getting a Pulitzer Prize. They worked it. And not only did they get the Pulitzer Prize for helping to close it down. They had undercover people in the hospital that were reporting and telling stories about the problems of the hospital" (C-SPAN Online, "State of the Black Union 2009, Morning Session," *C-SPAN Archives Video Library*, February 28, 2009, http://www.c-spanarchives.org/library/ index.php?main_page=product_video_info&products_id=284355-1).

131. More than half of the articles in our random sample—fifty-two articles —appeared between 2000 and the end of 2006.

132. Herb Wesson, interview by one of the authors, November 17, 2008.

133. Dr. Richard S. Baker, interview by one of the authors.

134. For example, see Gans, *Deciding What's News*; Herman and Chomsky, *Manufacturing Consent*; and Hunt, *O. J. Simpson Facts & Fictions*.

135. See Joint Commission on Accreditation of Healthcare Organizations, "1998 Hospital Performance Report," and Joint Commission on Accreditation of Healthcare Organizations, "2001 Hospital Performance Report."

136. The *Times* rests most of its case that funding wasn't the problem at King/ Drew on a head-to-head comparison of the facility with another Los Angeles County hospital, Harbor/UCLA (see n. 106). This argument, of course, says nothing about whether Harbor/UCLA might also have been under funded and faced similar problems (if not as prominent) to those faced by King/Drew. It also says nothing about the health characteristics of the patient populations treated by the two hospitals, which is problematic given the fact that the population in King/

Drew's service area, SPA-6, exhibited the most health problems of any population in the county. A balanced consideration of the funding issue at least would
have mentioned a report on the status of King/Drew released by the California
State Assembly just the month before (November 2006) that makes these points,
concluding that "King/Drew has functioned remarkably well with fewer funds."
The report, in fact, presents an entirely different view of King/Drew's financial
performance than the one presented in the *Times* series. The report notes that
among the nation's top ten most profitable teaching hospitals, King/Drew was
ranked number one in 2003, posting a profit margin of 36.9 percent. Rather than
doing less with more, as the *Times* charges, King/Drew actually did more with
less, according to the report. See California State Assembly, "A Status Report on
the King/Drew Medical Center."

137. In chap. 1, Paul Robinson documents some of these early portrayals. The
black Los Angeles politician Mervyn Dymally recounted how he regularly received bad press in the *Times*. When he complained in person to Otis Chandler,
publisher of the *Times*, Chandler "told me then that the *Examiner* [the *Times*'s
major competitor at the time] had more black readers than the *Times*" (Mervyn
M. Dymally, interview conducted in 1997 by Elston L. Carr, Center for Oral History Research, Young Research Library, University of California, Los Angeles. Audio recording, tape no. 4, Side A; transcript, 165).

138. For example, see "Angels on Assignment Take Measures into Their Own
Hands to Help King-Drew," *Los Angeles Sentinel*, December 23, 2004, A6. See also,
"In Defense of King/Drew: A Triumph and Promise Born of Struggle," *Los Ange-
les Sentinel*, October 5, 2006, A7).

||||||||||||||||||||||||||||||||||||||||||||||||||||

Part 4

Action

Unity of the entire community could win any good cause.

—Charlotta Bass

Life is not a spectator sport. If you're going to spend your whole life in the grandstand just watching what goes on, in my opinion you're wasting your life.

—Jackie Robinson

Chapter 13

||||||||||||||||||||||||||||||||||||||||||||||||||||||

Bass to Bass

Relative Freedom and Womanist Leadership in Black Los Angeles

Melina Abdullah and Regina Freer

On August 8, 2008, a beautiful Friday morning in Los Angeles, patrons are waved through the gates of the California Science Center at Exposition Park, a sprawling urban oasis and educational center that sits at the gateway to South Los Angeles. The parking lot, which is normally bordered by yellow school buses and only sparsely populated by the cars of parents bringing their children to the Center and the nearby Natural History Museum, is filled to capacity. A few steps away, housed within an impressive building, is Muses Auditorium.

Every seat in the auditorium is filled, and dozens of people line the walls. Attendees are young, old, and middle-aged. Every racial group is represented, with people of color constituting the clear majority and African Americans comprising the plurality. The usual suspects—bureaucrats and heads of community-based organizations—are present but appear out of place and are certainly outnumbered as they are joined by individuals who are far less common in gatherings of this sort—parents, teenagers, area residents and a few babies making an occasional fuss in the rear corners of the room. Some are dressed in business suits, others in jeans, with a large, organized contingent wearing brightly colored, turquoise T-shirts identifying them as members of Community Coalition, a South Los Angeles grassroots organization.

What prompted this motley crew to decide to skip work, miss school, turn off the television, or opt out of a visit to the beach or the park? They have come from all regions, but especially South Los Angeles, for a special hearing on foster care convened by California State Assembly Speaker Karen Bass. The convener and the issue are notable exceptions to the rule, as is the presence of state legislators who come from places like Visalia and San Jose, which are literally and figuratively far from Los Angeles.

Eyes well up, applause echoes, and the sense of pride and determination is palpable as eighteen-year-old Meshay Broadnax, a foster child who is transitioning out of the system, concludes her testimony to the panel of elected officials and agency mucky-mucks at the front of the room. "I am not what the statistics have painted me to be. I am worth the fight. I believe that lots of us are worth the fight."

It is rare that an issue of concern to some of the most disenfranchised should find a place at the top of a political agenda, but Karen Bass, who elevated this issue, departs from the traditional model in countless ways. In the first decade of the twenty-first century, foster care disproportionately impacted *Black*[1] and poor communities, with African Americans comprising 41 percent of the children in foster care, a drastic overrepresentation of the 15 percent share that Blacks comprised of the United States youth population.[2] Politically, Bass's prioritization of foster care made little pragmatic sense. The majority of Forty-seventh Assembly District residents were not directly connected to the foster care system; the district was diverse in both racial and economic terms, with non-Blacks comprising 71 percent of the district and neighborhoods that boasted home values exceeding $1 million.[3] Karen Bass's connection to the issue came less from a concern for traditional models that connect elected officials to the most affluent of constituents and more from her trajectory as a leader. Hailing from a background in community organizing as the founding executive director of Community Coalition, only four years prior to becoming Speaker, Karen herself would have been seated in the audience wearing a turquoise T-shirt.

The seamlessness between Karen Bass's activism and more formal leadership inherits a legacy forged by Black women in Los Angeles who came before Karen Bass. Rewind to 1960 and the publishing of Charlotta Bass's *Forty Years: Memoirs from the Pages of a Newspaper*. No relation to Karen Bass, Charlotta Bass—a Los Angeles–based newspaper editor and publisher, activist, and Progressive candidate for the vice presidency of the United States in 1952—pays homage to another pioneering woman, Biddy Mason, who arrived in the Los Angeles region in 1851 as a slave.[4] Mason had fought for and won her freedom in a Los Angeles courtroom and went on to become a successful landowner and co-founder of the First African

Methodist Episcopal Church. In Charlotta Bass's discussion of Mason, she connects her own "forty years" legacy to the remarkable story of Mason, a Black Angelena who had charted a course for her own freedom, defying stereotypes and the boundaries imposed by race and gender.

But Charlotta Bass's connection with Biddy Mason goes beyond a shared identity or even being inspired by her achievements as an individual; what resonated most with Bass was Mason's commitment to collective liberation, empowerment and the legacy of Black women leaders that she inherited. "Her desire to achieve freedom for herself and her family was the great urge that encouraged her to follow in the footsteps of those great Negro women pioneers, Sojourner Truth and Harriet Tubman."[5] What Charlotta Bass pulled from Mason's example was a model of leadership that can be traced as far back as pre-colonial Africa and emanates from the struggles of the countless Black women who took part in antislavery activism, the struggle for women's rights, and the anti-lynching movement. This style of organizing and leadership resonated with Charlotta Bass because it was fundamentally radical and a marked departure from traditional, white male leadership models.

Much as Charlotta Bass looked to Biddy Mason as a model, Karen Bass looked to Charlotta Bass—so much so that when she served as executive director of the Community Coalition, the group inaugurated the "Charlotta Bass Award" in recognition of community leadership. While Karen Bass is often assumed to have familial ties to Charlotta Bass, the relationship between them is not one of blood but is a strong kinship nonetheless, as they are tied by the style and substance of their political lives and their commitment to a particular style of organizing and leadership. Karen Bass rose to political leadership from a background in community organizing. Even after being elected to office, Karen Bass is careful to note that electoral politics is only one part of creating change. In 2007 she stated, "I am an activist, being an elected official is my current occupation."[6]

In this chapter, we examine parallels between the cases of Charlotta Bass and Karen Bass, in order to outline a tradition of "womanist" leadership that emerged out of the particulars of Black Los Angeles. The theory of womanist leadership that we have developed serves as the foundation for this investigation.[7] Our analysis of womanist leadership in Los Angeles lifts up two of the model's core tenets[8]: group-centered leadership, and the use of both traditional and nontraditional methods. This group-centered leadership model has a long history in Black women's organizing and served as the foundation for the work of Black clubwomen in the late nineteenth and early twentieth centuries. It was articulated most clearly, perhaps, in the work of Ella Baker.[9] While taking full advantage of traditional methods (i.e., voting, lobbying, running for office), womanist leaders also employ nontraditional methods to build their visions of change, including protests and grassroots organizing.

This work relies on the womanist model as we consider the leadership of Charlotta Bass and of Karen Bass, and the role of place in shaping the leadership of these women. We propose that Black Los Angeles has been a unique home for such leadership. While womanist Black leaders certainly existed and operated elsewhere into the early twenty-first century, we argue that the Los Angeles context, and the Black community in particular, offered particularly fertile ground for this style of leadership. However, just as the multicultural promise and sunshine of the city made Los Angeles ripe for a sort of leadership and organizing that seeks to forge a new vision, there was also a very palpable racial and gender reality. In many ways, it was not simply the hopeful optimism of the city but also the stark reminders of a racialized reality that breathed life into womanist leadership.

Leading the Way: Black Angelenas

Echoing a western tradition, Black Angelenas have been political trailblazers, establishing a track record of "firsts," willing to try new strategies and promote unconventional styles of leadership. Operating in a multicultural milieu, these women forged unconventional coalitions across racial and ideological lines, significantly standing at the forefront of political leadership in the city's Black community. Central to the unique space that Black Los Angeles occupies in the broader political context is the way in which Black women, such as Charlotta Bass and Karen Bass, have shaped the community's structure and have been influenced by that same community. The contours and evolution of this prescient community, as well as the particular shape that gender took within it, can be better understood by examining the lives of these two women, who provided political and community leadership that spans the twentieth and early twenty-first centuries.

Charlotta Bass was a community activist who published and edited the premier Black newspaper of the day, the *California Eagle*, from 1912 to 1951.

Karen Bass is a Los Angeles–based community organizer who founded the grassroots organization Community Coalition in 1990 and served as its executive director, until she was elected to the California State Assembly in 2004 and went on to be named Speaker in 2008. The elder Bass paved the way very clearly for the younger, and their connected stories not only highlight Black social and political development in Los Angeles but also reveal important lessons for Black communities elsewhere.

Although Karen Bass is the first Black woman to lead a state legislative body,[10] it's important to note that Black women's ascent to leadership in Los Angeles was not through electoral politics alone. In fact, when considering "Black politics" in Los Angeles, it is outside activism that is most prominently seared into history. The phrase "outside activism" fills our collective memories with images of Black leather jackets, berets, and dashikis. We remember Black mothers who fought for access to schools and safe conditions for their children. Afro-haired women with raised fists emerge before we peer more deeply into the eyes of these statuesque, determined figures. We recall the leadership of Elaine Brown, the first and only woman to serve as chairman of the Black Panther Party from 1974 until 1977, as well as one of the leaders of the Los Angeles chapter, which she joined in 1968.[11] Along the periphery of the gang violence that peaked in the late 1980s, we see images of mothers who joined forces with one another to preserve their communities, to protect the lives of their children, and to call on government to provide additional resources.

What these women represent is a balancing, a recognition that Black empowerment comes not only through inside participation but also through outside agitation. It is the outsiders as well as the insiders who primed the ground for the ascent of Karen Bass. Karen Bass certainly shared many of the policy priorities of the host of other Black women leaders who hailed from Los Angeles. However, she departed from many of them in her conceptions of leadership. It was her distinct conception of leadership that inherited the legacy of Charlotta Bass. For both Charlotta Bass and Karen Bass, it was not enough to simply be a Black woman leader; for them, their identity shaped their outlook—the lens through which they viewed the world. Such a lens offered a particular gaze, a vision that allowed them to adopt a womanist perspective or frame. And just as identity shaped perspective, that perspective informed the way they led. Neither Charlotta nor Karen Bass served as Black female bodies in a space defined by white supremacist patriarchy. They were both actors with the will to transform the spaces they occupied.

Fighting Despite Relative Freedoms

The presentation of womanist praxis as a progressive or even revolutionary form may initially seem unlikely in the context of Los Angeles, a city
with a history of relative openness and freedom. The rigidity of divisions
(class, race, gender, ideological, and others) that were well entrenched
elsewhere in the nation were generally more flexible in Los Angeles. Los
Angeles was not home to mass lynchings, to the harshest of Jim Crow
laws, or the strictest of segregation policies. For most Blacks, Los Angeles
was a dream city—a place to which they might escape the economic, political, and social oppressions of the South (see Introduction). However,
once they arrived, it became apparent that relative freedom was not full
freedom. For example, Blacks in the city have historically enjoyed greater
levels of homeownership than those in any other U.S. city.[12] Yet, they have
also been subject to some of the harshest residential restrictions and segregation in the nation.[13] Housing access and residential quality of life issues
were at the heart of the struggle for Black advancement in Los Angeles for
more than a century. As womanist leaders, Charlotta Bass and Karen Bass
were on the frontlines of these struggles, ignoring any temptation to rest
on the laurels of relative freedom but instead fighting for total equality.

In fact, we assert that it is precisely this relative freedom in Los Angeles that made ripe a call for *full* freedom. The relative freedoms enjoyed
by Black Angelenos, in a sense, offered space to imagine the possibility of
more, which fed into a womanist leadership model forming the base for a
proactive agenda. Charlotta Bass's and Karen Bass's particular biographies
within Los Angeles—being women who were basically middle-class, educated, and centered in groups where critical thought and engagement was
not a rarity—fall in line with the legacy of women who inherit the mantle
of womanist leadership. Their own relative freedom within a relatively free
space allowed them to use their own access and position to launch collective
movements that demanded gains for the whole of the Black community.

The *California Eagle*'s December 20, 1945, front-page headline declared,
"Mass Meeting Sunday—Protest Racist Covenants—Hear Facts on Laws
Case." As she so often did, Charlotta Bass used her power as owner and
editor of the *Eagle* to rally support for community members on the front
lines of the battle against racially restrictive covenants. The Laws family
case was perhaps the most famous of these interventions. Three months
after the close of World War II, Black defense workers Anna and Henry
Laws were arrested, found guilty, and fined for violating a restrictive cov-

enant in their deed when they tried to occupy their home in Watts. Their case triggered a grassroots movement for civil rights and better housing, and Charlotta Bass was among the leaders of this cause.

As a Black woman owner of a prominent newspaper, Charlotta Bass was undoubtedly a rarity. Rather than becoming enamored with her own prestige, Bass envisioned and utilized the *Eagle* as a vehicle for collective empowerment.[14] She used the paper to inform her readers about terrorist intimidation perpetrated by neighbors determined to maintain restrictions. She publicized the fire bombings of Black residents' homes and other less violent efforts to maintain a white line in Westside neighborhoods. In addition to relaying news of such attacks, she urged the community to rally to protect the rights of Black homeowners, publicizing meetings and protests organized by the Home Owners Protective Association, a group devoted to the pursuit of fair housing. It was not her fight alone. Drawing from a group-centered model, she and others who worked in this organization were not satisfied with the "better than elsewhere" description of Black residential conditions, nor did they stop at "preserving gains and preventing backsliding" of conditions.[15] Rather, they pushed for new opportunities. Literally and figuratively, they forged a new frontier of integrated residential settlement.

Two issues encapsulated Charlotta Bass's vision for fair residential conditions in 1940s Los Angeles: improving existing Black neighborhoods, and expanding Black residential mobility. For Bass, residential questions were tied to broader quality of life concerns:

> While white citizens try to oust . . . highly respected Negro families from their homes in the Van Ness Avenue district, a group of property owners in the vicinity of 20th Street and Compton Avenue ask the City Planning Commission for relief from noise and street blocking caused by the presence of a heavy machinery factory running top speed night and day in the community. At the end of the day's shift, the persons who own and operate this factory no doubt retire to Van Ness or some other like district where Negroes are not welcome, for a quiet night's repose.

She continues:

> It is staggering to realize that 95 [percent] of this great sprawling city is restricted against occupancy by Negroes. It is a challenge to the equilibrium of those who hold faith with the West as part of democratic America. . . .

[Only through] a considered, militant campaign can the destiny of the Negro's future in Los Angeles be assured. Only through such a campaign can the grasping hands of Southern custom be torn from local housing and shoved back to Dixie.[16]

Bass clearly points to an expectation of opportunity in the West. Her admonition is not only an attempt to prevent backsliding but also a call for full freedom. Such a liberating call, she argued, would not come simply from a polite push for reform but would likely require the use of "militant" methods that moved Black communities and shook white society. Like womanist leaders before her, Bass was moving forward with a proactive agenda, rather than simply pushing back against restrictions. Instead of relying on inside participation to move such an agenda forward, Bass called for nontraditional outside methods.

The battles fought by Charlotta Bass in many ways brought about the fall of housing restrictions in Los Angeles, directly benefiting Karen Bass's family, which raised her in a Venice/Fairfax neighborhood on the predominately white Westside. Like Charlotta Bass, Karen Bass resisted settling for relative freedom. She chose instead to focus on community organizing in South Los Angeles. "I grew up in Venice/Fairfax," she noted, "I went to Hamilton High [School]. I was in a predominately white context. I *selected* to be in a Black context" (emphasis added).[17]

For Karen Bass, this Black context was the neighborhoods of South Los Angeles that she became more familiar with in her job as a physician's assistant in the 1980s. In hospital interactions, Bass struggled to treat people whose lives had been torn apart by the increasing crisis of crack cocaine and its ravishing impacts on South Los Angeles's Black community (see chap. 5). South Los Angeles had become a community medicating itself against suffering in the wake of de-industrialization. In addition to crack, alcohol had become a second "medicine" of choice. As a health professional, Bass struggled to treat symptoms but became increasingly frustrated that the root causes were not being adequately addressed. Such dissatisfaction prompted her to initiate Community Coalition in 1990. One of the key priorities for the group was addressing nuisance businesses, including liquor stores, hourly motels, and recycling centers, while also preserving positive assets of the community, including strong, intact, single-family neighborhoods and further enhancing neighborhood livability by recruiting businesses that would offer valuable goods and services. By changing the landscape of South Los Angeles, Bass and Community

Coalition believed that negative outcomes could be lessened, opportunities developed, and organic leadership nurtured.

The emergence of Charlotta Bass and Karen Bass as challengers to traditional structures, which sought to pacify through the award of relative privilege to a few while offering false hope to many, is emblematic of womanist leadership. Their perspective as Black women is significant in explaining their approach to the relative freedom offered by Los Angeles. With the doubling of identity-based oppression at the intersection of race and gender, they experienced even less of the freedom that the city had to offer. Thus, they had more motivation and less to lose from a full-court press toward total equality. This vision of freedom and equality was, in many ways, a radical departure from the norm, thus requiring efforts and strategies that extended beyond standard engagements with inside politics.

Womanist Praxis and Improvisation

In January 1945, Charlotta Bass was selected as "the people's candidate" for the Seventh District seat on the Los Angeles City Council. This run for office was unique in many ways, including the fact that the candidate was a Black woman activist who emerged from a collective, deliberative process rooted in the Black community. In Bass, the collective had a candidate who had earned her dues and demonstrated her allegiances through a track record of outside engagement and agitation. They also had a candidate who had earned a great degree of name recognition with a weekly byline in one of the most important newspapers of the time and whose networks extended beyond Black Los Angeles to include labor and non-black constituencies. Bass, in this sense, was not only a significant ideological choice but also made the most pragmatic sense. Remarkably, Black men stepped aside and supported Bass's candidacy as a womanist leader.

In the case of Karen Bass, the group-centered model was central to the formation and development of Community Coalition, the South Los Angeles–based grassroots membership organization that she initiated in 1990. This commitment is one of the central reasons for the sustainability of the Community Coalition following Karen Bass's departure as executive director in 2004. The coalition was seen as a movement with rather amorphous and unidentifiable leadership. For many coalition members, Karen Bass was seen as just another member, rather than as the "head" of a movement that was dependent upon her for its survival. But this rejection of celebrity-style leadership made Karen Bass's fight to win her state assembly seat much more challenging, as she had not garnered the celebrity stature and accompanying name recognition that follows from leader-centered groups. This rejection of the celebrity style of leadership also challenged her as Speaker, as she often found herself restricted by the norms of the legislative system:

> I am very challenged by my rejection of celebrity-style leadership now. . . . I do have to accept a lot of the "celebrity" of it now, and if I don't, I diminish the role [of Speaker]. . . . There's a certain presence that I have to have when I walk into the room, and if I don't, it feeds into the idea that "Oh well, she's *sort of* the Speaker." This is one of those spaces where my beliefs and my job kind of part ways. So, I've learned how to get into character and be Speaker. They aren't clothes that I wear that comfortably, but I'm learning.[18]

The ascent of Speaker Bass was no minor accomplishment. "Karen Bass Becomes America's First Black Woman Speaker,"[19] "Bass Takes Office as History Takes Note,"[20] and "California Speaker Makes History,"[21] read newspaper and magazine headlines around the nation as Karen Bass was elected Speaker of the California State Assembly—the first Black woman to lead a state legislative body in U.S. history. This "first" was notable not simply because of her racial and gender identities but also because of her political trajectory, her ideological leanings, and the type of leadership to which Karen Bass ascribed:

> I still define myself as a progressive. It really defines a set of values. . . . I would define a progressive as somebody that really challenges the social and economic structure of this country and really feels that the root causes of a lot of social problems are economics and the inequity in our system and racism, and believes that there are fundamental changes that need to take place.[22]

Karen Bass's progressive ideology and worldview echoed much of what had been presented by Charlotta Bass before her. The twenty-first-century Bass inherited from the twentieth century one a commitment to not simply engage the system but to challenge it. A core difference, however, is the strategies that Karen Bass was able to employ. While the elder Bass had a desire to utilize the electoral process to advance the collective Black progressive agenda, her repeated runs for elected office were successful only in a more esoteric sense—they allowed for the building of a coalition and for the raising of issues. Perhaps the unwillingness of the electorate to actually place Charlotta Bass in any of the elected positions for which she ran is more indicative of a political system that was too inflexible to respond to the group-centered approach to leadership.[23] Despite her electoral losses, Charlotta Bass's ability to "raise the issues" in many ways helped to prepare the ground for Karen Bass's ascent.

Karen Bass's rise and victories in the realm of electoral politics were unlikely when viewed in light of traditional political models. In 2004 her name appeared on an electoral ballot for the first time. She had considered and announced a run for the Los Angeles City Council's Eighth District seat in 2002 but was, by many accounts, pushed out by the entrenched Black elite who favored a more traditional candidate.[24] Although there were indications that Karen Bass would receive a great deal of support from progressives—and she *had* received some endorsements and raised some funds—early indications that it would be a very tough race, coupled with the death of her father, caused her to drop out of the race at a fairly early stage. Few foresaw the 2004 victory in her legislative race and even fewer could have anticipated her election as Speaker.

Inside Outsider

While Karen Bass's climb to electoral leadership marked a turning of the page of history, it did not mean that the path was completely open for womanist leadership or that electoral politics was or should be the sole means for progressive advance. Once in office, progressives often found themselves constrained. The structures, norms, and constructs of government are usually built to ensure that any change is incremental and that the status quo is preserved. Progressive elected officials have to work to rally a majority of their colleagues but are usually stymied by a conservative "majority tyranny."[25] The question for womanist leaders like Karen Bass became the degree to which they might be able to transform the system of which they had become a part. How might they balance the required degree of assimilation to the norms of the system with a push for systemic change?[26] For Bass, shifting the fundamentals of the system was a high priority agenda item, which she realized could not be accomplished without agitation from the outside. Furthermore, arriving in Sacramento with an agenda, while a necessity for a womanist leader, became an exercise in futility without the engagement of outside actors. This outside/inside partnership proved even more necessary with electoral victories. However, forging, developing, and maintaining these partnerships was no easy task. Bass noted her frustration with the limited ways in which outsiders accessed her as an insider member of a movement that would benefit from the utilization of a combined strategy:

> In general, I've been disappointed [with the inside/outside relationship] . . . and the reason why is that I have really wanted to be more strategic with folks on the outside and I've had to work really hard at it. It's like people were so supportive of me running for office and then the minute I got there they were like "See ya'!" and I was like "Wait a minute now! What was my point in being here if it wasn't to figure out how to move what we were doing in LA or anyplace else?"[27]

Karen Bass's recognition of the central role that outsiders would play in advancing a progressive agenda, despite her high rank as a progressive Speaker, signals a key point often overlooked in analyses of movement building.[28] While it is generally thought that elected office is a core goal of a movement and that incorporative politics are the most viable means for empowerment, womanist praxis views electoral wins as a strategy rather than a goal. For womanist leaders like Charlotta Bass and Karen Bass, inside participation became stronger when paired with outside agitation. This dual approach worked to center the movement vision and goals, reaffirming the position of committed elected officials as a *part* of the movement rather than as *defining* the movement. In Los Angeles, particularly, outside methods were often equal in importance to inside ones as agitational methods in the city were often more accessible, more militant, and less foreign, and thus often garnered a greater measure of success than in other spaces. In contrast, electoral wins were usually less important than the advancement of a message through the electoral process. As highlighted in the campaign slogan of the Progressive Party that nominated Charlotta Bass for vice president in 1952, "Win or lose, we win by raising the issues."[29]

Despite Charlotta Bass's inability to move from the "outside" to the "inside," and the challenges that Karen Bass faced in maintaining and utilizing connections to the outside once on the inside, their ardent pursuit of inside/outside methods demonstrated their willingness to employ innovative strategies. As such, their shared leadership style, in many senses, expanded the pathways to empowerment and revisited ideals of collective uplift rather than ascribing to traditional models of individual leadership in the face of a stagnant system.

Coalition-Building in Los Angeles

In declaring his support for Charlotta Bass's candidacy for city council, Rev. Clayton Russell highlighted the significance of her ties to communities beyond the boundaries of Black Los Angeles, including labor and other racial groups. This process of incorporating non-black supporters as a part of both electoral and governing coalitions was and is central to womanist leadership, for both pragmatic and philosophical reasons. While Black women remained central, womanist leadership in Los Angeles recognized the history of the space as a multiracial city that was never exclusively Black and white. As such, the role of other people of color became crucial, as did the participation of leftist whites. Thus, womanist leadership in Los Angeles utilized coalition building as another innovative strategy, recognizing that by working in larger collectives toward shared goals, more could be accomplished. It is important to note that while occasional alliances developed, coalition building was much more common. Coalitions are distinguished from alliances in that they are based on mutual interest rather than shared vision.[30] Coalitions also allow tighter group-definitions to remain prioritized. In the cases of Charlotta Bass and Karen Bass, both were rooted firmly within a Black community that provided their base.

The coalitions developed by Charlotta Bass and Karen Bass can be thought of as concentric circles, with a Black progressive community at the center, expanding outward to a larger group of Black Angelenos, and then to labor, other people of color, and leftist whites. While this overall structure was essentially the same for both Basses, the trajectories to their development are almost inverse images. Charlotta Bass began her career firmly planted in Black Los Angeles, establishing her base among Black progressives as her vision became more radical and more defined, while also building her coalition out beyond the boundaries of the Black community. With memberships in the United Negro Improvement Association (UNIA), an organization founded by the Black nationalist separatist Marcus Garvey, and the more conservative NAACP as well as her status as owner of the *Eagle*, Charlotta Bass was clearly entrenched in the Black community.

However, she did not restrict her work to Black advancement but was active in organizations that addressed the conditions of other people of color. One such organization was the Civil Rights Congress—a national group affiliated with the Communist Party, which in Los Angeles expanded its approach beyond issues that affected working-class Blacks to include issues that affected people of color more broadly.[31] Additionally, she used the *Eagle* to educate and rally her base in support of the plight of other people of color whose conditions often mirrored those of Black Angelenos. This is best exemplified by the *Eagle*'s coverage of the Sleepy Lagoon murder trials where Mexican American youth were profiled and targeted by the sheriff's department; this situated Bass as one of the city's earliest advocates of a Black/brown coalition.[32] In addition to targeting her base, Charlotta Bass's advocacy of a larger coalition reached into her service on the county grand jury. In response to perceived racism on the part of fellow jurors, Bass admonished:

> Ladies and gentlemen of the jury . . . I consider what I have just heard an outrageous attack on our Mexican American citizens, and as a member of another minority group, a personal attack on me. For I am sure that what you have said about the Mexican people, in your subconscious mind, is precisely what you feel about my people. Do you realize that the very land you claim and live on was once the property of the Mexicans that you now despise? Did you buy it? . . . I am ashamed and afraid that your ignorance and prejudice will be your undoing unless you wake up and together all of us, you and I—Mexican, Negro, Asian, European, and African—create a world in peace dedicated to the real brotherhood of man."[33]

More than simply an advocate for racial justice, Charlotta Bass also built coalitions to advance the cause of workers' rights more broadly. An early supporter of the CIO (Congress of Industrial Organizations), Charlotta Bass was affiliated with much of the labor and white left-wing activism in the city. Such affiliations would result in Bass being Red-baited from within the Black community and beyond. Not only would she be under FBI surveillance and called to testify before the California State Un-American Activities Committee, many of the Black organizations that she had so diligently served sought to expel her.[34] Ultimately, she would be identified more heavily for her presumed affiliations with the Communist Party than for her diligent work for racial justice. As such, by the end of her life Charlotta Bass found herself pushed toward the margins of the circle that she had built.

Interestingly, as Charlotta Bass's political trajectory moved her from the center to the margins, Karen Bass would move from margin to center. Raised, not in a closed Black community but as a part of a multiracial progressive circle on the Westside of Los Angeles, Karen Bass's earliest political involvements were not initiated by Black progressives of the wider Black community but by broader calls for social and economic justice. In many ways, she inherited a space and a coalition that had been built by Charlotta Bass; the coalitions that gave rise to Karen Bass's political development were the very ones that Charlotta Bass had cultivated. Many of Karen Bass's early influences, as she notes, were among the city's most prominent white and Jewish leftists:

> It [the white Left] played a huge role for me. In Hamilton [High School] for example, a lot of the Jewish parents were activists and some of them were in the Communist Party. And so I grew up with a lot of red diaper babies. And there were some African American parents who were in the Communist Party. There were teachers who were in the Communist Party. So, white radicals were very influential. And at the same time you have the Panthers and the whole black movement.[35]

Beyond the white Left, Karen Bass's vision is tied strongly to the building of a multiracial coalition, with particularly strong ties to the Latino community. Her early work with the Venceramos Brigade[36] and Jobs with Peace,[37] highlighted the parallels in conditions experienced between Blacks and Latinos in the city. Two key elements emerged out of Karen Bass's early experiences and were further developed by the work that she was a part of in the 1980s—a commitment to coalition building, and the development of an international perspective. Bass's work with the Venceramos Brigade brought her together with Gil Cedillo, Antonio Villaraigosa, Mark Ridley-Thomas, and Anthony Thigpenn,[38] "a group of mostly grassroots progressives working in Black and Latino areas,"[39] and who were a part of the Jobs with Peace movement. Coming out of this broader coalitional perspective was also a grounding within the Black community. In the late 1980s and early 1990s, Bass became involved with the Free South Africa Movement, where she met and worked with Rep. Maxine Waters (D-Los Angeles) and other entrenched Black leaders who were usually thought of as a part of the political mainstream.

Ideologically, Karen Bass was moving from a more leftist, internationalist frame to a progressive one. It was an approach that still sought to make demands of the system but worked to be more strategic in its attempt to move forward particular agendas through policy work. By the 1990s Karen Bass began to define her work by "looking at specific issues in our communities and how to use public policy to deal with those issues";[40] Community Coalition was born out of this approach. After her election to public office in 2004, Bass saw her work in Sacramento as an extension of the work that she had done in the communities of South Los Angeles—"She went to Sacramento with an agenda."[41] Bass was very deliberate in her development of a political agenda and recognized this as a departure from the practices of many of her colleagues:

> One of the things that I try to do in my job is insert my politics every chance I get and I also try to look for some area where I can bring about change and push the envelope. That's why I focused on foster care. . . . One thing that a progressive can do is go in with an agenda, recognizing that there are a whole lot of folks that have no agenda and have no concern about having an agenda.[42]

She was clear that her agenda developed largely out of her work as an organizer. "My agenda in Sacramento totally meshes more [with my] former life. I mean, I looked at what I was doing with the Coalition to say 'What can I do on a statewide level?' So, most of my legislation is related to the work that I had done in the Coalition."[43] While remaining a self-defined progressive, Karen Bass's role moved from one of a clear outsider to a political insider with ties to the outside.

The evolutionary process is one shared by Charlotta Bass, although their work unfolded in different ways. Charlotta Bass maintained her Black and leftist politics for a period but moved away, or more accurately was pushed away, from the Black community as she became more closely aligned with the white Left. Karen Bass, on the other hand, was able to move closer to the Black community, while maintaining her ties to the white Left. This speaks to the passage of time and the easing of Red-baiting, but as Karen Bass points out, it also demonstrates the possibilities that Charlotta Bass opened for her:

> The multiracial part of LA has always been my exposure. . . . I was never a part of the black establishment. I guess I am now, but the black organizations, the black leadership, whether you are talking about elected or just community, I was never connected to it and didn't know half of them until 1990 when I started the Coalition.[44]

When asked if this distance from the Black establishment was a benefit or a hindrance, Karen Bass replied:

> It's been good because I didn't come in with any of the beefs, the turf, the relationships. . . . I defined myself as to the Left and I saw all that as being mainstream and I didn't really have an interest in being there. I didn't really connect up with it until the Free South Africa Movement in the '80s. That's when I met Maxine Waters, worked with her through the Free South Africa Movement.[45]

By contrast, Charlotta Bass was not able to escape these types of beefs and was certainly party to turf battle. Her early entrenchment in the Black mainstream, her grappling with diverse ideological leanings, her ultimate radicalization, and her move beyond the boundaries of blackness to join coalitions with white leftists and other people of color resulted in both internal and external questioning, and occasional battles. But her role in an evolutionary process of womanist praxis would pave the way for future generations of leaders to engage in the important work required for fundamental, substantive change to occur. Los Angeles offered fertile ground for the development of a special brand of Black politics. Its racial and ideological diversity offered a unique backdrop for the strategic quest for freedom.

The Basses' Legacy

It is tempting to lift up the lives of Charlotta Bass and Karen Bass as unique stories of remarkable individual achievement. But their connections to one another remind us of the broader political and spatial contexts that gave rise to them. In fact, these women's own shared core values rejected such an individualistic portrayal of greatness. They were self-conscious products of a collective. As womanist leaders who emerged in Los Angeles, they are very much the products of a unique Black community—a community that has at times enjoyed relative freedom, but nonetheless fought for full equality, a community with disparate class, ideological, and ecumenical membership that nonetheless experimented with participatory and open democracy stretching back to the turn of the twentieth century. While Los Angeles and the West fell short of the dreamlands that many came in search of, the setting provided a space where experimentalism was a norm, where political systems and power holders were less entrenched and rigid, and where innovation came fairly naturally and regularly. A part of that innovation was the realization that the world existed beyond Black/white divides; coalitions could be built with groups representing the range of racial groups that called Los Angeles home. Both Charlotta Bass and Karen Bass capitalized greatly off of the immense opportunities and relative openness that the Los Angeles context offered.

Just as it is important to move beyond the narrow significance of two individuals, it is also worthwhile to consider what is more broadly significant about lives lived in Black Los Angeles. The Basses' pathways to leadership and their strategic approach to exercising it offer cautionary lessons when compared to the 2008 election of President Barack Obama, a former community organizer who was politicized as a college freshman in Los Angeles.[46] These women's emergence from and consistent connection to collective community forces distinguished them as leaders who respected power from the bottom up. The "people's candidate" committed to raising issues, "win or lose," and the Speaker who fought against "celebrity style leadership" and "transactional politics" prefigure President Obama's own admonition upon winning the presidency: "This victory alone is not the change we seek. It is only the chance for us to make that change."[47] For both Bass women, electoral strategies were part of a larger strategic approach to empowerment.

As fighters, despite relative freedom, the Basses telegraph an interesting approach to Black empowerment at the end of the first decade of the twenty-first century. Their refusal to become enamored with relative privilege, including their own and that of larger Black Los Angeles, parallels what appears to be the most strategic Black position for the new century: celebrating the unprecedented gains symbolized by the election of a Black president while also recognizing that the battle for full freedom and equality has yet to be won.

NOTES

1. Editors note: For political reasons, this chapter's authors elected to capitalize "Black" in all references to people of African descent, their culture, and their racialized experiences.

2. U.S. Government Accountability Office, "African American Children in Foster Care," i.

3. California State Assembly, "Karen Bass, Speaker of the Assembly, 47th Assembly District," 2008, www.democrats.assembly.ca.gov/Speaker/District/ (accessed August 15, 2008).

4. See chap. 1 for further background on Biddy Mason.

5. Bass, *Forty Years: Memoirs*, 7.

6. Karen Bass, speech presented to the California Faculty Association, Sacramento, California, March 5, 2007.

7. See Abdullah and Freer, "Toward a Womanist Leadership Praxis."

8. While not fully explored in the case studies presented, the additional components of womanist leadership, the connection between theory and practice, and proactivity, are also factors. The connection between theory and practice (or praxis—as defined by Paolo Freire) maintains that in addition to theorizing about change and progress, actual engagement is also required, with those actions then informing and reframing theory. More simply, the process is one of thinking, doing, and then rethinking. See Freire, *Pedagogy of the Oppressed*.

9. See E. Baker, "We Need Group-Centered Leadership." See also Marable, *Black Leadership*, xv–xvii.

10. Decades earlier, another Black Angelena, Yvonne Brathwaite Burke, had become the first Black woman elected to the California state legislature in 1967. See chap. 12 for more on Brathwaite Burke.

11. E. Brown, *Taste of Power*. See chap. 5 for more on the Los Angeles chapter of the Black Panther Party.

12. Bunch, "A Past Not Necessarily Prologue."

13. See chap. 1 and 2 for a detailed account of racially restrictive covenants.

14. See chap. 2 for a discussion of the origins of the *Eagle* on Central Avenue.

15. Charlotta Bass, "On the Sidewalk," *California Eagle*, August 7, 1941, 1.

16. Ibid.

17. Karen Bass, interview by authors, Los Angeles, California, August 8, 2008.

18. Ibid.

19. Jason Lewis, "Karen Bass Becomes America's First Black Woman Speaker," *New York Beacon* 15, no. 20 (2008).

20. Jim Sanders, "Bass Takes Office as History Takes Note: New Assembly Speaker Compares Economy to a Natural Disaster," *Sacramento Bee*, May 14, 2008, A3.

21. Tamara E. Holmes, "California Speaker Makes History," *Black Enterprise* 39, no. 1 (2008).

22. Karen Bass, interview by authors, Los Angeles, California, August 8, 2008.

23. Charlotta Bass was a candidate for the Los Angeles City Council, Seventh District in 1945, a candidate for U.S. Congress in 1950, and ran for the U.S. vice presidency in 1952 after having been nominated by Paul Robeson with a second from W. E. B. DuBois under the Progressive Party ticket (Regina Freer and Marti Tippens, "Charlotta Bass: Her Story," *Charlotta Bass and the California Eagle*,

Southern California Library for Social Studies and Research, http://www.socallib.org/bass/story/ [accessed February 13, 2009]).

24. Bass would have faced former police chief Bernard Parks, who had been ousted from the position by former mayor James Hahn, despite commitments made to the Black community. Much of Black Los Angeles, embittered by Hahn's betrayal, supported Parks in his subsequent electoral bid (Abdullah and Freer, "Pushing and Pulling toward Coalition").

25. Guinier, *Tyranny of the Majority.*

26. Junn, "Assimilating or Coloring Participation."

27. Karen Bass, interview by authors, Los Angeles, California, August 8, 2008.

28. Browning, Marshall, and Tabb, *Racial Politics in American Cities.*

29. Jeter, "Rough Flying: The *California Eagle.*"

30. A. Davis and Martinez, "Coalition Building among People of Color."

31. Civil Rights Congress Collection, Los Angeles, Southern California Library for Social Studies and Research, Los Angeles.

32. Gottlieb et al., *Next Los Angeles.*

33. Charlotta Bass, Addn. Box 1, "Grand Jury 1943," speech excerpt, Charlotta A. Bass Papers, MSS 002, Southern California Library for Social Studies and Research, Los Angeles.

34. Gottlieb et al., *Next Los Angeles.*

35. Karen Bass, interview by authors, Los Angeles, California, August 8, 2008. For an overview of the role of Black Panthers in Los Angeles, see chap. 5.

36. A group of young multiracial youth who worked to challenge U.S. policies toward Cuba.

37. A national coalition of progressives, with a multiracial coalition that emerged in Los Angeles in the 1980s to address the ways in which military spending desecrated funding for social programs and disproportionately affected people of color.

38. Karen Bass, interview by authors, Los Angeles, California, August 8, 2008. For more on these figures, see chap. 15.

39. Greg Akili, interview by one of the authors, February 13, 2009.

40. Ibid.

41. Ibid.

42. Karen Bass, interview by authors, Culver City, California, December 22, 2008.

43. Karen Bass, interview by authors, Los Angeles, California, August 8, 2008.

44. Ibid.

45. Ibid.

46. Barack Obama attended Occidental College in Glendale, California, from 1979 to 1981.

47. Barack Obama, "Presidential Acceptance Speech," Chicago, Illinois, November 4, 2008.

Chapter 14

IIIIIIIIIIIIIIIIIIIIIIIIIIIIIIIIIIIIIIIIIIIIIIIIIIIIIIIII

Concerned Citizens

Environmental (In)Justice in Black Los Angeles

Sonya Winton

In August 1985, two African American women learned that the City of Los Angeles had selected their neighborhood as the site for a thirteen-acre, municipal solid waste incinerator plant. They immediately took action by establishing the Concerned Citizens of South Central Los Angeles (CCSCLA)—"one of the first African American environmental organizations in the country."[1] Through their locally based environmental justice organization, Robin Cannon and Charlotte Bullock—who possessed moderate grassroots activism experience[2]—launched a large-scale protest campaign against a $535 million bond issue for the development of the Los Angeles City Energy Recovery (LANCER) Municipal Waste Incinerator.[3] According to Cannon, "The minute LANCER sprang up, we saw it as a health threat, but we also considered it an environmental issue. An incinerator has the potential to impact the air, the land, and the water. LANCER [could have] affected the totality of where we lived and worked."[4]

Los Angeles's economically disadvantaged communities of color already faced more than their fair share of environmental hazards, and LANCER posed yet another potentially adverse health risk to the predominantly black and poor inhabitants in Cannon's neighborhood.[5] Initial reports estimated that LANCER would have emitted "nearly 5 million tons of ash —most destined for landfills—of which over 8 million pounds would . . . [have] spewed into adjacent neighborhoods from its 280 foot main stack, as well as an additional 150,000 pounds of cooling tower particulate matter emissions."[6]

Undeniably, the two-year battle between CCSCLA, a politically disenfranchised, under-funded community organization, and an all-powerful
Los Angeles City Council resembled the biblical narrative of David and
Goliath. In the absence of national organizational support by mainstream
environmental groups (MEGs),[7] which are politically powerful and rich
in resources, members of CCSCLA accessed their *organic resource* base
and "mobilized a citywide network of community organizations and local
political and business leaders."[8] When CCSCLA emerged victorious, the
city council reluctantly suspended the construction of the $170-million
LANCER facility and reevaluated "their long prioritization of incineration
in its waste management policy . . . to pursue instead a commitment to
recycling."[9]

Like so many other multiracial, locally based environmental justice organizations in the United States, CCSCLA was established by lower- to
moderate-income African Americans because the dominant, indigenous
institutions in their community[10] failed to address hazardous environmental afflictions that disproportionately plagued minority communities.
Meanwhile, prominent, national environmental groups also had little to
contribute to their cause:

> [W]hen members of Concerned Citizens [of South Central Los Angeles]
> first approached these organizations [the Sierra Club and the Environ-
> mental Defense Fund] in the mid-1980s for support to fight LANCER,
> they were informed that the poisoning of an urban community by an
> incineration facility was a "community health issue, not an environmen-
> tal one."[11]

At the heart of this dismissive rejoinder was the long-standing neglect
by MEGs to "sufficiently address the fact that social inequality and im-
balances of social power are at the heart of environmental degradation,
resource depletion, pollution, and even overpopulation."[12] By combining
the issues of race, concentrated poverty, social isolation, and environmental health, leaders of CCSCLA not only made certain that South Central
Los Angeles emerged as a significant focal point of the burgeoning modern environmental justice movement that was sweeping the nation, but
they also effectively challenged an overly narrow definition of "the environment." MEGs had long employed this definition to prioritize public
policies related to conservation, preservation, and aesthetics, all at the expense of environmental inequity in historically marginalized communities

of color.[13] The emergence of a thriving environmental justice movement, as embodied by CCSCLA, challenged MEGs to develop more inclusive discourses and policies—a move that was met at times with hostility from their predominantly white membership base.[14] By contesting the city's plan to locate a potentially harmful municipal waste incinerator in their neighborhood, the founders of CCSCLA ensured that Los Angeles became a site of contestation over how environmental issues would be framed.

The goal of this chapter is to chronicle the process by which CCSCLA overcame the challenges confronting it and became a model to be emulated by other community groups committed to social justice. By pooling *organic resources* (e.g., community members and volunteer legal and policy experts), which allowed them to offset much of the financial burden associated with CCSCLA's start-up, group members created an effective *triangle approach* to their grassroots campaign. CCSCLA thus built an impressive cooperative partnership comprised of city and state officials, academicians, scientists, and national environmental justice activists. By the early twenty-first century, decades after its embroiled battle with the city, CCSCLA had evolved into a key social justice organization in the Greater Los Angeles area.

Toward the Politics of Inclusion

During the 1970s, emerging reports and studies identified communities of color as bearing a disproportionate burden of hazardous waste facilities and poor air quality. In 1971, the Council on Environmental Quality (CEQ) published one of the first reports to "document the correlation between a community's involvement in environmental protection, and a community's race and income." The report identified several factors as impacting urban environments: "inadequate housing, high crime rates, poor health, unsanitary conditions, inadequate education and recreation, and drug addiction."[15] The correlation between housing patterns and environmental inequity is significant, as the inequitable distribution of environmental hazardous sites can be traced to historical patterns of residential segregation.[16] The CEQ report also revealed that African American respondents living in cities, such as Cleveland, Boston, Detroit, and Los Angeles, felt that MEGs monopolized the environmental decision-making process. Many "expressed concern over whether or not their environmental issues would be lost in the shadows of the national environmental movement's policy agenda."[17] There were a number of published reports that linked poor air quality to higher rates of asthma in African American communities.[18]

Despite the findings of these reports, environmental equity concerns in economically disadvantaged black communities failed to enter the national decision-making agenda, which was due in large part to established MEGs refusing to incorporate disproportionate risk onto their legislative agendas. For example, a 1971 national membership survey of the Sierra Club had found that 58 percent of the group's members either strongly or somewhat strongly opposed the idea that the organization should "concern itself with the conservation problems of such special groups as the urban poor and ethnic minorities."[19] Annual reports of the other leading environmental groups (from 1950 to 1970) do not detail any provisions to address environmental concerns in communities of color. Nor do they show an active record of discussing a need to take action on this issue.

By the early 1980s, when protests demanding environmental justice erupted in communities of color nationwide, MEGs—who wielded a significant amount of political power over the national environmental agenda[20]—remained resistant to broadening their organizational agendas to include the environmental injustice that plagued these politically powerless neighborhoods. With MEGs' long history of systematically excluding people of color from their organizations, it is not surprising that they intentionally prevented environmental crises in communities of color from being fully incorporated onto the national environmental agenda. In the face of public outcry by environmental justice activists, MEGs argued that people of color had very little to no interest in environmental issues. Studies showed, however, that minorities were very concerned about neighborhood environmental problems—even if they had less to say about environmental quality in general.[21]

Concerned Citizens of South Central, Los Angeles (CCSCLA)

In 1984 the California Waste Management Board commissioned the infamous Cerrell Report, which identified for polluting industries "vulnerable sectors" of the population. According to the report, economically disadvantaged communities of color with low educational levels were ideal locations for the construction of garbage incinerators as they would offer considerably less resistance than "middle and upper socioeconomic strata [who] possess better resources to effectuate their opposition."[22] According to Robin Cannon, once she read the Cerrell Report she knew instantly why her community was chosen for the LANCER Project.[23]

The proposed site for the LANCER project was a vacant lot located in the Central Avenue Corridor at Forty-first Street and Alameda Street. According to a *Los Angeles Times* story, "the area combined heavy industrial with a residential population of about 16,000, as well as Jefferson High School[24] and a large public recreation center."[25] This location was just blocks away from the historic Central Avenue communities (see chap. 2). When Los Angeles city officials voted in support of the multimillion-dollar bond for LANCER's construction, they were confident that they were one step closer to solving the city's mounting "waste woes."[26] It was estimated that by 1993, all of the city's landfill sites would be filled to capacity.[27] When compared to previous mass burn incinerators that spewed filthy debris into both the air and lungs of affected populations, city officials praised LANCER as an "environmentally friendly project." However, reports of LANCER's projected emissions present a very different picture. According to a CCSCLA Fact Sheet, LANCER's emissions would contain "a wide variety of hazardous emissions, including heavy metals, toxic organic compounds, and other carcinogens, totally apart from the air pollution generated by the 600 to 700 garbage truck trips per day to and from the facility."[28]

In August 1985, when Cannon—then a senior data processor technician for the City of Los Angeles—reviewed the notification of the city's public hearing regarding the LANCER project, she knew immediately that the city planned to build the incinerator in a poor neighborhood where many of the residents already suffered from respiratory ailments.[29] "My family has a history of asthma; one my brothers, some of my sisters as well as myself suffer from asthma," Cannon noted.[30] She said that she had suspected for some time that air pollutants associated with established industries in her neighborhood contributed to her family's chronic asthma condition. So the moment she reviewed the Environmental Impact Report (EIR) for LANCER, she added, she was convinced that the city was trying to kill her and her family. Without hesitation, Cannon picked up her telephone receiver and dialed her co-worker and neighbor, Charlotte Bullock, in order to organize a rideshare to the public hearing. Despite several attempts, Cannon was unable to reach her because of busy signals. "Charlotte's line was busy," she recalled, "because she received the same notice and was trying to call me to say that she was going to the public hearing scheduled for the following week."[31]

When Cannon and Bullock arrived at the El Pueblo Housing Development building, they were greeted by Gilbert Lindsay, the Los Angeles City Council's first black councilman,[32] Delwin Biagi, director of the Los Angeles Bureau of Sanitation, and forty skeptical community residents. With the sole intent of selling concerned residents on the LANCER project, city officials rolled out an elaborate film presentation that starred African American actor Brock Peters detailing "how the towering, $170 million plant, disguised by walls and artful landscaping, would use state-of-the-art technology to burn tons of household trash to make electric power."[33]

In order to solidify their hard sell, city officials endorsed LANCER as an economic revitalization project vis-à-vis job creation. This is a strategy environmental justice scholars classify as "economic trade-offs," in which polluting industries offer residents in proposed site locations employment opportunities in exchange for their public support for the placement of polluting industries in their neighborhood. But these job opportunities rarely materialize for area residents, as employment opportunities at the proposed sites usually require employees to possess advanced educational degrees.[34] LANCER was no exception. According to the *Los Angeles Times*, the "majority of the 50 or so employment opportunities offered by such a high-tech operation would be specialized, meaning that most of its employees probably would be brought in from outside the community."[35]

By the close of the presentation, Cannon admitted, she "was already alarmed because they talked about emitting dioxins and furans, but said that was nothing for us to worry about."[36] Moreover, she continued, "They said that they would operate twenty-four hours a day, seven days a week, and would dispose of 100,000 gallons of waste water a day. I was worried about the water, the fumes, and the noise from the dump trucks."[37] Although Cannon had "tons and tons of questions," she waited patiently as other attendees had their respective turn at the microphone, her concerns growing:

> I had tons and tons of questions and when I started to ask my questions regarding the financing of the project as well as the potential health impact of the incinerator, city officials insisted that they would relieve my concerns by giving me an Environment Impact Report [EIR]. They stated that the EIR would normally cost $35, but that they were going to give it to me, as if they were doing me favor.[38]

Unbeknownst to Cannon—who stood center stage articulating her laundry list of concerns concerning the proposed landfill—Bullock was distributing her home telephone number to attendees on makeshift notebook business cards. "Charlotte passed out my number so freely that everyone thought that I knew more than they did," Cannon recalled. "But the truth was I knew just as much as they did."[39]

Cannon left the public hearing with the EIR in tow. Later on that evening, Cannon combed through the EIR and an EIR Fact Sheet—a cheat sheet that contained simplified scientific language. At 10 p.m., she phoned her sister, Sheila Cannon, and declared "Sheila, they are trying to kill us!"[40] Following the sisters' dialogue, Sheila made a decisive commitment to join her older sister in the fight to ensure that LANCER never saw the light of day. Over the course of a week, Cannon received countless telephone calls from a handful of concerned neighbors who inquired about her strategy to prevent the construction of LANCER.

The following week, the Cannon sisters, Bullock, Roberta Stephens, Randy Ross, Wilson Smith, and Halisi Price convened at the Vernon Public Library in order to develop a strategic plan for their oppositional campaign against LANCER.[41] Robin Cannon distributed EIR Fact Sheets, and as the small group reviewed the information, they decided that they were going to fight LANCER. "We named ourselves that very day: the Concerned Citizens of South-Central Los Angeles," Cannon recalled.[42] According to Cannon, the group met "every Saturday for two consecutive years."[43] When asked about her motivation to establish a locally based environmental justice organization, Cannon admits that "some of my education in community development and resource knowledge may have come from listening to the Black Panthers talk about the need for political, economic, and social empowerment in my community in the 1960s."[44] As a high school student at Jefferson High, Cannon passed by the Los Angeles Chapter of the Black Panther Party's (BPP) headquarters (located at Fortyfirst and Central) on her way home. One day she approached a BPP member to inquire about the group's community work and was so inspired by her dialogue with the member that she quickly volunteered for the BPP Free Breakfast Program. "I would get up early every morning to assist with the free breakfast program," recalled Cannon.[45] "When the BPP was destroyed, there was an organizational void in our community."[46]

During the inaugural meeting, CCSCLA organizers recognized that in order for their campaign to generate positive results they needed to immerse themselves in the scientific research associated with waste management, as well as acquire a greater understanding of the bureaucratic process (e.g., structural elements of local politics and key political actors) that led to the approval of LANCER's operating permit. In order to augment their knowledge base, CCSCLA's collective instituted an internal educational campaign comprised of Cannon and a fellow organizer poring over documents containing dense scientific and political language, and then creating simplified fact sheets detailing the information reviewed. CCSCLA's Fact Sheets were distributed at weekly meetings and review sessions followed. Simultaneously, CCSCLA organizers launched their public education outreach campaign, which involved an aggressive door-to-door campaign. Select CCSCLA organizers "would take a block and go door to door and talk to neighbors," said Cannon. "That's how we established the information and knowledge base in our neighborhood." This strategy proved rewarding for CCSCLA, as it illuminated *organic resources* that the resource-challenged organization subsequently accessed on a regular basis.

For example, Omawale Fowles, a former county health commissioner and community resident, was instrumental in informing fellow organizers that the EIR lacked the required Health Risk Assessment (HRA)—an analysis that identifies and assesses environmental risks to public health. Cynthia Hamilton, a Pan-African Studies professor at California State University, Long Beach, contacted national environmental justice figures —such as Dr. Robert Bullard, Charles Lee, and Dr. Benjamin Chavis, of the United Church of Christ Commission for Racial Justice—who traveled to South Central Los Angeles in an effort to shed some media spotlight on CCSCLA's local grassroots campaign.[47] This appeared to be an insurmountable task. While national media outlets had covered the Love Canal debacle, which involved working-class white citizens in Niagara Falls, New York,[48] they had been largely missing in action when it came to the coverage of environmental justice activists. Finally, Lewis Amand —a community resident and graduate student in the Urban Planning School at the University of California, Los Angeles (UCLA)[49]—petitioned his department to investigate the long-term health effects of "synergistic chemicals"[50] on the inhabitants in his community.[51] Hailed by Cannon as the "death nail to the LANCER project,"[52] Amand's investigation appropriately developed health standards tailored to the racial and ethnic makeup of his community.[53]

When members of CCSCLA arrived at the March 1986 Conditional Permit Hearing, it was the first time city officials learned that there was organized opposition to the LANCER project.[54] As members of CCSCLA crammed into the city council chambers, city officials deliberately closed the session off "so other people couldn't get in, because the chambers was so full." Cannon recalled that the presence of an organized black collective sent the media into a frenzy, whispering, "Why are so many black people here?" to one another.[55] Cannon's perception of the media continued to deteriorate as reporters frantically scurried about "looking for 'CCSCLA's white leader' . . . because you know as black people we can't speak for ourselves."[56] When the "media's ideal white leader" failed to materialize, reporters refused to interview CCSCLA's black organizers.

The media was not alone in its rejection of CCSCLA, as the black city councilman Gil Lindsay boldly protested the group's presence by pointing to members and declaring, "These people will never be able to impact my fellow councilmen!"[57] Lindsay's employment of the idiom "these people" was coded misogynist language, as he struggled with acknowledging that the disproportionately black female leadership of CCSCLA constituted legitimate adversaries. "He felt that black women should not have been challenging black male leadership." According to Cannon, Lindsay's public derision of Charlotte Bullock and her continued throughout their environmental campaign. "During numerous public hearings, Lindsay would point to me and Charlotte and loudly announce 'they work for the city, so they shouldn't be in here,'" recalled Cannon. Bullock also engaged in public sparring matches with Lindsay, whom she frequently encountered at her place of employment. "Charlotte said that Lindsay would point to her in front of her co-workers and loudly declare that she was 'stepping on his toes,' to which Charlotte would respond, 'I will continue to step on your toes until you change your mind about LANCER.'" When asked if she and Bullock ever feared losing their jobs with the City of Los Angeles, Cannon was adamant: "No! We confronted everyone who opposed what we believed in and most of the time that meant that we ruffled a few feathers."[58]

During the Conditional Permit Hearing, CCSCLA organizers took turns at the microphone outlining their list of demands. CCSCLA organizers insisted that because the first EIR failed to incorporate a Health Risk Assessment, the city council should bear the costs for producing a second, bilingual EIR. CCSCLA also demanded decision-making authority for choosing the peer reviewers for the HRA committee, along with new parameters to be employed in the HRA that were more culturally specific to the racial/ethnic makeup of the community. Finally, CCSCLA demanded more advance notification for city council hearings regarding LANCER.

While tensions ran high during the eight-hour session, CCSCLA effectively lobbied city council members to concede to the entire list of their demands. At the close of the meeting, CCSCLA members convened an emergency organizational meeting in order to formulate a strategy for effectively targeting the media and key political stakeholders. "We knew that we needed the media on our side to turn the tide in our direction," but garnering their attention would not be an easy task to achieve. For months CCSCLA participated in a number of rallies and lobbying tactics in an effort to garner media attention, but to no avail. "We were doing all of this work and getting no attention by the media. The [Los Angeles] Sentinel newspaper[59] wouldn't even cover our movement," added Cannon.

It was not until CCSCLA partnered with Laura Lake and the attorney Barbara Blinderman of the Not Yet New York political organization that the resistant media tide began to change. As founders of a powerful nonprofit organization in the affluent West Los Angeles area, Lake and Blinderman simply contacted their allies at the Los Angeles Times and strongly encouraged them to profile CCSCLA's movement. In a blink of an eye, CCSCLA was featured in the national newspaper. Cannon insisted that, "it wasn't until the white media did a story on us that our local black newspaper, the Sentinel, paid us any attention."[60] Cannon further noted that "when the media paid attention, an outpouring of support followed suit." CCSCLA strategically flexed their newly acquired media popularity in order to lobby political stakeholders for their support.

Although the Los Angeles Democratic political machine fully supported the LANCER project, two party members emerged as CCSCLA supporters.[61] Rep. Augustus Freeman "Gus" Hawkins (D-Los Angeles) was the first to emerge as a CCSCLA supporter.[62] According to Cannon, "Hawkins did not take much coaxing when we presented our concerns about LANCER to him, he put his full support behind us." Hawkins extended his political resources to CCSCLA by distributing anti-LANCER fliers to his entire congressional district. He also hosted a congressional hearing whereupon CCSCLA openly criticized LANCER as a potential threat to the public health of the Greater Los Angeles area. The leading environmentalist and city councilwoman Ruth Galanter also extended her support to CCSCLA's movement. According to Cannon, Galanter made LANCER a central part of her underfunded political bid to unseat the incumbent city council president Pat Russell.[63] Finally, CCSCLA organizers regularly interfaced with city and county officials in order to lobby for alternative waste disposal programs, such as recycling. To be exact, Bullock of CCSCLA argued vehemently for a 50 percent recycling law—a policy suggestion that was perpetually met with contestation and "laughter" by city and county officials.[64]

By the scheduled release date of the Health Risk Assessment Peer Review Committee's findings, CCSCLA amassed a substantial membership base and a broad coalition of partners, including national environmental justice figures (Dr. Robert Bullard, Charles Less, Dr. Benjamin Chavis, and Richard Moore),[65] scholars (Robert Gottlieb, Beverly Pittman, Lewis Amand, Cynthia Hamilton, and Baucus Johnson), scientists (Dr. Barry Commoner), city officials (Omawale Fowles), media ("Alex" of KNX radio), and nonprofit organizations (Not Yet New York and Labor Community Strategy Center). The coalition worked for months in order to strategically reposition LANCER supporters, putting them on the defensive —a power play that Councilman Lindsay resented. In a last ditch effort to sabotage CCSCLA, Lindsay convened a closed-door meeting with HRA Peer Reviewers. According to Cannon, "Lindsay had the peer reviewers upstairs in City Hall. We of course came into the meeting with the press and our supporters, so we were able to sit with the scientists and talk to them in depth about the health impact of LANCER."[66]

A few days later, the Peer Reviewers issued a negative report, citing that LANCER would pose a potential health risk to residents of the Central Avenue Corridor. The storm only strengthened when the publication of two additional studies warned of the adverse environmental and health impacts of the LANCER municipal landfill (i.e., UCLA's Urban Planning School 425-page report[67] and the United Church of Christ's study[68]). These reports created a groundswell of public criticism against LANCER, resulting in the municipal landfill's anguished death in June 1987, when Los Angeles mayor Tom Bradley announced that he was ending LANCER despite the fact that the city had already spent $12 million on it.[69] According to Cannon, Lindsay was so upset with the decision that he declared he "would never bring economic development to the Central Avenue community." As a final insult, Mayor Bradley invited leaders from mainstream environmental groups—who had refused to assist CCSCLA in their struggle to defeat LANCER—to take part in a photo-op marking LANCER's demise. CCSCLA organizers, the very group responsible for bringing Goliath to his knees, were not invited.[70] Cannon laughed when she recounted how she and Bullock learned of the gathering: "If it wasn't for one of our white allies, 'Alex' of KNX radio, we would have never known about the ceremony. The moment that Charlotte and I found out about the gathering, we rushed over to the public gathering and squeezed in as the final photograph was taken."[71]

"We're Not Going Anywhere!"

In this chapter, I examined how the lack of resources and unresponsive government policies engendered a perpetual cycle of political marginalization for an economically disadvantaged community besieged by the prospect of a lethal toxic-waste site. Without question, the Central Avenue Corridor's long-standing history of political marginalization significantly contributed to city officials prematurely investing considerable taxpayer dollars into the LANCER project prior to the project's public notification process. Los Angeles city official's reliance on the perceived political impotence of the Central Avenue Corridor's black residents also contributed to Councilman Lindsay's very public outbursts, as CCSCLA's intervention to defeat LANCER worked to dismantle traditional political processes that had disregarded the health of the urban community for years. Lindsay and other Los Angeles politicians had fully endorsed these processes in order to sustain their dominance. But in the face of insurmountable odds, CCSCLA strategically aggregated its *organic base*, and institutionalized a triangular organizational model (e.g., community education, science-based advocacy, and media outreach)[72] in order to challenge the status of area residents as marginalized and politically powerless.

Following LANCER's demise,[73] CCSCLA worked alongside its adversaries in order to tackle Los Angeles's solid waste problem. According to Cannon, CCSCLA co-authored numerous grants with the City of Los Angeles in an effort to secure funding for the institutionalization of city-wide recycling programs. CCSCLA also partnered with city and state officials to develop both the Los Angeles Environmental Affairs Office and the Office of Environmental Justice within the California Environmental Protection Agency (Cal/EPA), respectively. As a consequence, the establishment of an environmental justice structure within state government eventually led to the periodic proposal and passage of progressive legislation.[74]

As the first decade of the 2000s drew to a close, CCSCLA remained committed to addressing environmental inequity concerns. In 2008, for example, CCSCLA filed a lawsuit against the County of Los Angeles to challenge their "environmental impact report and oil drilling regulations covering the oil field adjoining the Baldwin Hills Park[75] . . . [and]

for failure to provide adequate health and environmental safeguards in a dense and diverse community that has long suffered from environmental degradation and discrimination."[76]

CCSCLA also gave birth to a new generation of young "Toxic Crusaders." In 2000 Fabiola Tostado (16), Maria Perez (16), and Nevada Dove (19) prevented Jefferson Middle School from opening for a full academic school year when the trio (who worked part-time at CCSCLA) publicized their findings that their school was "built on a toxic land that had once been used for munitions and other manufacturing, land whose emissions might cause illnesses ranging from the minor to the potentially fatal."[77] In many ways, the emergence of this new generation of grassroots environmental activists paralleled Cannon's politicization within the Black Panther Party. CCSCLA had become a conduit where intergenerational political efficacy could be transmitted. When asked if she believed that CCSCLA was filling the organizational void left by the demise of 1960s and 1970s community organizations, Cannon was unequivocal:

When the Panther's died, black political activism in my community died. CCSCLA is awakening the old and new guard in our community to confront the same issues that plagued our neighborhood in the 1960s and 1970s. But this time, no matter how hard the dominant system tries to get rid of us, we're [CCSCLA] not going anywhere![78]

NOTES

1. Concerned Citizens of South Central Los Angeles, "Developmental Fact Sheet," Los Angeles, 2008. See also Concerned Citizens of South Central Los Angeles, "CCSCLA Services: Environmental," CCSCLA, 2009, http://www.ccscla.org/environ.htm.

2. Robin Cannon revealed that during the 1960s, she was a volunteer for the Los Angeles chapter of the Black Panther Party's (BPP) Free Breakfast Program. She also states that CCSCLA's first official office was located in the former building of the BPP (interview by author, December 6, 2008).

3. Concerned Citizens of South Central Los Angeles, "CCSCLA Services: Environmental."

4. Connie Koenenn, "South-Central Stops an Incinerator," *Los Angeles Times*, December 23, 1991, 4.

5. See Janet Wilson, "California has Largest Number of Minorities Near Hazardous Waste," *Los Angeles Times*, April 12, 2007, B1. The article notes that a study

found California to have the highest concentration of minorities living near haz-ardous waste facilities and that Greater Los Angeles "tops the nation with 1.2 mil-lion people living less than two miles from 17 such facilities, and 91 [percent] of them, or 1.1 million, are minorities." Also see Building a Regional Voice for Envi-ronmental Justice Collaborative, "Building a Regional Voice."

6. Reynolds, "LANCER and the Vernon Incinerator," 95.

7. By the term "mainstream environmental groups," I mean environmental groups that disproportionately focus on environmental policies concerning pres-ervation and conservation issues. The leadership positions within these organiza-tions are comprised predominantly of white men from privileged socioeconomic backgrounds and the constituent base is also composed of white citizens who are middle- to upper-middle class.

8. Cronon, *Uncommon Ground*, 299.

9. Ibid.

10. Robin Cannon states that indigenous institutions such as the National As-sociation for the Advancement of Colored People, National Urban League, South-ern Christian Leadership Conference, and black churches were resistant to their claims of environmental exploitation and thus refused to provide them with re-sources in order to aid in the creation of their local community organization (in-terview by author, December 6, 2008). See Winton, *All Things Being Equal*.

11. Cronon, *Uncommon Ground*, 299.

12. Bullard, *Dumping in Dixie*, 23.

13. See Bullard, *Dumping in Dixie*; Dowie, *Losing Ground*; Taylor, "Race, Class, Gender and American Environmentalism"; Bullard, *Confronting Environmental Racism*; Taylor, "Can the Environmental Movement Attract and Maintain"; and Winton, *All Things Being Equal*.

14. See Winton, *All Things Being Equal*.

15. Lester, Allen, and Hill, *Environmental Injustice in the United States*, 25.

16. See Massey and Denton, *American Apartheid*.

17. Lester, Allen, and Hill, *Environmental Injustice in the United States*, 25–26.

18. See Gianessi, Peskin, and Wolff, "The Distributional Effects of Uniform Air Pollution Policy"; Asch and Seneca, "The Incidence of Automobile Pollution Control"; Freeman, "Air Pollution and Property Values."

19. Cole and Foster, *From the Ground Up*, 30.

20. President Carter appointed a number of key environmental leaders from leading environmental groups to the Environmental Protection Agency (EPA), the Department of Interior (DOI), and the Justice Department. This inside access consolidated "leading environmental group's influence over environmental policy making to such a degree that one publicly pronounced, 'before, we filed lawsuits and held press conferences. Now we have lunch with the assistant secretary to discuss a program'" (Mosher, "Environmentalists Question," 212).

21. Mohai and Bryant, "Is There a "Race" Effect."

22. Cerrell Associates, Inc., "Political Difficulties Facing Waste," 43.

23. Interview by author, December 6, 2008.

24. Jefferson High School graduated many of Black Los Angeles's luminaries over the years, including Nobel Prize–winner Ralph J. Bunche in 1922.

25. Connie Koenenn, "South-Central Stops an Incinerator," *Los Angeles Times*, December 23, 1991, 4.

26. John Haywood, "Incineration Plan Is Garbage and Worse," *Los Angeles Times*, November 30, 1986, 5.

27. Ibid.

28. Concerned Citizens of South Central Los Angeles, "Developmental Fact Sheet."

29. Connie Koenenn, "South-Central Stops an Incinerator," *Los Angeles Times*, December 23, 1991, 4.

30. Robin Cannon, interview by author, December 6, 2008.

31. Ibid.

32. In 1962, when Edward Roybal was elected to the U.S. Congress, he recommended that a special election be held in order to replace him on the Los Angeles City Council. The council decided instead to appoint Gilbert William Lindsay, the first person of African descent to serve on the Los Angeles City Council in the modern era. Between those 1963 victories and the early 2000s, blacks held on to three (20 percent) of the council's fifteen seats, despite accounting for only about 11 percent of the city's population in 2007. See Susan Anderson, "African American Clout Isn't Going Anywhere," *Los Angeles Times*, November 11, 2007, opinion, M4.

33. Connie Koenenn, "South-Central Stops an Incinerator," *Los Angeles Times*, December 23, 1991, 4.

34. For analysis of economic trade-offs, see Bullard, *Dumping in Dixie*.

35. Connie Koenenn, "South-Central Stops an Incinerator," *Los Angeles Times*, December 23, 1991, 4.

36. Robin Cannon, interview by author, December 6, 2008.

37. Ibid.

38. Ibid.

39. Ibid.

40. Ibid.

41. Cannon insisted that on their drive over to the Vernon Public Library, she and Bullock made a commitment to remain together to address other issues impacting their neighborhood even if they were successful in LANCER's defeat (interview by author, December 6, 2008).

42. Robin Cannon, interview by author, December 6, 2008

43. Ibid.

44. Robin Cannon, interview by author, December 28, 2008.

45. Ibid.

46. See chap. 5 for a detailed account of the BPP's demise and its impact on Black Los Angeles.

47. Cannon stated that CCSCLA was part of the creation of the SouthWest Network for Environmental and Economic Justice—a regional organization that linked more than eighty community-based grassroots organizations working in communities of color in six southwestern states and Mexico. According to Cannon, CCSCLA also participated in writing the now famous letter to the Big Ten mainstream environmental groups in order to protest their history of racial exclusion (interview by author, December 8, 2008).

48. See Winton, *All Things Being Equal.*

49. See chap. 16 for an overview of UCLA's impact on Black Los Angeles over the years.

50. "Synergistic" effects refer to the health risks associated with the combination of hazardous materials (e.g., the mixture of lead and mercury) on community members.

51. Amand was one of ten graduate students who produced the report. Robert Gottlieb and Beverly Pittman were the primary project managers on the study.

52. Robin Cannon, interview by author, March 22, 2009.

53. Amand's approach was significant as it replaced the healthy twenty-year-old white man, the usual standard for these types of analyses, with one that more accurately represented the South Central community.

54. Prior to this meeting, Cannon and Bullock went to the City of Los Angeles Planning Department and the Bureau of Sanitation and added their names to LANCER's notification process. According to Cannon, during this interface with city officials, she and Bullock learned of the appeal process for the Conditional Use Permit for LANCER. In an interview, Cannon insists that she "paid out of pocket for the appeal" (interview by author, December 6, 2008).

55. Robin Cannon, interview by author, December 6, 2008.

56. Ibid.

57. Ibid.

58. Robin Cannon, interview by author, December 28, 2008.

59. See chap. 2 for more on the *Los Angeles Sentinel,* the West's largest black-owned newspaper.

60. Ibid.

61. Victor Merina argues, "Campaign finance statements show that investment banking firms and their employees that contributed the most to the campaign of Los Angeles city councilmembers and to mayor [Tom Bradley] were the firms that obtained the city's bond business to finance the LANCER trash disposal project" ("Money Is Muscle in Bond Sale Field: LANCER Project Shows Link between Contributions, Contracts Series," *Los Angeles Times,* August 11, 1986, 5).

62. In 1963 Hawkins became the first African American from California to serve in the United States Congress. He was one of the founding members of the

Congressional Black Caucus and the oldest person to serve in Congress. He died at the age of 100 in 2007.

63. In 1987 Galanter successfully secured the city council seat in District Six. According to Cannon, Galanter based her campaign chiefly on her opposition to massive environmentally hazardous development projects that included the LANCER project (interview by author, December 8, 2008).

64. Cannon noted that "Charlotte's recycling policy recommendation was instituted three or four years later, which resulted in the city receiving accolades for their 50 [percent] recycling program" (interview by author, December 8, 2008).

65. Cannon stated that each of these national environmental justice figures traveled to Los Angeles in order to meet with CCSCLA organizers (interview by author, March 20, 2009).

66. Robin Cannon, interview by author, March 26, 2009.

67. See Bills, Gottlieb, and Pitman, *The Dilemma of Municipal Solid Waste Management*.

68. See Bullard et al., "Toxic Wastes and Race at Twenty."

69. The Environmental Research Foundation, "New Report Offers Insights into America's Recent Garbage Crisis," *Rachel's Hazardous Waste News # 55*, December 14, 1987, http://www.ejnet.org/rachel/rhwn055.htm (accessed December 28, 2008).

70. For more on Tom Bradley's complicated relationship to Black Los Angeles, see chap. 1.

71. Robin Cannon, interview by author, December 19, 2008.

72. Robin Cannon, interview by author, December 6, 2008.

73. The proposed site later housed the South Central Farm, a community farm that Jessica Hoffman argues has been the center of a "long and complicated series of land-use and property-rights struggles" ("History of the South Central Farm," *New Standard*, April 5, 2006, http://newstandardnews.net/content/index.cfm/items/3028).

74. Matsuoka, "Building Healthy Communities from the Ground Up," 16.

75. Darnell Hunt discusses the affluent black neighborhoods bordering this park in the Introduction.

76. This lawsuit was pending at time of printing, according to The City Project ("Concerned Citizens Sue County to Protect Baldwin Hills People, Homes, and Parks," *City Project Blog*, November 26, 2008, http://www.cityprojectca.org/blog/archives/1160 (accessed January 1, 2009).

77. Levine, Bettijane, "'Toxic Crusaders' Aren't Afraid of a Good Fight," *Los Angeles Times*, May 24, 2000, 1.

78. Robin Cannon, interview by author, December 28, 2008.

Chapter 15

A Common Project for a Just Society
Black Labor in Los Angeles

Edna Bonacich, Lola Smallwood Cuevas,
Lanita Morris, Steven Pitts,
and Joshua Bloom

On September 7, 2007, a standing-room-only reception was held in the lobby of the *Los Angeles Sentinel*.[1] The energized scene included Congresswoman Maxine Waters (D-Los Angeles), Kwanzaa founder and chair of the US Organization Maulana Karenga,[2] and the activist Rev. Eric Lee, head of the Southern Christian Leadership Conference[3] (SCLC) of Greater Los Angeles. They had come together to honor the appointment of Faith Culbreath, an African American firebrand from Detroit, as president of a newly formed security officers union.

"I am here because of you," were the first words uttered by the impressive thirty-something woman. As the new leader of the Service Employees International Union's (SEIU)[4] highly financed campaign—which was one of the largest national organizing drives of black men in decades—Culbreath spoke not only with humility; her statement also was a loud testament to the complex relationship between labor and Black Los Angeles in the first decade of the 2000s.

Consider that many of the community leaders attending the reception had used their political and moral capital over the past six years to organize the workers of a security union called SEIU Security Officers United in Los Angeles (SOULA) Local 2006. They had mounted a vigorous fight against Los Angeles commercial building owners who contracted with security firms notorious for paying low wages and offering unaffordable healthcare. The community leaders had participated at key junctures of

Figure 15.1. SEIU building on Washington Boulevard, near
downtown. Photo courtesy of Darnell Hunt.

the campaign with letter-writing campaigns, sit-ins, civil disobedience,
picket lines, delegations, petitions, and sermons. The city's black community was a powerful partner in the union's effort to unionize the largely
black private security workforce in commercial real estate.

In this chapter, we seek to examine the relationship between the African American community and the labor movement in Los Angeles, looking closely at the case of SOULA. How were working-class blacks faring
in Los Angeles at the turn of the twenty-first century? What impact did
immigration and perceived competition with Latinos have on black involvement in the city's labor movement? What can the case of SOULA
teach us that may serve as best practices for addressing the challenges
faced by black workers in other cities?

Our methods of study have been eclectic. We reviewed histories and
reports, collected statistics, conducted in-depth interviews with labor and
community leaders,[5] attended numerous meetings, and followed the *Los
Angeles Sentinel*'s accounts of the issue. One of the authors, Lola Smallwood Cuevas, worked as the community organizer for the SEIU (see
fig. 15.1), ran a leadership school for African American trade unionists,

and had considerable firsthand knowledge of the issues addressed in this chapter.[6]

The labor movement and the black liberation movement have been two of the most important social justice movements in the United States. Civil rights leaders like Rev. Martin Luther King Jr. recognized their mutual concerns, including the need for greater social and economic justice.[7] However, the relationship has been a complicated one because of the ongoing presence of racism in the United States. Some unions and their members were at the forefront of struggles for racial justice, while others took concrete steps to preserve white privilege.[8] This chapter considers the history of the struggle for racial and economic justice in Los Angeles with an eye toward proposing a plan for a more just future.

The Black Labor Crisis in Los Angeles

In the first half of the twentieth century, African Americans migrated to Los Angeles as part of the great migration out of the South. California in general, and Los Angeles in particular, had the reputation of being more open to blacks and affording greater economic opportunities (see chap. 1 for a more detailed account of black migration to and settlement in Los Angeles). While these opportunities were generally better than those in the South, the new migrants still faced racism and restricted job opportunities. Black workers, for example, tended to be confined to low-wage, service work. In 1930, 87 percent of black women and 40 percent of black men in Los Angeles worked in domestic service. Meanwhile, other black workers joined or formed unions. The American Federation of Musicians Local 47 had denied membership to African Americans, which led black musicians to establish their own independent Musicians Local 767. The largest all-black union of the day was the Waiters Union Local 17. In 1926, the musicians and waiters unions accounted for two-thirds of all unionized African Americans in Los Angeles.[9]

The World War II period marked the opening of industrial employment to black workers. Los Angeles had a large industrial sector, especially in the production of cars, tires, and steel. The plants were located in the Alameda Corridor, adjacent to areas of concentrated black residence. Federal regulations also forced employers to cease discriminatory hiring in certain industries. The CIO was organizing, and blacks joined. The result was the creation of a substantial black middle class rooted in good union jobs.[10] For example, one of our interviewees, Gary Phillips,[11] pointed out that his father had a union job, which allowed his family to buy a house without having to rely on the GI Bill.[12] Neighbors of the Phillips family also had union jobs.

The public sector afforded another union route into the middle class. As part of the welfare state, public services were expanding and thus providing blue-collar jobs such as sanitation, custodial work, health care, and food services. In Los Angeles, 80 percent of the sanitation workers who collected the city's garbage were African Americans, and they belonged to a CIO public employees union. As city councilman Gilbert Lindsay noted: "Garbage collection is dirty work, but the sanitation department pays good wages to people who couldn't get a good job otherwise."[13]

Then in the 1970s and 1980s, the country faced global economic restructuring. Major industries moved offshore, and plants shut down. In Los Angeles, the automobile plant was replaced by the garment sweatshop as the main industrial employer. Aerospace grew in importance, but it was located mainly in suburbs shaped by housing covenants that had prevented black families from moving nearby.[14] Given the Los Angeles area's notoriously weak public transportation system, few blacks were able to work in these growing industries. The result for blacks was a loss of good, industrial union jobs.

Another feature of the restructuring of the 1970s and 1980s was the rise of "flexible production." By contracting out elements of work, including services, to independent contractors, employers were able to break unions and lower the price of labor. Although the SEIU was ultimately able to stop it, even the city attempted to contract out garbage collection in 1981.[15] Meanwhile, contractors would seek out the most tractable sources of labor, such as immigrants who were moving to the city because of the impact of globalization and warfare in their homelands that was supported by the United States. Blacks lost jobs as a result of these processes as well.

In the 1980s, crack cocaine was introduced into Black Los Angeles neighborhoods (see chap. 5). Coupled with rising unemployment, this development created a "perfect storm," according to the former Los Angeles city councilman Martin Ludlow.[16] The result was a rise in gangs and violence, police abuse and brutality, and increased rates of incarceration. Black youth faced increasing criminalization, and the public school system was eroding. Opportunities for employment, especially for decent employment, were evaporating.

By 2000, 43 percent of Los Angeles's black working-age population was unemployed, while 29 percent were employed in low-wage, dead-end jobs that offered neither retirement nor health benefits, no protection from the arbitrary authority of the employer, and little opportunity for moving up and improving one's situation. Thus, while unemployment was typically the primary focus of those concerned with the black jobs crisis, substandard jobs were equally significant. Nearly 70 percent of black Angeleno adults were either not working or working in low-wage, dead-end jobs.[17]

A 2008 study of South Los Angeles, which included the Watts area, described the social characteristics of this section of the city.[18] In the early twentieth century, South Los Angeles was majority white. By mid-century it was mainly black, and by 2000 it was majority Latino (62 percent Latino versus 31 percent black). Nevertheless, South Los Angeles remained a major center of black residence. The study found a severe shortage of available local jobs, coupled with a lack of transportation, and the presence of job discrimination when black workers could get to the jobs. In addition, education levels were relatively low: 43 percent had not completed high school, while only 11 percent had a college degree (compared to 27 percent for the county as a whole).

It must be noted here that immigrants were not to blame for the crisis in the African American community. While there was indeed job competition between working-class black Angelenos and immigrants, global restructuring, de-industrialization, the shift to flexible production, crack, and criminalization were more fundamental causes. However, some jobs had moved from union jobs employing African Americans to lower-wage, non-union jobs employing Latino immigrants. A prime example of this transition was in janitorial services. Black janitors were members of SEIU. In order to lower costs, building owners contracted out their janitorial services to firms that employed non-union immigrants at lower wages. SEIU's Justice for Janitors subsequently organized immigrant janitors and won back some (but not all) of the previous wage levels. But black workers were forever eliminated from these jobs, their displacement a ploy of the employers, not of the immigrant workers.

Indeed, a Los Angeles–based study found clear evidence of employer preference for immigrant workers for certain types of jobs.[19] Both black and white workers were seen as more demanding, as knowing and insisting upon their rights, as complaining of ill treatment, and as having clear notions of decent pay and the amount of energy they should be expected to exert for a given level of pay. In the words of one employer: "The white factory worker is a whining piece of shit. They [feel that they] never make enough money. They [feel they] always work too hard. They never want to work over eight hours a day and they feel that, as soon as you hire them, you owe them."[20] Black workers faced the same stereotypes with exaggerated force. These beliefs added up to the image of the "lazy" native-born worker, in contrast to that of the hard-working immigrant. While black and white workers faced similar resistance at the low end of the labor market in Los Angeles, whites had far more opportunities than blacks at the higher end. Indeed, in managerial and professional jobs, whites constituted the preferred workforce, and blacks faced considerable discrimination. Blacks were thus squeezed out of jobs at both ends and faced declining employment opportunities as a result.

Blacks and the Labor Movement

Despite the labor movement's checkered history when it came to race, black workers traditionally were among the strongest supporters of unions. Martin Luther King Jr. saw a strong connection between the struggle for civil rights and the fight for economic justice. He was assassinated while supporting an AFSCME[21] sanitation workers' strike in Memphis, Tennessee, which exemplified the link between racial oppression and worker exploitation.[22]

Table 15.1 shows the union membership rates of the largest racial/ethnic groups in the United States and Los Angeles in 2008. The first column shows that the rate of union membership for employed African American

TABLE 15.1
*Membership in Unions of Employed Workers
by Different Ethnicities, 2008*

Ethnicity	Percentage of Group Belonging to Unions	
	United States	Los Angeles
Total	12.4	17.0
Whites	12.2	17.9
Latinos	10.6	14.9
Asians	10.6	15.0
Blacks	14.5	27.6

Source: U.S. Bureau of Labor Statistics, "Economic and Employment Projections," 2009, http://www.bls.gov/news.release/ecopro.toc.htm; Ruth Milkman and Bongoh Kye, "The State of the Unions in 2008: A Profile of Union Membership in Los Angeles, California, and the Nation," (Los Angeles: UCLA Institute for Research on Labor and Employment, 2008).

workers (14.5 percent) was higher than for any other group in the nation. In the second column, union membership rates are shown for each group in Los Angeles. Here we find that the African American rate (27.6 percent) was far higher than any other group. As Anthony Thigpenn, president of SCOPE (Strategic Concepts in Organizing and Policy Education, a major African American community organization) observed: "South Los Angeles is the bedrock of the L.A. unions."[23] And consistent with this observation, African Americans occupied prominent positions of leadership in the Los Angeles labor movement in the early years of the twenty-first century.

Until the early 1990s, the Los Angeles labor movement was dominated by the building trades, which tended to focus on protecting their own members and not upon expanding the movement to new industries and new groups of workers. In 1994 Miguel Contreras became the political director of the County Federation of Labor, and in 1996 he took over the head position of secretary-treasurer. Miguel shifted the focus of the movement to low-wage workers, new organizing, and building power for labor. In 2005 Antonio Villaraigosa became mayor of Los Angeles. This new, progressive Latino leadership of both the city and labor came in with a basic ideology. First, they saw it as essential to organize immigrant workers, including the undocumented. Taking an anti-immigrant stand would have been self-defeating, so the movement prioritized fighting for immigrant rights. Second, the new leadership determined that the labor crisis in the black community must be addressed, which meant that a coalition including the black community had to be developed and nurtured.

Nevertheless, some African American community leaders felt that Black Los Angeles was not getting sufficient attention during this period, though they did not necessarily blame the Latino leadership. Dr. Maulana Karenga, head of the black-nationalist US Organization, addressed the issue this way:

> Too often blacks in the labor movement are conceived and cultivated not as leaders but as dependents. Thus, they are pushed to seek favor rather than position and equal respect. This means that our interests are placed last. Meanwhile, Latino interests are placed first, as the most important rising constituency. This is true in labor and it is true in the state. The issue, then, becomes how do we change this without blaming Latinos and missing the opportunity for alliance? Demographics play a role in Labor's attitude and actions, but there is another important factor. There

is a general sense by many white liberals that they have "done enough" for us, and that Latinos represent the rising point of focus. We don't see it that way. We think we are in a common project of creating a just society. Many whites see themselves as giving us an entitlement, instead of meeting the requirements of a just society. With such an approach, they will eventually become exhausted with Latinos too when a new constituency emerges.[24]

Another criticism concerned the tendency of some unions to use African American community leaders when they needed them to support a union campaign, only to quickly lose interest in the community when the campaign was over. According to Rev. Eric Lee, head of the Los Angeles area SCLC:

Unions, when they are in a campaign, come to the clergy and the community under the banner of justice, and lure us into being the voice of moral authority. But rarely do the jobs mean economic opportunity for the African American community. Union leaders never say to community leaders that what they are proposing is important to the black community. They just don't focus on that issue. I'm looking for true collaboration between labor leaders and the community, where we collectively identify issues and put resources into creating equity for both the black and brown communities. They come when they have a campaign, but they never say, "This is an issue of importance to the black community, so what can we do to help?"[25]

Dr. Karenga put it this way:

There is a need for a mutually beneficial relationship between the community and labor, so that when labor needs support, there is already a relationship in place—so that the community is constantly engaged with labor issues, and vice versa. A. Philip Randolph[26] talked about this. He felt that if the relationship worked as it should, the community would embrace labor as its own. If labor supported the community on a regular basis, the community would be ready to support labor when it needed help. But it doesn't always work that way.[27]

But other leaders spoke about the strength of the connection between labor and community, seeing the struggles for labor rights and civil rights as closely connected. While recognizing that the labor movement had had its racist past, there was a belief that in Los Angeles, in particular, a progressive labor leadership was striving to represent all groups and to build a multiracial, labor-community alliance.

Anthony Thigpenn, president of SCOPE, suggested that labor came to the relationship as an institution that was bigger and better organized than the local black community. Labor was an institution with its own pressing requirements to service and build its membership. By contrast, Los Angeles's black community had numerous organizations but no real organizational base or united agenda. So the black community came to the relationship with labor, he maintained, from a much weaker position. Labor, said Thigpenn, tended to emphasize tactics over strategy. By this, he meant that unions got caught up in winning a specific campaign. They faced intense pressures to succeed and grow, and they turned to the community for help in achieving their immediate campaign goals. The goal of establishing a strategic vision for community development tended to fade into the background when unions were faced with pressing tactical needs.

Nevertheless, Thigpenn concluded: "The character of the labor-community coalition in Los Angeles is exceptional. Black/Latino division is *not* the dominant approach in Los Angeles. There is a long-term connection with good cooperation. The coalition works here." This was in contrast to the rest of the country, especially the East Coast. Thigpenn attributed Los Angeles's exceptionalism to long-standing personal relationships, where trust had been built over the years. Both Latinos and blacks participated in such organizations as Jobs with Peace[28] and the United Farm Workers, and had maintained those ties. Indeed, Thigpenn and Los Angeles mayor Antonio Villaraigosa had been friends since 1975, and Thigpenn played a key role in both of Villaraigosa's mayoral campaigns.

The SOULA Campaign

In 2008, after a multiyear, multimillion-dollar campaign, SEIU successfully organized more than 4,000 security officers in Los Angeles, ratifying a union contract providing for a 40 percent pay raise over five years, as well as health benefits and job security. Providing a model, perhaps, for how blacks can leverage their power within the labor movement, Los Angeles's black community strongly urged SEIU to appoint an African American as head of the new union and pushed for the union to ensure that blacks continued to have a stronghold in the industry after unionization.

This campaign was a milestone for SEIU and for the Los Angeles labor movement as a whole because the centerpiece of the security campaign was the union's carefully constructed alliance with black community leaders.[29] If SEIU's deep and sustained partnership with black community leaders was crucial to winning recognition and a contract, it was also rather unusual for a unionization campaign.

The organizing of SEIU's SOULA Local 2006 is an example of how far the labor movement had come in realizing the need for allying with the African American community in its struggle to win strong contracts and organize new industries. The campaign also illuminates how far unions and the black community still had to go in order to develop a true alliance of equal power and partnership in the fight for social and economic change. In the mid-1990s, Los Angeles became the epicenter of labor organizing, particularly of immigrant workers.[30] Organizing in the city also achieved distinction because of labor's progressive coalition with the black community, which increasingly applied its civil rights tradition of struggle against powerful elites to the cause of workers' rights.

In 1999, for example, SEIU organized 74,000 Los Angeles County homecare workers, led by a team of persistent African American women. This organizing effort was the largest organizing victory since the unionization of the Ford Motor Plant in the 1920s.[31] Then, in 2000, the Justice for Janitors campaign rewrote the book on organizing and unionized thousands of immigrant Los Angeles janitors, restoring wages and health benefits in the industry.

The stage was thus set for SOULA. SEIU launched the national security organizing campaign in 2001, assigning management of the campaign to the powerful Los Angeles janitors union, SEIU Local 1877. The campaign required long-term, extensive funding by SEIU and skilled staff. At the time, SEIU was the largest union in the country, boasting 1.9 million members and a pension fund of approximately $1 trillion. SEIU was determined to win unionization and took advantage of its unparalleled assets, expertise, political connections, and leverage in the city's building services industry.

According to a 2006 study[32] commissioned by SEIU, most security officers employed in Los Angeles's major office buildings had little training and, prior to unionization, were paid an average of $8.50/hour. Turnover rates were high, rivaling the fast-food industry. Almost 60 percent of the workers in these buildings were black. And because security is a 24/7 industry with rolling shifts and no large physical concentrations of workers, union organizing was especially challenging. Security officers were under constant surveillance by anti-union supervisors. Moreover, security officers typically worked in isolation, stationed far apart, and were assigned breaks at different times, thereby providing little opportunity for on-the-job interaction.

To meet these challenges, SEIU deployed its signature comprehensive campaign approach, perfected in previous organizing drives. As with the earlier Justice for Janitors organizing in Los Angeles, SEIU adopted an industrywide strategy, simultaneously targeting the five security contractors —Securitas, Allied Barton, Guard Systems, Universal Protective Services, and American Commercial Security Service—that comprised 80 percent of the city's market in large, commercial real estate. Early on, these contractors signed pre-recognition agreements pledging to recognize the union if the other contractors and the building owners agreed.

The security campaign relied on the close coordination of strategic research, community-alliance building, public relations, and worker organizing to gain leverage over the building owners. The research uncovered building owners' vulnerabilities, the community allies attacked those vulnerabilities, the union's public relations staff secured news coverage, security officers participated in actions, and thousands of these officers signed unionization cards.

Given the racial composition of the security workforce in Los Angeles, SEIU believed that building an alliance with black community leaders could prove pivotal to its multifaceted organizing effort. But this presented a challenge in its own right, thanks in part to the long-standing mistrust of the SEIU janitors union in the black community—mistrust rooted in the history of ethnic succession in the building services industry discussed earlier. As black community leaders often pointed out, until the 1970s most Los Angeles janitors had been black. In those days, many were also SEIU members, earning good pay and benefits. But as the building service industry was restructured in the 1970s and 1980s, the union lost power, and a low-wage, non-union immigrant workforce replaced black workers. In 2000, SEIU's Justice for Janitors campaign restored unionism to the janitorial sector, but by then the workforce was largely Latino. In the union's ranks, recent immigrants from Mexico and Central America, many of them undocumented, had replaced black janitors.

Many black leaders were troubled by this history. They were also troubled by the absence of African American leadership in the power structure of the local labor movement, as well as a lack of focus on the broader issue of ballooning black unemployment and the proliferation of bad jobs in Black Los Angeles. They understood the union would gain new members, hundreds of thousands of dollars in union dues and control of the industry, but were wary of the union's commitment (or lack thereof) to protecting the prominent black presence in the industry. In other words, would the organizing, in the end, really benefit the black community? Finding a way to offer the black community some tangible institutional advantage was critical, especially in light of the chronic resource shortages faced by institutions in Black Los Angeles.

As the union's community organizer, co-author Lola Smallwood-Cuevas put together a series of honest dialogues to unpack the history of the janitors union and SEIU's failure to respond. Conversations on worker retention and long-term partnerships between the new union and the black community were also discussed. Behind closed doors, relationships were built between union leadership and community leaders. For example, SEIU Local 1877's president, Mike Garcia, explained it was not the union but union-busting building owners who actively undermined the black janitorial union by bringing in immigrant labor. He also made it clear that the union's response reflected the incompetence of the all-white union leadership structure at the time. As the son of immigrants, Garcia explained how the union's institutionalized racism and bias had paralyzed any defense of black or brown workers in the 1970s and early 1980s. These frank and often heated discussions between the union and black community leaders were facilitated by the union staffers, who not only understood the importance of unionizing the security jobs but also pressed the union to utilize its power to address community concerns. The community coalition attempted to facilitate a new level of union alliance building, which led to honest and open dialogue and provided a seat at the union organizing table for the community to give input and exchange ideas on strategies and tactics.

After months of discussion, the community agreed to support the campaign under certain conditions. For one thing, the community demanded that the union preserve the mostly black demographics of the workforce and provide assurances that the leadership of the union would reflect the workforce. Black community leaders believed this would ensure the union's continued participation in its efforts to address economic injustice in the black community beyond the conclusion of the security organizing campaign. Ultimately, black leadership saw participation in the campaign as an effort to promote its own social justice agenda.[33]

With its major concerns addressed, the community began to move its campaign forward. In January 2003, the union and the SCLC of Greater Los Angeles jointly organized "King Week," a series of actions to advance security officer unionization in celebration of Martin Luther King's birthday. The week's events emphasized that most of the security officers were black, with more than half living in South Los Angeles, and framed the plight of security officers as an issue that affected the entire black community. Several black security officers spoke at these events, and the week culminated in the annual Dr. Martin Luther King Jr. Birthday Dinner at the downtown Los Angeles Biltmore Hotel, which featured the noted black intellectual Cornel West[34] as the keynote speaker. The Rev. Norman Johnson later recalled SCLC's decision to make the security campaign the central focus of this annual event:

> This is the Southern Christian Leadership Conference, and in my mind, we were doing what Dr. King would do. . . . This is not just about security officers. When you look at the fact that an overwhelming majority of them are African American, these are the working poor, they live in our communities. These are the folk that have children that go to these schools. They are in these neighborhoods. What it is doing . . . is impoverishing . . . South Los Angeles. And so we have a community interest in this.[35]

Over the next five years, the clergy, the NAACP, South Los Angeles social and economic justice organizations such as AGENDA,[36] the Community Coalition, ACORN, and others would join the effort. They wrote letters to building owners and organized delegations to security companies and building management. They walked picket lines and got arrested in acts of civil disobedience. They met weekly to develop community strategies to support and enhance the organizing, and they integrated the campaign into community events in order to raise its visibility among the black press and community.

For example, wearing pictures of security officers on placards, the protestors marched to the corner of Fifth and Flower streets in downtown Los Angeles, proceeded into the intersection between two buildings—one owned by Maguire Properties and the other by Thomas Properties—and sat down, completely blocking traffic. Police reinforcements arrived and ordered protestors to disperse. When they refused, the police physically removed black clergy and community members from the intersection, arresting thirteen protesters.

Days later, the campaign had its first real breakthrough. Thomas Properties had not initially been a major target of the campaign since it owned only two buildings. But when James A. Thomas wrote to the SCLC in June 2004, stating that, like Maguire, he opposed having security officers in a mixed union with the janitors in his buildings, the union began to target his company along with Maguire. The key point of leverage with Thomas was the California State Teachers Retirement System (CalSTRS), which had invested approximately \$270 million in a joint venture with Thomas Properties to purchase Arco Towers, a prime 2.7 million-square-foot, fifty-two-story office complex in downtown Los Angeles. CalSTRS was a union pension fund with a responsible contractor policy (originally developed partly through SEIU efforts) that called for union neutrality.

A few days after the civil disobedience and arrests of black community leaders, the SEIU leader Jono Shaffer, drawing on SEIU's longstanding relationships with key trustees, arranged for a delegation of union representatives and black community allies to speak at the CalSTRS board meeting in Sacramento. Terence Long, the security campaign's communications director, provided CalSTRS staff with documentation of the economic injustices Thomas was imposing on security officers and the black community, and why he was not a responsible investment manager. The day before the board meeting, CalSTRS's CEO Jack Ehnes met with Thomas to discuss the matter. Later that night, Thomas became the first downtown building owner to formally agree to neutrality in the SEIU bid to unionize security officers. At 2 a.m., just hours before the community and union delegation was scheduled to speak to the CalSTRS board, Thomas faxed Ehnes a letter agreeing to follow the CalSTRS fund policy and stating that his company "is neutral on whether the guards organize or not."[37] This was an important victory for the campaign, demonstrating the efficacy of applying intense focused pressure on one target at a time. As Terence Long recalled, "The Thomas victory . . . made folks realize that there is a way to get to these guys."[38]

Energized by this breakthrough, the campaign intensified its mobilization against Maguire. On June 7, 2005, a coalition of black organizations, including the NAACP and the SCLC, announced their support for the security officers' efforts to join SEIU, and explicitly charged Maguire with racism. The SEIU press release quoted Rev. James Lawson[39] as follows:

> Maguire Properties is in effect practicing a policy of institutionalized racism by denying security officers their civil rights and freedom to form a union of their choice with SEIU. The mostly Latino janitors that do work for Maguire Properties have the union of their choice. The predominately Anglo-operating engineers that do work for Maguire Properties have the union of their choice. Only the disproportionately African American private security officers that protect Maguire Properties are still struggling to raise standards by forming a union of their choice.

The Rev. "Chip" Murray, then pastor of the influential First AME Church, led a protest outside Maguire's shareholders' meeting, stating that: "Maguire Properties is in effect practicing a policy of institutionalized racism by denying security officers their civil rights and freedom to form a union of their choice with SEIU."[40] Security officers Willie Hunter, Troy Hammond, and Joe Matthews wore white tape over their mouths and carried signs reading "Maguire Properties: Stop Silencing Security Officers."

The spirited participation of black community leaders and the explicit charge of racism lent powerful moral authority to the campaign. But in addition to moral authority, as the Thomas victory had shown, direct pressure was essential to force individual owners to agree to neutrality.

Five months later, on May 20, 2007, after a second blitz to collect union authorization cards, the contractors recognized SEIU's new local, SOULA 2006, and began contract negotiations. With Rev. Eric Lee and Rev. Lewis Logan on the hiring committee, the union appointed Faith Culbreath as SOULA's president (as noted earlier). Culbreath in turn appointed Rev. Logan to the contract negotiating committee as a community liaison. The final victory came on January 26, 2008, when more than 4,000 security officers ratified their first union contract. It provided a 40 percent increase in wages and benefits over the five-year contract term as well as medical insurance and job security.

Community partnership in decision-making and organizing campaigns that are relevant to community constituencies is vital.[41] While community support for union organizing is not unusual, few campaigns delve into the gritty work of relationship-building that unpacks the causes of historic mistrust, addresses them, and sets the foundation for future, ongoing collaborative work. The security campaign took an historic step forward in

Los Angeles by providing community leadership with direct involvement in the organizing campaign. The union also hired organizers who acted as bridge builders, who understood the broader community concerns and attempted to incorporate those themes and resources into the campaign. The union continued into the early 2000s to organize non-union security contractors with the support of the community. But as successful as the alliance between SEIU and the black community was, it was unclear whether it was strong enough to deliver the longer-term goal of strategic partnership needed for addressing the labor crisis in Black Los Angeles.

Black Worker Center: Addressing the Labor Crisis in Black Los Angeles

The preceding story of the successful struggle to organize security officers brings to light one strategy to improve the lives of black working families. Typically, employment issues in the black community are expressed as joblessness issues. This focus attempts to help the jobless find employment by increasing their skills or increasing access to certain jobs. The building of SOULA, by contrast, represents the use of resources to attack another problem: the overabundance of low-wage work in the black community. There is a need to transform these jobs so that they are better quality jobs. This job-quality focus holds that no job is inherently bad—it is the absence of collective bargaining power on the part of workers that results in unacceptable levels of wages and benefits. The employment concerns of Black Los Angeles encompass the need to both reduce unemployment *and* improve job quality.

The emphasis on job transformation is particularly important given the growth of certain industries in the United States (retail, health care, leisure and hospitality, logistics) that were relatively immune in the early 2000s from pressures to outsource the jobs. These industries were major contributors to the net job growth in the United States. A large number of the jobs in these industries paid poorly, and they employed substantial numbers of black workers. Strategies to improve the well-being of black workers must take these realities into account and find ways to improve these jobs.

There are two ways to transform and improve the quality of jobs: unionization and public policy. As shown with the security officers' campaign, unionization empowers groups of workers at the workplace so that they can bargain collectively with their employers over working conditions. Alternatively, public policy can establish certain labor standards that set a floor in the workplace and labor market, minimum conditions that employers must maintain (e.g., minimum wages, overtime provisions, health and safety regulations, employee benefits).

African Americans have a long history of being the group with the highest percentage of unionized workers, and this was still the case in the early 2000s. But as the African American proportion of Los Angeles declined, there was a feeling in the community (as portrayed in this chapter) that the labor movement had not made the black job crisis a distinct priority. We believe that one answer to the double crisis of unemployment and poor jobs in Black Los Angeles is to put more effort into union organizing. In 2008 workers in unions nationwide received 13.3 percent higher wages than their counterparts who were not in unions. For black workers, the gain to joining a union was larger—15.8 percent.[42] Black workers in unions also had a higher likelihood of securing employer-based health care and a pension compared to non-union black workers (16 percent and 19 percent, respectively).[43]

If more African American workers could be unionized, job quality definitely would improve in the community. Traditionally, the black community has seen job training as the primary tool for addressing inadequate employment. Training programs, however, are rarely linked to guaranteed job placement. Moreover, well-paying jobs with strong benefits are not readily available in the urban core, where most black Angelenos work and live.

We thus propose the development of a Black Worker Center for Los Angeles. Because the purpose of the Worker Center would be to strengthen the position of the African American working class in the city, the center would adopt a "race and class" perspective. It would focus on improving the situation of Black Los Angeles as a whole, but would be especially concerned with the empowerment of workers and potential workers, so that community development is rooted in social justice and aimed at the collective benefit of all community members. In particular, the Worker Center would aim to increase union membership, participation, and leadership among African American workers in Los Angeles. It also would aim to direct the attention and some of the resources of the Los Angeles labor movement to African American concerns. We view the Los Angeles labor movement both as a partner in this project and as an institution that the Worker Center would try to influence and improve in order to better represent the interests of the African American community. Too often the local labor movement shied away from the concerns of particular communities, fearing that addressing group-specific concerns would be divisive. We, on the other hand, believe that having strong communities among its constituents only strengthens the labor movement.

The proposed Black Worker Center would target the one entity that has been most constant in union and community organizing in Los Angeles: the black church. As noted in this chapter, black church leadership was involved in supporting union organizing struggles in Los Angeles from the late 1990s and into the early 2000s. The Los Angeles County Federation of Labor, under the leadership of the late Miguel Contreras, understood that the moral authority and civil rights tradition of the black church was needed in the fight for workers' rights. From 1996, when Contreras took over as head of the federation, through the first decade of the 2000s, a relationship was nurtured with leaders of the South Los Angeles black faith and social justice community. However, it had not translated by the end of the decade into a strategic alliance that jointly developed campaigns and initiatives to address the broader black jobs crisis. Through the establishment of a community-based network, the Worker Center would connect organized labor to community organizations, including churches, worksource centers, and GED-youth programs that are already involved with job placement, job training, and employment support services, thereby sharing resources and developing joint initiatives.

Additionally, the Worker Center would concentrate on training and educating unorganized black workers, leaders, and neighbors. This would create a true conversation about worker rights in the black community and build a foundation for organizing that originates in the black community and is facilitated by the community. It would facilitate the development of campaigns that address key employment problems facing the community. It also would put the black church and, to some degree, the community in a stronger position when partnering with labor, by establishing an infrastructure and framework for joint organizing initiatives. For unions, the Worker Center would educate a generation of black workers, particularly youth, who did not grow up in the post–World War II heyday for black labor, when good union jobs were linked to black advancement into the middle class. For youth, the Worker Center would introduce the notion of collective struggle for quality jobs.

The Worker Center would emphasize two primary areas of work: countering discrimination and improving job quality. Too often African

Americans face job discrimination when they are not hired or promoted. Discrimination is often subtle and systemic. Rarely can it be proven in court, and even if it could, the time and resources it would take to prevail could be out of proportion to the results. One possibility is to try and make discrimination a central union issue. The Worker Center could educate and put pressure on unions to put anti-discrimination clauses in their contracts as well as make sure the clauses are enforced.

In terms of improving job quality,[44] the challenge is to gain black access to good union jobs, such as construction work. Alternatively, the focus could be on organizing and developing strong union contracts in those jobs where African American workers are already concentrated. African Americans have proven their commitment to the ideals of unionization. While the SEIU SOULA Security Officers campaign successfully focused on organizing black workers, much more attention in early-2000s Los Angeles was given to organizing immigrants. The Worker Center would ensure that adequate attention is given by unions to organizing African American workers, and it could perform various roles in furthering this goal. It could serve as a center for research on African American workers, pointing to where political intervention is needed. It could provide trainings of various sorts, including job training and the soft skills of job acquisition. Most importantly, it could help workers and unions develop organizing campaigns in industries of African American concentration.

In short, the focus of our proposal is not on developing job skills. Nor is it on developing black entrepreneurialism or capitalism. Our vision entails the development of forms of *collective* ownership and collective (and democratic) responsibility, with workers and unions playing a key role in the planning and implementation process. The Worker Center would receive strong support and resources from the Los Angeles labor movement, including the unions that have benefited from community support in winning campaigns. It could serve as a central clearing house for research, curriculum, and campaign models pertaining to black workers. It would serve not only as a place that helps African American workers thrive in their workplace and that develops union consciousness, but it also would build alliances among black community workforce development, empowerment, and advocacy groups who partner, albeit on an inconsistent basis, with organized labor in Los Angeles. The Worker Center would facilitate a core group of service providers in the areas of ex-offender services, employment and civil rights law, housing, and health and safety training. It would serve as a place to develop ideas for building an alternative economic development plan for Black Los Angeles as a whole.

NOTES

1. The largest black-owned newspaper in Los Angeles and the West is discussed further in chap. 2.

2. For background on Maulana Karenga and the US Organization, see chap. 5.

3. The Southern Christian Leadership Conference (SCLC) emerged in 1957 out of the civil rights movement. It brought together protest groups from the South and incorporated nonviolent action as its foundation. Dr. Martin Luther King Jr. was elected as its first president. The SCLC grew nationally and internationally to champion human rights. See SCLC, "Our History," http://www.sclcnational.org.

4. In 2009 the SEIU was America's largest and fastest-growing union with more than 2 million members. See SEIU—Service Employees International Union CTW, CLC, "Our Union: Fast Facts," SEIU.org, http://www.seiu.org/our-union/index.php.

5. We interviewed twenty-seven people involved in the labor movement in Los Angeles. Because of limits on the length of this chapter we have not been able to do justice to the richness of the interviews. However, we plan to publish them in a more extended form later.

6. All authors have worked closely with the labor movement and have a special interest in the challenges faced by black workers. For this chapter, we focused on our work in Los Angeles.

7. Honey, *Going Down Jericho Road.*

8. Zieger, *For Jobs and Freedom.*

9. Flamming, *Bound for Freedom.*

10. Sides, *L.A. City Limits.*

11. Gary Phillips was a local author at the time of the interview.

12. Ibid.

13. Jones, "The Infrastructure of South-Central Los Angeles."

14. See chaps. 1, 2, and 5 for detailed accounts of the impact of racially restrictive housing covenants in Los Angeles.

15. Jones, "The Infrastructure of South-Central Los Angeles."

16. Martin Ludlow, interview by one of the authors, October 1, 2008.

17. Pitts, *Job Quality and Black Workers.*

18. Ong et al., "The State of South L.A." See chap. 8 for a discussion of how this area has been portrayed in popular media.

19. Waldinger and Lichter, *How the Other Half Works.*

20. Ibid., 158.

21. The American Federation of State, County and Municipal Employees (AFSCME) was founded in 1932 and had 1.6 million members by 2009. See AFSCME, "About AFSCME," American Federation of State, County and Municipal Employees, AFL-CIO, http://www.afscme.org/about/aboutindex.cfm.

22. Honey, *Going Down Jericho Road*.

23. Anthony Thigpenn, interview by one of the authors, January 27, 2009.

24. Maulana Karenga, interview by one of the authors, August 12, 2008.

25. Rev. Eric Lee, interview by one of the authors, July 21, 2008.

26. A. Philip Randolph was the leader of the Brotherhood of Sleeping Car Porters, the first national black union in the United States. He was a strong advocate for trade unionism among African Americans and fought for their inclusion in the mainstream, often racist, labor movement.

27. Maulana Karenga, interview by one of the authors, August 12, 2008.

28. Jobs with Peace was a broad-based coalition that formed to counter the Los Angeles economy's reliance on military-related industries.

29. Bloom, "Ally to Win."

30. Milkman, *L.A. Story*.

31. Delp and Quan, "Homecare Worker Organizing in California."

32. See Bloom, "Ally to Win."

33. For a brief and powerful statement by one of the community leaders involved in the campaign, see Maulana Karenga, "The Unfinal Fact of Freedom: The Ongoing Struggle for Justice," *Los Angeles Sentinel*, April 19, 2006, A7.

34. West is a civil rights activist, professor of African American Studies and Religion at Princeton University, and a leading scholar on race.

35. See Bloom, "Ally to Win."

36. Strategic Concepts in Organizing and Policy Education (SCOPE), a community-based organization in Los Angeles, created Action for Grassroots Empowerment and Neighborhood Development Alternatives (AGENDA) "following the 1992 civil unrest in Los Angeles to address chronic poverty in South Los Angeles. AGENDA is a membership-based organization that seeks to reverse the trend of declining civic participation and disinvestment in this community" (SCOPE, "AGENDA," http://www.scopela.org).

37. Gilbert Chan, "Union Effort Clears Hurdle: A CalSTRS Pension Fund Partner Says It Won't Block Security Guards in L.A. who Want to Organize," *Sacramento Bee*, April 8, 2005, D1.

38. See Bloom, "Ally to Win."

39. Rev. James Lawson is a major figure in the struggle for civil rights and labor rights. He was a close friend of Rev. Martin Luther King Jr., and a strong advocate of nonviolent struggle. He has been a supporter and ally of the Los Angeles labor movement.

40. SEIU 1877 Security, "African American Clergy, Community Leaders Call

on Maguire Properties Inc. to Honor Security Officers' Civil Rights, Freedom" [Press Release], June 2005, in authors' possession.

41. Bloom, "Ally to Win."

42. Lawrence Mishel, Jared Bernstein, and Heidi Shierholz, "The State of Working America 2008/2009,"Economic Policy Institute, 2009, http://www.stateof workingamerica.org/tabfig/2008/03/SWA08_Wages_Table.3.32.pdf (accessed October 12, 2009).

43. John Schmitt, "Unions and Upward Mobility for African-American Workers," April 2008, http://www.cepr.net/documents/publications/unions_2008_04 .pdf (accessed October 11, 2009)

44. Co-author Steven Pitts has given considerable attention to the issue of job quality in his work at the University California, Berkeley Center for Labor Research and Education.

Chapter 16

||||||||||||||||||||||||||||||||||||||||||||||||||||||

Reclaiming UCLA
The Education Crisis in Black Los Angeles

Ana-Christina Ramón and Darnell Hunt

UCLA—which boasts such storied black alumni as Jackie Robinson, Tom Bradley, and Ralph Bunche, and is in a county that is 9.8% African American—now has a lower percentage of black freshman than either crosstown rival USC or UC Berkeley, the school often considered its top competitor within the UC system.[1]

On a Sunday morning in June 2006, Los Angeles woke up to the above words under the headline "A Startling Statistic at UCLA." Media throughout the nation soon picked up the news, reigniting a long-standing debate about higher education, race, and access.[2] For much of the city's black community, the revelation that fewer than one hundred African Americans were expected to enroll in a freshman class of more than 4,900 students was indeed startling. Black students stood to account for only about 2 percent of the freshman class at the University of California, Los Angeles (UCLA)[3]—a public university located in a county where blacks made up nearly 10 percent of the population. For those better acquainted with UCLA, the news was not really all that new. This latest crisis reported in the pages of the *Los Angeles Times* was merely reflective of a promising yet often disappointing relationship between black Angelenos and the campus that could be traced to the origin of that relationship.

UCLA was a place of contrasts for black Angelenos. Established near Hollywood in 1919, when Black Los Angeles was experiencing tremendous growth, the campus relocated farther west to what would become the exclusive, white enclave of Westwood in 1929[4] (see figs. 16.1 and 16.2), just as the Central Avenue black community was coming into its own (see

Figure 16.1 (*top*). Aerial view of UCLA, Westwood in background, 1930. Photo courtesy of UCLA University Archives, Los Angeles, California.

Figure 16.2 (*bottom*). Aerial view of UCLA campus and Westwood, Calif., July 8, 1984. Photo courtesy of *Los Angeles Times* Photographic Archive, Department of Special Collections, Charles E. Young Research Library, UCLA.

chap. 1). Yet, in times when traditionally white colleges typically excluded blacks and other minorities, UCLA was known for producing black luminaries and pioneers such as Dr. Ralph J. Bunche, Jackie Robinson, and Tom Bradley.[5] In 1949, five years before the Supreme Court rendered Jim Crow unconstitutional with its landmark *Brown v. Board* decision, UCLA became the first predominantly white college in the nation to elect a black, Sherrill Luke, as student body president.[6] But like Los Angeles, UCLA was never a racial paradise. Beneath the veneer of UCLA's proud legacy of black achievement were the realities of a pre–Civil Rights Act America—token blacks admitted largely because of their athletic prowess and unacceptable levels of segregation and alienation on campus.

Still, UCLA was a symbol of promise for blacks from Los Angeles and elsewhere who sought access to a first-rate college education and a better future for themselves. Because of its association with black pioneers, UCLA represented a prime path to the American Dream for many blacks. Perhaps it is no accident that as the Black Power movement challenged the status quo at traditionally white campuses across America in the mid-1960s,[7] UCLA again would lead the way, as black Angelenos proclaimed the campus their own, pushing for what became a model program for opening the campus to inner-city minorities with high potential[8] and organizing for the establishment of one of the nation's first Black Studies research centers.[9] So it seemed quite ironic that in the spring of 2006—in the afterglow of this legacy, and when the County of Los Angeles boasted the second-largest black population in the nation—that the *Los Angeles Times* could report such a "startling statistic" about black admissions and enrollments at the campus.

The day after the "startling statistic" became news, a coalition of African American community organizations in Los Angeles came together in order to demand equity for black students applying to UCLA. The group's action was reminiscent of organized efforts during the civil rights and Black Power periods—which was fitting given that the number of expected black enrollees to the campus had dropped to levels not seen since the 1960s. Unlike any other education-focused coalition that Black Los Angeles had seen in decades, the group brought together mainline civil rights organizations and other community-based organizations in the city that had traditionally pursued their own separate agendas in different ways. The group called itself the Alliance for Equal Opportunity in Education (AEOE). We served as consultants to the AEOE, providing the group with data from our *Bunche Research Report* series on the education crisis confronting black students in California,[10] which the group used to develop its case for progressive change. The AEOE's crusade quickly produced results when UCLA switched to a fairer admissions system the following year and doubled its black enrollment.

In this chapter, we present a case study of the AEOE's response to the admissions crisis that plagued UCLA in the early 2000s. With the help of a team of graduate student researchers, we conducted an ethnographic study[11] that sought to gain a comprehensive understanding of the purpose and functions of the AEOE. We sought to document how and why the organization was founded, how it functioned, its challenges and accomplishments, its membership's commitment, and plans for the future. With these goals in mind, members of our research team attended weekly AEOE meetings, observing the proceedings and taking notes. They also conducted and transcribed in-depth interviews with fifteen AEOE members, ranging from UCLA students to heads of prominent Los Angeles–based civil rights organizations.

Hegemony theory[12] provides a useful framework for understanding the history of black struggle at UCLA, which has included periodic black demands for access and inclusion, white acquiescence, and a gradual opening up of the campus in ways those in power never really thought would threaten white control. Through this theoretical lens, we attempt to trace the promises and pitfalls associated with Black Los Angeles's efforts to "reclaim UCLA" in the early 2000s, looking closely at the inner workings of a community alliance that may serve as a model for racial advocacy in "colorblind" times.

Prelude to a Crisis

African Americans have long believed that education is the key to success and access.[13] However, many scholars have argued that the white, middle-class model of individual success in a white-controlled education system restricted blacks by diverting their attention away from the possibilities associated with claiming a place of power in the system.[14] The Black Power movement pushed these issues to the forefront, and UCLA became a central location where questions regarding education and Black Power played out. Although Black Studies programs were initiated at many universities in the late 1960s, the issues of power and control remained in question.[15] As the black psychologist Kenneth Clark observed in 1969:

If a university administration can restore harmony and the image of innovation by a no-strings-attached financial grant to a separate black studies program that may cover a few salaries or subsidize a gas station, it need not move to transform itself into a genuinely nonracial institution dedicated to developing human beings and to helping them develop effective strategies for fundamental social change. No more power is granted than is necessary to yield.[16]

Indeed, despite the many symbolic and real advances that had been made over the years, setbacks in the struggle for black access and equity at UCLA would continue into the twenty-first century. The latest setback in 2006 reflected a new hegemonic order in UCLA admissions that was marked by three major factors: the death of affirmative action in California's public institutions of higher education, the dismal failure of public education at the K-12 level in Los Angeles, and the skyrocketing popularity of UCLA.

In the 1970s, a white backlash against the group-based civil rights and Black Power gains of the 1960s paved the way for a sharp turn to the right in the 1980s. One of the defining characteristics of this "Reagan Revolution" era was the routine dismissal of collective notions of racial justice and equity in favor of a radical focus on individual rights.[17] By the 1990s, a policy such as affirmative action,[18] which had been instituted in the 1960s to level America's historically tilted racial playing fields, was itself redefined as "reverse discrimination" and gradually dismantled by conservative jurists appointed during the twenty-year rule of presidents Reagan, Bush 1, and Bush 2. California, perennially a bellwether state on racial matters due to its diverse populations, again established a significant racial precedent in 1996, when 54 percent of voters passed Proposition 209 and effectively eliminated the use of affirmative action in the state's public institutions like UCLA. A steady decline in black admissions to UCLA soon followed, reaching a nadir of less than 250 admits (out of more than 12,000) in 2006.[19]

In a "colorblind" era when commonsense understandings of racial dynamics worked to minimize the reality of racial discrimination and privilege, the steep decline in black admissions to UCLA could be blamed on the failure of black applicants to measure up to their white and Asian counterparts—to "merit" admission to the campus. These views were reinforced by the abysmal failure of public, K-12 education in Los Angeles, where only 56 percent of black students in Los Angeles Unified School

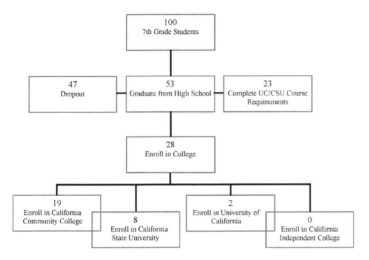

Figure 16.3. The Pipeline to College for Black Los Angeles Unified School District (LAUSD) Students, 2005 Graduates. Sources: California Department of Education and California Postsecondary Education Commission.

District (LAUSD) schools graduated with their class in 2003.[20] Moreover, the education received by most of these graduates was hardly comparable to the education received by their white and Asian American counterparts in the state, students who attended high schools with more experienced teachers, vastly superior physical plants,[21] and the availability of advanced placement and honors courses that allowed them to inflate their grade point averages (GPAs) to competitive levels.[22] The pipeline to college for black LAUSD students, particularly to the University of California, was a sobering one (see fig. 16.3). Collectively, these racial realities obfuscated deep-seated problems with UCLA's admissions policies, problems that worked to severely disadvantage black applicants to a campus with a legacy of producing black firsts.

At the same time, UCLA had become America's most popular university by the early 2000s, attracting more applicants than any other institution.[23] Skyrocketing demand for admission to UCLA during this period, combined with minimal if any increases in the supply of freshman slots, resulted in the inevitable increase in the costs of admission. While UCLA, as a public institution, remained a bargain relative to private alternatives,[24] the campus necessarily became much more selective in its admissions. The standardized test scores and GPAs of admitted students went through the roof,[25] as students fortunate enough to come from affluent families and attend richly resourced high schools benefited from test preparation courses and taking as many honors and advanced placement courses as possible in order to inflate their GPAs.[26] Because of K–12 disparities associated with race, most black applicants to UCLA were severely disadvantaged in this numbers component of the college admissions game. Indeed, competition for admission to UCLA had become so intense that more than a few of the black students denied admission to UCLA in 2006 were admitted to *more* prestigious universities like Stanford, Princeton, and Yale.[27]

A Call to Action

I came into the office early one morning, even though I rarely come in early and read an *LA Times* article on the low number of African American students admitted to UCLA. . . . This made my stomach turn. . . . I knew something had to be done so I talked to three or four people saying, "This is not right, we need to do something!" It was spontaneous! Everyone that I talked to agreed that this was wrong and that something needed to be done.[28]

Following a call to action by Dr. Geraldine Washington, president of the Los Angeles branch of the National Association for the Advancement of Colored People (NAACP), the AEOE emerged in June 2006 as a multi-organization collaborative comprised of national, state, and local African American organizations. These organizations included the Los Angeles branch of the NAACP, the Los Angeles Urban League, the Southern Christian Leadership Conference (SCLC) of Greater Los Angeles, the Brotherhood Crusade, prominent black church leaders, educators, community leaders, California state assembly members, the UCLA Black Alumni Association, and the UCLA African Student Union. With research support provided by the Bunche Center for African American Studies at UCLA, the AEOE pressed for change in the UCLA admissions process.

In September 2006, just three months after the AEOE's founding, UCLA implemented a *Bunche Research Report* policy recommendation and changed to a more holistic admissions process[29] that considered student achievement in the context of student challenges and opportunities.

Soon after, a UCLA press release noted that "this change is the most sweeping reform since the comprehensive review process was adopted by the University of California Board of Regents five years ago, ending a practice of allowing a portion of students to be admitted solely on academic criteria."[30] In spring 2007, the implementation of holistic review led to a 60 percent increase in African American admissions and a doubling of black enrollees, which was maintained the following year. UCLA admissions officials acknowledged that public pressure about the rapidly declining number of African American freshman enrollees was a major factor in the university's decision to overhaul its comprehensive review process.[31] The AEOE's efforts to make the UCLA admissions process fairer for black students had succeeded.[32]

Throughout the course of this study, the AEOE met weekly, as it had done since it was created in June 2006,[33] and representatives from all of the major organizations continued to participate. The meetings were organized and run by a moderator, Greg Akili, from Community Call to Action and Accountability in Los Angeles, and the group was headed by three co-chairs: the head of the local NAACP, the president of the Los Angeles Urban League, and a former president of the UCLA Black Alumni Association. In order to facilitate its agenda, the AEOE established three subcommittees that focused on the group's most pressing issues: UCLA-specific policies and procedures, UC systemwide policies and procedures, and community education and media. Three basic issues seemed to motivate AEOE members and orient the organization: (1) holding UCLA accountable for black access and inclusion, (2) raising awareness of the admissions issue in the broader community and maintaining it as a priority, and (3) having a personal sense of duty and obligation to the community.

Holding UCLA Accountable

AEOE members were clearly outraged that UCLA, a public, land-grant institution supported by California taxpayers of all races, could have such a disproportionately low number of black students. Recall that black freshmen were underrepresented by a factor of about 5 to 1 in the fall 2006 class. This seemed completely unjust to AEOE members, and they were determined to hold the university accountable. Blair Taylor, president and CEO of the Los Angeles Urban League, was blunt on this point: "Diversity is not optional. It's mandatory! We are 10 percent of the [county] population and thus we should be 10 percent of the population at UCLA."[34] Another member, Jennifer White from the UCLA Black Alumni Association, further explained the AEOE's position on the issue of representation:

> [AEOE's goal is] that we ensure African American students get their fair share of public resources, including access to higher education, because as taxpaying citizens, we pay taxes and our children deserve to have access to these resources that we're paying for.[35]

At the time of the interviews, the AEOE's bylaws had not been set. However, the group's mission was clear. Each of the fifteen members interviewed considered the AEOE to be a "community watchdog"—an overseer that would monitor UCLA and ensure access and equity for black students at the campus. Nefertiti Austin from the Brotherhood Crusade summed up this assumed role by saying:

> The purpose and the goals—the purpose is really to serve as a community watchdog agency to really support students on campus, because ultimately the students are the ones who will have to be here and deal with whether or not there are other African American students on or not on campus. And so the purpose is to provide backup and to let the university know that there are people in the community, some are alums, such as I'm an alum, and others are not, who are watching to make sure that everyone has access.[36]

In holding the university accountable, the group asserted its position as an important stakeholder of the public institution. Although the AEOE had won a victory when it pressured UCLA to overhaul its admissions system, its members still did not trust the campus to police itself when it came to ongoing equity and access for black applicants. So the AEOE assumed this role itself.

The sometimes adversarial relationship between the black community and UCLA was discussed by about half of the members who responded to a question regarding the external challenges faced by the AEOE. Most of these respondents mentioned they had perceived "subtle" or "passive resistance" from university officials on the matter of changing the campus's admissions policies, policies whose shortcomings had been well documented. These respondents pointed to how university administrators wanted to maintain control of the admissions issue, pushing back at times if they felt the AEOE was infringing upon their domain. Greg Akili, a well-known community activist who moderated AEOE meetings, noted:

> Well, it's interesting. It was never seen as opposition, that is, it was never —like, "What you all are doing's wrong, we're opposed to it." UCLA wanted to do it they're own way. It was more, "That's okay, we got it. We'll handle this now."[37]

Kevin Johnson,[38] a leader in the UCLA African Student Union, described how the administration's actions seemed to move at a slower pace, at times, which seemed to signify an underlying opposition or lack of motivation for changing the status quo:

> There's still a tone, there's an overtone, or underlying theme that us having problems moving forward, still is somewhat of like an uphill battle. . . . I think the administration and just like, I think, local government, and you know, the people, a lot of times, they've gotten so sophisticated to a point that, where they can hide their opposition but still ensure that people are not moving you forward as fast as they need to.[39]

Karume James, who began as a UCLA African Student Union leader and transitioned after graduation to become a labor union organizer, echoed this view:

> Man, maybe a little bit of push back, you know, . . . in terms of . . . "Well, do you really wanna meet with the Chancellor on this quota?" . . . they [administrators] might get, you know, not necessarily brushed off but . . . not immediately jumping to . . . get that taken care of, kind of thing.[40]

In the so-called "post-racial" era of the early twenty-first century, administrators' resistance to institutional change and racial equality may have appeared subtler than the more confrontational stances associated with the Black Power era of the 1960s. But AEOE members were still keenly aware of this resistance, and it shaped the strategies that members pursued. Rather than viewing the administrators as partners in pursuing diversity, AEOE members maintained their mistrust of the administration's agenda, which often rendered the campus-community relationship rather precarious.

Meanwhile, other AEOE members pointed out that administration opposition was at times not so subtle. Lamar Hale, who was a prominent student leader and former UC Student Regent,[41] was rather blunt: "There are people within the university who don't want to see diversity increase in the university."[42] Daniel Johnson, an officer with the UCLA Black Alumni Association who was a student in the 1960s, concurred and described the response to the AEOE by key power brokers in the university as "patronizing:"

> The university has been very patronizing of the [AEOE]. They've treated us as if they take us seriously as an institution. But they don't take us seriously because the key people within the university like [an unnamed administrator][43] and people who advise the Chancellor know that we're nothing more than a paper tiger. . . . So it's almost like a treadmill that we're on where we're both going over the same territory, not going anywhere at either level.[44]

Although AEOE members were proud of their early accomplishments as a group—namely pressuring UCLA to overhaul its admissions procedures—they knew that more needed to be done to sustain UCLA's accountability to the black community over the long run. And this task was complicated by the incorrect impression many casual observers had that the crisis confronting black students had been resolved.

Keeping the Admissions Crisis in the Headlines

By 2008, the UCLA black admissions crisis may not have appeared as dire as it had immediately after Proposition 209 passed in 1996 or in the spring of 2006, when the "startling statistic" headline flashed across the front page of the *Los Angeles Times*. But the crisis continued due to the fact that the top UC campuses still admitted a disproportionately low number of black students. In fact, many AEOE members pointed out that UCLA appeared to be in violation of the federal disparate impact standard associated with Title VI of the Civil Rights Act of 1964. In the arena of college admissions, the federal standard holds that policy may adversely impact individuals of a particular group when the group's admission rate is less than 80 percent of the admission rate for the most highly admitted group. After the admissions overhaul at UCLA and the doubling of black enrollments in 2007, the campus still appeared to be out of compliance with the standard. That is, the admission rate for black students *rose* to only about 63 percent of the admission rate for Asian American students, the most highly admitted group (admission rates of 17 percent and 27 percent, respectively).[45]

Although the black admissions crisis at UCLA continued to receive periodic public attention, AEOE members expressed concern that public interest in the matter—which had supported their effort to pressure the administration into overhauling campus admissions procedures—was waning. Indeed, the AEOE itself increasingly struggled to keep its most prominent members engaged in alliance activities. These members were active heads of other organizations and had difficulty keeping up with the AEOE's weekly meeting schedule. A UCLA African Student Union leader, Christina Walter, summed up how these issues were connected:

I think the internal and external issue is one in the same. Because the alliance is valued around the admissions issue and because [admissions] numbers have gone up for the past three years, there's no sense of urgency and there's no sense of crisis anymore—regardless of the fact that if you actually break down the numbers, the increases are proportional to the increases in applications received. . . . And so it's just kind of, that whole crisis thing really, it was good and bad in the sense that it brought us together, but you know, when the fire's out, everybody goes home.[46]

AEOE members recognized that the mainstream media were not committed to keeping the issue in the headlines. As NAACP representative and UCLA alumnus, Ernest Smith, noted:

The challenges outside [are] how to reach the community because of mass media. They don't always share our concerns. And they may not —the media does not feel that the issues we're concerned about are major issues enough for them to give us any kind of public support. Once we had a mass meeting forum at a couple of churches here. We were able to get one radio program to go on and give some coverage to it. We got in some of the community papers.[47]

Despite the expectation by some alliance members that local black media would make up for the mainstream media's disinterest, black media only sporadically covered the issue after the initial crisis, disappointing members like the Brotherhood Crusade's Nefertiti Austin:

> Externally, I think [another AEOE member] has mentioned this several times and he's right. In the court of public opinion we—not so much that we're losing, we don't even have a—I don't think we have a place. The black media hasn't done what they said they were going to [do], kinda no surprise there. But it is unfortunate.[48]

Other alliance members, like Lamar Hale, were more critical of the AEOE's own role in helping to keep the message in front of the black press and relevant to the black community:

> At this point, people aren't aware of the issue, 'cause they don't see it as an issue. And so we have to repack the rooms, and we have to repack the rooms by making the issues relevant to people. We're not in the black media consistently. We don't produce the articles like we said we would, the editorials like we said we would.[49]

AEOE members who were critical of UCLA's diversity efforts knew they had to find a way to promote UCLA to the black community, despite the campus's more recent image as an alienating place for black students. Without a large influx of black applicants, members realized that admissions numbers would not increase significantly because the campus was so selective—by mid-decade, the campus only admitted about one out of every five applicants. For black applicants, the odds were even worse, about one in every eight applicants was admitted. The African Student Union's Christina Walter discussed the challenges the AEOE faced in recruiting students to apply to UCLA:

> I think it's been difficult because a lot of people are still very, in general, turned off about UCLA because that, you know, the whole "UCLA doesn't like black people" is definitely ingrained in a lot of people in the community. Like, you can hear it just dialoging with students—will be, like, "Yeah, I don't wanna go there," and, "They don't like my people," or "There's only two black people at UCLA." Well there's not gonna be three if you don't apply. You know?[50]

As mentioned earlier, the lack of urgency also extended to prominent members of the alliance itself. Although most alliance members remained committed to meeting every week since the group formed in June 2006, the group experienced its own growing pains once its initial UCLA campaign was completed and the black enrollment numbers doubled for the fall 2007 freshman class. A few respondents noted that two of the AEOE co-chairs—who were leaders of the most high-profile member organizations of the alliance—had not been to any of the meetings in months. Instead, they had sent representatives in their place. Some AEOE members perceived the sending of substitutes as a sign of waning interest on the part of the prominent members that was rooted in the short-term successes of the alliance. But others—like Chris Strudwick-Turner, vice president of the Los Angeles Urban League—perceived it as a need for the alliance to better define its focus, a task that was complicated by the differing agendas of member organizations:

> Internally, I think it's the focus—where we're going, what are the priorities? Everybody has their different priorities, I think. And I think that's manifesting itself in the fact that the leaders of organizations are not present. . . . But I don't know that that's necessary. . . . I don't know that in terms of getting the work done that needs to be done, and then sticking to the mission, that they have to be present.[51]

As a new organization consisting of numerous community groups, the AEOE's challenge was not only keeping the admissions issue at the forefront in the present, but also learning to refocus their goals for the long term in order to maintain member interest and a strong, united front that could effectively address the issue and related challenges in the future.

Duty to the Community

AEOE members routinely expressed their sense of duty to the local black community when talking about the struggle for equity and access at UCLA. For the UCLA Black Alumni Association, however, the relationship between a duty to UCLA and to Black Los Angeles was sometimes a conflicted one. For the obvious reason of supporting prospective black UCLA students, the black alumni of UCLA had maintained a strong and steady involvement in the AEOE. Most study informants agreed that the black alumni association was one of the groups that carried a disproportionate load of the AEOE's work. But despite their allegiance to the institution where they had learned to become community activists, these alliance members felt compelled to publicly condemn UCLA at times—to pressure the campus to step up and offer future generations of black students the same opportunity to learn and grow. Jennifer White put it this way:

> I'm an alumni [sic] of UCLA . . . and I was a student activist and so on. I have an affinity for the campus and what it can provide to develop black students and, therefore, I have a vested interest in ensuring more black students get access to it.[52]

Similarly, Daniel Johnson remarked on his memories as a student leader at UCLA during the 1960s, which energized him to continue with the AEOE the fight for equality that he had started as a student:

> All of this experience at UCLA has defined, not my existence, but it's defined my life. I came here fulfilling a decision I made at 12 years old, to try and come to be the next Ralph Bunche. . . . And I got caught up in the spirit of self-sacrifice that was prominent in the '60s both in terms of civil rights and in terms of those who went to Vietnam and didn't come back . . . and those who were at Campbell Hall and lived to tell the tale of those who died at Campbell Hall [in the 1969 shootings].[53] All of that has left me with a sense of obligation that I can't stop until the job that I was allowed to begin is finished. . . . And the [AEOE] is a forum, is a vehicle in which I can continue to do that.[54]

Mandla Kayise, who attended UCLA in the late 1970s and early '80s, discussed his affinity for the campus when describing the role he assumed as one of the three co-chairs of the AEOE:

> I look at it as kind of akin to like church. Because people ask me when are you going to stop working with UCLA or higher education? I tell them, "Never." It's the institution I've chosen, that I think I need an ongoing connection to, to maintain my development and also to maintain the development of all the folks and the institutions and organizations with which I work. I think that's why higher education exists.[55]

This idea of giving back to the community is a common mantra among ethnic minorities,[56] which further supports the importance of diversity in higher education. Often it is alumni who play a key role in efforts to ensure that future generations of ethnic minority students have equal opportunities to learn.

Other AEOE members' equating of duty to the community and making UCLA accessible was just as strong a motivating force, even if they weren't alumni of the campus. The Urban League's Chris Strudwick-Turner discussed why she got involved in the AEOE:

> So my motivation is to just turn this ship around. To think that from when I went to school to now nothing had really changed was just mind-boggling to me. And I have kids. I mean I have a daughter who's out of college, but I have a son that's coming up as well. And when I think about him, like he's facing the same crap that I did way back when. I mean it's just—and here in California of all places, what used to be the most innovative. So for the kids I just decided, "You know what, enough is enough." And when I met all the people who were involved at the school, are committed, they are the like the alumni, 'cause I'm not from here.[57]

With respect to community awareness of their efforts, most members felt people had heard something about a group of individuals from their community focused on UCLA admissions. Nonetheless, they believed the black community was not aware there was an organization called the AEOE that pursued the alliance's specific agenda. While some members felt this was a failure of the group that needed to be addressed, others felt it was not a failure as long as the community was aware of the efforts and took advantage of the opportunities afforded by them. Chris Strudwick-Turner subscribed to this latter view:

> I don't even know that it's that important that they know about the [AEOE] so much as they know about our efforts. And if we get out there and let them know about how to get your kid to UCLA, if that's what your kid wants, and making sure that kids know that they are wanted at UCLA and should apply at UCLA. I mean, I think that's the more important piece than awareness about the organization itself.[58]

Other members noted the significance of the alliance's work to the black community in general. The Rev. Eric Lee,[59] head of the Southern Christian Leadership Conference (SCLC) of Greater Los Angeles, summarized what he thought the AEOE's efforts would accomplish for the black community in terms of civil rights:

> [E]ducation to me has always been and continued to be the civil rights issue of the day. So access to the institutions of higher education are about African Americans' access to seats of power and influence. And, so being denied access to that hinders our progress to a more equitable society. The struggle has always been about access. Not about racial equality. It is about access.[60]

Mandla Kayise echoed this point about the importance of education to the black community: "So I think we've just lost as a community an understanding of just how central education is to our development, to our viability economically, but also to just our general development."[61]

These sentiments underscore the idea discussed earlier that African Americans have always viewed education as key to attaining status and power in society, that they see it as something worth fighting for. Toward this end, alliance members committed themselves, week after week, taking time from their busy schedules to attend meetings and work together on a crisis that many outside the group believed had been resolved. In so doing, alliance members found themselves regularly taking aim at the hegemonic understandings of the situation that permeated mainstream media and, unfortunately, much of the black community in the city. In this sense, alliance members participated in what amounted to a counterhegemonic movement, which occurs when members move from skepticism of the dominant ideology to deciding to take collective action based on their own personal experiences.[62]

Toward a Model of Community Mobilization

Although there were many internal and external challenges, AEOE members seemed dedicated to the collaborative not only because of the immediate matter of UCLA admissions but also because they perceived themselves as a unit, much like a family, that could serve as a model for community mobilization in an era of political fragmentation. Members often talked about how they perceived the AEOE as a model that could be replicated elsewhere in a Black Los Angeles sorely in need of political organization. Ernest Smith, an NAACP member and longtime activist, put it this way:

> Coming from—as I said, my background, I see the difference of it and it can be broadened. This is just microscopic of what's achievable. It says "We're doing this on a small basis and we can broaden this out. We can expand this."[63]

We identified five simple lessons that AEOE members took from their experiences in the UCLA crisis, lessons that could be useful to other black community alliances attempting to forge progressive change.

1. *Stay focused and committed to the group's original goals, but not so inflexible that the group can't adapt to changing circumstances.* AEOE members learned that it's important to stay committed to their group's original goals because other issues invariably threatened to distract them from this focus. AEOE members also realized they had to be proactive after they had won the initial battle to improve the admissions process, as public interest in the matter waned. They maintained a resolve to serve as a community watchdog that would monitor admissions practices at UCLA and throughout the UC system over the long haul. The AEOE gained a commitment from UCLA's Chancellor to meet with the group quarterly to discuss its questions and concerns about admissions and diversity on the campus. Meanwhile, the AEOE remained flexible to the changing circumstances of its own membership, as well as to pulls from within and outside the group to expand the group's focus to the K–12 issues that plagued educational opportunity in Black Los Angeles.

2. *Stay connected to the community in order to remain relevant.* The AEOE set up an interactive website and conducted quarterly community town hall meetings, particularly in their first two years of existence, when rapid changes were occurring in the group's struggle to achieve a fairer admissions policy at UCLA. As the AEOE branched out to include other educational issues, the group's strong connection to the community became even more essential for developing the understanding of community needs and "state of mind" necessary for staying relevant and communicating effectively.

3. *Present a unified voice to the public.* As a group comprised of preexisting, independent organizations, AEOE members learned at the onset that they had to function as a cohesive unit in order to win the public

relations aspect of the struggle to achieve AEOE goals. The alliance relied on the expertise of its members who knew how to effectively conduct public relations campaigns in order to ensure that the group communicated a coherent message. These experts served on the AEOE's Community Education and Media subcommittee, which coordinated the alliance's public statements, press conferences, and media advisories. A critical aspect of their work was strategizing with AEOE members to determine who would speak or ask questions at public presentations or closed meetings with outside entities.

4. *Treat all members equally and make each of them feel useful.* AEOE members understood that promoting equity among collaborative partners, regardless of the resources or history of any given member organization, would be key to maintaining the alliance. Although AEOE members included both up-and-coming leaders and well-established figures from major national civil rights organizations, all members were given the space to speak, they were all treated with respect, and their contributions were all equally valued. The group's democratic proceedings, facilitated by a strong moderator, ensured that all members bought into the group's evolving agenda and strategic activities.

5. *Acknowledge the indispensable role of allies to the collaborative.* In any counterhegemonic movement, allies are needed for support, reinforcement, and sustainability. AEOE members were aware, early on, that the alliance needed help in areas where members were not experts. For example, the AEOE requested assistance from the Bunche Center for African American Studies to provide it with the research data necessary for understanding exactly what was wrong with the admissions process at UCLA. From these data, alliance members were able to develop key talking points on the admissions issue, which led them to create a more persuasive argument in which to encase their demands for equity. Moreover, although the AEOE was primarily focused on access for black Angelenos, it also reached out throughout its battle to organizations representing other ethnic groups facing similar challenges. AEOE members were aware that other underrepresented groups also had been negatively affected by inequities in the admissions process and that collaboration with these groups would be key to generating more support and advancing the AEOE's agenda.

By 2007 UCLA had responded to the "startling statistic" crisis and implemented a new "holistic" admissions process. Although the new process was fairer than the one it replaced, it still failed to admit black students at rates compliant with the federal disparate impact standard. Nonetheless, the AEOE's short-term victory had largely quelled public dissent over the issue of black underrepresentation at UCLA, and the AEOE continued to work with campus administrators on outreach and fundraising initiatives geared toward protecting the rather precarious gains.

While those hoping to "reclaim UCLA" celebrated the recent increases in black freshmen as progressive change, critics invoked commonsense understandings of "merit" to dismiss the increases as proof that the campus had lowered its academic standards. News media, mainstream and black, generally grew weary of the matter. The AEOE continued to wrestle with these complicated issues as the decade drew to a close. But as is always the case in hegemonic orders, the final outcome of this struggle was far from determined.

NOTES

1. Rebecca Trounson, "A Startling Statistic at UCLA," *Los Angeles Times*, June 3, 2006, A1.

2. For example, see "At UCLA, Black Freshman May Drop to Lowest Number in 33 Years," *Chronicle of Higher Education News Blog*, June 4, 2006; http://chronicle.com/news/article/522/at-ucla-black-freshmen-may-drop-to-lowest-number-in-33-years; Elaine Korry, "Black Student Enrollment at UCLA Plunges," *Morning Edition*, NPR, July 24, 2006, http://www.npr.org/templates/story/story.php?storyId=5563891; and David Leonhardt, "The New Affirmative Action," *New York Times Magazine*, September 30, 2007, http://www.nytimes.com/2007/09/30/magazine/30affirmative-t.html?ref=magazine.

3. The Master Plan for Higher Education of 1960 established a hierarchical system of public higher education for the state of California. It defined the distinct missions of two four-year systems of postsecondary education, as well as a single two-year community college system. UCLA is one of ten campuses in the University of California system, which was designated as the public research university and mandated to select from only the top 12.5 percent of the state's high school graduating class (Kerr, "The California Master Plan for Higher Education"; R. Johnson et al., "Gaming the System").

4. From 1914 to 1929, UCLA was located on Vermont Avenue in Hollywood, a campus that would later become Los Angeles City College (Andrew Hamilton, "(UC) Los Angeles: Historical Overview," *University of California History Digital Archives*, The Regents of the University of California, June 18, 2004, http://sunsite.berkeley.edu/UCHistory/general_history/campuses/ucla/overview.html).

5. Bunche was valedictorian of UCLA's 1927 graduating class. He went on

to become a scholar and statesman and was awarded the Nobel Peace Prize in 1950. In 1940, Bradley left UCLA before graduating to join the Los Angeles Police Academy. He went on to lead a distinguished career in public service as the first elected black city councilman and the city's first black mayor in modern times. About a year later, Robinson also left UCLA before graduating to help his mother financially. He went on to play baseball and break the color barrier in the major leagues.

6. Sherrill Luke would go on from his leadership role at UCLA to become a Los Angeles Superior Court judge.

7. See Williamson, "In Defense of Themselves."

8. According to the UCLA High Potential Program (HPP) 1968–1969 report, "This program was designed to allow those students not meeting regular admission requirements to be granted special admissions and then be involved in an academic program designed especially to accommodate their special needs, while at the same time giving them valid experience in higher education and preparing them for successful, independent matriculation at UCLA" (Barbara A. Rhodes, "UCLA High Potential Program 1968–1969," Academic Support Program files, UCLA"). "The High Potential Program was an attempt to engage underprivileged African American and Chicano students in higher education and to have them return to their communities and to make meaningful change" (Rhodes, "UCLA High Potential Program 1968–1969"). In 1969–1970 Asian American, American Indian, and Engineering components were added to the program. In its three years of operation from 1968 to 1971, 586 students were admitted to UCLA under HPP (Susan Meives, "A Summary of the Academic Progress of High Potential Program Students at UCLA," Folder "High Potential Program, 1969, 1970–1971 March," University Archives, Charles E. Young Research Library, UCLA").

9. Based on a Black Student Union proposal for Black Studies (John Dreyfuss, "Ethnic Studies in State Mostly Promises, Plans," Los Angeles Times, April 25, 1969, A1), UCLA announced in 1969 that African Americans, Chicanos, Asians, and American Indians would each have their own programs and centers to "study and conduct research into the problems of ethnic minorities in society" (Robert Rawitch, "UCLA Creates Culture Project to Research Minority Problems," Los Angeles Times, January 24, 1969, E1).

10. These Bunche Research Reports were products of the College Access Project for African Americans (CAPAA), a six-year study funded by the Ford Foundation that sought to understand the barriers faced by black students who sought access to the University of California in the post-Proposition 209 era.

11. The portion of the study discussed in this chapter includes the 2007 and 2008 admissions cycles and ends in October 2008.

12. As developed by Gramsci (Selections from the Prison Notebooks), hegemony describes how the dominant group in society can maintain power over the subordinate group and even exploit that group without relying on physical force.

The dominant group rules with the consent of the subordinate group. However, a "compromise equilibrium" must be maintained with the dominant group making some kind of concession. Hegemony is an ongoing struggle between classes. Hegemony can also be viewed through the racialized struggles that occur between groups (Arena, "Race and Hegemony").

13. See Jones-Wilson, "Race, Realities, and American Education."

14. See J. Williams and Ladd, "On the Relevance of Education for Black Liberation."

15. For an analysis of these issues, see Rooks, *White Money/Black Power.*

16. Clark, "A Charade of Power," 146.

17. See Omi and Winant, *Racial Formation in the United States.*

18. Affirmative action policy originated with the Civil Rights Act of 1964 and was reinforced with executive orders by President Johnson in 1965 and 1967. Affirmative action policies in college admissions were implemented throughout the 1960s and 1970s at postsecondary institutions in response to student demands for increased access and equity for underrepresented minorities and to increase campus diversity (R. Johnson et al., "Gaming the System"). Also, see Bowen and Bok, *Shape of the River.*

19. Ralph J. Bunche Center for African American Studies, " 'Merit' Matters."

20. United Way of Greater Los Angeles and Los Angeles Urban League, "The State of Black Los Angeles." Los Angeles Unified School District (LAUSD) was the second-largest school district in the nation in the early 2000s. Hypersegregated by race, its 688,138 students in 2009 were 72.8 percent Latino, 11.2 percent black, but only 8.9 percent white and 3.7 percent Asian. See Los Angeles Unified School District, "Fingertip Facts 2009-2010," www.lausd.net.

21. Ralph J. Bunche Center for African American Studies, "Separate but Certainly Not Equal."

22. Ralph J. Bunche Center for African American Studies, "Admissions and Omissions."

23. In 2005, UCLA was already receiving the highest number of undergraduate applications of any UC system campus and one of the highest in the nation with 42,223 applicants, when the numbers began to markedly climb, increasing to 47,317 in 2006, 50,746 in 2007, and 55,423 in 2008 (University of California, "Table 1-2005/2006/2007/2008, Fall Applicants, Fall Admits, Fall Enrollees, Admit Rate and Fall Applicant Yield Rate: First-Time Freshmen, Universitywide and by Campus: Fall 2005/2006/2007/2008," August 29, 2008 [for table 1-2005/2006/2007] and March 16, 2009 [for table 1-2008], http://statfinder.ucop.edu/library/default .aspx). See also Claudia Luther, "UCLA Admits 12,098 Freshman Students for Fall 2009," *UCLA News*, UCLA Office of Media Relations, April 7, 2009, http://www .newsroom.ucla.edu/portal/ucla/ucla-admits-12-098-freshmen-students-87095 .aspx, which also notes that UCLA had 55,676 undergraduate applicants in 2009.

24. "For example, annual in-state fees to attend UCLA in 2007–08 totaled

$7,711.23. By contrast, tuition and fees to attend the University of Southern California totaled $35,810" (R. Johnson et al., "Gaming the System," 7).

25. For example, the *average* high school GPA for entering black students in 2007 was 4.08, compared to 4.33 for Asian Americans and 4.31 for whites (UCLA Office of Analysis and Information Management [AIM], "New Undergraduate Enrollment Summary, Fall 2007," UCLA, http://www.aim.ucla.edu/Statistics/enrollment/NewStudentsFall2007.pdf [accessed November 7, 2007]; R. Johnson et al., "Gaming the System").

26. A key disparity in California public schools that impacted student access to the UC was the number of Advanced Placement (AP) courses offered at each high school. Students learned college-level material in these courses, and if they passed a standardized AP exam, they could receive college credit. The successful completion of AP courses positively impacted students' college applications. Students taking these courses could also boost their GPAs up to a maximum of 5.0. This value placed on AP courses explains why many students who took them were able to earn GPAs greater than 4.0 (R. Johnson et al., "Gaming the System").

27. While UCLA was regarded by 1984 as the nation's fifth-best graduate research university and its second-best public university, it was still not considered in the early 2000s to be in the ranks of colleges like these and other Ivy League campuses. See Anne C. Roark, "UCLA: New Standing in Academia," *Los Angeles Times*, July 8, 1984, A1.

28. Dr. Geraldine Washington, interview by CAPAA researcher, October 17, 2008.

29. According to a 2008 *Bunche Research Report*, UCLA admissions officials stated that "holistic review requires that applicants be concurrently evaluated on academic achievement, life challenges, and personal achievement. Academic achievement is evaluated based on traditional measures of merit such as test scores, GPA, and college preparatory courses. Personal achievement is measured by student participation in extracurricular activities, honors and awards, volunteer work, and community service. Life challenges include the evaluation of environmental, family, and personal situations that may require extraordinary student effort to overcome. In UCLA's holistic review process, academic achievement receives the most weight in admissions decisions. However, consistent with the core tenet of holistic review, UCLA admissions officials claim they are looking for students who are living up to their full academic potential in light of life challenges and school contexts" (R. Johnson et al., "Gaming the System," 15).

30. "UCLA Adopts a Holistic Approach to Reviewing Freshman Applications; Change Is Most Sweeping Since Systemwide Revisions Five Years Ago," *UCLA News*, UCLA Office of Media Relations, September 28, 2006. http://newsroom.ucla.edu/page.asp?RelNum=7375.

31. R. Johnson et al., "Gaming the System."

32. For a report of their efforts, see Ronald Roach, "Black Student Enrollment

Rebounds at UCLA," *Diverse Issues in Higher Education*, December 13, 2007, http://www.diverseeducation.com/artman/publish/article_10358.shtml.

33. Initial meetings were held in the offices of the Los Angeles branch of the NAACP, only to move between the NAACP, SCLC, and Brotherhood Crusade before stopping and remaining at the Los Angeles Urban League offices.

34. Blair Taylor, interview by CAPAA researcher, October 30, 2008.

35. Jennifer White, interview by CAPAA researcher, June 9, 2008.

36. Nefertiti Austin, interview by CAPAA researcher, June 2, 2008.

37. Greg Akili, interview by CAPAA researcher, March 12, 2008.

38. All names of informants who were students at the time of printing are pseudonyms.

39. Kevin Johnson, interview by CAPAA researcher, April 25, 2008.

40. Karume James, interview by CAPAA researcher, August 16, 2008.

41. "The student Regent is a voting member of The Regents of the University of California [which governs the University of California], attending all meetings of the Board and its Committees and serving a one-year term commencing July 1" (The Regents, "Student Regent," The Regents of the University of California, http://www.universityofcalifornia.edu/regents/studentreg.html).

42. Lamar Hale, interview by CAPAA researcher, March 4, 2008.

43. The direct reference to the university administrator's name has been removed for privacy reasons.

44. Daniel Johnson, interview by CAPAA researcher, April 28, 2008.

45. University of California, "University of California Application, Admissions and Enrollment of California Resident Freshmen for Fall 1989 through 2008," UC Office of the President, Student Affairs, Admissions, CSG, January 2009, http://www.ucop.edu/news/factsheets/flowfrc_8908.pdf.

46. Christina Walter, interview by CAPAA researcher, April 25, 2008.

47. Ernest Smith, interview by CAPAA researcher, August 13, 2008.

48. Nefertiti Austin, interview by CAPAA researcher, June 2, 2008.

49. Lamar Hale, interview by CAPAA researcher, March 4, 2008.

50. Christina Walter, interview by CAPAA researcher, April 25, 2008.

51. Chris Strudwick-Turner, interview by CAPAA researcher, May 20, 2008.

52. Jennifer White, interview by CAPAA researcher, June 9, 2008.

53. See chap. 5 for an account of the Campbell Hall shootings.

54. Daniel Johnson, interview by CAPAA researcher, April 28, 2008.

55. Mandla Kayise, interview by CAPAA researcher, May 6, 2008.

56. See Bowen and Bok, *The Shape of the River*; Lempert, Chambers, and Adams, "Michigan's Minority Graduates in Practice."

57. Chris Strudwick-Turner, interview by CAPAA researcher, May 20, 2008.

58. Ibid.

59. See chap. 15 for more on Rev. Lee's role in Black Los Angeles politics.

60. Rev. Eric Lee, interview by CAPAA researcher, August 19, 2008.

61. Mandla Kayise, interview by CAPAA researcher, May 6, 2008.

62. See A. Kebede, "Grassroots Environmental Organizations in the United States."

63. Ernest Smith, interview by CAPAA researcher, August 13, 2008.

Bibliography

Abdullah, Melina, and Regina Freer. "Pushing and Pulling toward Coalition: The Election of Antonio Villaraigosa and the Black Vote." Paper presented at the American Political Science Association's Annual Conference, Boston, 2006.

———. "Toward a Womanist Leadership Praxis: Electoral/Grassroots Alliances in Black California." In *Racial and Ethnic Politics in California*, edited by Bruce Cain and Sandra Bass. Berkeley: University of California Press, 2008.

Abrahams, Roger. "Playing the Dozens." *Journal of American Folklore* 75, no. 297 (1962): 209–20.

———. *Deep Down in the Jungle: Negro Narrative Folklore from the Streets of Philadelphia*. Chicago: Aldine, 1964.

Adler, Patricia R. "Watts: From Suburb to Black Ghetto." PhD diss., University of Southern California, 1977.

Almaguer, Tomás. *Racial Fault Lines: The Historical Origins of White Supremacy in California*. Berkeley: University of California Press, 1994.

Alonso, Alex. "Territoriality among African American Street Gangs in Los Angeles." Master's thesis, University of Southern California, 1999.

Anderson, Elijah. *A Place on the Corner*. Chicago: University of Chicago Press, 1978.

———. *Streetwise: Race, Class, and Change in an Urban Community*. Chicago: University of Chicago Press, 1990.

———. *Code of the Street: Decency, Violence, and the Moral Life of the Inner City*. New York: Norton, 1999.

Arena, John. "Race and Hegemony: The Neoliberal Transformation of the Black Urban Regime and Working-Class Resistance." *American Behavioral Scientist* 47, no. 3 (2003): 352–80.

Asante, Molefi K., and Ama Mazama. *Encyclopedia of Black Studies*. Newbury Park, CA: Sage, 2005.

Asch, Peter, and Joseph J. Seneca. "The Incidence of Automobile Pollution Control." *Public Finance Review* 6, no. 2 (1978): 193–203.

Ayoub, Millicent Robinson, and Stephen A. Barnett. "Ritualized Verbal Insult in White High School Culture." *Journal of American Folklore* 78 (1965): 337–44.

Baer, Hans, and Merrill Singer. *African-American Religion in the Twentieth Cen-*

tury: Varieties of Protest and Accommodation. Knoxville: University of Tennessee Press, 1992.

Bailey, Amanda, and Joseph M. Hayes. *Who's in Prison: The Changing Demographics of Incarceration.* Vol. 8, no. 1, California Counts. San Francisco: Public Policy Institute of California, 2006.

Baker, Donald. *Crips: The Story of the L.A. Street Gang from 1972–1985.* Los Angeles: Precocious, 1988.

Baker, Ella. "We Need Group-Centered Leadership." In *Let Nobody Turn Us Around: Voices of Resistance, Reform, and Renewal: An African American Anthology,* edited by Manning Marable and Leith Mullings, 398–99. Lanham, MD: Rowman & Littlefield, 2003.

Bancroft, Hubert H. *History of California.* Vol. 1. Berkeley: University of California Press, 1963.

———. *History of California.* Vol. 2. Berkeley: University of California Press, 1963.

Bandini, Hellen E. *History of California.* New York: American Book Company, 1908.

Banks, Patryce. *A "Choc' Let" State of Mind: Poetry and Short Stories.* Elk Grove, CA: Motion Publishing, 2005.

Banks, Phyllis. "Spotlight on Teri Brown-Jackson." *OBS Writer* 1, no. 2 (2008): 7.

Barker, Lucius. *Black Electoral Politics.* New Brunswick, NJ: Transaction Press, 1990.

Barongan, Christy, and Gordon C. Nagayama Hall. "The Influence of Misogynous Rap Music on Sexual Aggression against Women." *Psychology of Women Quarterly* 19, no. 2 (1995): 195–208.

Bass, Charlotta A. *Forty Years: Memoirs from the Pages of a Newspaper.* Los Angeles: self-published, 1960.

Beatty, Phillip, Amanda Petteruti, and Jason Ziedenberg. *The Vortex: The Concentrated Racial Impact of Drug Imprisonment and the Characteristics of Punitive Counties.* Washington, DC: Justice Policy Institute, 2007.

Becker, Howard. *Outsiders: Studies in the Sociology of Deviance.* New York: Free Press, 1963.

Beveridge, Andrew A., and Susan Weber. "Race and Class in the Developing New York and Los Angeles Metropolises, 1940–2000." In *New York and Los Angeles: Politics, Society, and Culture,* edited by David Halle. Chicago: University of Chicago Press, 2004.

Bills, Terry, Robert Gottlieb, and Beverly Pitman. *The Dilemma of Municipal Solid Waste Management: An Examination of the Rise of Incineration, Its Health and Air Impacts, the LANCER Project, and the Feasibility of Alternatives: The UCLA Urban Planning Program: Incineration Study.* Los Angeles: University of California, Graduate School of Architecture and Urban Planning, 1987.

Blackstock, Nelson. *Cointelpro: The FBI's Secret War on Political Freedom.* New York: Anchor Foundation, 1988.

Blakeley, Edward J., and Mary Gail Snyder. *Fortress America: Gated Communities in the United States.* Washington, DC: Brookings Institution Press and Lincoln Institute of Land Policy, 1997.

Bloom, Joshua. "Ally to Win: Black Community Leaders and SEIU's L.A. Security Unionization Campaign." In *Low Wage Worker Organizing and Advocacy: The L.A. Model,* edited by Ruth Milkman, Joshua Bloom and Victor Narro. Ithaca, NY: Cornell University Press, forthcoming 2010.

Bogle, Donald. *Blacks in American Films and Television: An Encyclopedia.* New York: Garland, 1988.

———. *Toms, Coons, Mulattoes, Mammies, and Bucks: An Interpretive History of Blacks in American Films.* New York: Continuum, 1989.

Bollens, John C., and Grant Geyer. *Yorty: Politics of a Constant Candidate.* Pacific Palisades, CA: Palisades Publishers, 1973.

Bond, J. Max. "The Negro in Los Angeles." PhD diss., University of Southern California, 1936.

Bowen, William G., and Derek Bok. *The Shape of the River.* Princeton, NJ: Princeton University Press, 1998.

Braman, Donald. *Doing Time on the Outside: Incarceration and Family Life in Urban American.* Ann Arbor: University of Michigan Press, 2004.

Braman, Donald, and Jenifer Wood. "From One Generation to the Next: How Criminal Sanctions Are Reshaping Family Life in Urban America." In *Prisoners Once Removed: The Impact of Incarceration and Reentry on Children, Families, and Communities,* edited by Jeremy Travis and Michelle Waul. Washington, DC: The Urban Institute, 2003.

Brewer, Rose M., and Nancy A. Heitzeg. "The Racialization of Crime and Punishment: Criminal Justice, Color-Blind Racism, and the Political Economy of the Prison Industrial Complex." *American Behavioral Scientist* 51, no. 5 (2008): 625–44.

Brown, Elaine. *A Taste of Power: A Black Woman's Story.* New York: Anchor Books, 1993.

Brown, Scot. *Fighting for US: Maulana Karenga, the US Organization, and Black Cultural Nationalism.* New York: NYU Press, 2003.

Browning, Rufus, Dale Rogers Marshall, and David H. Tabb. *Racial Politics in American Cities.* Third ed. New York: Longman, 2002.

Building a Regional Voice for Environmental Justice Collaborative. "Building a Regional Voice for Environmental Justice." Los Angeles: Center for Justice, Tolerance & Community, 2004.

Bullard, Robert D. *Dumping in Dixie: Race, Class and Environmental Quality.* Boulder, CO: Westview Press, 1990.

———. *Confronting Environmental Racism: Voices from the Grassroots.* Boston: South End Press, 1993.

Bullard, Robert D., Paul Mohai, Robin Saha, and Beverly Wright. "Toxic Wastes and Race at Twenty: A Report Prepared for the United Church of Christ

Justice & Witness Ministries." Cleveland, Ohio: United Church of Christ, Justice & Witness Ministries, 2007. http://www.ucc.org/environmental-ministries/environment/toxic-waste-20.html.

Bullock, Paul. *Watts: The Aftermath.* New York: Grove Press, 1969.

Bunch, Lonnie G., III. "Introduction." In *Vernon-Central Revisited: A Capsule History,* edited by Neighborhood Reinvestment Corporation for Los Angeles Neighborhood Housing Services Inc. Washington, DC: Neighborhood Reinvestment Corporation/NeighborWorks Publication, 1989.

———. "A Past Not Necessarily Prologue: The Afro-American in Los Angeles." In *20th Century Los Angeles: Power, Promotion, and Social Conflict,* edited by Norman M. Klein and Martin J. Schiesl. Claremont, CA.: Regina Books, 1990.

Burnett, Robert. *The Global Jukebox: The International Music Industry.* London and New York: Routledge, 1996.

Butler, John Sibley. *Entrepreneurship and Self-Help among Black Americans in America.* New York: Harcourt, Brace, Jovanovich, 1971.

Caldeira, Teresa P. R. *City of Walls: Crime, Segregation, and Citizenship in São Paulo.* Berkeley: University of California Press, 2001.

Caldwell, Ben. "Kaos at Ground Zero: Video, Teleconferencing, and Community Networks." *Leonardo* 26, no. 5 (1993): 421–22.

California Department of Corrections and Rehabilitation. "One and Two Year Follow-up Recidivism Rates for All Paroled Felons Released from Prison for the First Time in 2005." 2008. http://www.cdcr.ca.gov/Reports_Research/Offender_Information_Services_Branch/Annual/RECID2/RECID2d2005.pdf.

California Governor's Commission on the Los Angeles Riots. "Violence in the City: An End or a Beginning? A Report of the Governor's Commission on the Los Angeles Riots." Los Angeles: Governor's Commission of the Los Angeles Riots, 1965.

California Legislative Analyst's Office. "California Spending Plan 2007–08: The Budget Act and Related Legislation." Sacramento: State of California, 2007. http://www.lao.ca.gov/2007/spend_plan/spending_plan_07-08.aspx.

California State Assembly. "A Status Report on the King/Drew Medical Center." Los Angeles: The Assembly Select Committee on the Status of Health Facilities, 2004.

Campbell, Marne. "Heaven's Ghetto?: African Americans and Race in Los Angeles 1850–1917." PhD diss., University of California, 2006.

Cannon, Lou. *Official Negligence: How the Rodney King and the Riots Changed the LAPD.* Boulder, CO: Westview Press, 1999.

Cardman, Denise A. "Letter to Federal Communications Commission from Deputy Director." American Bar Association Governmental Affairs Office, 2007. http://www.abanet.org/poladv/letters/crimlaw/2007may01_fccphone_l.pdf (accessed February 2, 2009).

Cerrell Associates, Inc. "Political Difficulties Facing Waste-to-Energy Conversion

Plant Siting." Los Angeles: California Waste Management Board, Technical Information Series, 1984.

Chang, Jeff. *Can't Stop Won't Stop: A History of the Hip-hop Generation.* New York: St. Martin's Press, 2005.

Chapman, Rachel Rebekah. "I Am My Mother's Daughter: The Transfer and Transformation of Motherwit in an Urban African American Community." Master's thesis, University of California, Los Angeles, 1991.

Charles, Roland, Toyomi Igus, and Nathaniel Bellamy. *Life in a Day of Black L.A.: The Way We See It: L.A.'s Black Photographers Present a New Perspective on Their City.* Los Angeles: CAAS Publications, University of California, Los Angeles, 1992.

Churchill, Ward, and Jim Vander Wall. *Agents of Repression: The FBI's Secret Wars against the Black Panther Party and the American Indian Movement.* Boston: South End Press, 1990.

Clark, Kenneth B. "A Charade of Power: Black Students at White Colleges." *Antioch Review* 29, no. 2 (Summer 1969): 145–48.

Clear, Todd R. "The Impacts of Incarceration on Public Safety." *Social Research* 74, no. 2 (2007): 613–30.

Cohen, Cathy. *The Boundaries of Blackness: AIDS and the Breakdown of Black Politics.* Chicago: University of Chicago Press, 1999.

Cole, Luke W., and Sheila R. Foster. *From the Ground Up: Environmental Racism and the Rise of the Environmental Justice Movement.* New York: NYU Press, 2001.

Collins, Keith. *Black Los Angeles: The Maturing of the Ghetto, 1940–1950.* Saratoga, CA: Century Twenty-One Publishing, 1980.

Collins, Patricia Hill. "The Meaning of Black Motherhood in Black Culture and Black Mother/Daughter Relationships." *Sage: A Scholarly Journal on Black Women* 4, no. 2 (1987): 4–11.

———. *Black Feminist Thought: Knowledge, Consciousness, and the Politics of Empowerment.* Boston: Unwin Hyman, 1990.

Comfort, Megan L. "In the Tube at San Quentin: The 'Secondary Prisonization' of Women Visiting Inmates." *Journal of Contemporary Ethnography* 32, no. 1 (2003): 77–107.

Comstock, Gary David. *A Whosoever Church: Welcoming Lesbians and Gay Men into African American Congregations.* Louisville, KY: Westminster John Knox Press, 2001.

Cronon, William, ed. *Uncommon Ground: Rethinking the Human Place in Nature.* New York: Norton, 1996.

Cunningham, Lynn. "Venice, California: From City to Suburb." PhD diss., University of California, Los Angeles, 1976.

Cutler, Cecilia. "Yorkville Crossing: White Teens, Hip-hop and African American English." *Journal of Sociolinguistics* 3, no. 4 (1999): 428–42.

D'Emilio, John. *Sexual Politics, Sexual Communities: The Making of a Homosexual Minority in the United States, 1940–1970.* Chicago: University of Chicago Press, 1983.

Dang, Alain, and Somjen Frazer. "Black Same-Sex Households in the United States: A Report from the 2000 Census." New York: National Gay and Lesbian Task Force Policy Institute and the National Black Justice Coalition, 2004.

Davis, Angela Y. "The Black Woman's Role in the Community of Slaves." *Black Scholar* 3, no. 4 (1971).

Davis, Angela, and Elizabeth Martinez. "Coalition Building among People of Color." In *Inscriptions: Enunciating Our Terms—Women of Color in Collaboration and Conflict.* Santa Cruz: University California, Center for Cultural Studies, 1994.

Davis, Mike. *City of Quartz: Excavating the Future in Los Angeles.* New York: Vintage Books, 1990, 1992.

Dawson, Michael. *Black Visions: The Roots of Contemporary African-American Political Ideologies.* Chicago: University of Chicago Press, 1991.

Dear, Michael J., ed. *From Chicago to L.A.: Making Sense of Urban Theory.* Thousand Oaks, CA: Sage, 2002.

De Graaf, Lawrence B. "The City of Black Angels: Emergence of the Los Angeles Ghetto, 1890–1930." *Pacific Historical Review* 39, no. 3 (1970): 323–52.

De Graaf, Lawrence B., K. Mulroy, and Q. Taylor eds. *Seeking El Dorado: African Americans in California.* Berkeley: University of California Press, 2001.

Decker, Scott H., and G. David Curry. "Gangs, Gang Homicides, and Gang Loyalty: Organized Crimes or Disorganized Criminals." *Journal of Criminal Justice* 30, no. 4 (2002): 343–52.

Delp, Linda, and Katie Quan. "Homecare Worker Organizing in California: An Analysis of a Successful Strategy." *Labor Studies Journal* 27 (2002): 1–23.

Deriane, Muna. "Benjamin Horowitz." *Resonance.* Vol. 1, no. 1, February 1997.

Domanick, Joe. *To Protect and to Serve: The LAPD's Century of War in the City of Dreams.* New York: Pocket Books, 1994.

Dowie, Mark. *Losing Ground: American Environmentalism at the Close of the Twentieth Century.* Cambridge, MA: MIT Press, 1995.

Drake, St. Clair, and Horace Cayton. *Black Metropolis: A Study of Negro Life in a Northern City.* New York: Harcourt Brace, 1945.

Du Bois, W. E. B. *The Philadelphia Negro.* New York: Schocken, 1999.

———. "Colored California." *Crisis* 6 (August 1913): 192–96.

Dymski, Gary, and John Veitch. "Financing the Future in Los Angeles: From Depression to 21st Century." In *Rethinking Los Angeles*, edited by Michael Dear, H. Eric Shockman, and Gregg Hise, 35–55. Thousand Oaks, CA: Sage, 1996.

Egan, Patrick J., and Kenneth Sherrill. "California's Proposition 8: What Happened, and What Does the Future Hold?" Commissioned by the Evelyn &

Walter Haas, Jr. Fund in San Francisco. Released by the National Gay and Lesbian Task Force Policy Institute, 2009.

Ellingson, Stephen, Nelson Tebbe, Martha Van Haitsma, and Edward O. Laumann. "Religion and the Politics of Sexuality." *Journal of Contemporary Ethnography* 30, no. 3 (2001): 3–55.

Estrada, Leobardo F., and Sylvia Sensiper. "Mending the Politics of Division in Post-Rebellion L.A." In *South-Central Los Angeles: Anatomy of an Urban Crisis*, 123–37. Los Angeles: Lewis Center for Regional Policy Studies, 1993.

Ettinger, David S. "The Quest to Desegregate Los Angeles Schools." *Los Angeles Lawyer* 26, no. 1 (2003): 55–67.

Evans-Campbell, T. "Historical Trauma in American Indian/Native Alaska Communities: A Multilevel Framework for Exploring Impacts on Individuals, Families, and Communities." *Journal of Interpersonal Violence* 23, no. 3 (2008): 316–38.

Farmer, Paul. "The House of the Dead: Tuberculosis and Incarceration." In *Invisible Punishment: The Collateral Consequences of Mass Imprisonment*, edited by Marc Mauer and Meda Chesney-Lind, 239–57. New York: New Press, 2002.

Flamming, Douglas. *Bound for Freedom: Black Los Angeles in Jim Crow America*. Berkeley: University of California Press, 2005.

Fogelson, Robert M. *The Fragmented Metropolis: Los Angeles, 1850–1930*. Berkeley: University of California Press, 1967.

Foley, Barbara. "History, Fiction, and the Ground Between: The Uses of the Documentary Mode in Black Literature." *PMLA* 95 (May 1980): 389–403.

Forbes, Jack D. "The Early African Heritage of California." In *Seeking El Dorado: African Americans in California*, edited by Lawrence B. De Graaf, K. Mulroy and Q. Taylor, 73–97. Berkeley: University of California Press, 2001.

Frazier, Franklin E. *The Negro Family in Chicago*. Chicago: University of Chicago Press, 1932.

———. *The Negro Family in the United States*. New York: Dryden Press, 1939.

Freeman, A. Myrick, III. "Air Pollution and Property Values: A Methodological Comment." *The Review of Economics and Statistics* 53, no. 4 (1971): 415–16.

Freire, Paolo. *Pedagogy of the Oppressed*. 30th Anniversary ed. New York: Continuum, 2000.

Fricke, Jim, and Charles Ahearn. *Yes Yes Y'all: The Experience Music Project Oral History of Hip-Hop's First Decade*. Cambridge, MA: Da Capo Press, 2002.

Gamblo, Vanessa Northington. *Making a Place for Ourselves: The Black Hospital Movement, 1920–1945*. New York: Oxford University Press, 1995.

Gans, Herbert. *Deciding What's News*. New York: Pantheon, 1979.

Garland, David. *Mass Imprisonment: Social Causes and Consequences*. London and Thousand Oaks, CA: Sage, 2001.

Gates, Gary, Holning Lau, and R. Bradley Spears. "Race and Ethnicity of Same-

Sex Couples in California." The Williams Project on Sexual Orientation Law and Public Policy, UCLA School of Law, February 2006. http://www.law.ucla .edu/williamsinstitute/publications/Race_and_ethnicity_of_same-sex_couples _in_california.pdf.

George, Nelson. *The Death of Rhythm & Blues*. New York: Plume, 1988.

Gianessi, Leonard, H. M. Peskin, and E. Wolff. "The Distributional Effects of Uniform Air Pollution Policy in the U.S." *Quarterly Journal of Economics* (1979): 281–301.

Gladwell, Malcolm. *The Tipping Point: How Little Things Can Make a Big Difference*. Boston: Little, Brown, 2002.

Goffman, Erving. *Asylums: Essays on the Social Situation of Mental Patients and Other Inmates*. New York: Doubleday, 1961.

Gottlieb, Robert, Mark Vallianatos, Regina Freer, and Peter Dreier. *The Next Los Angeles: The Struggle for a Livable City*. Berkeley: University of California Press, 2005.

Gramsci, Antonio. *Selections from the Prison Notebooks*. New York: International Publishers, 1971.

Gray, Herman. *Watching Race: Television and the Struggle for Blackness*. Minneapolis: University of Minnesota Press, 2004.

Griffin, Horace L. *Their Own Receive Them Not: African American Lesbians and Gays in Black Churches*. Cleveland: Pilgrim Press, 2006.

Guinier, Lani. *Tyranny of the Majority: Fundamental Fairness in Democracy*. New York: Free Press, 1994.

Hairston, Creasie Finney. *Focus on Children with Incarcerated Parents: An Overview of the Research Literature*. Baltimore: The Annie E. Casey Foundation, 2007.

Halle, David, Robert Gedeon, and Andrew A. Beveridge. "Residential Separation and Segregation, Racial and Latino Identity, and the Racial Composition of Each City." In *New York and Los Angeles: Politics, Society and Culture: A Comparative View*, edited by David Halle, 150–90. Chicago: University of Chicago Press, 2004.

Harman, Jennifer, J., Smith, E. Vernon, and Louisa C. Egan. "The Impact of Incarceration on Intimate Relationships." *Criminal Justice and Behavior* 34 (2007): 794–815. http://cjb.sagepub.com (accessed January 24, 2009).

Harris, Mary G. *Cholas: Latino Girls and Gangs*. New York: AMS Press, 1988.

Hayden, Dolores. *The Power of Place: Urban Landscapes as Public History*. Cambridge, MA: MIT Press, 1995.

Herek, Gregory M., and John P. Capitanio. "Black Heterosexuals' Attitudes toward Lesbians and Gay Men in the United States." *Journal of Sex Research* 32, no. 2 (1995): 95–105.

Herman, Edward S., and Noam Chomsky. *Manufacturing Consent: The Political Economy of the Mass Media*. New York: Pantheon, 1988.

Hilliard, David, and Lewis Cole. *This Side of Glory: The Autobiography of David Hilliard and the Story of the Black Panther Party*. Boston: Little, Brown, 1993.

Honey, Michael K. *Going Down Jericho Road: The Memphis Strike, Martin Luther King's Last Campaign*. New York: Norton, 2007.

Hooks, Bell. *Ain't I a Woman: Black Women and Feminism*. Boston: South End Press, 1981.

Horne, Gerald. *Fire This Time: The Watts Uprising and the 1960s*. Charlottesville: University Press of Virginia, 1995.

Hudson, Karen E., and Paul R. Williams. *Paul R. Williams, Architect: A Legacy of Style*. New York: Rizzoli, 2000.

Hughes, Everett C. "Institutional Office and the Person." *American Journal of Sociology* 43, no. 3 (1937): 404–13.

———. "Careers." *Qualitative Sociology* 20, no. 3 (1997): 389–97.

Hunt, Darnell M. *Screening the Los Angeles "Riots": Race, Seeing, and Resistance*. New York: Cambridge University Press, 1997.

———. *O. J. Simpson Facts & Fictions: News Rituals in the Construction of Reality*. Cambridge: Cambridge University Press, 1999.

———. "Representing 'Los Angeles': Media, Space and Place." In *From Chicago to L.A.: Making Sense of Urban Theory*, edited by Michael J. Dear. Thousand Oaks, CA: Sage, 2002.

———. *Channeling Blackness: Studies on Television and Race in America*. New York: Oxford University Press, 2005.

Hussey, Andrew. "Le Temps Modernes." *Observer*, April 2, 2006.

Hutchinson, Sikivu. "The Northern Drive: Black Women in Transit." In *Gender and Planning: A Reader*, edited by Susan S. Fainstein and Lisa J. Servon, 256–74. New Brunswick, NJ: Rutgers University Press, 2005.

Hutson, H. Range, Deidre Anglin, Demetrios N. Kyriancou, Joel Hart, and Kelvin Spears. "The Epidemic of Gang-Related Homicides in Los Angeles County from 1979 to 1994." *Journal of the American Medical Association* 274, no. 13 (1995): 1031–36.

Jackson-Brown, Grace. "Media Coverage of South Central Los Angeles, the *Los Angeles Times* and the *Los Angeles Sentinel*, 1990–2000." PhD diss., Indiana University, Bloomington, 2005.

Jah, Yusuf, and Sister Shah'Keyah. *Uprising: Crips and Bloods Tell the Story of America's Youth in the Crossfire*. New York: Scribner, 1995.

Jeter, James Philip. "Rough Flying: The California Eagle (1879–1965)." Paper presented at the 12th Annual Conference of the American Journalism Historian's Association, Salt Lake City, Utah, October 7, 1993.

Johnson, Daniel M., and Rex R. Campbell. *Black Migration in America: A Social Demographic History*. Durham, NC: Duke University Press, 1981.

Johnson, James, Lee Anderson Jackson, and Leslie Gatto. "Violent Attitudes and

Deferred Academic Aspirations: Deleterious Effects of Exposure to Rap Music." *Basic and Applied Social Psychology* 16, no. 1 (1995): 27–41.

Johnson, James, Mike Adams, Leslie Ashburn, and William Reed. "Differential Gender Effects of Exposure to Rap Music on African American Adolescents' Acceptance of Teen Dating Violence." *Sex Roles* 33, no. 7 (1995): 597–605.

Johnson, Maria. "Black Women Electric Guitarists and Authenticity in the Blues." In *Black Women and Music: More Than the Blues*, edited by Eileen M. Hayes and Linda F. Williams. Urbana: University of Illinois Press, 2007.

Johnson, Robin N., Cynthia Mosqueda, Ana-Christina Ramón, and Darnell M. Hunt. "Gaming the System: Inflation, Privilege, and the Under-representation of African American Students at the University of California." *Bunche Research Report*. Vol. 4, no. 1. Los Angeles: Ralph J. Bunche Center for African American Studies, UCLA, 2008.

Johnson-Mitchell, Cheryl. "When Is a Collect Call Cruel and Unusual Punishment?" Panel discussion summary. 2002 Mid-year Meeting of the National Association of State Utility Advocates, Utility Consumer Protection Committee, Austin, Texas, 2002.

Joint Commission on Accreditation of Healthcare Organizations. "2001 Hospital Performance Report for Martin Luther King Jr./Charles R. Drew Medical Center." Oakbrook Terrace, IL, 2001.

———. "1998 Hospital Performance Report for Martin Luther King Jr./Charles R. Drew Medical Center." Oakbrook Terrace, IL, 1998.

Jones, William P. "The Infrastructure of South-Central Los Angeles: Unions, Public-Service and the New Black Middle Class." Paper presented at the Center for the Study of Work, Labor, and Democracy, UC Santa Barbara, Santa Barbara, February 23, 2009.

Jones-Wilson, Faustine C. "Race, Realities, and American Education: Two Sides of the Coin." *Journal of Negro Education* 59, no. 2 (Spring 1990): 119–28.

Junn, Jane. "Assimilating or Coloring Participation: Gender, Race and Democratic Political Participation." In *Women Transforming Politics: An Alternative Reader*, edited by Cathy Cohen, Kathy Jones, and Joan Tronto. New York: NYU Press, 1997.

Katz, Jack. "Metropolitan Crime Myths." In *New York and Los Angeles: Politics, Society, and Culture*, edited by David Halle. Chicago: University of Chicago Press, 2004.

Kebede, AlemSeghed, "Grassroots Environmental Organizations in the United States: A Gramscian Analysis." *Sociological Inquiry*, 75, no. 1 (2005): 81–108.

Kelley, Robin D. G. *Yo' Mama's Disfunktional!: Fighting the Culture Wars in Urban America*. Boston: Beacon Press, 1997.

Kennedy, Rick, and Randy Mcnutt. *Little Labels—Big Sound*. Indianapolis: Indiana University Press, 1999.

Kerr, Clark. "The California Master Plan for Higher Education of 1960: An Ex

Ante View." In *Higher Education Cannot Escape History: Issues for the Twenty-First Century*, edited by Clark Kerr, Marian L. Gade, and Maureen Kawaoka, 111–28. Albany: State University of New York Press, 1994.

King, Ryan S. *Disparity by Geography: The War on Drugs in America's Cities*. Washington, DC: The Sentencing Project, 2008. http://www.sentencingproject .org/PublicationDetails.aspx?PublicationID=614.

Klein, Malcolm. *Street Gangs and Street Workers*. Englewood Cliffs, NJ: Prentice-Hall, 1971.

Kochman, Thomas. *Black and White Styles in Conflict*. Chicago: University of Chicago Press, 1981.

Labov, William. *Sociolinguistic Patterns*. Philadelphia: University of Pennsylvania Press, 1972.

Lapp, R. M. *Blacks in Gold Rush California*. New Haven, CT: Yale University Press, 1977.

Lark, Raymond. "Drawings and Paintings by an Afro-American Artist." *Leonardo* 15, no. 1 (Winter 1982): 7–12.

Lee, Jooyoung. "Battlin' on the Corner: Techniques for Sustaining Play." *Social Problems* 56, no. 3 (2009): 578–98.

Lefebvre, Henri. *The Production of Space*. Oxford, UK: Blackwell, 1974.

Lempert, Richard O., David L. Chambers, and Terry K. Adams. "Michigan's Minority Graduates in Practice: The River Runs through Law School." *Law and Social Inquiry* 25 (2000): 395–506.

LeoGrande, William. "Did the Prestige Press Miss the Nicaraguan Drug Story?" *Harvard International Journal of Press/Politics* 2, no. 4 (1997): 10–31.

Lester, James P., David W. Allen, and Kelly M. Hill. *Environmental Injustice in the United States: Myths and Realities*. Boulder, CO: Westview Press, 2001.

Lewis, Oscar. *Five Families: Mexican Case Studies in the Culture of Poverty*. New York: Basic Books, 1959.

———. *La Vida: A Puerto Rican Family in the Culture of Poverty—San Juan and New York*. New York: Random House, 1966.

Lewis, Sandra. "Background Information: Service Area of the Los Angeles County–Martin Luther King Jr. General Hospital Drew Postgraduate Medical School." Los Angeles: Department of Community Medicine, 1971.

Lewis, Samella S. *African American Art and Artists*. Berkeley: University of California Press, 1990.

———. *African American Art for Young People*. Vol. 1. Los Angeles: Unity Works Press, 1991.

Liebow, Elliott. *Tally's Corner: A Study of Negro Streetcorner Men*. New York: Rowman & Littlefield, 2003.

Los Angeles County Probation Department and the Youth Studies Center. "Study of Delinquent Gangs: Progress Report." Los Angeles: University of Southern California, 1962.

Lott, Tommy. *The Invention of Race: Black Culture and the Politics of Representation*. Oxford, UK: Blackwell, 1998.

Low, Setha. *Behind the Gates: Life, Security and the Pursuit of Happiness in Fortress America*. New York: Routledge, 2003.

Lubiano, Wahneema. "'But Compared to What?': Reading Realism, Representation, and Essentialism in *School Daze*, *Do the Right Thing*, and the Spike Lee Discourse." *Black American Literature Forum* 25, no. 2 (Summer 1991): 253–82.

Mahon, Maureen. "Race, Gender and Genre: The Power Dynamics of Rock." In *African American Music: An Introduction*, edited by Mellonee V. Burnim and Portia K. Maultsby. New York: Routledge, 2006.

Marable, Manning. *Black Leadership*. New York: Columbia University Press, 1998.

Martin, Darnise C. *Beyond Christianity: African Americans in a New Thought Church*. New York: NYU Press, 2005.

Mason, William M. *Los Angeles under the Spanish Flag*. Burbank, CA: Southern California Genealogical Society, 2004.

Massey, Douglas S., and Nancy A. Denton. *American Apartheid: Segregation and the Making of the Underclass*. Cambridge, MA: Harvard University Press, 1993.

Massoglia, Michael. "Incarceration, Health, and Racial Disparities in Health." *Law and Society Review* 42, no. 2 (2008): 275–306.

Matsuoka, Martha. "Building Healthy Communities from the Ground Up: Environmental Justice in California." National City, CA: Environmental Health Coalition, 2003. http://www.environmentalhealth.org/PDFs/PDFs_Archive/EJ Report.pdf.

Mauer, Marc, and Ryan S. King. *Uneven Justice: State Rates of Incarceration by Race and Ethnicity*. Washington, DC: The Sentencing Project, 2007. http://www .sentencingproject.org/PublicationDetails.aspx?PublicationID=593.

Maxson, Cheryl, and Malcolm Klein. "Defining Gang Homicide: An Updated Look at Member and Motive Approaches." In *Gangs in America*, edited by C. R. Huff, 3–20. Thousand Oaks, CA: Sage, 1996.

McEvilley, Thomas. *Art & Otherness: Crisis in Cultural Identity*. Kingston, NY: Documentext/McPherson, 1992.

McKenzie, Evan. *Privatopia: Homeowner Associations and the Rise of Residential Private Government*. New Haven, CT: Yale University Press, 1994.

McQueeney, Krista. "'We Are God's Children, Y'all': Race, Gender, and Sexuality in Lesbian- and Gay-Affirming Congregations." *Social Problems* 56, no. 1 (2009): 151–73.

McWhorter, John. *Winning the Race: Beyond the Crisis in Black America*. New York: Penguin, 2005.

Milkman, Ruth. *L.A. Story: Immigrant Workers and the Future of the U.S. Labor Movement*. New York: Russell Sage Foundation, 2006.

Miller, Loren. *The Petitioners: The Story of the Supreme Court of the United States and the Negro*. Cleveland: Meridian Books, 1967.

Miramontes, Bonita. "Research Resource Materials on the Origins of 'Nigger Slough' in the Dominguez Family Papers." Carson, CA: Ranch San Pedro Museum Reference Collection, California State University, Dominguez Hills, 1977.

Miranda, Dave, and Michael Caels. "Rap Music Genres and Deviant Behaviors in French-Canadian Adolescents." *Journal of Youth and Adolescence* 33, no. 2 (2004): 113–22.

Mitchell-Kernan, Claudia. "Language Behavior in a Black Urban Community." In *Monographs of the Language-Behavior Research Laboratory.* PhD diss., University of California–Berkeley, February 1971.

———. "Signifying and Marking: Two Afro-American Speech Acts." In *Directions in Sociolinguistics; the Ethnography of Communication,* edited by John J. Gumperz and Dell Hymes, 161–79. New York: Holt, Rinehart & Winston, 1972.

Mohai, Paul, and Bunyan Bryant. "Is There a 'Race' Effect on Concern for Environmental Quality?" *Public Opinion Quarterly* 62, no. 4 (1998): 475–505.

Moore, Mignon R. "Invisible Families: Gay Identities, Relationships and Motherhood among Black Women." Unpublished manuscript, University of California, Los Angeles.

Mosher, Lawrence. "Environmentalists Question Whether to Retreat or Stay on the Offensive." *National Journal* 12 (1980): 2116–21.

Myers, Brenda T. "An Afternoon with Dick Griffey: His Philosophy and Thoughts on Business, with Reflections." *African American Review* 29, no. 2 (1995): 341–46.

National Advisory Commission on Civil Disorders. "Report of the National Advisory Commission on Civil Disorders." New York: Bantam Books, 1968.

National Coalition of Anti-Violence Programs (NCAVP). "Anti-Lesbian, Gay, Bisexual and Transgender Violence." NCAVP, 2008. http://www.ncavp.org/common/document_files/Reports/2007HVReportFINAL.pdf.

Ngozi-Brown, Scot. "The US Organization, Maulana Karenga, and Conflict with the Black Panther Party: A Critique of Sectarian Influences on Historical Discourse." *Journal of Black Studies* 28, no. 2 (1997): 157–70.

O'Conner, George M. "The Negro and the Police in Los Angeles." Master's thesis, University of Southern California, 1955.

O'Toole, J. *Watts and Woodstock: Identity and Culture in the United States and South Africa.* New York: Holt, Rinehart & Winston, 1973.

Omi, Michael, and Howard Winant. *Racial Formation in the United States: From the 1960s to the 1990s.* New York: Routledge, 1994.

Ong, Paul, Theresa Firestine, Deirdre Preiffer, Oiyan Poon, and Linda Tran. "The State of South L.A." Los Angeles: UCLA School of Public Affairs, 2008.

Park, Robert E., Ernest W. Burgess, Roderick D. McKenzie, and Louis Wirth. *The City.* Chicago: University of Chicago Press, 1926.

Pattillo, Mary. *Black on the Block: The Politics of Race and Class in the City*. Chicago: University of Chicago Press, 2007.

Pattillo-McCoy, Mary. *Black Picket Fences: Privilege and Peril among the Black Middle Class*. Chicago: University of Chicago Press, 1999.

Pattillo, Mary, David Weiman, and Bruce Western, eds. *Imprisoning America: The Social Effects of Mass Incarceration*. New York: Russell Sage Foundation, 2004.

Payne, J. Gregory, and Scott C. Ratzan. *Tom Bradley, the Impossible Dream: A Biography*. Santa Monica, CA: Roundtable Press, 1986.

Perry, Anthony. *Original Gang Truce*. Beverly Hills, CA: Ant Valley Book Productions, 1995.

Person-Lynn, Kwaku. "Insider Perspectives on the American Afrikan Popular Music Industry." In *California Soul*, edited by Eddie Meadows and Jacqueline DjeDje. Los Angeles: University of California Press, 1998.

Pitts, Steven C. *Job Quality and Black Workers: An Examination of the San Francisco Bay Area, Los Angeles, Chicago, and New York*. Berkeley: Center for Labor Research and Education, University of California–Berkeley, 2007.

Porter, Eric. *What Is This Thing Called Jazz? African American Musicians as Artists, Critics, and Activists*. Berkeley: University of California Press, 2002.

Posner, Gerald. *Motown: Music, Money, Sex, and Power*. New York: Random House, 2002.

Quinn, Eithne. *Nuthin' but a "G" Thang : The Culture and Commerce of Gangsta Rap*. New York: Columbia University Press, 2004.

Ralph J. Bunche Center for African American Studies. "Separate but Certainly Not Equal: 2003 CAPAA Findings." Vol. 1, no. 2. Los Angeles: Ralph J. Bunche Center for African American Studies, UCLA, 2004.

———. "Admissions and Omissions: How 'the Numbers' Are Used to Exclude Deserving Students, 2005–2006 CAPAA Findings." Vol. 3, no. 2. Los Angeles: Ralph J. Bunche Center for African American Studies, UCLA, 2006.

———. "'Merit' Matters: Race, Myth & UCLA Admissions, 2006 CAPAA Findings." Vol. 3, no. 3. Los Angeles: Ralph J. Bunche Center for African American Studies, UCLA, 2006.

Reynolds, Joel R. "LANCER and the Vernon Incinerator: Protecting Communities from the Projects That 'Have to Go Somewhere . . .'/Chapter 5: Environmental Justice." In *Everyday Heroes Protect the Air We Breathe, the Water We Drink, and Natural Areas We Prize: Thirty-Five Years of the California Environmental Quality Act*. Sacramento: Planning and Conservation League Foundation and The California League of Conservation Voters, 2005.

Richardson, John D., and Karen Lancendorfer. "Framing Affirmative Action: The Influence of Race on Newspaper Editorial Responses to the University of Michigan Cases." *Harvard International Journal of Press/Politics* 9, no. 74 (2004).

Riggs, Thomas. *St. James Guide to Black Artists*. Detroit: St. James Press, 1997.

Roberts, D. E. "The Social and Moral Cost of Mass Incarceration in African American Communities." *Stanford Law Review* 56 (2004): 1271–1306.

Robinson, Cedric. *Black Movements in America*. New York: Routledge, 1997.

Rooks, Noliwe M. *White Money/Black Power: The Surprising History of African American Studies and the Crisis of Race in Higher Education*. Boston: Beacon Press, 1998.

Sandoval, S. J. "Ghetto Growing Pains: The Impact of Negro Migration on the City of Los Angeles." Master's thesis, California State University, Fullerton, 1974.

Sanjek, David. "One Size Does Not Fit All: The Precarious Position of the African American Entrepreneur in Post–World War II American Popular Music." *American Music* 15, no. 4 (1997): 535–62.

Schiesl, Martin J. "Behind the Badge: The Police and Social Discontent in Los Angeles since 1950." In *20th Century Los Angeles: Power, Promotion, and Social Conflict*, edited by Norman Klein and Martin Schiesl, 101–30. Claremont, CA: Regina Books, 1990.

Schou, Nick. *Kill the Messenger*. New York: Nation Books, 2006.

Schrank, Sarah. *Art and the City: Civic Imagination and Cultural Authority in Los Angeles*. Philadelphia: University of Pennsylvania Press, 2009.

Schudson, Michael. *The Power of News*. Cambridge, MA: Harvard University Press, 1995.

Sides, Josh. *L.A. City Limits: African American Los Angeles from the Great Depression to the Present*. Berkeley: University of California Press, 2003.

Simpson, Richard. *Soho: The Artist in the City*. Chicago: University of Chicago Press, 1981.

Smith, R. J. *The Great Black Way: L.A. in the 1940s and the Lost African-American Renaissance*. New York: Public Affairs, 2006.

Sociocultural Research Consultants. "Ethnonotes: The Future of Mixed Methods Research." Los Angeles: Sociocultural Research Consultants, 2006–2007. http://www.ethnonotes.com.

Soja, Edward W., and Allen J. Scott. "Introduction to Los Angeles: City and Region." In *The City: Los Angeles and Urban Theory at the End of the Twentieth Century*, edited by Scott Allen and Edward Soja. Berkeley: University of California Press, 1996.

Soja, Edward W. *Postmetropolis: Critical Studies of Cities and Regions*. Oxford, UK: Blackwell, 2000.

Spergel, Irving. *The Youth Gang Problem: A Community Approach*. Oxford: Oxford University Press, 1995.

Stack, Carol. *All Our Kin*. New York: Basic Books, 1974.

Stanford, Karin L. *Beyond the Boundaries: Reverend Jesse Jackson in International Affairs*, SUNY Series in Afro-American Studies. Albany: State University of New York Press, 1997.

Stotzer, Rebecca. "Gender Identity and Hate Crimes: Violence against Transgender

People in Los Angeles County." *Sexuality Research and Social Policy* 5, no. 1 (2008): 43–52.

Streatfeild, Dominic. *Cocaine: An Unauthorized Biography.* New York: Thomas Dunne Books/St. Martin's Press, 2002.

Swearingen, Wesley. *FBI Secrets: An Agent Exposé.* Boston: South End Press, 1995.

Taylor, Dorceta. "Can the Environmental Movement Attract and Maintain the Support of Minorities?" In *Race and the Incidence of Environmental Hazards: A Time for Discourse,* edited by Bunyan I. Bryant and Paul Mohai. Boulder, CO: Westview Press, 1992.

——. "Race, Class, Gender and American Environmentalism." U.S. Department of Agriculture, Forest Service, Pacific Northwest Research Station, 2002.

The PEW Center on the States. *One in 100: Behind Bars in America 2008.* New York: PEW Charitable Trusts, 2008. http://www.pewcenteronthestates.org/uploadedFiles/Onepercent2oinpercent2o1oo.pdf.

Tolnay, Scott, and Suzanne C. Eichenlaub. "Inequality in the West: Racial and Ethnic Variation in Occupational Status and Returns to Education, 1940–2000." *Social Science History* 31, no. 4 (2007): 471–507.

Travis, Jeremy, and Michelle Waul, eds. *Prisoners Once Removed: The Impact of Incarceration and Reentry on Children, Families, and Communities.* Washington, DC: The Urban Institute, 2003.

Travis, Jeremy. *But They All Come Back: Facing the Challenges of Prisoner Reentry.* Washington, DC: The Urban Institute, 2005.

Tucker, Sherrie. *Swing Shift: "All-Girl" Bands of the 1940s.* Durham, NC: Duke University Press, 2000.

Tyler, Bruce M. "Black Radicalism in Southern California, 1950–1982." PhD diss., University of California, Los Angeles, 1983.

U.S. Census Bureau. "Seventh Census of the United States, 1850 (NARA Microfilm Series M432, Roll 35)." Washington, DC: National Archives and Records Administration, 1850.

——. "Tenth Census of the United States, 1880 (NARA Microfilm Series T9, Roll 67)." Washington, DC: National Archives and Records Administration, 1880.

——. "Twelfth Census of the United States, 1900 (NARA Microfilm Series T623, Roll 89)." Washington, DC: National Archives and Records Administration, 1900.

——. "Thirteenth Census of the United States, 1910 (NARA Microfilm Series T624, Roll 81)." Washington, DC: National Archives and Records Administration, 1910.

U.S. Congress, House Un-American Activities Committee (HUAC). "Subversive Influences in Riots, Looting, and Burning, Pt. 1 (Los Angeles-Watts), October 25, 26, 31, 1967." Washington, DC: Government Printing Office, 1967, 1968.

——. "Subversive Influences in Riots, Looting, and Burning, Pt. 3 (Los Angeles-

Watts), November 28, 29, 30, 1967." Washington, DC: Government Printing Office, 1967, 1968.

U.S. Department of Health and Human Services, Substance Abuse and Mental Health Services Administration, Office of Applied Studies. "National Survey on Drug Use and Health, 2007." Computer file distributed by Inter-university Consortium for Political and Social Research: ICPSR23782-v1. Research Triangle Park, NC: Research Triangle Institute, 2007. http://www.icpsr.umich.edu/SAMHDA/using-data/quick-tables.html.

U.S. Department of Justice. "Recidivism of Prisoners Released in 1994, Bureau of Justice Statistics Special Report (NCJ 193427)." Washington, DC: U.S. Department of Justice, 2002. http://www.ojp.usdoj.gov/bjs/pub/pdf/rpr94.pdf.

U.S. Government Accountability Office. "African American Children in Foster Care: Additional HHS Assistance Needed to Help States Reduce Proportion in Care." GAO-07-816. Washington, DC, 2007.

U.S. Senate, Select Committee to Study Governmental Operations with Respects to Intelligence Activities. "Supplementary Detailed Staff Reports on Intelligence Activities and the Rights of Americans, Book III." Washington, DC, April 23, 1976.

Umemoto, Karen. *The Truce: Lessons from an L.A. Gang War*. Ithaca, NY: Cornell University Press, 2006.

United Way of Greater Los Angeles, and Los Angeles Urban League. "The State of Black Los Angeles, 2005 Full Report." Los Angeles: United Way and Los Angeles Urban League, 2005. http://www.unitedwayla.org/pages/rpts%5Fresource/stateofblackla/SBLA%5Ffinal%5Ffull%5Frpt%5F090905.pdf.

van Dijk, Teun A. *Elite Discourse and Racism*. Newbury Park, CA: Sage, 1993.

Vigil, James D. "Cholos and Gangs: Cultural Change and Street Youth in Los Angeles." In *Gangs in America*, edited by Ronald D. Huff, 146–62. Newbury Park, CA: Sage, 1990.

Waldinger, Roger, and Michael I. Lichter. *How the Other Half Works: Immigration and the Social Organization of Labor*. Berkeley: University of California Press, 2003.

Walker, Juliet. *The History of Black Business in America: Capitalism, Race, Entrepreneurship*. New York: Macmillan, 1998.

Washington, Joseph. *Black Sects and Cults*. Garden City, NY: Doubleday, 1972.

Webb, Gary. *Dark Alliance: The CIA, the Contras, and the Crack Cocaine Explosion*. New York: Seven Stories Press, 1999.

Western, Bruce. *Punishment and Inequality in America*. New York: Russell Sage Foundation, 2006.

Wheeler, Gordon. *Black California: The History of African Americans in the Golden State*. New York: Hippocrene Books, 1993.

White, Charles, and Benjamin Horowitz. *Images of Dignity: The Drawings of Charles White*. Los Angeles: W. Ritchie Press, 1967.

Widener, Daniel. *Black Arts West: Culture and Struggle in Black Los Angeles, 1942–1992.* Durham, NC: Duke University Press, 2009.

Williams, Brett. *Upscaling Downtown: Stalled Gentrification in Washington, D.C.* Ithaca, NY: Cornell University Press, 1988.

Williams, Joyce E., and Ron Ladd. "On the Relevance of Education for Black Liberation." *Journal of Negro Education* 47, no. 3 (Summer 1978): 266–82.

Williams, Stanley Tookie. *Blue Rage, Black Redemption.* Pleasant Hill, CA: Damamli, 2005.

Williamson, Joy A. "In Defense of Themselves: The Black Student Struggles for Success and Recognition at Predominantly White Colleges and Universities." *Journal of Negro Education* 68, no. 1 (1999): 92–105.

Willis, Deborah. *Reflections in Black: A History of Black Photographers, 1840 to the Present.* New York: Norton, 2000.

Wilson, William Julius. *The Declining Significance of Race: Blacks and Changing American Institutions.* Chicago: University of Chicago Press, 1980.

——. *The Truly Disadvantaged: The Inner City, the Underclass, and Urban Social Policy.* Chicago: University of Chicago Press, 1987.

——. *When Work Disappears: The World of the New Urban Poor.* New York: Random House, 1996.

Windsor, Charles E. "A Summary of the History and Plan for Development of the Los Angeles County Martin Luther King Jr. General Hospital." Hospital administrator document. Los Angeles: Martin Luther King Jr. General Hospital, 1972.

Wingood, Gina M., Ralph J. DiClemente, Jay M. Bernhardt, Kathy Harrington, Susan L. Davies, Alyssa Robillard, and Edward W. Hook III. "A Prospective Study of Exposure to Rap Music Videos and African American Female Adolescents' Health." *American Journal Public Health* 93, no. 3 (2003): 437–39.

Winton, Sonya. *All Things Being Equal: The Politics of Environmental (In)Justice.* New York: NYU Press, forthcoming.

Wolch, Jennifer. *Malign Neglect: Homelessness in an American City.* San Francisco: Jossey-Bass, 1993.

Wormley, Roy. *World Prison Population List.* 5th ed., Findings, 234. London: Home Office, 2003. http://www.homeoffice.gov.uk/rds/pdfs2/r188.pdf.

Zieger, Robert H. *For Jobs and Freedom: Race and Labor in America since 1865.* Lexington: University of Kentucky Press, 2007.

Zimmerman, Paul R., and Susan M. V. Flaherty. "Location Monopolies and Prison Phone Rates." *Quarterly Review of Economics and Finance* 47 (2007): 261–78.

About the Contributors

Melina Abdullah is associate professor of Pan-African studies at California State University, Los Angeles. She has contributed to the edited volumes *Racial and Ethnic Politics in California, Black Women's Intellectual Traditions*, and *The Black Urban Community*.

Alex Alonso is a geographer and gang expert who has testified and consulted in more than two hundred criminal court cases.

Dionne Bennett is an anthropologist and assistant professor of African American studies at Loyola Marymount University in Los Angeles. She is the author of *Sepia Dreams: A Celebration of Black Achievement Through Words and Images*.

Joshua Bloom is a doctoral candidate in sociology at the University of California Los Angeles (UCLA). He is author of *Black Against Empire: The Rise and Fall of the Black Panther Party* (with Waldo E. Martin Jr.), and editor of *Low Wage Worker Organizing and Advocacy: The L.A. Model* (with Ruth Milkman and Victor Narro).

Edna Bonacich is professor emeritus of sociology and ethnic studies at the University of California, Riverside. She has written extensively on labor issues, including the classic article, "A Theory of Ethnic Antagonism: The Split Labor Market."

Scot Brown is associate professor of history at UCLA. He is the author of *Fighting for US: Maulana Karenga, the US Organization, and Black Cultural Nationalism*.

Reginald Chapple is director of the West Coast Center of the School of Community Economic Development at Southern New Hampshire University, former president and CEO of the Dunbar Economic Development Corporation in the historical Central Avenue community of Los Angeles, and a doctoral candidate in Anthropology at UCLA.

Andrew Deener is assistant professor of sociology at the University of Connecticut. He is currently writing a book based on six years of ethnographic and historical research on demographic and political changes in Venice, California.

Regina Freer is professor of politics at Occidental College in Los Angeles. She is co-author of *The Next Los Angeles: The Struggle for a Livable City* and has contributed to the edited volumes *Racial and Ethnic Politics in California* and *The Los Angeles Riots*.

Darnell Hunt is director of the Ralph J. Bunche Center for African American Studies and professor of sociology at UCLA. He is the author or editor of many books, including *Channeling Blackness: Studies on Television and Race in America* and *Screening the Los Angeles "Riots": Race, Seeing, and Resistance*.

Jooyoung Lee is a sociologist and postdoctoral Fellow in the Robert Wood Johnson Foundation's Health and Society Scholars at the University of Pennsylvania. He has published articles in *Social Problems, Social Psychology Quarterly*, and *Ethnography*.

Mignon R. Moore is assistant professor of sociology and African American studies at UCLA. Her work on black sexuality has been published in the *American Sociological Review, Ethnic and Racial Studies*, and *Signs: Journal of Women in Culture and Society*.

Lanita Morris is a labor organizer and a project coordinator at UCLA's Labor Center.

Neva Pemberton is a doctoral candidate in the Department of Education at UCLA.

Carrie Petrucci is a senior research associate at EMT Associates, Inc., a private evaluation firm in Encino, CA. She has authored several book chapters on juvenile justice and social work.

Steven C. Pitts is a labor policy specialist at the University of California, Berkeley Center for Labor Research and Education. His research and training projects focus on black workers and job quality.

Ana-Christina Ramón is a social psychologist and assistant director of the Ralph J. Bunche Center for African American Studies at UCLA.

Gwendelyn Rivera is a doctoral student in the Department of Education at UCLA. Her research focuses on risk and protective factors in adolescent development, and academic achievement of ethnic minority and immigrant populations.

Paul Robinson is assistant professor, investigator in Informatics Core, and director of the Medical Geographic Information Systems Laboratory at Charles R. Drew University of Medicine and Science. His work has been published in *Social Science and Medicine, Ethnicity & Disease,* and *Alcoholism: Clinical and Experimental Research.*

Lola Smallwood-Cuevas is a labor organizer and project director at the UCLA Labor Center.

M. Belinda Tucker is professor of psychiatry and biobehavioral sciences at UCLA and associate dean in UCLA's Graduate Division. She has authored numerous publications on family formation, couple relationships, interethnic relations, and research methodologies.

Paul Von Blum is senior lecturer in African American studies and communication studies at UCLA. His books include *The Art of Social Conscience; The Critical Vision: A History of Social and Political Art in the U.S.; Other Visions, Other Voices;* and *Resistance, Dignity, and Pride.*

Mary Weaver is executive director of Friends Outside in Los Angeles County. She previously served on the Board of Directors of the Restitution Center, California Department of Corrections.

Sonya Winton is a political scientist and adjunct professor in African American studies at UCLA. She is currently completing a book on the environmental justice movement.

Nancy Wang Yuen is assistant professor of sociology at Biola University in Los Angeles. Her recent work focuses on how race affects the performances of actors in the Hollywood entertainment industry.

Index

Aaron, Yardenna, 198–99
ABC Records, 267, 272
Action for Grassroots Empowerment and Neighborhood Development Alternatives (AGENDA), 372
activism: cultural, 249, 255; educational, 391, 396, 399; environmental, 343, 345; gay rights, 188–89, 198–201; and Pan Africanism, 277–78, 279; role of black press in, 372, 393–94, 401; role of women in, 324–25; after Watts, 145–50
Adams Boulevard, 66, 67–68
Adams-Washington Freeway Committee, 70
affirmative action, 386
Africa, 160, 277–78, 279, 325
African American Religious Science, 205–6; and Transcendentalism, 205
African Development Public Investment Corporation, 279
Africans, 22, 25, 27, 336
Afro-Mexicans, 32–33
AFSCME, 365
Agape International Spiritual Center, 205–7
Akili, Greg, 389, 391
Alliance for Equal Opportunity in Education (AEOE), 384–85, 388–401
alliances: educational, 385, 388, 398, 399, 400; gang, 153; labor, 368, 370, 377, 378; versus coalitions, 335
Alta California, and skin color, 27
Amand, Lewis, 350, 353
American Dream, 4–5, 11, 14, 384; and ambivalence, 4; and Puritans, 4
Amos 'n' Andy, 220
Ankrum Gallery, 250
Ankrum, Joan, 250
Anti-Drug Abuse Act (1986), 172
Architectural Digest, 6, 9
art: as activism, 243–44; and European

tradition, 243; parental support for, 126; and resistance, 263
Art West Associated (AWA), 246–47, 249, 256
Asian Americans: attitudes about gay marriage, 202; and coalition-building, 336; and college admissions, 386; and union membership, 365; in West Adams, 260
Aspect One, 125
Associated Press, 156, 188
Austin, Nefertiti, 390, 394

Bailey, William, 42
Baker, Ella, 326
Baker, Richard, 309–10
Balasubramaniam, Subramaniam, 301, 303
Baldwin, E. J. "Lucky," 6
Baldwin Hills, 1, 3, 14, 205–6; and black immigrants, 56; and celebrity, 9, 10; and class distinction, 44, 46, 48, 71, 124, 222; history of, 5–11; and "The Jungle," 6, 8, 14, 222; as "Pill Hill," 7; and Spanish land grant holders, 6
Baldwin Hills, 1–2, 5
Baldwin Hills Company, 6, 9
Baldwin Hills Crenshaw Plaza, 74
Ballou, Robert, 46, 152, 153
Bamboozled, 237
Barbara Jordan/Bayard Rustin Coalition, 192, 199–200
Barnes, Ernie, 247, 248, 251, 252
Barrows v. Jackson, 70
Barthe, Richmond, 245, 256
Bass, Charlotta, 40, 321; as activist, 324–25; and coalition-building, 335–37, 338, 339; and Communist Party, 336–37; and grand jury, 336; and residential segregation, 328–30
Bass, Joe, 62, 63

429